Shower Posse

The Most Notorious
Jamaican Criminal Organisation

Shower Posse

The Most Notorious
Jamaican Criminal Organisation

DIAMOND ◆ PUBLISHING

www.showerposse.com

Copyright © 2002, 2004 by Duane Blake

All rights reserved, including the right of reproduction whole or in part in any form

Published by Diamond Publishing, New York, New York

Manufactured in Canada

Library of Congress Cataloging-in-Publication Data
Blake, Duane
  Shower Posse; The Most Notorious Jamaican Criminal Organization
TXu 995 402

ISBN 0-9724371-0-X

First Paperback Edition

10 9 8 7 6 5 4 3 2 1

This book is dedicated to my family and MOST

IMPORTANTLY GOD, FOR GIVING

ME THE STRENGTH TO COMPLETE THIS

PROJECT.

Table of Contents

INTRODUCTION

Jamaica's most notorious posse leader Vivian Blake sits in his jail cell awaiting word of his final appeal for his stay of extradition to the United States on charges which stem from murder to drug trafficking. His story is an incredible journey into the life of a "Don". A story which takes place primarily during the Reagan era, a time Jamaican gangs proliferated the American landscape, capitalizing on the emerging crack cocaine epidemic which became synonymous with the eighties.

But, Vivian's story is not a story of crack cocaine, nor is it a story simply about drug dealing and murder. Vivian's story encapsulates the universality of brotherly love, familial bonds and basic entrepreneurship in a country built on capitalism. As a result of his unyielding desire to succeed, Vivian became a victim of his own making. His generosity was to be his downfall. His love of family and close friends was to be his undoing. Like Julius Ceaser, he too had a Brutus. Though, he only wanted the best for himself and those around him, he eventually became a scapegoat of all their wrongdoings.

Though he was no ordinary "Kingpin" Vivian became a legend in his own time because of his ability to earn the respect of some of the most vicious murders to emerge out of homeland Kingston, Jamaica. As part of his genius, Vivian saw the necessity of having those criminal elements around him, in an effort to further his business. As a result, he created opportunities for them to establish themselves in a foreign land. Earning their loyalty and their support by sharing his wealth and his knowledge with them selflessly.

What emerged out of those relationships was the creation of the "Shower Posse". The most dangerous drug gang to ever emerge in recent American history. Though vicious himself, Vivian was able to manipulate and orchestrate these thugs who had body counts in the hundreds to do his bidding. With a strong cadre of violent criminals as his closest allies, Vivian Blake was able to build a drug empire which spanned from Jamaica to Miami to New York to Philadelphia to California.

What follows is his story, as told to his son, Duane Blake. A story that will shock and enlighten you.

Chapter 1: Jamaica, West Indies

The antiquated cut-stone structures at the St. Catherine District Prison swelter under the hot May sun. Outdated sentry boxes are evenly placed atop the twenty-foot wall that surrounds the facility. Housed within the compound are two buildings—South Block and New Hall, commonly called the "Ship" as it is three times larger than the South Block. Manning the sentry posts are newly hired security guards from a private security firm, replacements for the prison warders who were summarily fired by the Commissioner of Prison, Colonel John Prescod, for being ineffective and irresponsible.

The climate at the prison is as hot as the mid-afternoon sun, which scorches the ground and renders humans fatigued and restless. Inmates are locked down for their afternoon count.

Vivian Blake is lying down on his makeshift bed, admiring his stylishly furnished cell, and talking on his illegal cell phone with one of his many girlfriends. "I should've been an interior decorator," he chuckles quietly to himself. His cell is tastefully decorated, the walls painted in white, with black borders at the floor level, and complimented with black-and-white plastic tiles decorating the floor in a checkered pattern. To top it off, a shaggy, fire-engine-red throw rug has been placed carefully in a designated section of the cell, which is filled with red, white, and black accessories. Even his *Rubber Maid* chair is fire-engine red, although his desk is black and white. Hanging on the wall, is a red shoe bag filled with ten pairs of Italian designer shoes and a few expensive sneakers. Vivian Blake has four cell phones in his cell, a television, a VCR, a fan, a CD and cassette player. He's living like a king in his jail-cell palace.

Vivian is interrupted from admiring his surroundings by shouts coming from Sexy Paul's cell. "Coach, Coach. Soldiers and police inna de prison, and they headin' over here!"

Alarmed, Vivian immediately terminates the call with his girlfriend and hastily throws his illegal gadgets into a plastic bag, attaches the bag to a lengthy stick, which he passes through his grilled cell door to the next-door cell, and is then passed to another cell down the corridor that has a proper hiding place.

Within moments, police officers and soldiers—some in uniform and others in plain clothes—surround the South Block Building. All are armed with M-16 and AR-15 rifles. The prison warders, a few soldiers, and police officers run into the building all the way up to the third floor where Vivian Blake and other inmates are housed. The prison warders fan out in front of all twenty-two cells on the third floor, but the majority are standing in front of Vivian's cell door. The warders proceed to open Vivian's cell and order Vivian to come out with his bucket. The cells have no toilets, and prisoners are usually locked down for up to twenty-four hours—a bucket is used to collect urine and feces.

Vivian steps out of the cell with his bucket, as a warder searches him and his bucket, but finds nothing. Two warders, and a soldier who carry a sophisticated metal detector, enter Vivian's cell and begin to search it thoroughly. With perspiration drenching their clothing, they continue to search in vain. They find nothing. No cell phone. No weapons. As if under specific instructions, they do not disturb anything else in Vivian's cell.

Vivian's mind is racing, *why soldiers and police? The warders could have handled the situation on their own. Must be something very serious.*

The warders, soldiers, and police officers search every cell on the third, second and first floors. A few knives, some cooking pots, and makeshift stoves are found and seized. Four soldiers with metal detectors proceed with a comprehensive search of the prison yard.

Watching the frantic undertaking, Vivian silently muses, *what the fuck's going on?*

One of the warders responds to Vivian's puzzled look. "The Security Minister, K. D. Knight, received an intelligence report from a United States Intelligence source. Said guns were on South Block."

Immediately, Vivian surmises that he is the target of the so-called intelligence report. *Next time, the government might take it a step farther, like plant a gun in my cell. I'll be shot to death.* Lying on his back, Vivian shivers at the thought, "Next time they might kill me," he says out loud, to no one in particular. Staring at the ceiling, he ponders his fate. *What next? What the fuck next?*

The third floor was noisy, though the inmates were all locked down. Everyone was discussing the search that just took place. Sexy Paul shouted to Vivian, "Oh, Bossie! Coach!"

Vivian rose from his bed and slowly walked toward his grilled cell door, "Yeah, yeah, Paul. What's up?"

"I don't like that search, Boss. You have to be careful. Keep your eyes open." There was concern in his voice.

The third floor became silent as Sexy Paul and Vivian reasoned. "Things are going from bad to worse, Paul. But, I'm strong. They can't break me … but, as you say, I definitely *will* keep my eyes open." Moving toward his bed, Vivian shouted, "I'll talk to you later. Going to lay down and meditate."

Sexy Paul shouted back, "Bossie, don't let them get to you. You must win this extradition."

Vivian lay down and looked up at the ceiling, wondering, *what's going to happen to me?*

The following Saturday, about two o'clock in the afternoon, Vivian was enjoying steamed butterfish with vegetables—expertly prepared by Mackerel, one of his close friends in the prison—outside his cell, which overlooked the prison yard. Mackerel and Steel Belly, another one of Vivian's close friends, were the best at preparing food in the South Block and usually cooked for Vivian.

As he was finishing his tasty meal, a shout from an orderly informed Vivian that his attorney was there for a visit. With no further ado, he finished his lunch, went to his cell, and reached for his *Gentleman Polo* shorts, a *Polo* shirt, and a pair of *Polo* sneakers. Always an impeccable dresser—in and out of prison—he sprayed his clothes with expensive cologne, brushed his hair, then left the cell. As he headed out the building, he met Mackerel and Sexy Paul on the steps. Seeing the way he was dressed, they scampered down the steps behind him.

Mackerel spoke. "You going in the Visiting Box, Bossie?"

Vivian laughed. "You forget this is Saturday evening. No visits in the Visiting Box on Saturday evenings," Vivian reminded him.

Mackerel sniggered. "You're the Boss. Anything is possible for you, Bossie."

Vivian smiled at Mackerel. "No. Going to see my lawyer."

Sexy Paul and Mackerel accompanied Vivian to the gate separating the South Block from the rest of the prison. "My lawyer's here to see me," Vivian told the two warders manning the gate. The one on the left opened the gate to allow Vivian passage, but Sexy Paul and Mackerel followed.

The warder shouted at Sexy Paul and Mackerel, "Where you two think you're going?"

"We're with the Boss," Mackerel tossed back. "We have to watch the back of his head. Security for surety!" The three inmates laughed together. The two warders laughed with them and allowed all three to leave the South Block compound.

Vivian walked toward the office where his lawyer, George Soutar was waiting, while Sexy Paul and Mackerel walked toward the building that housed the prison's Superintendent—Mr. Jones—directly in front of the office where Vivian was to meet with his attorney. Mackerel and Sexy Paul stood by the steps of the Superintendent's office building and watched Vivian as he proceeded.

No need to appear anxious, he calmed himself. As he stepped into the office, he extended his hand in greeting, "How you doing, George?"

Soutar looked away and shook his head. "Bad news, Vivian. Bad news."

Vivian sat down in front of Soutar, a deadly look in his eyes. "What's wrong?" Soutar looked away from Vivian's earnest gaze. "England turned down your application for Special Leave to the Privy Council."

Vivian remained silent a while. The attorney's words gouged him, like a knife thrust into his chest. He looked at Soutar, his eyes sad, his heart broken. "What'll I do next, Boss?"

Soutar could give no comfort. "This is the end of the extradition fight."

Vivian's face turned angry. "You mean there's no other avenue?"

Soutar responded, "Legally, as far as I know … no." He paused and cleared his throat, "I could make a suggestion, though."

Vivian looked up eagerly. "What?"

"You could try to get in touch with Hilare Sobers, the Human Rights Attorney, to see what he suggests."

"Why don't you contact him for me? This is Saturday. You know I can't get to Sobers until Monday."

"I'd prefer you make the initial contact. I'll do the follow-up," Soutar ended the parley.

Vivian looked at Soutar seriously, "All right, I'll jump on it immediately …George, come see me Monday afternoon, okay?"

Soutar nodded his head in agreement. "Right. I'll see you Monday." He rose from his chair while Vivian led the way out. Sexy Paul and Mackerel were surveying the situation from across the street.

Vivian looked at Soutar and affirmed, "Monday. All right, Boss," then walked away.

Mackerel and Sexy Paul followed Vivian to the South Block entrance gate, where Sexy Paul said in a mere whisper, "Bossie, what wrong? You don't look so pleased."

"It's just a business disagreement," Vivian lied to relieve the worried looks on his friends' faces.

Sexy Paul breathlessly ventured, "For a moment, I thought it was something about your extradition."

Vivian scoffed at the remark, but kept walking.

Returning to the South Block building, Vivian immediately went to his cell to change clothes. His head was pounding, and he shook it in disbelief, trying to dispel the throbbing anger. *This is a dream. I'll wake up soon.* He stopped short. *No. This is real fucking reality, not a fucking dream. Shit!* Vivian held his head with his hands. Talking to himself, he said out loud, "Look what my friends did to me … this shit would've never come down if it wasn't for Tony. Fucking power struggle! Fucking brother and his Shower Posse shit! Fuck you, Tony!" He flopped down on the bed, pounding his fists into the thin mattress and bloodying his knuckles on the hard metal frame, not caring that his friends were waiting for him.

Mackerel was a slender-built guy, with an earring—a knob—in his nose, who had come from a community called Hannah Town, close to Vivian's home in Tivoli Gardens, Jamaica. Hannah Town, along with Matthews Lane, was a PNP stronghold within the JLP-controlled Western Kingston constituency.

Sexy Paul was an exercise fanatic and an avid reader of novels. Short and stocky, with a hefty scar across his left cheek, he was once a strong community leader in Tivoli Gardens in the 1980s, along with Lester Lloyd Coke—a.k.a. Jim Brown—until Jim migrated from Jamaica. Sexy Paul didn't get along with the area leader of the time, Baskin, so he left Tivoli Gardens for Bull Bay in St. Thomas.

Vivian summoned the courage to leave his cell and walked over to where Sexy Paul, Mackerel, and some of his other friends were sitting. The humid Saturday evening wore on oppressively as the inmates went about their last-minute business before lock-down.

Vivian gladly retreated to his cell and asked the warder to lock his door immediately. "Aren't you gonna help me put the inmates in their cells?"

Vivian gave him a wan smile. "I don't feel well. Sexy Paul and Mackerel will help."

Locking the cell with the padlock, the warder tried to cheer Vivian up with a reassuring look, but Vivian closed the curtain across the front of his cell, blocking all contact with others. The whole world was closing in on him. He didn't want to leave Jamaica and had been fighting his extradition to the United States for nearly five years. Now, it seemed the fight was over. *I have only one snowball's chance in hell.* Other than that, the Jamaican Government would surrender him to the US Marshals.

Vivian picked up his phone and dialed the number of the one friend whom he thought might have a way of getting him through to Hilare Sobers on a weekend. On his first call, he struck gold. Without hesitation, he dialed Sobers' home number.

A woman answered the phone.

"Hello, may I speak to Mr. Hilare Sobers?"

"Hilare is not in, but he'll be back soon. You could call back around seven this evening," she informed him.

"Thanks a lot. I'll call back then. Thank you." He hung up the cell phone, not wanting to sound too anxious. All four cell phones were laid out on the floor and rang continuously, but Vivian was in no mood to talk to anyone unless the person was directly connected to his freedom. He quickly terminated the conversations. TV held no appeal, as his mind wouldn't release the impending doom of the extradition proceedings.

Waiting for the stroke of seven to arrive was torture. Vivian dialed Sober's house once again.

A male voice spoke, "Hello."

"May I speak with Mr. Sobers?"

"Who is this?" The voice on the other end was gruff.

Vivian hurried on, hoping the man wouldn't hang up. "You don't know me, but you might've heard about me. My name's Vivian Blake. I'd like to retain you as my Human Rights Attorney—an extradition case. I was turned down in England where I'd applied for Special Leave. If my case has any Human Rights' issue, I would appreciate it if you could represent me."

"You'll have to call me back. I'm busy right now," was Sober's unpleasant response.

Vivian merely said, "Okay." But, as he hung up the phone, he yelled into the air. "Who does that piece of shit think he is? I'm not gonna call that motherfucker again. What a piece a shit!" Vivian immediately dialed his attorney, George Soutar.

"Hello," came Soutar's familiar voice over the phone.

"I called that bastard Sobers and he acted like I was a beggar asking him a fucking favor!" screamed Vivian into the mouthpiece.

Soutar's voice softened into a gentler tone, "All right, cool down. Now, I'll deal with it as a matter of business."

Vivian backed off, "All right, let me know what's happening … *quickly*."

"I'll see you Monday or Tuesday," Soutar acknowledged.

Vivian let his phone fall through his fingers to the floor. The carpet muffled the thud and kept the phone from breaking. "When will this fucking nightmare end?" He cursed at the tiny spot on the ceiling until sleep overtook him, then rolled over on his stomach and fell into a fitful sleep.

Chapter 2: Memories of Tivoli Gardens

Vivian Blake was born on May 11th, 1955 to sixteen-year-old Gloria Henriques. Although she gave birth to Vivian at Kingston's Jubilee Hospital, Gloria lived on Metcalfe Street in Western Kingston. When Vivian was a year old, his maternal grandmother—Miss Daisy, who lived on Prince Albert Street in Allman Town—took custody of Vivian from his mother, who liked to party and have a good time.

Vivian spent most of his time with his grandmother, but he visited his mother often. Vivian's resemblance to his mother was quite evident, for he inherited Gloria's strong build and dimpled cheeks. In the fourth month of her pregnancy with Vivian, Aston Blake—Vivian's father, a tailor with a shop on Maxfield Avenue—asked Gloria to migrate to England with him. She refused; she was not in love with Aston.

By the time Gloria turned eighteen, she bore another child—a girl she named Vivienne. Gloria's daughter was the result of a relationship she'd had with a man known as Altiman Bruce, a very short, dark-complexioned man, who was a Rastafarian. Gloria bore three more children by him—Paul Anthony (Tony), Donovan, and Errol (Kong) Hulsin. At the time of Gloria's fifth pregnancy with Errol, Gloria separated from Altiman Bruce, and her boyfriend—whose surname was Huslin—adopted Errol; hence the name, Errol Huslin.

When Vivian was four years old, he went to live with his mother on Chestnut Lane. While attending a kindergarten school on Regent Street—one block from his house—Vivian got into an altercation with a student, which resulted in a spanking by the teacher with a ruler.

At four years of age, Vivian was walking to school by himself. Instead of walking to his usual school the next day, Vivian walked one block west and found himself at St. Anne's Infant School where he ventured into a class taught by Sister Gertrude. Seeing Vivian seated in her classroom, Sister Gertrude beckoned Vivian to approach her.

"Son, what is your name?"

Vivian gave his name.

The nun then inquired, "What are you doing in this class?"

"I come kool [school]."

The nun smiled and walked over to Vivian lovingly and hugged him. "Where's your mother?"

"She at home."

The nun then stooped down to Vivian's level. "Go home and tell your mother to come and see me now." Vivian left the school and went to fetch his mother. That was how Vivian started going to St. Anne's Infant School.

When Vivian was six years old, his grandmother, Miss Daisy—who was a maid for a Chinese family—moved from Allman Town to North Street, at the corner of Milk Lane in Western Kingston. Vivian continued to divide his time between his grandmother's house and his mother's house.

That Christmas, Miss Daisy bought some cloth and gave it to Vivian's mother to have a pair of long pants made for Vivian's Christmas present. She also gave Gloria a two-seater tricycle for Vivian's Christmas. Gloria's common-law husband, Altiman Bruce, was given the responsibility to have a tailor sew the pair of trousers for Vivian. What Altiman Bruce did was the exact opposite, though. Alty, as he was called, took his son Tony along with Vivian to the tailor shop, and told the tailor to make a pair of long pants for Tony, and a pair of short pants for Vivian out of the cloth that Miss Daisy had bought for Vivian.

On Christmas day, Vivian was dressed in a pair of short pants, while Tony, the younger brother, was dressed in long pants. Vivienne and Tony ecstatically rode Vivian's tricycle while Vivian watched sadly, unable to ride the tricycle given to him by his grandmother. He decided to do something about the injustice and walked from his mother's house to his grandmother's house on North Street. He told Miss Daisy about his sister and brother taking over his tricycle. His grandmother went straight Gloria's house, took away the tricycle, and brought it to her house. Vivian rode it happily there.

In 1966, Vivian was still alternating between living with his grandmother and his mother. Gloria lived at 17 Wellington St., next door to the JLP headquarters—Cho-Co-Mo Lawn—run by the JLP Member of Parliament for Western Kingston, the Right Honorable Edward Seaga. Miss Daisy lived very close by on Nelson Street.

Mr. Seaga had just finished building Phase I of the government-housing scheme, Tivoli Gardens, and Miss Daisy bought one of the two-bedroom houses in the complex. Vivian by her side, she stopped by Gloria's house, while on her way to take up residence in Tivoli Gardens, and told Gloria that she and the rest of the children could come and live with her and Vivian. Gloria accepted the offer and moved to Tivoli Gardens the next day.

Because of the upcoming general election in 1967, the political climate was filled with violence in 1966. While living with his family in Tivoli Gardens, Vivian took the common entrance examination and passed it to attend St. George's Boys College(high school) on North Street, beginning in September 1967. Gloria was an activist for the Jamaica Labour Party and went to see Mr. Seaga when Vivian earned the scholarship to St. George's, explaining that she and Vivian's grandmother couldn't afford Vivian's schoolbooks. Seaga composed a letter for Gloria to take to the Ministry of Education, by which Vivian was awarded a grant for schoolbooks and uniforms for five years.

While Vivian and four friends were walking in Tivoli Gardens on Mammoth Highway—now known as Bustamante Highway—on their way to Port Royal, they saw Seaga driving his big black car and waved for Seaga to stop. Vivian, being the vocal one, said, "Good day, Mr. Seaga, we're going to Port Royal and are short of lunch money."

Mr. Seaga smiled and took out five one-dollar bills and gave one to each of the five boys, then said to them, "You kids try not to stay out too late on the streets. Get back home before dark."

They boys gratefully nodded to Seaga, then told him "thanks" in unison and went on their way.

Vivian did well in his first year of school and continued to excel in his schoolwork. He represented St. George's College in soccer and cricket at the first-form level against other high schools. The residents of Tivoli Gardens and Western Kingston praised Vivian, because few children from that area were able to attend high school, and Vivian was attending the prestigious catholic school, St. George's College.

After Vivian's first year at St. George's, every resident of Tivoli Gardens, even the area leaders, knew him. One day, while on summer holidays, Vivian was playing soccer on the concrete pavement by Top Ten—a section of Tivoli Gardens where sports were played—and was picked to play on the team captained by Lester Lloyd Coke, a.k.a. Jim Brown.

During a game, Vivian, who was a very skillful player, tried to put a ball over the head of a representative of the Jamaica Under-Nineteen squad, Seymour Daley. The ball accidentally hit Seymour in the mouth. Seymour picked Vivian up by his shirt and was about to punch him when Jim intervened. "Leave the youth alone. It was an accident. Is football we playing."

Seymour's respect for Jim Brown made him restrain himself and release his hold, although he clearly wanted to punch Vivian in the face.

After the game, Jim put his arm around Vivian's shoulders and they walked away together. Jim sent out for two box lunches, one for Vivian, the other for himself, and proceeded to counsel Vivian as they ate. Jim said, "I don't want you to become any gunman around here. I want you to become the first lawyer out of Tivoli Gardens. If you need anything, just come to me. No stealing, remember?"

Vivian took Jim at his word on his offer, and Jim assisted Vivian with lunch money, extra clothes, and any other items that weren't covered by his grant. The assistance from Jim came to an unfortunate end, though, when Jim was arrested in 1971 and remanded to the General Penitentiary for over two years, where his spine became infected. While he was hospitalized at the Kingston Public Hospital for several months, Vivian visited Jim every day.

At this time, Vivian was representing St. George's College in the Manning Cup Soccer League, under the coaching of Bunny Goodison. Bunny took up where Jim left off and supported Vivian in every way he could.

Jim Brown and Bunny Goodison were worlds apart concerning socio-economic differences; however, they were the same in many ways. Jim, like Bunny, was very loving with children, but Jim was a criminal, with a deep association with crime and violence. However, many people failed to recognize his affectionate side. Bunny was also a very caring man who'd grown up in the roughest area of western Kingston, but was a man in love with music and sports. Bunny owned Soul Shack—a popular sound system—and was once a manager at D'Aguilar's Sports Shop.

Vivian graduated from St. George's in 1972 with three GCE O'level passes out of five taken. It was a sad time, for he'd lost his mother in a car accident in 1969, and she wasn't there to witness her firstborn graduate from high school. With this in mind, Father Tom Bradley—a priest at St. George's—arranged for Vivian to receive a soccer scholarship to attend St. Joseph's College in Philadelphia. Unfortunately, Vivian passed on the scholarship, because his grandmother had lost her job, and his friend, Jim Brown, was in prison. The only other person he could turn to was his mentor, Bunny Goodison, but Bunny had his own family to take care of. Instead, Vivian opted to work for the PNP Government in the Pubic Works Department of the Ministry of Works, located next door to Tivoli Gardens.

Even though the only thing that separated the Public Works Department from Tivoli Gardens was a retaining wall, Vivian couldn't use his Tivoli Gardens address to obtain the job at the Public Works. He had to use a Washington Gardens address in order to secure it. His wages of $52 (Jamaican) every two weeks had to support Vivian, his grandmother, four brothers, and sister.

In his spare time, Vivian played cricket and represented the Customs Tourers Cricket Team sometimes. With the insistence of Bunny Goodison, he was issued a visa by the American Embassy to go on a US tour with the team on August 10th, 1973.

After receiving his passport with the visa on Thursday, the 9th, he was faced with the dilemma of finding money to purchase a return ticket to New York. His grandmother contacted some of her friends, and they gave Vivian what they could, but it wasn't enough. His last resort was to go to some of his mother's old friends and her ex-boyfriend. The day he was scheduled to leave, Vivian was on the road begging. His flight was scheduled to leave that afternoon and Vivian was desperate. He visited an old boyfriend of his mother's, Mr. Simpson, and was given some money. Still, he didn't have enough. Going by faith, Vivian visited his mother's best friend, Smokey Barbara, who provided Vivian with the rest of the money he needed.

He went downtown happily, picked up his plane ticket, and then returned to his home in Tivoli Gardens, packed his clothes, showered, and with little time to spare, said goodbye to his friends at Top Ten. Vivian was accompanied to the airport by his girlfriend, Norma, and met his teammates at the airport. After checking his luggage, he kissed his girlfriend goodbye, then vanished inside the restricted area of the airport, his girlfriend waving to him as he ascended the plane's steps.

Chapter 3: The Arrival

On a hot summer night, the 10th of August 1973, Vivian Blake stepped out of customs at the John F. Kennedy Airport in New York, one of the team members of Jamaican cricketers called *The Custom Tourers*. Vivian had a cricket bat strapped between the cricket pads in his hands and had pulled the strap tightly around his over-sized, partially empty suitcase. Vivian touched the two dimes and two quarters in his pocket to make sure they were still there, and strolled to the phone booth quickly, while taking the piece of paper with addresses and phone numbers of family friends out of the same pocket. He reached for the phone, inserted a dime, and proceeded to dial a number that his friend Killo, who'd recently visited Jamaica, had given to him—a phone number to contact Killo if Vivian ever reached the shores of America. A frown came over Vivian's face as he held the receiver to his ear. "Shit. Out of service!" Vivian had no more phone numbers, only addresses, so he retrieved the coin from the phone box and rejoined the cricket team.

A van and three cars took the cricketers from the airport to the Bronx. Vivian was seated in the van looking out at the bright lights of New York City, fascinated by the scenery. Opening the van window, he inhaled deeply to fill his lungs with the wonderful fresh air, a joyous smile on his face. "New York, New York."

The convoy of vehicles drove through the Triborough Bridge tollbooth and headed for the Bronx. Finally, they exited the expressway, drove through the streets of the Bronx, and pulled up in front of an apartment building in the South Bronx. Clutching the handle of his over-sized suitcase, along with his bat and pads, Vivian stared at the apartment building in amazement, as they exited their transports. The other guys left their belongings inside the vehicles.

There was a welcome party in progress in a fourth-floor apartment. All the members of the cricket team and the drivers of the vehicles went inside, where the sound of Reggae music filled the air. Vivian looked oddly out-of-place, pulling his suitcase, bats, and pads along with him, and his face was full of woe. Everyone in the touring party had relatives or friends with whom to stay, but Vivian had no one. He'd been depending on getting in touch with Killo upon his arrival.

The party was pumping; everyone was having fun, except Vivian. He didn't have a place to stay after the party ended. "Excuse me," he said, approaching one of the partygoers, "Can you tell me where in New York we are?"

"The Bronx."

Vivian reached in his pocket for the piece of paper with the addresses and phone numbers, and proceeded to scan it. "Do you know where Home Street is?"

Shaking his head, the youngster said, "No."

Vivian was overcome with emotion, not knowing what to do. He asked two more people for directions to Home Street, but neither could help. Frustrated, Vivian leaned against the bare wall of the living room, cleared of its furnishings to accommodate the party. He nervously fingered his jaw, considering what to do. An elderly Jamaican man, who was drinking heavily and having the time of his life, glanced over and saw Vivian with his hand at his jaw, sadness filling his eyes.

The drunken man strolled over to Vivian, "Son, this is a party. You should be enjoying yourself." The man spoke in a steadier voice that his drunken state suggested, but it didn't help Vivian's sad state. "What's wrong?" the elderly man asked.

Vivian looked at the man for a second. "I need to find an address … Home Street."

The elderly man smiled. "Home Street's not too far from here. I know where it is."

A smile came over Vivian's face, but quickly vanished, wondering if the man would be of any help, as drunk as he was. "Can you take me there?"

"Sure, kid, but you'll have to wait until I'm finished partying."

Relieved, Vivian happily replied, "Thank you, Sir … I'll wait."

As the party went on and on, and the elderly man partied on and on—growing drunker by the minute—Vivian watched, hoping his last hope of finding Home Street didn't pass out. Eventually, the partygoers started to leave, trickling out, one by one.

"Kid, wait for me downstairs … the blue Monte Carlo in front of the building's mine. Wait by the car."

Vivian eagerly nodded to the man, "Yes, Sir," then gathered his baggage and went downstairs. Leaning against the car, he waited … and waited … and waited … for what seemed like an eternity ... until he fell asleep with his suitcase, bat, and pads gripped in his hands.

The old man abruptly startled Vivian. "Wake up, son. Let's go."

Jolted out of a dead sleep, the intrusion frightened Vivian. The sun was rising. *It must be close to six-thirty.* Vivian hurriedly tossed his belongings in the back seat of the Monte Carlo, and then jumped into the front passenger seat beside the drunken old man. He didn't care if the man driving the car was blind, as long as he could deliver Vivian to his destination. So tired and weary, Vivian just wanted to reach Home Street.

As the man pulled up to an apartment building, he announced, "This is the apartment building your piece of paper says, son. Let's go and find your friend."

Vivian took his belongings out of the car and followed the elderly man to the entrance.

The Monte Carlo driver looked at Vivian's piece of paper with the address on it again. "There's no apartment number on the paper, just the building number. I'll have to find out from the superintendent of the building."

Vivian panicked. "You have to check with the police?"

Patting Vivian on his shoulder, the drunk said, "No, not the police. A superintendent takes care of the apartment building."

Vivian heaved a sigh of relief as his companion rang a bell with the word *Superintendent* written beside it. An apartment door opened on the ground floor, and a middle-aged Spanish gentleman approached them.

"May I help you?"

The drunk must have felt as though he should take charge of the situation. "I'm trying to find Lloyd Reid. This is his address, but I don't have an apartment number."

"There's no Lloyd Reid living here. I know all the tenants."

"He's Jamaican," the elderly man persisted, while Vivian looked on, worry causing perspiration to dampen his shirt.

"There's only one Jamaican living in the building, and he lives on the fifth floor, but his name isn't Lloyd Reid."

The elderly man paused for a second, then cajoled, "Take me to see this Jamaican. He might know Lloyd Reid."

The Superintendent beckoned the two to follow him as Vivian dragged his luggage all the way up to the fifth floor, where the superintendent stood, ringing the doorbell. Within a few seconds, the door opened and a stocky, bearded Jamaican looked out. The face peering at them wasn't Lloyd Reid, but Vivian smiled for the first time since landing in New York, as he recognized him as a man who'd lived in West Kingston. Finally, a familiar face.

"What's up, Super?" said the Jamaican man.

Turning towards Vivian and the elderly man, the superintendent said, "These guys are trying to find a Lloyd Reid, a Jamaican. Know him?"

When the occupant of the apartment hesitated, Vivian quickly jumped forward and offered, "It's me who wants to find Lloyd Reid. They call him Law." To better explain his situation, Vivian continued, "I just came up from Jamaica, and I got this address from his mother...."

The stocky man studied Vivian for a few seconds before answering. "Yes, I know Law. Come inside. I'll call him for you."

Vivian's companion said, "Kid, I guess you're in good hands now. Take care of yourself."

"Thanks a lot for helping me, Sir."

"No problem, kid. Just take care of yourself."

Vivian went into the apartment as his ride to the apartment walked away, a bit more sober. Turning to the stocky bearded man, Vivian reassured him, "I know your face from Jamaica."

"You should, if you know Law. We grew up together. Law uses this as his mailing address. "Er ... uh ... well, anyway, my name's Neville. What's yours?"

While taking a moment to observe his surroundings, he gave the man his name.

Neville dialed a number and began speaking into the mouthpiece, "Yeah, Law, a youth, named Vivian, is here to see you from Jamaica." Neville paused while Vivian looked at him anxiously. "Hold on," Neville handed the phone to Vivian.

"Wha'aappen Law?" asked Vivian, falling back into familiar jargon, as if it hadn't been such a long while since they'd seen each other.

"When did you come from Jamaica?"

"Last night."

"Just stay cool. I'll be over there to pick you up in a few minutes." Vivian was excited to see his old friend. "All right, see you soon." They both hung up and Vivian turned to Neville. "Law said he'll be here soon."

Appeased, a smile escaped from Neville. "Come. Let me show you a room where you
can rest 'til Law comes."

Vivian followed Neville into the large, moderately furnished five-bedroom apartment and was shown to a room decorated with a wooden bedroom set. After waiting at the drunk's car and falling asleep standing up, Vivian's look of satisfaction was read by Neville.

"Just get some rest 'til Law comes."

As Neville exited the room, Vivian gladly fell onto the bed, willing sleep to overtake him, but his adrenalin was still pumping. He lay on his back for about half-an-hour before the doorknob turned and Law was standing at the entrance, a smile splashed across his face.

"What's up, youth? You reached the Big Apple, eh?"

Calling Law a name his friends called him in Jamaica, Vivian jumped up. "Yes, Puru-Pang."

Stopping the reunion short, Law informed Vivian, "We have to leave now. I have a cab waiting downstairs."

"I'm ready." Vivian took up his belongings and walked behind Law, out of the bedroom toward the living room where Neville was sitting. "Thanks, Neville."

"No problem, man. Just take care of yourself, Vivian."

"Neville … later," came from Law as he and Vivian left.

Walking down the steps Law said, "We just going to drop off your luggage at my house. Then we going to take the train to Brooklyn to see Buggie (Barber) Clinton at his barbershop."

Every kid in West Kingston had his hair cut by "Barber" before Buggie migrated to the States, and Vivian was pleased that he would see another familiar face.

Law was a tall, slim, black male who was one of the first residents of Tivoli Gardens to migrate to America. Law, his common-law wife, Linnette, and his children used to live across the street from Vivian in Tivoli Gardens, and although Law was much older than Vivian, he was a man Vivian respected ever since he was young boy. Buggie was also tall and dark—much taller than Law—and very firmly built. Buggie, his wife, Maggie, and their children had also lived across the street from Vivian in Tivoli Gardens.

As Law and Vivian stepped into Buggie's barbershop in Brooklyn that Saturday morning in August, Buggie's eyes lit up to see the little kid Vivian—now grown up. "How are you, Vivian? When did you come to America?"

"Last night."

"So, how was school? Did you graduate?"

"Yes, over a year ago. I was working with the Government," Vivian explained to his old friend.

"Are you going back to Jamaica?"

"I don't plan to. Jamaica's too rough," Vivian replied, shaking his head, before he continued. "I'd love to get a job and try to finish my schooling."

Vivian and Law began mingling with the Jamaican patrons and friends that came to have their hair cut, and spent the entire day at Buggie's barbershop. Finishing his work for the day, Buggie took Vivian up to Utica Avenue and bought him a pair of slacks and a shirt, and gave him twenty dollars. While Vivian and Buggie were walking back from the store, Buggie extended some solid advice. "Don't get mixed up in too much company up here. I mean ... bad company ... just get a job and work for your living."

Immediately understanding the seriousness in Buggie's voice, Vivian promised, "That's exactly what I plan to do."

Law was waiting at the barbershop for them to return.

Vivian was living now on Grant Avenue in the Bronx with Law and Law's second girlfriend, Norma, who was called "Nurse" ever since she lived in Tivoli Gardens. News got around and Vivian's friend Killo, who was living in Brooklyn at the time, heard that Vivian was living with Law up in the Bronx. About four days after Vivian moved in with Law, a telephone call came in at the apartment. Norma, Law, and Vivian were home at the time.

Law answered the phone, "What's happening, Killo?" Law then glanced at Vivian and handed him the phone.

"What's up, Harry-Quashy?" (a name Vivian usually called Killo).

"I'll be coming to see you today, I just heard that you were here," Killo said.

"I tired to reach you from the airport the night I came in, but your phone was disconnected," said Vivian.

"Yeah man, when I came back from Jamaica my phone was disconnected. Anyway, let me get the address from Law," Killo said.

Vivian handed the phone to Law, who gave Killo the address then hung up the phone.

Killo came to visit Vivian at Law's apartment and spent the night, reminiscing with Vivian about the past and joking around. Killo was a very flashy individual. He dressed like a pimp, talked like a pimp, and acted like a pimp, but didn't have the working girls to go along with his image.

When Killo invited Vivian to spend the weekend in Brooklyn in the presence of Law, Law approved, but Vivian was looking forward to taking the train that following Friday to Brooklyn by himself for the first time.

Killo met Vivian in Brooklyn that Friday at the train station, which was at the intersection of Sterling and Nostrand Avenues, and they walked to an apartment building where Killo was staying with a friend of his—Boomie. When Killo rang the apartment doorbell, a light complexioned young lady with huge breasts opened the door. She smiled pleasantly at Killo and Vivian, and then let them in.

Killo introduced Vivian to the very sexy-looking young lady, "Anne, this is my friend Vivian from back home."

Anne was tall and shapely and about twenty-two years old. She smiled as she spoke in an American accent, "Glad to meet you, Vivian. Strange name though…a name usually for a girl."

Vivian laughed, "In Jamaica, Vivian is a boy's name. The girl's name is Vivienne."

While Anne, Killo, and Vivian were becoming acquainted, a tall gentleman appeared from the bedroom area and walked into the living room area where Anne, Vivian, and Killo were.

Killo looked at the gentleman who was much older than himself and Anne and said, "Boomie, this is Vivian."

Boomie smiled and stretched his arm out to shake Vivian's hand, "Glad to meet you, man, Killo always spoke well about you."

Vivian smiled while shaking Boomie's hand, "Glad to meet you too, Boomie."

Boomie was a calm-looking, soft-spoken man, one who seemed like he was a real pimp and was teaching Killo the pimping game. Boomie spoke to Anne, his girlfriend, in that calm, but commanding manner, and Anne responded promptly and respectfully like that of a slave attending to her master. It was clear that Boomie was in charge.

That night Killo took Vivian to meet his girlfriend, Debbie. Vivian and Killo went inside Debbie's apartment building and Killo rang the buzzer on the building's front door. Not bothering to take the elevator, they walked up one flight of steps to Debbie's second-floor apartment, where a young lady waited with her door wide open.

Killo, with Vivian close behind him, approached the pretty girl.

"Hi, baby," was Debbie's greeting to Killo; then she kissed Killo on the lips. The very pretty, curvy, tall young lady smiled at Vivian and nodded pleasantly, then led Killo and Vivian into her beautifully decorated apartment. Another pretty girl—a sexy, little, American thing—who was sitting in the living room, rose from her seat and walked toward Killo, Debbie and Vivian. She smiled then hugged Killo.

"Hi, Clive. How are you?" she said.

Clive Cephas was Killo's real name. "Debbie, Shirley, this is Vivian," Killo said.

"Vivian? You must be joking, Clive."

Killo and Vivian laughed, "No," said Killo, "Vivian is a man's name in Jamaica, Debbie."

Then Debbie said jokingly, "Child, you better change that name. You're in New York now, not in Jamaica. Please."

Shirley looked at Vivian and smiled as if sympathetic to Vivian concerning his name. After the introductions, everyone sat down in the living room and talked, and Shirley and Vivian hit it off immediately.

Vivian and Killo left Debbie's apartment about twelve o'clock that night and went back over to Killo's home where Boomie and Anne were relaxing in the living room, watching television. Vivian and Killo joined them.

Boomie looked over at Killo and Vivian and said, "Killo, let's take Vivian for a drink by the corner pub."

"That sounds good," said Killo.

"Sounds good to me, too" Vivian said smiling.

Anne looked on and smiled at Vivian. Boomie got up from the sofa then slid his hands under the sofa, took out a gun, and put it in his waistband. Then he, Killo and Vivian left for the pub.

The next night, Killo had a party to go to at a club they called *The Keg Lounge* in East New York. He dressed like the mack, with a pink sleeveless jumpsuit with rhinestones on the upper section, a pink pair of platform shoes, a pink felt Stetson with a tall white feather protruding from the back, and an ivory-handled walking stick.

Vivian and Killo left the apartment and walked towards The Keg Lounge. They looked like the odd couple, Killo dressed so "fly," and Vivian dressed in below-average clothes that he brought with him from Jamaica.

Something popped up in Vivian's mind. "Killo, why did Boomie have to carry a gun with him last night when the bar we went to was just downstairs?"

Killo laughed then looked at Vivian, but then Killo got serious. "Boomie and some guys called "Untouchables" have some problems, so Boomie carries his gun to protect himself."

"So … what are you saying, Killo? If those Untouchables had seen Boomie and us it would have been a shoot out?" Vivian asked.

"Boomie would have to defend himself," Killo said.

Vivian looked at Killo seriously, "I won't be going out with Boomie again. Remember that."

Killo laughed out aloud and so did Vivian.

Killo and Vivian were walking past a bar on Nostrand Avenue by Rutland Road when they saw Killo's cousin Pauline, whom Vivian knew well. She was pretty with a slender body and very light complexioned. Vivian previously dated Pauline's sister, Lorna, back in Jamaica.

Pauline ran towards Vivian and hugged him. "How are you, Vivian?" Pauline said, happy to see him.

"I'm alright. Long time no see," answered Vivian.

Pauline turned to a gentleman and a girl who were standing next to each other and said, "This is Lorna's old boyfriend, Vivian."

The man and the girl responded by smiling.

Pauline, still hugging Vivian, walked over to the man and the girl and introduced them. "Vivian, this is another one of Lorna's sisters, Beverly, and this is Beverley's husband, Finey."

"Glad to meet you, Vivian," said Beverly, who was tall, strongly built, and very shapely. Beverly resembled Vivian's past girlfriend, Lorna.

Killo interrupted, "What happened? You mean none of my cousins don't see me? You mean I'm invisible?" quipped Killo.

Beverly laughed and teased, "The girls up the road will see you, Fly Baby."

Finey greeted Vivian warmly. "Where you going, youth? With Killo?"

"Yeah, Killo is taking me to a club named *The Keg*," answered Vivian.

Finey looked at Killo and said, "You, alone, go on to The Keg. Vivian is going to stay with us."

Killo looked at Vivian and said, "What you saying, V?"

"Yeah, man, I stay with them. I haven't seen Pauline in a long time and I would just be like a baggage on you tonight," answered Vivian, knowing his attire was out of place.

Killo laughed and said "Later." Then he walked away.

Vivian, Finey, Beverly, and Pauline watched Killo walk up the street with his walking stick looking "fly" like a pimp.

Finey looked at Vivian as they all stood outside the bar. "You want something to drink?"

"Yeah, a beer would be alright," said Vivian.

Finey went inside the bar, came back out with an eight-pack of Miller, and handed one to Vivian.

"Have you got an opener?" Vivian asked.

Finey smiled and jokingly teased, "You are in America now … just twist the cap."

Vivian twisted the cap off the beer, and then smiled. As they became acquainted, Vivian and Finey discovered they both liked each other's company. Finey was a middle-aged gentleman of medium build, with one gold tooth in his mouth, an acclaimed jeweler, and he dressed well.

Vivian, Finey, Beverly, and Pauline finished their all-night drinking and chatting at about two-thirty that Sunday morning. With Killo nowhere in sight, Vivian went home with Finey, Beverly, and Pauline, who were all living in Pauline and Beverly's mother's house close by on Midwood Street.

At the house, Pauline told Vivian he could sleep with her in her room, so he went to bed beside Pauline. All night he thought about this sexy lady sleeping beside him. A hard-on kept him in pain the whole time.

The next weekend, Killo invited Vivian and Law to a party in a basement on Eastern Parkway, run by an elderly man named Becky. Vivian was dressed in the outfit that his elder friend, Buggie, had bought for him, and he felt more at ease as he and Law rode the train from the Bronx to the party in Brooklyn. It was in full swing when Vivian and Law got there, and they saw that Killo and Pauline were already having fun. As a matter of fact, everyone was having fun in Becky's basement.

Vivian and Pauline danced together a couple of times. In the wee hours of the morning, while Pauline was standing next to Vivian and Law was fast asleep on a chair, a very tall guy dressed very "fly" approached Pauline for a dance, but Pauline told the guy she didn't want to.

"I see you dance with anyone again before the night is through, an' I'm going to spray my beer all over you," the guy angrily said to Pauline and walked away.

Vivian looked at Pauline and saw that she was visibly upset. "What's wrong, Pauline?"

"That guy over there said if he sees me dancing with anyone he is going to spray me with his beer," Pauline said with a frown.

Vivian got upset and said to Pauline, "Let's dance. I wanna see what he is going to do." He took Pauline's hand and started to dance with her, holding her closely.

At that moment, the same guy appeared in front of Pauline and Vivian with his shirt opened. A chrome, thirty-eight revolver was brandished in the guy's waistband. Vivian's eyes widened as he saw the guy's gun. The guy pulled the gun from his waistband and approached Vivian and Pauline. They stopped dancing and the partying crowd started to panic. People rushed to different corners of the basement, leaving only Vivian and Pauline in the middle with the gunman. Law was still fast asleep on a chair.

Pauline went behind Vivian for cover. Vivian panicked for a minute then said to the guy with the gun, "What is this for?"

"Your girl dissed me," said the guy with the gun, pointing the gun at Vivian.

"This is not necessary, brethren. There is no need for violence. We can talk this out," Vivian said nervously. He looked the guy over and saw that the he was trembling—he was a coward, armed with a gun. "This is not the way to solve this," Vivian said more confidently.

The guy with the gun started to retreat while putting his gun back in his waist. Law woke up just in time to see the guy putting the gun back in his waist. Feeling that the guy had embarrassed him, Vivian wanted to get even. He walked towards the guy with the gun but the guy kept backing up the basement step until everyone was outside on the street. Vivian wanted to get close to the guy with the gun to see if he could grab the gun out of his waistband, but the guy guarded the gun.

Vivian, Killo, Law and Pauline had followed Vivian out of the basement. Two of Killo's friends were also there behind Vivian. "Killo, haven't any of your friends got a gun?" whispered Vivian.

Killo's friends were reading Vivian's lips as he spoke to Killo. "No, I don't think so," answered Killo.

The guy with the gun slowly backed away from the crowd until he was out of sight. When the gunman was gone, Vivian discovered that one of Killo's friends had a gun. "Damn! You knew this guy disrespected me and you had a gun?" Vivian barked angrily.

Vivian hugged Pauline and told her, "I'll talk to you later, P," then he and Law walked to the subway station, which was just a few yards away. Upset about the fact that Killo's friend had a gun and did not come to his assistance, Vivian cried while on the train on their way back to the Bronx.

Three weeks had passed since Vivian had been in New York. Due to move the following week, Law and Norma were getting their stuff together to move to a bigger apartment on Edgecombe Avenue, between 145th and 146th Street in Manhattan.

Neville and a friend of his were over at Law's house that Saturday. "Neville, do you know of any job openings?" asked Vivian.

"No, not right now," replied Neville.

Neville's friend, a slim dark guy, young in age, looked at Vivian and said, "You can get a job where I'm working if you would do clean up work. The clean-up guy got fired yesterday, and I know they would definitely want someone to fill his place. If you want the job, I could recommend you."

Vivian looked at the guy and asked, "What type of work did the clean up guy do?"

Law, Norma, and Neville laughed.

"Rip carton boxes to pieces, tie them up, then throw them out. It's a factory that deals with clothing only," he said.

"I think I can handle that," Vivian replied confidently.

"I'll pick you up Monday morning early," he confirmed. "You can ride with me to work and apply for the job. I think you'll get it."

"That sounds good," Vivian's agreed.

Vivian was dressed and was waiting for Bobby to pick him up when the doorbell of Law's apartment rang. Norma went to the door and looked through the peephole. "Vivian, it's your school friend Bobby." She opened the door and let Bobby in.

"See you guys later," said Vivian then he left with Bobby, a tall, slim kid who was a classmate of Vivian's while they attended St. George's College in Jamaica. Vivian had just registered for night class at Morrisianna High School by Boston Road and 167th Street. He should have started classes the same night of his job interview.Bobby and Vivian walked to the number four train station at 170th Street and Jerome Avenue. Bobby was taking Vivian up to the house of one of his girlfriends to give her a helping hand in preparing for a party that was planned that same night. Bobby and Vivian changed trains and got off at the Dyer Avenue stop, uptown Bronx.

Upon reaching Bobby's girlfriend's house, Bobby rang the bell. A girl answered the door of the private residence. "Come in, Bobby. Hi" she said to Vivian.

"This is Vivian, my school friend," Bobby said.

"I'm Pat. Glad to meet you, Vivian," she said, very courteously.

"I'm pleased to meet you too, Pat," said Vivian confidently.

They all went inside the house then Pat lead them down to the basement. While they were descending the steps, an attractive girl caught Vivian's eye. The girl was sorting some records around a stereo system as she looked up and saw them.

"We have company, Norma. This is Bobby, my friend from back home," said Pat, as she pointed to Bobby. "And this is his friend, Vivian, who is now our friend, too," Pat continued jokingly.

"Uh … hi," Norma said, acting rather shy. On the turntable, she was playing a Reggae tune that was the rave in Jamaica at that time.

Vivian, being fresh from Jamaica knew the popular tune well, because there was also a new dance that was created for the tune. Bitten by the music bug, Vivian walked over to the turntable where Norma was, while Bobby and Pat went down to the kitchen.

"Hi. You like that tune?" Vivian asked Norma.

"Yes, I love it!" Norma answered with a smile.

"There is a dance that goes with that tune," said Vivian, while showing Norma a sample of the new dance.

Norma said joyously, "I know how to do it, too," and showed Vivian some of her moves.

Astonished by his own naivete, Vivian started laughing. "You are good. I didn't know that the new dance is in America already."

"It's not. I just came up from Jamaica. I've been here about four weeks now," replied Norma.

Vivian looked at Norma, "Then you came a week before I did. I'm here three weeks yesterday," said Vivian. "This is where you live?" he asked.

Norma shook her head, indicating no. "I live on Anderson Avenue, near 166th Street, further down in the Bronx."

Vivian started getting more interested in Norma's whereabouts and informed her, "I live down in the Bronx, too, by Grant Avenue and 169th Street."

Norma looked at Vivian for a second. "My brother speaks about that Avenue all the time. That's where his friends hang out."

They got to talking and exchanged phone numbers and addresses. Bobby and Pat walked back into the sitting area where Vivian and Norma were and found the two people deep in conversation, as if they had known each other for a long time.

"This looks like a match made in heaven," Pat joked.

Then Bobby said, "Viv, you look like you're okay, man ... well at home."

Vivian smiled at Bobby's jovial remark, and so did Norma. The day stretched on until it was party time, which turned out wonderful. Vivian and Norma danced the night away, doing the new dance moves from Jamaica to the delight of the guests at the party.

Vivian got the job at the factory with the recommendation from the guy who took him. The job paid eighty-six dollars per week before taxes. After taxes, Vivian took home sixty-eight dollars. It was a far cry from the fifty-two Jamaican dollars he was earning every two weeks while working for the government in Jamaica. That was like earning twenty-six American dollars every two weeks.

He could now send twenty dollars per week to his grandmother in Jamaica to support his brothers and sister.

A lot of stealing took place at the factory where Vivian worked. The guys would put the stolen clothes in the rubbish that was handled by Vivian, then they'd retrieve the stolen clothes from the garbage when they left work. The guys were putting Vivian's job at risk, so he decided that if his job was going to be put at risk, he would have to benefit from it, too. So, all the guys had to give Vivian half of what they stole from the factory. He was now earning an extra one hundred and fifty to two hundred dollars each week. He sent a lot of clothes to Jamaica for his brothers and sister, plus extra money for his grandmother. Vivian was also giving Norma fifteen dollars a week for room and board now, for they were living together in Manhattan.

Norma was by now deeply in love with Vivian, and he was also deeply in love with her. He used to sleep by Norma almost every night. Norma's father was the Superintendent of a beautiful apartment building on Anderson Avenue. He was a short, stocky, elderly man with a bald head, who held down two jobs; he was the Superintendent by day, and he had a job that he went to at night. He would leave his building at ten o'clock every night to go to work and returned at six-thirty in the morning.

Norma's father had two apartments in the building—one on the first floor, given to him rent-free because he was the Superintendent, and another one on the second floor he rented for his three eldest children; Norma, Junior, and Little Dread. He had three other young children who lived with him on the ground floor.

Norma was not permitted by her father to have boyfriends. For one thing, she was married to a fireman in Jamaica, and her father was a Christian man who did not believe in adultery. Secondly, her father was paying the rent for the second floor apartment. His routine was cleverly watched by Vivian so that Vivian could sneak into Norma's apartment after her father had left for work at night and sneak out before six-thirty in the morning. It was very inconvenient for Vivian, but he was in love with Norma and vice versa. Sometimes, Vivian would have to wait at the top of the hill on Anderson Avenue in the cold until Norma's father left for work, sometimes up to an hour and a half in the freezing weather, but it was well worth it because he was in love.

After three months on the job, Vivian was caught with stolen clothes in his garbage container—set up by a Polish worker who envied him. Vivian's employer paid him his wages, then told him he was fired. Vivian protested that someone set him up, but it went on deaf ears. Vivian's loss of income caught him off guard. He had just spent a lot of money buying clothes and other stuff for his brothers, sister, and grandmother in Jamaica and was broke. The sixty-eight dollar check was all he had, and he had not yet sent any cash for his grandmother for Christmas.

Vivian bought a forty-dollar money order and sent it off to Jamaica to his grandmother. He put away fifteen dollars to pay Norma for room and board and had thirteen dollars to spend for himself until he picked up another job.

Norma's friend, Beverly, an elderly lady with a small physique and very light complexion, had promised to take the clothes down to Jamaica for Vivian. She was scheduled to leave two days after Vivian was fired from his job. After she had come home from work that evening, he took the suitcase full of clothes over to Beverly's apartment, which was two buildings down from where Norma lived. Vivian rang the bell to Beverly's apartment, she opened the door, and Vivian walked inside the apartment with the suitcase.

"What a big suitcase, Vivian," Beverly remarked astonished at its size. "You know you have to give me money for overweight."

Vivian's heart skipped a beat, because he had no money except the fifteen dollars to give Norma for room and board. He knew his relatives needed the clothes and thought that Norma would not bother to ask him for money since he was just fired. He had to make a quick decision, so he reached into his pocket and gave Beverly the fifteen dollars.

"Where in Tivoli Gardens your grandmother lives?" asked Beverly.

"On Chang Avenue … 98 Chang Avenue. You can't miss it. Just ask anyone for Gloria's mother," said Vivian quickly.

Beverly took a pen and wrote down the address.

"Alright, then, Bev, have a safe trip in case I don't see you again before you leave," Vivian wished Beverly, then she let him out of the apartment.

Vivian was starting to miss going to Norma's apartment during the daytime. He made up many excuses to tell Norma, but Norma was suspecting that he had another girlfriend. The sister of Vivian's former girlfriend, Lorna, had migrated to New York, and Vivian decided to go to Brooklyn to have an enjoyable weekend. After he left Beverly's apartment, he headed to the train station on his way to spend the weekend by Finey and visit with Lorna.

He had not made love to Lorna since she arrived in New York from Jamaica, so they both had big plans for this weekend. Vivian got off the train at Nostrand Avenue and walked to Midwood Street where Beverly, Lorna, Finey and Pauline were. Everyone decided that they weren't going out on the street that night, because it was too cold. Finey had plenty of beer in the house plus a very good smoke of marijuana. Vivian attacked the cassette player and started to play some cassettes, which Finey had made available, and the party started. Everyone had a ball.

Vivian and Lorna looked at each other constantly. Vivian rolled a cigarette with the marijuana, and then whispered into Lorna's ear, "Let's go upstairs to your room."

Lorna looked at Vivian with her sexy eyes then rose from her seat and Vivian followed.

"Tomorrow, you all," Vivian said, as he took one of the beers out of the case on the floor. Finey touched Beverly in her side and made a face at Vivian and Lorna as they left the room, then they both smiled at the couple as they walked up the stairs.

Vivian didn't wake up until about eleven o'clock the next morning, when Lorna woke him with his breakfast. Vivian put the breakfast tray aside and kissed Lorna passionately. "I love you," Vivian said softly.

"I love you too," Lorna replied convincingly.

Vivian then reached for the breakfast tray and started to eat as Lorna fed Vivian some of the food from the tray.

Vivian returned home in Manhattan at midday on Monday after the lovely weekend with Lorna. Law's second common-law wife, Norma, was home with three friends, playing cards, when Vivian entered the apartment, but Norma gave him an unpleasant look when Vivian's eyes met hers. He knew something was wrong, but he couldn't figure out what it was. He knew he hadn't done anything wrong, so he just left it at that and headed for the kitchen for something to eat.

"You all want me to cook some food? Dumplings and cabbage maybe?" asked Vivian of the gathering.

One of the girls said, "Yes, that sounds good." Then the others nodded in agreement. He went about the tasks of cooking up the boiled dumplings and steamed cabbage, and then served the food to the four ladies first, dishing his out afterward. Everyone ate and enjoyed the meal, indicating to Vivian that the food tasted good. After everyone finished eating, Vivian washed the dishes and the pots and turned them down to dry. He took a seat beside the ladies when he was finished cleaning up and watched them play cards.

They decided to call it a day after a couple more hours. While the visiting ladies were straightening up to leave, Norma looked over at

Vivian. "You have a fucking phone bill to pay, you don't remember?" she said disrespectfully, in the presence of the other ladies. "I don't want you to use my fucking phone again. It is for me and my fucking man," she continued. She threw the phone bill at Vivian.

He was so embarrassed that he held his head down and looked through the phone bill. There was only one call on the phone bill for him, made over a month ago to his friend, Norris, in Hartford, Connecticut. The cost of the call as listed on the phone bill was three dollars and fifteen cents.

Vivian had intended to pay for his long distance call because at the time he was working. Now, being out of a job made it difficult for him to pay until he picked up another job. The embarrassment to Vivian was uncalled for.

The visiting ladies looked at Vivian pitifully but did not intervene.

"You had fucking money to give Beverly to take clothes to Jamaica, but you don't have any to pay your fucking bills," Norma barked, trying to justify the disrespectful way she was treating him.

He now realized what had been eating at Norma. Beverly had told Norma that he had given her the fifteen dollars. Vivian kept his head down in shame with tears in his eyes, thinking about what he was going through at the hands of Norma. Things got worst in the ensuing weeks.

Vivian was hungry one evening, so he looked in the refrigerator and saw some slices of fried Jack fish in aluminum foil. He took out a slice and prepared it with some boiled dumplings. Norma had counted the slices of fish and knew one slice was missing.

She cursed Vivian disrespectfully in the presence of his friend, Law, saying, "My food is only for me and my fucking man. Buy your own fucking food."

That was the last straw for Vivian. He knew now that he had to find somewhere else to live.

Vivian picked up a job at a factory on 163rd Street in the Bronx named *Finer Chrome Products*. This company made furniture for residential and commercial properties, and his job was to assemble chairs made for Kinney Shoes Company.

At this time, Vivian was still having an affair with his girlfriend, Norma, so he slept at her house every night and avoided going to Law's apartment as much as possible. Law's girlfriend, Norma, left for work at nine o'clock every night, then Law would leave the apartment at about nine-thirty every night to go and sleep with another girlfriend. Norma did not suspect a thing, because she didn't get home until seven-thirty in the morning. By that time, Law would be at one of his many construction jobs. He was a labourer and was with the Manpower Union, which secured construction jobs for him on a regular basis. Norma worked with a hospital as a Nurse's Aid.

Vivian would sneak into Law's and Norma's apartment sometimes after ten at night to get a change of clothes and then leave for his girlfriend's place. Most evenings, when not hanging out with friends, he had to ride the subway for hours until his girlfriend's father had left for his second job at ten in the night. Vivian realized that he had to have somewhere to stay in the evenings after work and early mornings before work, because he couldn't stand living at Law's anymore.

He had a friend named Carlton, whom he knew as a decent guy back in Jamaica. Carlton and Vivian were neighbors in Tivoli Gardens, but they were not close back then. Carlton hung with the not-so-down-to-earth people in Jamaica, while Vivian's friends were more the down-to-earth, grass roots sort of people. But, moving to a different country changes people's views, and Vivian and Carlton became closer in New York.

One day, Vivian finally revealed to Carlton what he was going through at his present abode. Carlton was saddened and said, "I've got a room by my mother's and I am hardly there. Plus, as you know, I work at night," he continued, "you can live there. You know my mom very well. She's cool."

Vivian was very happy to hear Carlton's suggestion.

"Come, let's go for your belongings in Manhattan. You can move into my house today," said Carlton eagerly. Carlton and Vivian took the train to 145th Street and went down to Law's apartment. Law came to the door and let them in.

Vivian politely said, "Good day" to Law and Norma who were both at home, because it was a Saturday. Vivian proceeded to the second bedroom where his belongings were, to pack every bit of his belongings so that he would never have to return to the apartment for anything else. Carlton stayed in the living room and spoke with Law and Norma.

Law and Norma looked at Vivian as he entered the living room with his packed suitcase. "Thank you both for letting me stay with you all. I've got a place of my own now," Vivian said solemnly.

Norma nodded her head, but Law wished Vivian well, "Just take care of yourself, you hear?" said Law.

"I definitely will, Law," said Vivian. "I'll come by to visit from time to time," finished Vivian. Then he and Carlton left.

One cold winter night, Vivian walked down the hill atop Anderson Avenue as he watched his girlfriend's father leave for work. Norma's apartment window was on the second floor of the building with her bedroom windows facing the street. He threw a pebble at Norma's window as he always did. She looked outside, opened her window, and tossed out her front door key. Vivian caught the key and went into the building to her apartment.

Norma was all 'sexied' up and smelling good, waiting for Vivian to arrive. He smiled when he saw Norma's sexy body through her see-through nightgown, took her in his arms, and started to kiss her nipples, gently sucking on them through her nightgown. He placed her on the bed and quickly took off his clothes.

"I have something to tell you, Vivian," Norma said softly.

"What is it?"

Norma hesitated for a few seconds.

"What is it, Norma?" Vivian asked again, then turned and faced Norma.

"I'm pregnant," said Norma.

"What? That's the best news I've ever received!" replied Vivian happily.

Norma looked at Vivian with a half-smile. "Why aren't you happy, Norma? What's wrong?"

"You're forgetting one thing, Vivian. I'm married. I couldn't have your baby," said Norma sadly. "My parents are Christians; they would abandon me."

"But I could take care of you," begged Vivian.

Norma smiled and kissed Vivian on his lips. "It would be too much burden on you. You have to be looking out for all your relatives in Jamaica. It would be too much for you," said Norma, with tears in her eyes.

Vivian hugged Norma. "Let's think about this for a couple of days before we make a decision, okay?" asked Vivian.

"Okay," Norma answered slowly. They both hugged each other closely and kissed passionately until they were making love again.

Vivian was now settled in his new job. He and three Jamaican co-workers walked home from the work place after a very hard day at work. Vivian lived closest to the work place on Clay Avenue by 167th Street. He was now living with Carlton's family, which included Carlton's mother and stepfather, Miss Lou and Mr. Derrick, his sisters Pauline, Joan and Sharon, his brothers Emrick and one called Dogga-Putty.

Miss Lou was one of the sweetest, kindest people in the world, and she treated Vivian as though he were more than a son. Vivian loved her like a mother. She was a heavyset black woman, with a round cute face, who loved to cook for her family. Mr. Derrick was a very nice, easy-going man who didn't allow anything to bother him. His pleasure in life was to have a drink around him, but he didn't get too drunk.

Mr. Derrick was tall and slim and was the father of Sharon and Joan, who were twins. These were the two strangest twins; Sharon was dark complexioned like her mother, while Joan was light complexioned like her father. Joan was short like her mother, while Sharon was tall like her father, but they were both very cute.

Then there was Pauline, who kept to herself. She didn't leave the apartment, period—no social life, no job, no nothing, but she did have a boyfriend, by the name of Ryan, nicknamed Marble. Vivian, who was Marble's friend, introduced Pauline to Marble.

Emrick was a tall dark guy, the third child for Miss Lou. He sometimes acted a little crazy and was once institutionalized in a psychiatric home for a few months. Dogga-Putty was the youngest brother, but he was the radical one. He loved guns ever since he was a kid.

Last, but not least, there was Carlton. He was short, dark and good-looking, a flashy dresser with many girlfriends. He was an accomplished welder who worked at the Brooklyn Navy Yard and made a good salary.

Vivian was very comfortable with this family, and they treated him like he was part of the family. This particular evening when he returned home after work, Miss Lou was in the kitchen, fixing a side dish to go with the broiled sirloin steak, which she had in the oven. She smiled at Vivian as he walked into the kitchen on his way to Carlton's room (that Vivian occupied), next to the kitchen.

"You hungry?" Miss Lou asked Vivian.

"Sure, I could eat a cow," replied Vivian.

"You are just in time for my broiled steak with my special sauce," boasted Miss Lou. She took the steak out of the oven and dished out a plate of the food for Vivian.

When they both were finished eating, Vivian rubbed his belly and smiled heartily. "That was great Miss Lou. I enjoyed it," he said happily.

Miss Lou smiled and said, "I'm glad you enjoyed it."

Vivian rose from the table and placed his dirty dish in the sink, then reached for the telephone. He dialed Norma's house and her sister answered the phone.

"Hello, can I speak to Norma?" Vivian asked.

"She's not here. She went to Jamaica this morning," said Norma's sister.

Vivian froze. He had slept with Norma the night before, and she didn't tell him that she was going to Jamaica.

"Thank you," Vivian replied sadly, then hung up the phone. "Can you believe that, Miss Lou? Norma went to Jamaica this morning and didn't even tell me she was going."

"It probably was an emergency," said Miss Lou, defending Norma's action.

Vivian rubbed his head. "It's no emergency, Miss Lou. That's total disrespect."

"You are all young lovers, you all have to work out your problems," Miss Lou said, then walked away.

Vivian was now dating another girl from Brooklyn by the name of Jeanette who was about three years older than Vivian. She was pretty—the sophisticated type—and oh, so sexy! He'd met her at a nightclub in the Bronx on Tremont Avenue. Jeanette was spending the weekend with an African girlfriend in the Bronx, but Jeanette was Jamaican. While Norma was in Jamaica with her husband, Vivian and Jeanette were having fun. Now he had two girls in Brooklyn, Lorna and Jeanette.

Norma spent eight long weeks in Jamaica before she returned to New York, still pregnant, and tried to explain to Vivian. She begged Vivian to come see her, so he went about four days after she returned from Jamaica. Norma was irresistible to Vivian; she was his true love. With the first sight of her, even after eight weeks, he fell into her arms.

"Why, Norma? Why did you go to that god-damned husband of yours?"

"I didn't want to break up my marriage because of this pregnancy," Norma said. "I spoke to my husband yesterday and told him I was pregnant. He thinks it's his child."

"What?" said Vivian astonished.

"Yes, he thinks it's his child. It's better this way. He can provide for the child much better than you could, Vivian. At least you will know in your heart that it's your child, but no one else should know. I'm begging you," Norma pleaded.

He looked at her seriously for a while. "You are serious, aren't you?" Vivian said, "You know what you are asking me to do?" He paused. "To give up my own child, my first child, my own flesh and blood..." Vivian could find no other words.

Norma stared deeply into his eyes. "If you love me, you would. If you really loved me … your child will have a good life." She took a deep breath. "When the child becomes of age, I promise I'll tell him or her who the real father is. I promise."

Vivian was so in love with Norma, he honoured her wishes. Tears rolled down the young man's cheeks, thinking of the sacrifice he had just agreed to make in the name of love.

One spring evening in 1974, Norma, whose pregnancy was beginning to show, was visiting Vivian at Miss Lou's apartment. They were sitting in Carlton's room, talking, when the telephone rang.

Pauline answered the phone in the living room then shouted to Vivian, "Vivian, your call."

He reached into the kitchen for the kitchen phone and took up the receiver. "Hello," he said.

The voice on the other end of the line responded, "Hi, V, this is Jeanette. How are you?"

He panicked a bit then looked over his shoulder where his and Norma's eyes met. "I'm alright, and you?" replied Vivian politely.

Jeanette hesitated on the line, and then said, "You don't sound okay, what's wrong?"

"I'm okay. What's up?" said Vivian more firmly.

Norma looked at him from behind and started to grow suspicious. She walked toward him swiftly then yanked the phone from his ears. "Who is this?" Norma yelled.

"I'm Jeanette, and who are you?" answered Jeneatte politely.

"I'm carrying Vivian's baby, that's who I am, and don't you dare call back this number!" Norma shouted in the phone then slammed the phone down.

Vivian looked at Norma in astonishment. "Why the fuck did you do that?" screamed Vivian. "You've got your husband and I can't do shit about it. Now you trying to make my life hell," he shouted. Vivian was upset. He lunged at Norma, held her by her hair, and started to punch her.

Miss Lou and Pauline heard Norma's screams and rushed to her assistance. They pulled Vivian from atop Norma who was by now on the floor being punched in the face.

"You can't treat her like that, Vivian. She could lose the baby," said Miss Lou.

Vivian, very upset, said, "I don't care," then stormed out of the apartment.

Miss Lou and Pauline took Norma up from the floor and placed her on Carlton's bed. Pauline went for a damp towel to wipe the blood that was pouring from Norma's mouth and the rest of her face.

"What went wrong, Norma?" Miss Lou asked.

"He beat me up because of that bitch who called him on the phone," Norma cursed.

Pauline and Miss Lou just said, "Take it easy, Norma. Men will always be men."

Norma was crying profusely by then and Miss Lou hugged her, trying to comfort her.

Whenever Vivian called Jeanette, she just slammed the phone down, refusing to take his calls. That was the end of a fun-filled relationship between Vivian and Jeanette. After many months, Vivian decided to go out on his own and rented a studio apartment on Grant Avenue, almost at the corner of 167th Street. He bought a bed and a second-hand television set, plus his cooking utensils, but he still visited Miss Lou and the family regularly and had dinner with them.

Norma gave birth to a beautiful baby boy. She spent a few days in the hospital then she was released with her child. Vivian went to visit Norma when she got out of the hospital. He admired his little son who was lying in a bassinet in Norma's room, whom Norma had named Roger. The baby's birth paper had Norma's surname. It was upsetting to Vivian, but he had come to an agreement about this situation long ago. Vivian became attached to the boy and started to sleep with Norma and the boy on a nightly basis again. Most nights, Roger would fall asleep on Vivian's chest.

Getting back with Norma put a strain on his relationship with Lorna in Brooklyn. Not being able to see Vivian on a regular basis, Lorna started a relationship with a guy named Billy in Brooklyn, a short, dark, good-looking Indian guy—a drug dealer. Billy could afford Lorna more than Vivian, so Vivian lost out.

One Saturday night, Vivian went to visit Norma and asked her to loan him twenty dollars. When she obliged, he left Norma's apartment and went to pick up another girl named Paulette whom he had just met. Paulette was a Jamaican, dark-skinned and cute with a curvy body.

Vivian took Paulette to a club on Tremont Avenue where they had a fun time. He had previously told Norma that he would be back that night, but he didn't show. Instead, he took Paulette back to his studio apartment, straight from the nightclub.

Vivian and Paulette were both awakened by loud bangings on his apartment door. He jumped out of the bed, rushed to the door, and looked through the peephole. He froze. Outside his door was Norma, banging on the door with an umbrella. It was raining that Sunday morning. Vivian kept looking through the peephole at Norma without saying a word. Paulette came up close to Vivian, but he indicated to her to keep quiet.

"Open the fucking door, Vivian! I know you're in there!" shouted Norma.

Vivian started to panic, so he rushed back to the bedroom, "Put on your clothes," he said to Paulette. His apartment was on the ground floor with windows to the street, and Vivian contemplated going through the windows to avoid Norma and her screaming of obscenities in the hallway. He moved the shade at the window in his bedroom to see how clear the street was.

Norma rushed around to the window facing the street and saw Vivian looking out. "You dirty pierce of shit, you. You took my money to spend on your bitch! I know you got a bitch in there! I'm going to kill you and that bitch!" shouted Norma violently.

People on the street looked and listened as Norma cursed. Vivian had some dreadlocks Jamaican friends—Big George, Derrick, and Little

Mikey—who had a marijuana joint on the second floor. They were all alerted by Norma's loud shouts, so they came down to Vivian's apartment door. When Vivian heard George's voice, he rushed to the door. "George, you have to help me," Vivian said. "I want you to put my girlfriend up in your apartment."

By this time, Norma was back at the front door acting boisterous. Vivian walked back to Paulette. "I am going to lure her around to the front of the building. When you see me talking to her, just go out the door and up to the second floor to my friends' apartment, okay?" whispered Vivian.

Paulette nodded her head, indicating yes.

When she realized that Vivian wasn't at the door, Norma rushed back around to the street to try to stop him from going out the window.

He started talking to Norma, "Why you acting like this, Norma?" He indicated with his hand for Paulette to go, and she complied. Vivian was leaning on the window glass while talking to Norma.

Big George took Paulette up to his second floor apartment, then came back down to Vivian's door and shouted that everything was alright.

"You fucking dirty, stinking shit, you, Vivian!" Norma cursed, then with a swing of the hand, Norma used her umbrella to break the windowpane. Glass splinters flew and some got into Vivian's eyes.

He screamed, "Norma, I'm blind!" then rushed to the bathroom. He nervously washed his eyes until he realized he could see, and then went back into his bedroom. Norma came back to the window, but Vivian stayed far from the window this time. He wanted to leave the apartment, but did not know how. Big George's voice could be heard at the front door again, and an idea came to him. He walked swiftly to the front door and told George that he and Derrick should hold Norma so he could get out. George agreed.

With Vivian at the front door, Norma rushed back to the hallway. She had a pair of scissors and the umbrella in her hands. Big George and Derrick sneaked up behind her while she was cursing Vivian outside his door and held her, while Norma screamed and kicked.

Vivian, seeing that the guys had Norma covered, opened his door and ran past Norma, Big George, and Derrick, and into the streets, headed toward Miss Lou's apartment. When Big George and Derrick released Norma, she ran out the building, running after Vivian. Vivian could see Norma from a distance, so he ran faster to Miss Lou's house.

Vivian was tired when he reached Miss Lou's house. The cigarette smoking was taking a toll on him. He sat on Carlton's bed, breathing heavily, when he heard someone knocking on Miss Lou's front door. Pauline went to the door and looked through the peephole, then opened the door. It was Norma.

Vivian looked straight down the passageway to the door and shouted, "I don't want her near me, Pauline. Keep her down there."

Norma tried to push past Pauline, but Pauline kept her at bay.

"I'm just going to talk to him, Pauline," said Norma. "I won't make any trouble."

Pauline, still blocking Norma's path, walked in front of her toward Vivian who was lying flat on his back on the bed. "Vivian, she say she just want tot talk," begged Pauline.

"So let her talk quickly, then she just leave me alone," answered Vivian without looking at Norma and Pauline.

"Why you did that to me, Vivian?" Norma asked then walked around Pauline toward Vivian.

Vivian looked up and saw Norma in front of him. "Pauline, why you allow this girl to come in the room?" shouted Vivian.

Anger filled Norma as he spoke. Her hand rose in the air as she lunged at Vivian with the pair of scissors clutched in the hands, aiming for his chest. Quick reflexes and agility allowed Vivian to grab Norma's hand before the scissors could bore his chest cavity. He twisted Norma's hand vigorously until she released the scissors. He was really mad now and kicked Norma viciously like she was a soccer ball, non-stop, until blood was pouring from between Norma's legs. The beating had brought on her monthly menstruation.

Seeing the blood, Vivian stopped kicking her and walked away, headed through the door. Vivian sat outside, across the street from Miss

Lou's building, pondering. About an hour later, he saw Norma emerge from Miss Lou's building, and their eyes met. She started shouting obscenities at him, but he walked away.

"I'm going to put you in jail for what you just did to me!" Norma shouted. She looked up and down the street. "The first police car I see I'm going to have you locked up!"

Vivian started to panic at the sound of jail. He knew he was an illegal alien and could be deported. He tried to move away from her, but everywhere he moved, she was right behind him. He decided to make a run for it. She could not keep up the pace with him so he lost her. Vivian stayed away from Norma as of that day.

Vivian was still working at Finer Chrome Furniture Company. While at work assembling chairs one Monday, one of the Jamaica guys by the name of Tony came to Vivian. "I hear that Immigration Officers will be checking out the factory tomorrow. I was told by the Union Delegate."

Vivian's stomach trembled at what Tony had said. "Immigration? You sure?"

"That's what I was told," Tony answered.

Vivian kept on working. When no one was looking, Vivian who became so paranoid, snuck out of the factory and went home and never returned to the factory after that day. He was out of a job again and did not know what to do.

Vivian had a friend by the name of Mr. Barry—a tall, light-complexioned Jamaican—who grew up in Jamaica with Vivian's friend, Taddy. Mr. Barry had served fifteen years in a Jamaican prison. After his release, he migrated to New York City and to Taddy's house on Grant Avenue. Mr. Barry had an American girl by the name of Neicy who was also light complexioned and very sexy—the expensive type. She wore nothing but Minks and expensive clothes. She was a lady gangster, always knew who the drug dealers were, and she would have Mr. Barry rob them.

While talking to Mr. Barry after walking out on his job, Vivian was encouraged by Mr. Barry to assist him in robbing a drug dealer in Harlem. Being out of cash and flat broke, Vivian decided he would go along with Mr. Barry. They needed another man plus a driver, so they recruited big George and another dreadlocked guy named Kasa, who was a good driver.

It was a cold winter night in January, 1975. Mr. Barry, Vivian, Big George, Kasa, and Neicy drove in Kasa's cab down to a club on 125th Street in Harlem. Neicy went inside the club first with Mr. Barry, then a few minutes later, Vivian and Big George entered. They sat at separate tables from Neicy and Barry, pretending not to know each other. All four ordered drinks and just hung out in the club for a while. Barry and Neicy were watching a drug dealer who Neicy had identified.

About three o'clock in the morning, the drug dealer rose from his seat, leaving some cash on the table for the waitress, then headed out the door. Mr. Barry signaled Vivian and Big George and they all walked out behind the drug dealer, leaving Neicy still at the table. Barry, Vivian and Big George walked toward Kasa, who was sitting in his car with his engine running, while the drug dealer hailed a cab.

Vivian, Barry, and Big George jumped in the back of Kasa's cab and they kept a safe distance behind the drug dealer's cab. They tailed the drug dealer to Bradhurst and 145th Street where his cab turned down Bradhurst and drove to 147th Street. As the drug dealer got out of the cab, Kasa quickly drove alongside the cab. Vivian, Big George, and Barry alighted from the car with guns in their hands. Vivian pointed his gun at the taxi driver's head while Big George and Mr. Barry held the drug dealer at gunpoint. Vivian took the keys out of the cab driver's ignition and ordered him out of the car. He searched the cab driver and found thirteen dollars in his pocket, which he took.

"Please don't kill me," the Haitian cab driver said. "I've got my wife and kids," he nervously begged.

Vivian felt sorry for the cab driver and said, "No harm will come to you. Just remain still ... that's all."

Meanwhile, Big George and Mr. Barry were searching the drug dealer. George's gun went off by accident, and the explosion alerted several people in the surrounding neighborhood. Windows started to open and people peered out to see what was happening.

Kasa tooted his horn at Big George, Vivian, and Mr. Barry. They released the drug dealer and the cab driver in a hurry, for fear the police would soon be on the scene, and rushed to Kasa's car. Kasa put it in reverse, turned around, and sped away.

The days following that botched robbery were haunting for Mr. Barry. He was broke and desperate for money. He and Denise visited Vivian's apartment on Grant Avenue, and Barry told Vivian about another robbery plan.

"I want us to go hit the liquor store at the corner of Findlay and 167thth Street later."

"Alright, check with me later then," Vivian said.

Mr. Barry and Neicy left Vivian's apartment, but as soon as night started to fall, Mr. Barry and Neicy came back to get Vivian. They knocked on the door, but Vivian didn't answer. He knew it was Mr. Barry and Neicy, but he decided that he would not rob anyone again. That Haitian cab driver that he had robbed of thirteen dollars was constantly on his mind. Mr. Barry knocked the door a couple more times, but left with Neicy when he didn't get an answer.

The two of them went to rob the liquor store themselves, but the robbery didn't go as well as they had planned. The owner of the liquor store resisted, and Mr. Barry shot him twice in the stomach. Mr. Barry and Neicy ran from the liquor store but they both were caught by some police officers in patrol cars while they ran down Teller Avenue. Mr. Barry and Neicy were arrested and charged for robbery and attempted murder. They were both found guilty. Mr. Barry was sentenced to fifteen years and Neicy got ten years.

That same night when Mr. Barry and Neicy robbed the liquor store, some friends of Vivian and Big George had pulled off a robbery and went to Big George's apartment with the proceeds from the robbery. Vivian and Big George received three hundred dollars each.

The next day, Vivian and Big George heard what had happened to Mr. Barry and Neicy. Vivian had earlier decided that he was going to call Norris in Connecticut and tell him what had happened at his job. Norris told him to come live with him in Hartford, Connecticut.

With the three hundred dollars, Vivian bought a money order for two hundred dollars and sent it off to his grandmother in Jamaica. "That can keep her until I get another job," he said to himself. Then he went to Big George and gave him his spare key to his apartment. "I'll be leaving for Hartford tomorrow. I am going to try and get a job up there, so you can take the things that are in my apartment after I leave tomorrow," said Vivian.

"Take care," said Big George.

They both embraced each other.

Chapter 4: Hartford, Connecticut

It was mid-winter, 1975, as Vivian hustled amidst the crowd down by 42th St. at Port Authority. He walked swiftly to the Greyhound Bus Station to catch the morning bus to Hartford, Connecticut. The blistery cold morning offered little comfort as he boarded the Hartford-bound bus, which was over a two-hours' ride up I 95 North, through New England.

Norris was at the bus station to meet him. As Vivian hopped off the bus, Norris—a tall, handsome, broad-shouldered man—rushed over to greet him with a hug. Light complexioned and dressed like a pimp—as a matter of fact, he was a pimp of a different sort—he had about six girls who held down nine-to-five jobs and turned over their salaries to him every payday.

Waiting until the luggage compartment of the bus was opened, Vivian retrieved his suitcase, and then walked with Norris to the cabstand where they hailed a cab to take them to Norris' apartment. Peaches, a dark, good-looking girl with buckteeth—a result of sucking her finger as a kid—was living with Norris. Telling the cabbie to wait, Vivian dropped his suitcase at the apartment, and then departed with Norris to his parents house off Albany Avenue in Hartford. Norris paid the cabbie when the car stopped in front of the two-story house, and the pair walked to the front door and rang the doorbell. Norris' thirteen-year-old brother, Rupert, came down the steps and let them in. Rupert was just a baby when Vivian knew him in Jamaica, and hadn't seen him again until he spent a weekend with Norris in Connecticut two years ago, late in '73. Rupert, now with the Dreadlocks Gang, slim and handsome, greeted Vivian warmly, and then led them upstairs. Vivian marveled that all of Norris' brothers were slim and handsome.

The rest of the family was out, either at work or school. Later that evening, though, the whole family gathered for dinner to welcome Vivian—Norris' brothers, Stevie, Picker, Rupert and Michael, with his father (Mr. Garvey), mother (Miss Tiny), and baby sister, Karen.

Upon their return to Norris' apartment, Peaches greeted her man with a passionate hug and a kiss on his lips.

Norris made the introductions. "This is my friend, Vivian."

Peaches looked at Vivian and smiled pleasantly. "Hi, Vivian. Welcome to Hartford." She paused. "I've heard a lot about you."

"Glad to meet you, Peaches." Enthusiasm came through Vivian's smile.

"Likewise, Norris told me a lot about you, too."

Peaches was Norris' hardest working lady. She provided his clothing, paid his rent, and utility bills. Norris said he'd taken Peaches from a Jamaican pimp with the same name as one of his brothers, Picker.

Watching TV in the living room until they all were ready to pack it in, they all three enjoyed a comfortable evening.

The next morning, Peaches prepared a delicious breakfast of boiled green bananas with ackees and salt fish—the national dish of Jamaica—before she went to work. While enjoying his live-in's efforts, Norris announced, "I'll be going to New York next week to attend a players' ball at the Silhouette Night Club in Brooklyn. Have you brought any suits with you?"

"Yes, I have a nice burgundy one that I just had custom-made in the Bronx."

"Well that's good. Otherwise, I'd have to find something for you to wear, because you're coming with me." Norris continued, "Killo will be accompanying us."

"What's a players' ball?"

Norris explained to his friend, "A players' ball is a party where pimps and whores get together and have fun. But, on this particular night, the Mack of the Year will be crowned ... meaning the Pimp of the Year."

Vivian grinned, "It sounds like that party's gonna be fun.

"*More* than fun," said Norris, "more like *interesting*," The sly look and glint in Norris' eyes indicated a secret Vivian didn't yet know.

A week later, the two of them boarded a Greyhound bus to New York City, two flight packs in tow, braving the mid-winter cold. At Port Authority, they took a train to Brooklyn, then a cab to Killo's apartment.

Boomy, Killo and Boomy's girl, Anne, were home, and Killo lavished them with affection as he greeted them at the door. "Boomy, this is my friend, Norris, I always speak about. Anne, this is Norris … you all met Vivian already,"

Norris smiled and nodded at Boomy, and Anne shook Boomy's hand. Boomy and Anne were interested in something on the TV in the living room, so Killo led his two friends to his bedroom where they could stow their luggage. Norris and Vivian sat on the bed while Killo sat on the floor, spilling over with excitement.

"What's happening, Norris? Long time no see, man. We're gonna tear this motherfucking club apart tonight, yo … and show these pimping ass niggas what we are all about, yo."

Norris laughed, "It's gonna be our night, yo. I want me a couple of bitches tonight," said Norris confidently, as Vivian looked on at the two potential pimps talking.

A friend of Killo's, by the name of Garfield, was the proud owner of a brand new, white-on-white Coup de Ville Cadillac, which was the craze in 1975. He'd be the one driving the guys to the players' ball, so when it was time to dress, Garfield was fitted with some clothes from Killo's wardrobe, too.

Their attire was spectacular—Norris in a light, lavender jumpsuit, with a light, lavender bell-sleeve jacket, and a white shirt underneath. An Italian-style broad cap, and bow tie made from the same material as his jumpsuit completed the outfit. His feet were adorned with lavender shoes and matching socks. He carried an ankle-length, white rabbit fur coat, thrown over his shoulder.

Killo was dressed in a pink three-piece suit and matching bow tie around the collar of his white shirt. A pink, broad-rimmed felt hat with a long, white feather adorned his head. He also wore a pair of shoes of the same color, and an ankle-length rabbit coat, dyed pink.

Vivian wore a burgundy three-piece suit and a burgundy shirt with white polka dots. A burgundy bow tie matched the suit, and a pair of burgundy shoes donned his feet. Norris lent Vivian a white rabbit fur hat and a white rabbit fur collar to throw over the collar of his jacket. To top it off, Norris lent him a brown rabbit coat to throw over his shoulders.

Last, but not least, was Garfield. The only outfit from Killo's wardrobe that fit Garfield's short stature was a walking suit. Though not as flashy, Garfield looked damned great in Killo's duds. They left the apartment together, going in style to the players' ball, after Booby and Anne approved the effects of their show-stopping coverings. Garfield drove his Cadillac, Vivian in the front, Killo and Norris in back.

The crowd gathered outside the Silhouette—on Utica Avenue at the corner of Crown Street—made entrance difficult. Killo told Garfield to stop on Crown Street as they neared the crowded nightclub entrance. Garfield brought the car to a halt at a parking spot about twenty-five feet from where the crowd was milling. The four alighted onto the sidewalk and strutted toward the club. Vivian and Garfield flanked Norris and Killo. A low murmur penetrated the crowd. Mouths dropped open in wide amazement as the four *fly guys* approached. The silent crowd voluntarily opened a path down the middle to allow the four awesome guys passage without any hassles. The studs ravished the attention, smiling and returning waves to the beautiful girls admiring the sight before them.

When they finally reached the entrance, Norris paid the fees for all four. The club was packed with pimps and prostitutes, dressed in their finest, the pimps' hair permed; some at shoulder length. Champagnes bottles popped all over the club—they were having a grand time at this players' ball.

Norris, Killo, Vivian, and Garfield's grand entrance caught the pimps and prostitutes off-guard. Nobody had ever seen them before. Pimps were stunned to see their whores staring at the quartet, attracted to the magnificence of their attire as well as their handsomeness. *Who are these niggas?* was the whispered question flying around the room.

Norris—definitely the leader, the king—led the group to the bar where he ordered four bottles of Moët Champagne. The female bartenders scrambled to be of service to Norris and his entourage. Their champagnes were served, and then they all turned to face the pimps and

52

whores who were watching them keenly. The prostitutes couldn't keep their eyes off these marvelous new guys as they lazily strolled by.

A pimp bravely walked over and approached Norris, stretching his hand out to shake Norris' hand. "Yo, bro, what's happening man? I ain't never seen the brothers before, man. Where you all be at? I'm Skip, man."

Norris shook his hand. "I'm Norris, *the Fly*." Then he pointed to Killo, "My homeboy is Fly Baby and that's V and Garfield right there. We all niggas from out-of-town, yo, Connecticut."

"Glad to meet you all, man," Skip said, "You fly, yo, if you copy any-a my bitches yo, here's my number, man … no static, man … and that's word my man," while giving Norris a card.

"Appreciate the respect shown, Skip, my man." Nothing but confidence filled Norris' words.

"Have fun you all … catch up with you players later," said Skip while walking away.

"Peace, Skip. Stay true to the game, man. You a real player, yo," Norris said while Skip backed away, returning to his group of ten bitches.

The night progressed wonderfully for Norris and friends. A fine bitch strutted her stuff across the center of the club and drew everyone's attention. She was light complexioned with the curves of a Coca-Cola bottle. Pretty. She had long, natural hair that flowed down her back. A sexy, skin-tight, sequined dress hugged her slender body, as she walked slowly to the rhythm of the O'Jays slow jam that was playing and headed toward Norris and his friends. She stood in front of Norris' face and puffed on a cigarette while the entire club watched. She looked deeply into Norris' eyes and Norris stared back at her, cunning as a fox.

"I love what I see, daddy. I choose you to be my pimp if you would have me. I'll work hard and make you a lot of money." Norris looked at the girl from head to toe. She turned slowly so that Norris could scrutinize her properly.

"Did I pass, daddy?"

Norris looked in her eyes for a few seconds, as if undecided, then said sternly, "Your choosing fee is five thousand dollars, and, as of now, you're on a short vacation. Enjoy it, because you'll be going back with me to work on the track in Springfield, Massachusetts."

"Your wish is my command. May I sit beside you, daddy?"

Norris looked her up and down again, "You didn't say your name, Red," he demanded.

"You just said it, daddy. My name's Red."

"Nah, from now on, your name is Sexy Red, and, yes, you may sit beside me." Then he turned to one of the bartenders, "Champagne for Sexy Red." In lightening speed, Norris had a champagne glass in his hand and offered it to Sexy Red. "Here, baby."

Red smiled and took a seat beside her new pimp.

Across the club, there was a little commotion. Skip was restraining a pimp with shoulder-length hair, who was wearing a shiny suit that resembled Skip's and had processed tall hair that rested on his shoulder.

"Damn, I'm gonna kill that bitch!" said the pimp as Skip restrained him,

"Yo, it's a players' ball, Pretty Tony. No static, yo. You win some; you lose some, yo."

Pretty Tony looked at Skip and spat out, "That was my prize bitch, yo. She dissed me, man."

Four of Pretty Tony's whores looked at him as he talked about Red, jealousy written all over their faces.

"Daddy, let her go. She always be trouble, anyway," one of the whores spat out.

"Shut the fuck up, bitch! Speak when you are spoken to!" barked Pretty Tony. "Have some respect when you see players talking, bitch!" He slapped the girl across her face with the back of his hand.

Pretty Tony and Skip resumed their talking. "Yo, Skip. That fucking bitch, Red, should die, yo. She better not let me see her whoring ass out in the fucking street else that new nigga of hers better be strapped, yo."

"Let's have fun, man. Forget about that Red bitch, yo." Skip dismissed it.

Over in Norris' corner, the guys were having fun. A very cute, chocolate-colored, sexy whore chose Killo, and both pimps bought their new conquests as much sipping champagne as they could hold.

A woman in a mini skirt walked over to Vivian. "Can I ask you for a cigarette?"

"Sure," Vivian reached into his pocket for the cigarette, pleased that a bitch noticed him.

"What's your game, daddy?" asked the whore.

Vivian wasn't a pimp, so he was not familiar with the terms in the pimping world. He answered, "I sell nickel-and-dime marijuana."

The girl took the cigarette. "Thanks." Then she walked away. She wanted a pimp, not a two-bit hustler.

Vivian didn't take it personally. He knew he was not in league with Norris or Killo. The night progressed fine with Norris, Killo Vivian, Garfield and the two whores having fun together.

The announcement of the Mack of the Year was fast approaching. Everyone's attention was focused on the stage where the MC was talking into a microphone. "Now, this is the moment we've all been waiting for, the Mack of the Year for the year 1974. The votes have been tallied, and we're now ready to announce the winners." He opened an envelope and took out a piece of paper. "The third place winner is no other than our own Baby Face Ray," the MC announced.

A pimp hustled his way through the crowd onto the stage to receive his trophy. Baby Face held the trophy presented to him by the MC in the air and said, " I love you all," to thundering cheers. Then he walked off the stage with his trophy.

The MC opened a second envelope and shouted, "The second place goes to no other than Pretty Tony!"

Pretty Tony walked swiftly through the crowd and onto the stage. "Thank you all for making me number two in this competitive game. Thank you."

Down by the bar, Red, holding on to Norris' arm said, "I made him number two, daddy. At the next players' ball, you'll be number one."

55

Norris looked at Red and smiled, then turned his focus back to the MC on stage, but Red hugged Norris' arm closer to her breast, resting her head on his shoulder.

"Now … the number one pimp, the lady's man of the year, the undisputed one, the Mack of the Year is … no other than Skip. The ladies' pet!"

There was a loud applause from the audience as Skip ran onto the stage to collect the Mack of the Year trophy.

"I'm very honored from you ladies out there, to see fit to vote for me as your Mack of the Year. I thank you all. Stay true, ladies." He blew kisses to the thunderous applause of the crowd.

The night went on joyously, without altercations—everyone enjoying themselves, until the crowd started to trickle away in the wee hours of the morning. Norris and Killo strolled out of the nightclub with their new whores on their arms and with Vivian and Garfield by their sides.

Norris and Vivian went back to Hartford, and Norris started making plans to put Red on the streets in Springfield to work for him.

One cold evening, Norris and Vivian went to Norris' parent's house. Miss Tiny gave her son three containers with enough food in them to serve three people dinner—Vivian, Peaches and himself.

"Bring back my containers in the morning, Norris," said Miss Tiny. "Vivian, you make sure you remind him for me. Norris is very forgetful."

Always respectful of elder people, Vivian acknowledged, "I definitely will remind him, Miss Tiny." Then Norris and Vivian left for their apartment.

Sitting in the living room after breakfast next morning, Vivian lit up a cigarette.

Norris teased him, "This is how you gonna look in your coffin when cigarettes kill you," and lay on the floor, pretending to be stone-cold dead. "I'm gonna give you a wreath made like a cigarette," Norris went on, laughing hilariously, not for the slightest moment knowing he was enacting his own death.

Vivian playfully punched Norris in the arm and reminded him that Miss Tiny wanted her dishes back—today—so they both dressed to leave. After they gave Miss Tiny her dishes, they ambled out to the back verandah where Norris's brother, Rupert, was sitting. Rupert pulled a .22 revolver out, messing with Norris and Vivian, playing like he was threatening them with the piece. He explained that the night before, two Dreadlock's brethren, who lived across the street, gave him the gun to hide for them. The brethren were afraid the police were watching their house and didn't want to be caught with the illegal firearm in their possession.

Rupert pointed the gun in Vivian's direction, but Vivian instinctively moved out of the line of fire.

"Empty guns shoot people, man," he reprimanded Rupert.

Not to be thwarted, Rupert pointed the gun at Norris. Without warning, an explosion cracked the air and the concussion rang through their ears. Frightened by the explosion, Rupert dropped the gun to the floor.

"Rupert, I got shot," Norris said calmly, clutching his chest. "Go. Hide the gun. Police be coming soon."

Rupert picked up the gun and rushed outside. Vivian trembled with panic and rushed into the kitchen to Miss Tiny.

"Norris got shot, Miss Tiny. Call the ambulance."

Norris walked into Miss Tiny's kitchen, clutching his chest, with blood pouring down his shirt. Miss Tiny was unable to move. Vivian grabbed at the phone, dialed 911, then turned back to Norris.

Norris' fist was tightening and squeezing his chest. His breathless words could barely be heard as he muttered, "Rastafari, Rastafari, Rastafari."

Vivian shouted in the phone to the male voice on the other end, "My friend's shot and he's dying," then dropped the phone and rushed to Norris.

He commanded the hysterical mother, "Miss Tiny, tell them the address."

Crying uncontrollably, Miss Tiny rushed to the telephone while Vivian held Norris, blood pouring out of Norris' nose. Vivian felt his heart trying to burst through his ribs. Panic was about to disable him.

Think, Vivian, Think. He heard something inside himself take control. Tears pouring down his cheeks, he lifted Norris in his arms, carried him downstairs and out to the street, running and shouting at the cars passing by, "Help me, please. My friend's dying."

But, none of the cars stopped. Vivian's arms and hands grew weaker and weaker from the weight of Norris' limp body. He dropped to the sidewalk with Norris in his lap and waited for the ambulance. As it finally approached, Vivian felt Norris making his last gasping attempt for breath, and he knew Norris was gone.

The paramedics released Vivian's hold on Norris and placed him in the ambulance. Vivian climbed into the ambulance and watched the paramedics try everything they could, but Norris was dead. Nothing could revive him.

Rupert—only thirteen years old—was taken into the precinct for questioning, along with Vivian. Rupert told the police that he was the one who shot Norris, but it was an accident. Vivian was questioned and confirmed Rupert's story that it was, indeed, an accident. Norris' death affected Rupert to the point that he was admitted into the psychiatric ward of a Hartford hospital.

The hearse headed the procession that slowly rolled into the Hartford, Connecticut cemetery. Family members, along with Vivian and Killo, rode in family cars behind. Vivian, Killo, Norris' brothers—Picker, Steve, Mike—Uncle Bunny and Mr. Garvey removed the coffin from the hearse. They marched to the gravesite, and then lowered the casket via the pulley to Norris's resting place. The funeral was well attended.

Norris' girlfriend from Jamaica, Valerie Easy—nicknamed Kimeeka—saw Norris for the first time in America as his body lay in the coffin. She had arrived from Jamaica about two months before, and was staying with her mother in Philadelphia, Pennsylvania. Her reunion with Norris was supposed to have taken place the week after he died.

Kimeeka, a pretty, chocolate-colored girl stood out from the pack at the gravesite. She was dressed in black and white, as was nearly everyone. The brothers and other male members of the family were decked out in black suits. Vivian was, perhaps, the exception, dressed as he was in flashy, pimpish attire—black suit with white pinstripes, black-and-white shoes, and a black fur hat with a white band around it. He caught the eyes of all the ladies at the funeral.

After the eulogy and Norris' body was lowered completely into the grave, an attractive-looking girl approached Vivian. "Hi, how are you? You're Vivian, right?"

"Yes, I am," Vivian answered politely, flashing a veiled smile—the occasion did not merit smiles.

"My name is Opal, Opal Green. I'm a close friend of the family. I heard you were Norris' best friend. I can imagine how much you miss him."

They chatted a while, different topics coming to mind as they became acquainted.

"So, are you heading back to New York after the funeral?"

Vivian's thoughts traveled for a while as he contemplated his answer. "I don't really know," he finally said, "I gave up my apartment in New York to come live with Norris. Things have happened so quickly I don't even know my head from my toes."

Opal boldly looked him in the eyes. "Why don't you come live with me in Springfield, Massachusetts. It's only half-an-hour from here."

Vivian was surprised at Opal's forwardness. "Just like that? What about your man?"

"I'm free, single and disengaged. No man in my life. I live alone," was Opal's invitation.

Vivian realized he had very few options. Looking deeply into Opal's eyes, seeing her insight and beauty, Vivian decided in an instant. "I guess it's worth a try, ah, Opal?" He paused then said, "We might just work out."

They embraced, sealing the pact.

Norris' eldest brother, Picker, and Kimeeka were watching. "It looks like Vivian's found himself a lady … and, a good one, too. I know her well."

"It sure looks that way to me, too," Kimeeka returned.

Vivian and Opal held hands and walked toward Opal's car. "I want you to come back with me tonight, will you?" Opal pleaded.

"Sure, I'll drive back with you tonight." Vivian was grinning from ear to ear, marveling about the mysteries of the world. His best friend was gone, but a new life was beginning.

Opal spun around suddenly and hugged him, then kissed him on his lips. "Thanks for accepting, Vivian. I was so lonely up there; now my life is complete." She laughed a truly happy laugh. "You know what? Let's leave right now. Let's go pack your things and go."

"All right, all right, but I have to let the family know. Is that okay?" Vivian teased, then took her in his arms.

The drive to Springfield was not as far as Opal had said. As they crossed the Massachusetts State Line, they saw a sign that read: Gun Law, One-Year Mandatory for Possession of a Firearm.

Opal exited the expressway two exits past the state line, and drove to a two-family house in the suburbs. When they got out of the car, Opal walked around to the passenger side of the car and threw her arms around Vivian, clinging tightly as they walked to the back to retrieve Vivian's luggage. Vivian took out his large suitcase and flight pack, which Opal insisted on carrying as they proceeded up the steps to the upper half of the house.

As Vivian took in his new surroundings, he saw a beautiful two-bedroom flat, well furnished, except for the second, unoccupied bedroom. Opal hung the flight pack inside the closet of the bedroom and Vivian slid the suitcase inside. He couldn't help but admire Opal's figure from behind as she walked away from the closet.

They went to bed and didn't awake until noon the next day. Luckily, it was Sunday and Opal didn't have to go to work.

Opal prepared breakfast for Vivian and served him in bed—eggs, bacon, toast, coffee and orange juice. When he finished, she took the tray, kissed him, and went off to the kitchen to start preparing a wonderful dinner.

Vivian was watching TV in the living room when Opal sneaked up and kissed him on his lips. "Honey, dinner's ready." By five o'clock,

Vivian was savoring his favorite Jamaican dish—rice and peas along with oxtail—at the well laid out dining table. Opal was Jamaican. *How lucky can a man be?*

After dinner, Opal telephoned a friend to come over and meet the new man in her life. About eight o'clock her doorbell rang, and Opal buzzed in her friend so that she could come into the upstairs apartment. Vivian was in the living room watching TV, allowing all that wonderful food to digest, when Opal appeared with her friend, a sexy, pretty, chocolate-complexioned girl. "Vivian, meet Ameena."

He rose from the sofa and took Ameena's hand gently. "Glad to meet you, Ameena. I'm Vivian."

Opal sat beside Vivian on one sofa, while Ameena sat on the other one. After they chatted for a while, Ameena said, "Let's go to the club downtown and have a few drinks. What do you say, Opal? Vivian?"

"I don't have a problem with that," Opal agreed. "What do you say, Vivian?"

"No problem, I'm down."

Ameena waited for them to change clothes before they went clubbing.

After Norris died, Killo and his cousins, Lorna and Beverly came down from New York to Connecticut to be with Norris' family in their period of mourning. Lorna and Vivian rekindled their sexual relationship while Lorna was in Connecticut, but Lorna and Beverly had to go back home before the funeral, although Killo stayed on in Connecticut afterward.

The next morning after Vivian, Opal and Ameena had been partying up a storm, Vivian called up to Hartford after Opal left for work.

"Yo, Killo. What's up, man?"

"What's up, homeboy? You enjoying it up in Springfield?"

"I think I'm gonna like it from what I see. I went partying last night, man, and get this ... I've got a pretty little doll for you, man. Her name's Ameena, and she has no man. Ain't no nigga up here, yo," Vivian explained.

Killo started laughing, "Yeah, for real? I'm-a let Picker drive me up there, yo, tomorrow."

"Opal can give Picker directions when she get home from work."

Picker wasn't able to take Killo the next day, so he drove Killo up to Springfield that Wednesday night. Vivian didn't know that it was the beginning of the end of his relationship with Opal when he invited Killo for a visit in Springfield. Killo dazzled Ameena with his city slickers, and she fell for Killo immediately. Everything was fine in the beginning, but Killo spent about two months in Springfield with Opal and Vivian.

One Saturday night, Opal, Vivian, Ameena and Killo went to a nightclub. They were all having fun when Killo started his pimping profile in Ameena's presence, trying to talk some girls into working for him in Springfield. Killo and Vivian were dressed impeccably that night, and Vivian started profiling, imitating Killo, ignoring Opal.

Opal watched Vivian all night long, going up to girls, trying to pimp like Killo, and she was pissed! She was falling in love with Vivian and didn't want their relationship to be anything like Killo's and Ameena's.

That night Opal and Vivian rode home in silence. He suspected what was bothering Opal, but was too proud to apologize to her.

Killo left for New York about two weeks later, but Vivian and Opal were still living in tension. One evening, Vivian was in the living room watching TV when Opal came home with a man. She went straight into the bedroom with him, then came back out, alone, approached Vivian in the living room, and told him, "Vivian, I've started seeing someone and am terminating our relationship as of today. I'm not putting you out. You can use the second bedroom until you decide what you gonna do."

Vivian was dumbfounded. He didn't have anywhere to go, so he had to endure this self-induced embarrassment. He had some Jamaican friends he'd met at a nightclub, and was also in contact with a family he knew from back in Tivoli Gardens, but this family didn't live in Springfield.

After the break-up with Opal, he spent most of his days hanging around with Jamaican friends and came home late at night. He had to sleep on the floor, because there was no bed in Opal's second bedroom, while Opal and her new man slept in Opal's bed. This was killing Vivian, but he had no choice. While lying on the floor one night, Vivian swore into the unfurnished room, "I have to get rich. I'll never sleep on anyone's floor again."

That decision made, he went to New York to pay a visit to a drug dealer—Taddy—he'd met while living on Grant Avenue in the Bronx. He rode a Greyhound Bus to George Washington Bridge Station in Upper Manhattan, then a local bus to the Grand Concourse. The rest of the journey he covered by foot, arriving at Taddy's building and finding him outside, leaning against a car.

"What's happening, Vivi? Haven't seen you for a while."

"I'm living in Massachusetts, but things are rough up there."

Taddy looked at Vivian, sticking out his lower lip in mock sadness. "So what's up?"

"I made the trip to ask you a favor. I want to start doing something for myself, and I'm asking what you can do for me."

Taddy drew closer to Vivian. "What do you want?"

"I'd love to have some marijuana, if you could spare it."

Taddy took Vivian upstairs to his apartment and he gave Vivian a quarter-pound of Colombian Gold.

He could hardly believe his good fortune to get the high-grade marijuana. He shook Taddy's hand as if he wanted to shake it out of its socket. "Thanks, Taddy. One day I'll repay you." Vivian vowed to make his promise good.

Vivian doubled back to Springfield, arriving late in the night, so he went straight to Opal's place. Early the next morning, he called one of his friends to pick him up. His friend drove him to the park where the other Jamaican friends hung out. It didn't take Vivian a minute to spot a male member of the family he knew from back in Tivoli Gardens, named Cous, and told Cous he had a quarter-pound of Colombian Gold.

Cous allowed a smile to break across his face. "I can definitely sell that for you, in nickel-and-dime bags."

So, Cous and Vivian went to Cous' house close by and bagged up the marijuana in small quantities.

Business boomed, and money jingled in his pocket once again.

Opal noticed a change in Vivian when she realized he was starting to make money. She started making up to him, but even though they became friends once again, nothing intimate happened between them. She continually borrowed money from Vivian, which she could never repay, because her new man was not contributing to the bills.

Vivian ran to Hartford once a week to buy a quarter-pound of marijuana to keep his business going, while Cous did the selling, profiting a hundred and fifty dollars—a lot of money in 1975. Cous' cut was fifty.

One weekend, when Vivian went to Cous to collect his money from the sale of the marijuana, Cous came up short of the hundred and fifty dollars, and couldn't give Vivian a satisfactory explanation. Vivian had no more money, not even enough to buy another quarter-pound. "Yo, Cous, I want my fucking money, man. I don't care where you get it, but get my fucking money." Then Vivian walked away.

He took a bus to Hartford and went to see Norris' brother, Picker, who had a .32 revolver stashed away. Vivian told Picker about Cous and his money, then confided in Picker. "I want to borrow your gun. This guy has to pay me my money, man."

"All right, I'll lend you the gun, but be careful up in Springfield. Remember, they say it's one year mandatory for possession of a firearm."

Vivian didn't care about the law; all he wanted was his money back. Picker gave Vivian the gun, and he took a bus straight back to Springfield, going directly to the park where he knew he'd find Cous.

Vivian caught Cous off-guard and pointed the gun at his head. "Where's my fucking money?" Vivian's voice was dripping with anger, as he spat out the words.

The other Jamaicans in the park screamed and one of them said, "No, Vivian, no. Don't shoot him."

Cous was shaking like a leaf on a tree on a windy day. "Please, I'll get the money for you later."

Vivian was still holding the gun at Cous' head. "I'm giving you until *later*... I mean, tonight, *later* ... to get my fucking money, pussy!" He kicked Cous in his ass and removed the gun from Cous' head. Cold sweat ran down Cous' face as he walked away, breaking into a frightened sprint.

Cous' mother came to see Vivian in the park later that evening. "Vivian, what wrong between you and Cous? He told me he owes you a hundred and fifty dollars?"

Vivian had respect for this lady, so he couldn't look her directly in the eyes and tell her what the money was for.

"Look at me, Vivian. Is this true?"

"Yes, he owes me one hundred and fifty dollars."

She reached into her pocketbook, took out one hundred and fifty dollars, and gave it to Vivian. "Don't give Cous any more money to keep again, 'cause he *loves* to spend money." Then she left. She never suspected it was drug money that Cous owed.

That night, Vivian packed his belongings and told Opal he was leaving for Hartford the next day, never to return to Springfield. In the morning, they hugged each other at the house before Opal drove Vivian to the bus station. They embraced one more time at the bus station, then Opal drove away.

Vivian reached Miss Tiny's house within an hour. Picker was there to open the door for him, and he immediately told him, "Lorna just called from New York for you. You can use my phone to call her back."

Vivian put his suitcase and flight pack in a room adjoining Picker's rooms, then used the phone to dial Lorna's number.

"Hello."

"What's up, babes?"

Lorna became very excited when she heard his voice. "When are you coming to look for me? When you wanna see me? Now?"

He pondered for a moment and decided not to rush into anything. "I'll call you back and tell you when I'm coming, okay?"

"All right … later." They both hung up.

Two days later, Vivian took the bus to New York to visit with Lorna at her mother's house. It was a happy reunion. When Lorna greeted him at the door, they hugged and kissed passionately. That night the two lovebirds had a fun time.

It was the last two weeks of spring when Vivian returned to New York. After three weeks, Vivian still had no income, so Lorna had to support him the best she could. Killo had an old girlfriend from Canada who came to New York to find him and ended up bunking at Lorna's mother's house at the same time that Vivian was there. Killo's girlfriend's name was Peaches—light skinned, but not very attractive—who supported Killo well in earlier times.

Lorna's mother, Miss May, took a liking to Peaches. Miss May was one of those Jamaican ladies who worked hard; she had two jobs. For an elderly lady, she looked good and was very well built. Miss May had a sister by the name of Miss Gladys who lived about three blocks away. Miss Gladys was a short and stocky black Jamaican woman, but she was sweet and kind-hearted, unlike Miss May. Then there was Kicks, Miss May's husband, a very jovial and free-spirited man who acted as though he was sixteen years old. He was a very small-bodied black man with a gold tooth—a distinguishing characteristic.

With Vivian not supporting Lorna, it started to pose a problem for Miss May. She started grumbling about it, taking Peaches into her confidence.

While they were down in the basement of the house one day, Miss May—Peaches by her side—accosted her daughter. "All you do every day is fuck, fuck, fuck with Vivian, and feed him with my food, and this boy don't have dry shit in his ass to give you. Why you don't find a man to support you?"

Beverly—Lorna's sister—and Finey had come out of the bedroom when they heard Miss May shouting at Lorna.

Vivian was upstairs in Lorna's bedroom, but he overheard Miss May when she was shouting at Lorna. He felt bad—it was embarrassing—but he just stayed in the room, unable to do the right thing.

After embarrassing Lorna with her disgusted shouting, Miss May walked back upstairs, leaving Lorna, Peaches, Beverly and Finey in the basement.

"She can't tell you how to live your life," Beverly said to Lorna. "She's out of order."

66

Lorna was crying, "When Vivian was working and giving me money, Mamma was happy, but now that he's not working she don't like him any more."

Finey and Beverly went back into their bedroom leaving Lorna with Peaches.

For the next week, there was a lot of was uneasiness between Vivian and Lorna. One hot summer night, Vivian, Lorna, Peaches, Beverly, Pauline and Pauline's lover, Derrick, were sitting on the steps outside Miss May's house. A car pulled up and a guy exited the car. Everyone watched as he walked toward the fence that surrounded Miss May's house. Lorna rose from her seat on the steps, walked toward the gate, opened it and greeted the guy on the sidewalk. They stepped away from the gate and started talking. Everyone was astonished at Lorna's boldness in front of Vivian, except Peaches, who had a grin on her face.

Vivian was so embarrassed he couldn't speak. He rose from the step, went inside the house, packed his traveling bag, and then came back out. His head bent, steps that of a very sad man, Vivian gave the appearance of being totally dejected. "I'm going back to Hartford."

"I'll drop you at the train station," Derrick offered.

Without saying a word, Vivian walked out of the yard toward Derrick's car.

Lorna's new guy, Barney was familiar. He was one of the lead members of a feared Jamaican gang called the *Untouchables*, who were in control of Brooklyn's drug trade. Their leader was an elderly man by the name of Peter Blackity, who originated from Tivoli Gardens, but used to hang out at Rae Town in Kingston.

Derrick drove Vivian to the train station. "That was total disrespect what Lorna did. Women … women, they're the most unpredictable things on earth. You can't trust 'em,"

A sly grin crossed Vivian's face. Already he was plotting out what he had to do. "One day things are gonna change, Derrick."

Vivian took the train to Port Authority then took a Greyhound to Hartford. While on the bus to Hartford, Vivian thought out aloud, "Why am I going back to Hartford? If I'm going to make it, New York would be the best place to start." He was only fifteen minutes from Hartford when he made the decision to move back to New York.

He spent two days in Hartford, then called his long-time friends—Miss Lou and the family—in the Bronx.

"Hello, who's this?"

"This is Vivian, Miss Lou. How are you?"

Miss Lou was excited to hear his voice. "Why, Lordy. It's been a long time since we heard from you. How is everything?"

"I was planning on coming to New York to spend a week or two with you." Vivian was checking her out to see if she would invite him to stay.

"You know you're welcome here anytime. The door's always wide open for you."

Yes! "Then tell the rest of the family that I'll be up there in two days."

"Emrick is here … talk to him." She handed the phone to her son.

"What's happening, V? Momma said you coming up?"

"You bet. Two days."

Chapter 5: Back to the Bronx

On a very hot summer's day, the Greyhound bus pulled up at the George Washington Bridge bus station in upper Manhattan. Vivian departed with all of his worldly belongings in tow, the usual suitcase and flight pack. The street was crowded, Hispanics and blacks buzzing around, cold beers in their hands, trying to alleviate the heat radiating all around.

Vivian hailed a cab, and as it came to a halt inches away from his feet, threw his suitcase and flight pack in the back seat, and hopped in alongside them. "Grand Concourse and 174th," Vivian shouted to the cabbie as he lowered the back windows. *The Bronx again* he said to himself, shaking his head and smiling.

The cab whisked him over the bridge, into the Bronx, and continued on its way to Vivian's destination. Rolling down the Grand Concourse off the express lane, the cabbie came to a halt at a huge complex of four apartment buildings. Vivian paid the fare, and then took his suitcase and flight pack inside the courtyard to the building of Miss Lou's apartment.

Taking the elevator to the third floor, he reached out to ring the doorbell. Emrick, Sharon, and Joan opened the door. "Vivian!" Their delighted shouts reassured Vivian that he was welcomed.

Pauline and Miss Lou threw their arms around him in a warm greeting. Miss Lou took the flight pack and Emrick took the suitcase as they showed him to Carlton's room, depositing his belongings in the closet. They all went into the living room and reacquainted themselves, laughing and joking, exchanging stories and tales.

"Emrick, let's take a walk down to Grant Avenue," said Vivian.

"I'm ready whenever you are."

Vivian rose from the sofa and told Miss Lou and the kids that they would be back soon, as the two took their leave of the apartment.

They walked down the Grand Concourse to 170th St., then east on it to Grant Avenue. Some Jamaican kids were muzzling the water at the hydrants—which were on full-blast—using empty condensed-milk tins, so that it sprayed the passing cars forcefully. Drivers had to keep their windows shut tight, which caused them to shake their fists and swear at the kids, the heat building inside their cars on such a sweltering day.

Vivian's friend, Taddy, spotted them and pointed out Vivian to a guy leaning on the car beside him, named Sisko. "There goes, Vivi."

Taddy was a tall, dark, elderly man from Tower Hill in Kingston, Jamaica. In order to look more like an American, he always wore sneakers, a hat over his kinky-curly hair, and rarely smiled, for he sported a gold tooth, hopefully unnoticed by the cops who patrolled the area looking for Jamaicans hustling on the street corner.

Sisko was a very light complexioned, short, and a good-looking young man, who originated from Matthews Lane in Kingston, Jamaica. The dreadlocks he once wore were now cut off, and he, too, sported a gold tooth.

Vivian, followed by Emrick, returned the greeting. "What's up, Taddy? Sisko? What's going on, man?"

"Long time no see, man," came from Sisko.

Taddy followed with, "So, how's things in Connecticut, V?"

"Slow … very slow." Vivian shook his head.

Taddy had been around for a while, and understood Vivian's dislike. "I don't like those country states. Money's slow and you get busted quickly. Try and see if you can do something in the city."

"I'd love that, Taddy, but it takes money to start up a business, which I ain't got."

"So where are you heading to?"

"I came to visit with you, but I'm going to check with Big George down the block, then check back with you later."

"All right. Do your business, then check with me later, okay?"

"See you soon, Taddy … Sisko." Sisko merely nodded.

Big George and some of his Dreadlock friends were playing with a soccer ball in front of the apartment building where he had his marijuana spot. Big George spotted Vivian and Emrick coming down the street and hailed them loudly.

"What's happening, Vivian? Long time no see." The other Dreadlocks eyed Vivian cautiously.

"I've been in the country, man. The Connecticut bushes. Just chilling, yo." He joined in the sidewalk soccer game. After keeping the ball in the air for a while, the game came to a halt as everyone was dripping with perspiration.

Vivian took George aside for a little chat. "I feel like I'm going to live back here in New York, man. It's slow up in the bushes, man."

"That's mighty wise of you, man. Money is in New York. Yo, you can make a lot of shit here." George was leaning on a car and straightened his stance. "Some ital stew's cooking upstairs. Want some?"

"Sure." Vivian jumped at the offer of friendship and free food, and he and Emrick followed behind Big George into the apartment building.

Later on that evening, Vivian and Emrick went back to see Taddy and Sisko. All four guys leaned back on a car while Taddy and Vivian spoke.

"Vivi, you can come hustle with me upstairs. It's just me and Sisko. Sisko sells ounces … you could sell the nickel bags, and help Sisko sell my pound marijuana."

"Sounds good, Taddy. I'm ready. When do I start?"

"Tomorrow or the next day if you like … within a week … no immediate rush."

Sisko accepted Vivian into the business with a pound (handshake). "Yes, nigga, you and I will be at the control."

Vivian could hardly believe his good fortune.

Two days later, Vivian reported to Taddy. The morning was boiling hot, but Vivian walked swiftly from Miss Lou's apartment to Taddy's marijuana house. He reached the house about ten o'clock, but over an hour passed before Sisko arrived, and they could go up to Taddy's fourth-floor apartment together. Sisko unlocked the door and immediately proceeded to show Vivian how the operation worked. He took him into the bedroom and showed him a barrel filled with marijuana. "You weigh the marijuana into one-pound parcels from this barrel. Take out a pound each time and package it into nickel-and-dime bags—I'll show you how. After you've finished them, you repay Taddy for the pound of marijuana you used—four hundred dollars."

Vivian was a smart. Sisko didn't have to repeat the directions twice. He weighed out a one-pound parcel of marijuana from the barrel, and then they both proceeded toward the kitchen, where Sisko poured the pound of marijuana on the table. He taught Vivian how to wrap the nickel-and-dime bags, which were larger than the regular ones sold on the street corners—to attract the customers. After they finished bagging up the dope, the total number of bags equated to eight hundred dollars, which meant Vivian would make four hundred dollars after he'd paid Taddy his share. This was Vivian's chance. After the first four weeks of sales, Vivian started to sell three pounds of marijuana every two weeks, earning twelve hundred dollars every two weeks, tax-free.

Vivian was still living with Miss Lou, so he gave Miss Lou fifty dollars—sometimes a hundred—every week. Miss Lou was able to move from 174th and the Grand Concourse to a posher building on Grand Concourse by 166th St.

One August night, Vivian, Sisko, Taddy and one of Taddy's friends, named Joe, were all watching TV in Taddy's living room. Sisko had accidentally shot himself in the hand a couple of days prior, so his fingers were wrapped in bandages. There was a knock on the door and Taddy went to check it out. Three of Taddy's friends came in for a visit. Taddy and two of the friends stayed in the kitchen and talked, while the other friend came into the living room to see who was in there. The guy recognized Sisko.

"What's happening, Sisko? How's Bird?"

"He's okay. Back in Jamaica."

The guy then went back into the kitchen where Taddy and his two other friends were talking. Vivian, Joe and Sisko were deep into the movie playing on the TV. All of a sudden, three explosions were heard coming from the kitchen and they watched Taddy run around to the living room and then the bedroom, screaming, "Police! Police!"

Everyone panicked and ran toward the bedroom, but Taddy had locked them out. Vivian was the last one to rise from the living room sofa. The sounds of two more explosions filled their ears. Sisko was the only one with a gun, but with his hand bandaged, he couldn't hold it properly.

With the bedroom door locked and inaccessible, everyone ran inside the bathroom. Vivian headed for the bathroom window and was hanging out from the ledge, ready to jump. His hat fell to the ground, and he realized how far he was from the ground—four floors plus the basement.

He proceeded to climb back into the window when Joe's foot stomped him in the face as Joe prepared to jump through the window. Vivian fell back from the force of the blow, but clung to the concrete windowsill for dear life. If he fell he would surely die, or at least be crippled. He pulled himself up through the window and went back into the bathroom. Joe should've thanked his lucky stars that Vivian hampered his jump, because he would have surely died, too.

The shots had ceased, so Vivian took the gun from Sisko, tiptoed out of the bathroom and peeked into the living room. The TV was still on, and Taddy's German shepherd lay bleeding on the floor, but no one else was present. The front door was open … the intruders had made their escape. Vivian shouted at the bedroom door to Taddy. "They're gone!"

Taddy opened the door slowly and peeked out, then made a dash toward the front door, bleeding and holding his chest. He ran straight downstairs and drove himself to the hospital.

Sisko and Joe came out of the bathroom cautiously and looked around. Sisko's voice was filled with apprehension. "Let's lock up the apartment and go downstairs—outside."

After a few hours, Taddy came back from the hospital with Mr. Mel—another friend of his. Minor flesh wounds from two bullets had been cleaned and bandaged. "Might as well go upstairs and clean the place up."

After throwing out the dead German shepherd, it was business as usual. Within a couple of days, Taddy was as good as new.

Sisko's hand being in bandages, Vivian had to stand guard at the apartment with the automatic pistol. One evening while Sisko was out and Vivian was alone at the apartment, he felt hungry, but couldn't leave the apartment, because there'd be no one to tend to customers. He called the Chicken Delight restaurant on 167th St. at the corner of the Grand Concourse, and ordered a five-piece chicken with fries and soda, to be delivered to Taddy's apartment.

Within a few minutes, there was a knock on the door. Vivian approached with the gun in his hand. He looked through the peephole and saw a Hispanic man with the chicken dinner. Not realizing that he had the gun in his hand—as if it were a marijuana sale—he opened the door and waved the guy in with the gun.

"$5.35," said the Hispanic man. Catching the sight of the gun, he dropped the dinner to the ground in panic, and ran. He tumbled down four flights of steps, coming very close to breaking his legs, and then ran like wildfire.

Watching the frightened man, Vivian realized he had a gun in his hand. He panicked for a minute, thinking that the guy might call the police. Instinct told him to close up the apartment and get the hell out of the building. Not knowing what to do, he decided to walk to the restaurant and peek in. The Hispanic man was behind the restaurant counter, wide-eyed and trembling.

Vivian didn't want to leave the situation as it was—it might've resulted in a visit from the police—so he entered the restaurant and decided to talk to the man. On seeing Vivian enter the restaurant, the Hispanic man panicked even more. His eyes widened as he pointed to Vivian, jabbering in Spanish to a man who seemed to be the restaurant owner.

Vivian thought of stepping back out, but opted to face the situation bravely, and walked up to the man. "I'm very sorry for what happened, but I was robbed at my house a couple of days ago, and have been on edge ever since." Turning toward the owner, he apologized. "I didn't realize he was the deliveryman. I'm really sorry, Sir."

The owner listened patiently. "I understand. I was recently robbed myself. Just pay for the food and let's forget this whole thing ever happened."

Vivian reached in his pocket and gave the man twenty dollars, "Give him the change … for his trouble, please, and thanks again."

The boss nodded his head and smiled as Vivian walked out of the restaurant, knowing he'd done the right thing.

The number one sound system for hire in the Bronx was Down Beat International, owned by one Tony Screw. He was given that name because of a deformity that made one side of his face three times the size of the other. Sisko and Vivian asked him to come see them at Taddy's apartment, for they were planning a party at Miss Lou's the third Saturday in October '75.

"That date's still open. You can have the sound system that Saturday night."

Invitations were printed for Saturday, October 22, 1975.

Big George, who was then living on Mount Eden Avenue with his parents George and Adina Taylor Williams—Mother Will and Father Will—also had three sisters and one brother.

George's eldest sister, Valerie, would be perfect for my wife, Vivian thought to himself. He'd never spoken to her before but had seen her on a couple of occasions when he went to visit Big George. Vivian decided to invite Valerie to his party—personally—so, he went to their home the next Sunday morning, about eleven o'clock. That's when he figured Valerie would be home. He rang the doorbell and Mother Will opened the door.

I'll just pretend it's George I want to see. "Morning, Mother Will. Is George in?"

"Yes, dear, he's around the back." Mother Will was one of the most polite, most charming ladies ever born—warm and loving with a pleasant smile. She treated all young people as if they were her own.

As Vivian entered the apartment, right across from the doorway, over in the living room, his eyes met Valerie's. She was sitting on the floor, sorting out some papers. Vivian smiled at her and walked over boldly, invitation in his extended hand. "I'm inviting you to my party."

Valerie accepted the invitation with a smile, then read the date. "I have a party to go to that night, but I'll stop by yours first," she said, politely and appreciatively.

"I'm looking forward to seeing you there," Vivian said, turning on the charm.

"I'll be there."

Vivian couldn't help but stare at her for a few seconds then said, "I'll see you, then."

She acknowledged him with a smile and nodded. Then he walked toward Big George's bedroom.

Finally, the night of the party came. Liquor was in place, food cooked and everything set to go. They removed the furniture from both Miss Lou's living room and a bedroom. Sisko was in charge of the bar and Vivian was in charge of the admission fees.

Vivian was looking dapper that night. He wore a powder-blue, custom-tailored, three-piece suit with matching platform shoes. A bow tie fit snugly underneath the collar of his white after-six shirt, and a powder-blue-and-white beaver tilted on his head. Immaculate.

Down Beat International was playing the latest in Reggae music, while the patrons trickled inside the apartment. The crowd increased as Vivian anxiously waited for Valerie to arrive. Big George was already there and partying with his girlfriend, Pat.

Pat came to the party dressed like an African Queen, in her African-print dress, and matching head wrap. She always looked good in her African garb and had a smile that could knock a person out. Pat was dark and strong, a real African Queen.

Vivian's anticipation came to an abrupt end when he saw in front of him a sexy, light complexioned nineteen-year-old girl approach the door—Valerie. She was dressed beautifully and her face radiated confidence in her appearance. Marie—a short, small-bodied chick, fair complexioned and a few years older than Valerie—accompanied her.

Vivian's heart was pounding. "How are you, Valerie?"

"I'm fine."

He allowed Valerie and Marie to enter before he said anything else to Valerie. "I want talk to you … I'll come and see you in a few minutes."

"All right, I'll be inside." She walked away with Marie.

Vivian had to do his duties at the gate's and it was killing him. He wanted so badly to go and talk to Valerie. Twenty minutes passed before he decided to call on Sisko to help him out for a few minutes—Sisko was at the bar with his girlfriend, but he obliged.

Vivian straightened himself … the bow tie and hat, and then headed into the living room to find her. Confident on the outside, butterflies in his stomach on the inside, he approached her. Valerie and Marie were dancing to the Reggae beat without partners.

"May I have this dance?" He took her hand and they started to dance. He spoke into her ear while they danced. "I'd like to see you again … take you out."

Valerie smiled but didn't say anything.

"Can I call you tomorrow?"

"Sure," said Valerie with an inviting smile.

They danced until the song was finished. "I'll call you tomorrow. I have to go back to the door. See ya, okay?"

While at the gate, Vivian couldn't stop thinking about Valerie. Of the two girls he had had on his mind, one of them had come to reality—Valerie. The other girl—Tessy—was the sister of Taddy's wife. Tessy was tall and very shapely, like a model, and dark complexioned. Vivian had always favored very light complexioned girls, but Tessy was an exceptional chocolate, and above all, she was a Christian.

The party was a success—everyone was having fun, and Vivian and Sisko made a ton of money. Valerie and Marie had to leave early, because they had another party to attend. They walked together up to the door where Vivian was standing. "We have to leave now, but I enjoyed the party."

"I'm glad you had fun. Talk to you tomorrow. Enjoy yourselves, wherever you're going."

"Thanks." Marie nodded her head at Vivian approvingly.

What a lady she is. She's gonna be mine.

The party went on until five-thirty the next morning, and everyone who assisted with the party arrangements was drained. Miss Lou and Pauline worked tirelessly until the wee hours of the morning. Vivian didn't manage to get much sleep. His mind was on Valerie when he went to bed and when he awoke up at ten in the morning. He figured he'd call her about eleven o'clock, and watched the clock every minute until then. It was the longest hour he'd ever spent.

"Hello," said the voice of an elderly lady.

"May I speak with Valerie?"

"Sure, hold on," said the elderly voice.

He waited for a few seconds then he heard a female voice on the line. "This is Valerie."

"Hi, this is Vivian? How are you?" He could hardly contain his excitement.

"Great, and you?"

"I'm fine, especially now that I'm talking with you." Vivian was putting on the charm. He didn't want to mess this one up. They spoke for about half-an-hour and Vivian promised to visit her at her home later that Sunday evening.

Before Sunday dinner at Miss Lou's, Vivian showered and immediately afterward dressed to see Valerie. He wore the same powder-blue pants, shoes, and hat as he had at the party, but added a powder-blue turtleneck sweater, and a leather jacket for the look. Walking on the Grand Concourse from 166th St. to Mount Eden Avenue, he caused a stir with the ladies. Making a right turn on Mount Eden, he continued toward Valerie's apartment building.

Big George's girlfriend, Pat, and his sister, Lorna, were looking through the window, anticipating Vivian's arrival. When they saw him, they were ecstatic.

Lorna was friendly with Miss Lou's son, Emrick, in the earlier days. She was always the withdrawn, the quiet one in the family.

Vivian waved at Pat and Lorna as he approached, and the girls were soon joined at the window by Valerie's younger sister, Grace—the crazy one. She was light complexioned and a little shorter than Valerie.

Vivian entered the apartment building and was let in by Valerie. Mother Will greeted him pleasantly, but Father Will's greeting was anything but affable. The mean look on his face told Vivian, *Watch out. That's my daughter.*

Valerie escorted Vivian to the living room where they sat and talked for a while, getting to know each other. The other girls joined them later and everyone laughed and talked. Vivian invited Valerie to the movie the next day—Veteran's Day. She asked if she could bring Marie along, and he told her it wasn't a problem.

The next evening, Vivian arrived at Valerie's apartment as the family was finishing their Veteran's Day dinner. Valerie, Marie, and Vivian left for a theater by Fordham Road. They enjoyed the newly released flick, *Let's Do It Again,* and continued laughing as they left the theater. A cab was hailed for Marie, because she lived across town.

"Let's go have a drink." Vivian wasn't ready to take Valerie home.

"Where?"

"There's a nightclub close by your apartment on Jerome Avenue. I'd like to take you there."

"Sounds good to me."

It was a very slow night at the nightclub—only one other couple in the whole place—but it turned out to be the perfect setting. Vivian ordered Harvey's Bristol Cream for both of them. As they sipped their drinks and talked, Valerie told him she had a man, but that the relationship was on the rocks—her man was in the Navy. It was just a matter of time before it ended.

Vivian convinced Valerie of his genuine feelings for her, that he wanted an intimate relationship. She agreed to start seeing Vivian on a regular basis, but didn't totally commit to ending the relationship with her boyfriend—Trevor—called Ten Man.

He could live with the arrangement for the present, he surmised, but he intended to override it in the near future. He rose from the table, went to the jukebox, inserted some coins, and punched his favorite tune six times, *For the Love of You,* by the Isley Brothers, then sat back at the table. As the tune started playing, he held Valerie's hands in his palms and said, "This tune's for you. Never forget it." He clutched her hands lovingly and sang along with the song, while looking deeply into Valerie's eyes. It was a very romantic occasion and Vivian ended the night knowing he'd won Valerie's heart.

The following weekend, Valerie wanted Vivian to take her to a nightclub in the Bronx—Epiphany—where most of her friends and associates hung out on Saturday nights. Vivian picked her up at her home. She wore a beautiful dress.

Dressed to kill likewise, Vivian was wearing a three-piece black suit, with white pinstripes, white shirt, black-and-white tie, and black-and-white shoes. His hat was black fur with a white band around it. There was a white pompom on his lapel, and he carried a white, ivory-handled walking stick to top it off.

Valerie was impressed—so proud to be the girl entering Epiphany with this young man on her arms—as they hopped out of the cab to numerous stares.

They walked into the club arm-in-arm. Valerie didn't leave Vivian's side but for a few brief moments when she spoke with some friends.

There were some slick Jamaican guys who lived in Queens, led by a guy named Lance. They were the fly guys who had the girls all over them. But, with the look in Valerie's eyes, it was clear that she was on top with the flashiest man in the club that night, outshining the boys from Queens. The night went well.

When they left the club in the wee hours of the morning, Valerie didn't want to leave Vivian's side, so they took a cab down to Taddy's apartment on Grant. No one was at the apartment and Vivian had the keys. It wasn't the best apartment for their first romantic interlude, but it sufficed. The bedroom was their destination.

The next morning, Vivian hailed a cab, and paid in advance for the driver to take Valerie home. He gave her a final, passionate kiss before seeing her off. She waved to him from the back seat, smiling, and he waved back happily.

Now, he thought, *I have conquered! That's my woman now. No turning back.*

In the weeks that followed, there was tension. Valerie's family was close to her boyfriend Ten Man, and Ten Man was due to visit Valerie in a few days. She was certain the relationship with Ten Man was over—she was going to tell him so. On the other hand, she was young, so family pressure could prevail.

Vivian was sure that one person, Pat—Big George's girlfriend—was on his side. Valerie's mother was neutral; she said Valerie should make her own choice.

That day, Valerie and Vivian met before Ten Man came to her home. She assured Vivian that she was going to tell Ten Man it was over, but Vivian was still nervous. Ten Man stayed at Valerie's house for about three hours.

Vivian was waiting nervously by Miss Lou's apartment to hear what had happened. He left his apartment and walked slowly up the Grand Concourse, figuring the meeting should be over. He walked to Mount Eden Avenue and looked at Valerie's apartment building. There was no sign of life at the window where the girls would sometimes look out. He went to a phone booth and dialed Valerie's phone number nervously.

Valerie quickly answered the phone, telling him, "I just called you at Miss Lou's, but you weren't there … I told him it was over … he's gone … you can come over."

"I'll be right there."

Chapter 6: Start Hustling

Sisko and Vivian were still working with Taddy, but Vivian and Taddy's relationship was showing strain. The marijuana supply was coming up short and Taddy thought Vivian was stealing from him. Vivian had taken a quarter-pound out of Taddy's marijuana only once and had given it to a friend—Marble—because he'd seen Sisko do so on numerous occasions. Taddy never suspected Sisko; he thought Vivian was the one who was pilfering the marijuana, but it occurred *after* Vivian came to work for him.

Vivian took the blame, anyway, and he and Taddy had an argument in the presence of Sisko and Mr. Mel. Taddy held his pistol in his hand in the heat of the argument and Vivian left, very upset.

Vivian swiftly walked to a friend's apartment—Crusty—who lived on 165th St. at the corner of the Grand Concourse. Crusty was a real black individual—black and cool—from Tower Hill in Kingston, Jamaica.

Vivian banged on the apartment door, still steaming, and Crusty let him in.

"Man, I want to borrow a gun. A guy just disrespected me."

"Cool down, V. What happened?"

"A guy named Taddy just pulled his gun on me saying, I stole his weed …and I didn't."

Crusty pulled a .38 revolver from his waistband, emptied out the six bullets, and then handed the revolver and the six bullets to Vivian, separately. "Just be careful," he said with a sly grin on his face.

Vivian took the gun and ammo from Crusty and rushed out of the apartment, loading the pistol in a dark corner at the top of Grant Avenue, then putting the pistol back in his waistband.

As Vivian approached Taddy's apartment building, Mr. Mel was walking up Grant Avenue in his direction. He saw Vivian's suspicious look and accosted him. "Youth, don't put yourself in any trouble. Forget what happened upstairs a moment ago. Taddy don't have much sense.

He's illiterate." He continued to talk to Vivian and convinced Vivian to forget the problem.

Vivian took Mr. Mel's advice and went home.

Vivian's first real taste of money came from working for Taddy. He locked himself in his room at Miss Lou's apartment and thought. With the money he had made working for Taddy, he had been able to stock his closet with custom-built suits, designer wear, and was also able to send large stacks of cash to his grandmother in Jamaica. He had to keep earning. *I can't quit now.*

The next day, after his run-in with Taddy, Vivian went apartment hunting, in order to start a nickel-and-dime marijuana spot. Luck was with him on his first try; he found an apartment on Gerard Avenue between 182nd and 183rd St. The second-floor apartment was ideal for a marijuana spot. That same week he signed the lease, and by the weekend, the apartment was sparsely furnished, but ready for business.

Vivian bought himself a half-pound of marijuana and started selling. His first customers were a couple of Puerto Rican gay men who lived in the apartment directly above him. Business wasn't big, but the bills could be paid with a little change left over.

He had previously sent money to Jamaica to buy a visa for his kid brother, Tony, and an airline ticket for his best friend, Caltman Daley. Caltman came up the week after Vivian opened up the marijuana spot and joined him.

The following month, Vivian's grandmother called and said that Tony received his visa, so Vivian was to pick up Tony in Miami the next day. Grandmother, not knowing the cost of airline tickets, took for granted that going to Miami was an easy task. Money was tight with Vivian, as the marijuana business wasn't yet flourishing, but he had to go to Miami. He took five hundred dollars from his thousand-dollar stash and went to Miami the next day.

When he arrived at Miami International Airport that afternoon, he could see from inside the airport that the day was sunny, but he didn't go outside to enjoy the weather. Instead, he hustled to the terminal section where the Air Jamaica plane would arrive and scanned the monitor to find the time of arrival for his brother's flight. An hour early, he waited anxiously. Finally, after two hours, the restricted-area door slid open and there was Tony, looking very suspicious. As Vivian happily approached Tony, Tony waved him away, as if he had experienced a problem inside the customs or immigration area. Vivian followed behind him until they were far away from the Air Jamaica terminal, then Tony stopped and relaxed.

"I didn't want you to talk to me there, for fear that someone would see us talking."

Vivian laughed out loud. "Are you stupid? You're not traveling illegally. You have a valid visa."

Vivian didn't stop laughing at Tony until they reached the Eastern Airline's ticket counter to purchase their tickets to New York. They had two hours to kill before flight time, so dinner at an airport restaurant seemed the thing to do.

At end of springtime, 1976, Paul Anthony Bruce—a.k.a. Tony—arrived in New York as a seventeen-year-old teenager. He was lanky and very dark in complexion. Vivian managed to get him out of Jamaica before anything fatal—or otherwise injurious—happened to Tony. A few days before his arrival in the States, Tony was chased by the police and fired at several times, but, luckily, the shots missed him. He clung to an old man for dear life.

Tony was deeply involved in crime and violence in Jamaica, from the tender age of fifteen. Surprising, he made it safely to the United States, since he was wanted for the brutal assassination of a senior Spangler member from Bread Lane—Skitta—but, fortunately, the police didn't know Tony's identity.

Now Tony had a chance for a fresh start in the Bronx, but he missed his friends in Jamaica. He asked Vivian to find someone who could bring his friend, Waxy, to America. Waxy had money, he said, and would pay his way to the United States, so Vivian decided to help. Tony said a friend of Vivian's resembled Waxy, so Vivian asked his friend if he would lend Waxy his Alien Registration Card. The friend agreed, saying he would fly to Jamaica on a return ticket, then have Waxy return instead of him. He'd return later in the year, because he hadn't been to Jamaica in a long time, and wanted to visit.

Waxy escaped a huge dragnet in Jamaica and flew to New York. Although only seventeen, Waxy was heartless. He was the most vicious person in Jamaica at the time—number one on Jamaica's Most Wanted List. He admitted to Vivian, Caltman, and Tony that he had brutally murdered over a hundred and fifty people back in Jamaica. Tony and Waxy walked the streets together that summer.

Vivian, Caltman, and Tony were still living on Gerard Avenue, while Waxy was staying with a friend over by Fulton Avenue and 169th St. in the Bronx. Business was slow for Vivian, so his cash became rapidly depleted with so many mouths to feed and bodies to clothe.

Obliged to take care of Tony, Vivian bought some fabric to have some pairs of pants custom-made for him, and a tailor on the Grand Concourse was hired. When Tailor Brown completed the pants, Vivian's was still short on cash flow. He told Tony to wait a couple of weeks before paying for the pants, because there was no money around.

Tony told Waxy about his pants at Tailor Brown's shop, and Waxy organized two guns. They both went to Tailor Brown's shop to take the pants by force. Tailor Brown was very determined and decided he was not giving Tony and Waxy the pants, despite looking down the barrels of two loaded pistols. Since Brown refused to give up the pants, Tony shot Brown in his abdomen, took the pants, and the pair ran from the scene.

When Vivian heard of the incident, he and Tony had a fight, and he punched Tony several times. During the fight, Tony tried to reach for the gun he'd used on Tailor Brown.

"What the fuck you reaching for that gun for?" Vivian shouted.

Vivian beat the crap out of Tony and took the gun, giving it back to Waxy later. The thought of what Tony might have done if he had reached the gun before him, kept playing through his head. *Would he have killed me?* He dispelled the thought. *No, I'm his brother.* He tried to convince himself of it, but deep down, he knew the anger on Tony's face spelled the truth. *Tony would have shot me.*

The feeling never left Vivian. He loved his brother, but he didn't trust him, especially with a gun.

Vivian was finally served with an eviction notice, because he didn't have the money to keep up with the rent. With no money to rent another apartment, Vivian didn't know what to do. He went to see Valerie and told her of his problems, but Valerie was broke too, as she was attending Lehman College in the Bronx, and was mainly supported by her elder brother, Big George.

Big George used to be Vivian's closest friend, but the relationship started to dwindle every since Vivian had taken up with Valerie. Big George had purchased a Toyota Corolla for Valerie, in which she taught Vivian how to drive. Big George later bought her a '73 green Pontiac LeMans, which Vivian drove even more than Valerie did, and Big George didn't like that either.

Big George liked Vivian, but he also knew Vivian had several girls and feared that Vivian was only using his sister. Since Big George's support of her had been slashed, Valerie was invariably broke, and she worked evenings at a Burger King to earn a few extra bucks.

Listening to Vivian's problems, Valerie felt she had to try to help him, so she borrowed a hundred and fifty dollars from one of her friends, even though she didn't know how she was going to repay it. She gave the money to Vivian, but never repaid the money to her friend.

Vivian went apartment hunting with the hundred and fifty dollars—which wasn't much—so he had to shop for a place in the Harlem slums. Luckily, he found one on 144th St., between Seventh and Lennox Avenues. The first-floor apartment was a dump, but for one hundred dollars, it was a steal—two bedrooms and a tiny area that could be used for a living/dining room.

Vivian—along with Tony and Caltman—cleaned up the place and painted it, bringing new life to the rooms and making it a bit more habitable for the three of them. Vivian fixed up the small room as his quarters, acquiring a box spring and mattress, and a little component set he received from a junkie for a nickel bag of marijuana. He painted the room a special color and adorned the walls with fluorescent posters that his black light captured, and illuminated in the dark.

With no marijuana to start any business, Vivian visited his old friend Law, who was still living a few blocks away—the same apartment where Vivian had lived with him and his woman, Norma. Law was selling some pound-parcel marijuana for a friend, and Vivian told him his hard-luck story, that he needed some marijuana to start up a new business. The man gave him a quarter-pound of some outstanding marijuana. Law was his savior.

Money was so scarce before he moved to Manhattan, that Vivian couldn't even find food one Sunday while at the apartment on Gerard Avenue. The only thing in the cupboard was salt, plus two bottles of water in the refrigerator. Valerie went without food some days and took her dinner to Vivian, so he, Tony and Caltman could eat. Sometimes she stole slices of bread, and eggs, and took them to Vivian.

This particular Sunday, with no food in the house, Vivian walked to the apartment of a girlfriend—Dawn Shorter. He conjured up a story to tell Dawn, which he breathlessly told her the minute she answered the door. "I just lost my wallet in a cab and I need five dollars to borrow until the weekend."

Dawn was a good friend of Vivian's from back in Jamaica, and he was very close with her family too, so she gave him double the amount. Vivian beamed inside, although he was careful not to allow Dawn to see the extent of his happiness. *God knows how much I need the money for food,* clearing his conscience of the lie. He left Dawn's apartment, hiked straight to the supermarket, and bought enough food to feed four people for an entire week, plus a pack of Marlboros. He counted every penny as he totaled up the cost of the items, careful not exceed the ten dollars. The money was well spent.

Back at the new apartment in Manhattan, he bagged up the marijuana he received from Law, then made some thin, sample cigarettes to give to prospective customers. Within a week, the sales of marijuana in the Manhattan apartment exceeded that of the entire time at Gerard Avenue. Within two weeks, Vivian was purchasing a pound of marijuana. He split the pound in two, kept half-a-pound for himself, then gave a quarter-pound, each, to Tony and Caltman. Each took turns selling their marijuana.

Valerie stayed over at the Harlem apartment, sleeping in Vivian's little room, which he'd made as comfortable as he could. She didn't leave his side, no matter what, all through his struggle, so he had access to her car to run his errands. The relationship between Big George and Vivian remained strained.

Waxy, who was living in Manhattan, and a friend—Wendell—came to visit Vivian's apartment in Manhattan. Law was the father of Waxy's sister's—Linnette—kids. In the presence of Vivian, Caltman, and Tony, Waxy said he was going to send Wendell to rob Law of his marijuana. Neither Vivian nor Caltman liked the idea, but they could not stop Waxy, so they said nothing. To make matters worse, Law was Waxy's brother-in-law. All of Law's kids were Waxy's nieces and nephews.

Tony was in agreement with Waxy openly. Vivian tried to caution Tony with a look out of the corner of his eye, but Tony didn't care one way or the other, even though he read Vivian's stare.

Wendell followed through and robbed Law, but Law escaped through a window and breathlessly ran down to Vivian's house. Waxy was not at the apartment, only Vivian, Caltman and Tony. Trembling, Law told them what happened. Everyone already knew, but said nothing for fear of reprisal from Jamaica's Most Wanted—Waxy.

Vivian had a pistol in the apartment, so he tucked the pistol in his waistband and he and Caltman accompanied Law back to his apartment. They spent the night at Law's place, wanting to tell Law who had set him up, but they knew it would have been a problem for them in the future with Waxy. They both kept that secret for over twenty years.

A few months after Law was robbed, Waxy came to Vivian's apartment again and invited Tony to go on a robbery up by Bradhurst Avenue and 145th St. Tony, the robot, did not hesitate. He just grabbed a pistol and went out the door with Waxy. About an hour later, there was a loud knocking on Vivian's apartment door. Vivian thought it was the police, so he tiptoed quietly and peeked through the peephole to find Tony holding his abdomen, blood oozing out of his belly.

"I just got shot."

Vivian hustled him into the room to lay him down. "Who shot you?"

Tony, in pain and still bleeding, said, "I was shot at the scene of the robbery."

Vivian ran out of the apartment to get Law. Out of breath and panting furiously, he banged on Law's door.

"Law, Tony just got shot. I want you to take him to the hospital."

Law threw some clothes on and they headed back to Vivian's apartment. Law got a cab and took Tony to Harlem Hospital where he was rushed to the operating room. The operation was a success and he survived, but Tony resumed his criminal life, not caring that he'd split hairs with death.

It was now the year 1977, and Vivian brought back another one of his brothers—Donovan—after an illegal trip to Jamaica. Donovan, too, was living at the drug house in Manhattan. Tony, unsatisfied with the earnings at the drug house, organized with Rudy—Caltman and Vivian's friend—to rob a store that sold marijuana on Seventh Avenue, close to 145th St. The robbery was successful, so Tony and Rudy robbed the store a second time.

Vivian didn't say anything to Tony, because Tony declared he was his own man—Vivian couldn't tell him what to do.

Early in 1977, Valerie made a trip to the doctor, complaining that she wasn't feeling well at all.

"Miss Williams, you are eight weeks pregnant."

Valerie was shocked, so she went to see Vivian after she left the doctor's office. Vivian was at his apartment when Valerie arrived and they both went into his room.

Valerie began nervously, "I have something to tell you, Vivian."

Vivian didn't like the look in Valerie's eyes, so he panicked. "What's wrong?"

"You don't have to look so frightened. It's nothing bad," said Valerie, managing a grin.

Vivian relaxed. "What's up?"

"I'm pregnant." Valerie couldn't contain her joy.

Vivian's face lit up like a Christmas tree. He was the happiest man in the world at that time. His girlfriend, Valerie, was having *his* baby.

As one month turned into another, Valerie's abdomen expanded, and Vivian was anxiously awaiting the birth of his kid. While he was driving Valerie home one night, his brother Tony sitting in the back seat, he was pulled over by two detectives in an unmarked car. He brought Valerie's car to a halt to talk to the detectives.

Tony took a gun from his waistband and threw it under the driver's seat, and escaped through the back door of the car, running as fast as he could up the road. Quick to respond, one of the detectives chased after Tony. Tony ran inside an apartment building to the fourth floor, and the detective pursued him. Tony suspended himself from one of the window ledges on the fourth floor stairwell. The detective saw him hanging from the ledge, losing his grip and begging for help. He smiled at Tony and went back downstairs to the basement, where he looked up at Tony, smiled, then waited for Tony to fall. Finally he lost his hold on the window ledge and fell, breaking his legs on contact with the concrete pavement. Tony was taken to the hospital and placed under police guard.

The other detective searched Valerie's car, while Vivian and Valerie stood outside. Two patrol cars had been radioed to the scene.

"Ah, ha, illegal firearm, eh?" The policeman was menacing.

Vivian and Valerie went blank. They couldn't believe their eyes. Valerie, in the advanced stage of pregnancy, and Vivian were handcuffed and carted off to the precinct. Valerie cried uncontrollably as Vivian tried to comfort her, but none of his apologetic words could take the edge off the situation.

Valerie and Vivian were charged with illegal possession of a firearm. Vivian was also charged with criminal impersonation of Carlton Depass. He was using Carlton's driver's license as his own identification. The gun charge was later dropped, because the detectives realized that the gun was Tony's, who was later charged with illegal possession of a firearm.

Prior to the charges being thrown out, Vivian and Valerie were released from jail without bond. By this time, an elderly friend of

Vivian's—Freeman—was making regular trips from Miami, transporting lots of marijuana.

Freeman was a very short, stocky fellow with a fair complexion whom Vivian had known back home in Jamaica—a goalkeeper for Boy's Town School. Vivian hooked up with Freeman in the Bronx and made an arrangement with him while sitting in Pepito's—Freeman's friend's—apartment

"I'll help you sell your marijuana, if you give me a reasonable price, so I can make some money for myself."

Pepito was also from Miami and had brought marijuana to be sold in New York, too. Both Pepito and Freeman agreed to give Vivian the marijuana at a reduced rate. Vivian had established a customer base through Mr. Mel.

Packing twenty pounds of marijuana at a time in a traveling bag, and taking a cab to Grant Avenue and 167th St., he sold the marijuana with the assistance of Big George. Things weren't too bad for Vivian, now that he'd managed to save up four thousand dollars from sales of the pounds-parceled marijuana he was selling for Freeman and Pepito.

During his final court appearance concerning the gun-related charges, he and Valerie were cleared of the charges. Vivian and Valerie were ecstatic, but their happiness didn't last long. An officer from the INS headquarters in Manhattan showed up in court.

"Vivian Blake, I have to take you downtown. You've overstayed your one-year entry Visitor's Visa."

The officer handcuffed Vivian, and Valerie cried as the immigration officer walked away with Vivian.

Later that day, Vivian was offered bond of three thousand dollars. He quickly arranged for Valerie's mother to get the three thousand dollars from his four thousand dollar savings, and he was bonded out of immigration the next morning. Valerie and her mother were waiting outside, anxiously awaiting Vivian's release.

By this time, Valerie was six months pregnant with Vivian's child, and Vivian was scheduled to appear at an immigration hearing, on the verge of being deported. The only option open to him was to marry the soon-to-be mother of his child. Neither of them was ready for marriage or planning a future together. On the other hand, Vivian was happy about the marriage because he would have preferred that his child be born to married parents. Valerie agreed to his proposal, for she was the holder of an Alien Registration Card.

For sixty dollars, Vivian bought a wedding band in downtown Manhattan. They made all the preparations, and on the first of August 1978, Vivian and Valerie were married at the Bronx City Hall on the Grand Concourse. Valerie's sister, Grace, was the only witness at the casual ceremony.

The following day, Vivian and Valerie went to see an immigration attorney—Mr. Friedman—in mid-town Manhattan. Friedman agreed to file for Vivian's Permanent Residency in the United States of America with a down-payment deposit of two hundred and fifty dollars. A monthly schedule was set up for Vivian to pay the balance of the attorney's fee, which was a thousand dollars in total.

Being married with a child on the way, little money, and no home for his wife and unborn child, did not sit well with Vivian. Valerie was still living with her family. Doubling his efforts in marijuana sales, Vivian took to the streets earlier in the day and stayed out later at night. It paid off.

Tony was still in the hospital, recuperating from his broken legs, so Vivian decided to rent a store to sell nickel-and-dime marijuana—his third marijuana spot. He'd already started a second marijuana spot by the Projects on Washington Avenue in the Bronx, in an apartment building. He and Donovan painted the store, which was located in front of a project on Courtland Avenue in the Bronx. After they finished painting, they both went up to the marijuana spot on Washington Avenue.

Vivian's friend, Killo, was manning the spot for Vivian, along with another associate of Vivian's—Junior Screw. No sooner had they entered the apartment before Killo asked Vivian to lend him the car for a while.

"Screw and I are going to look about some money."

Vivian was so tired after painting the store, he threw the keys to Killo then laid outstretched on the living room sofa.

"I'm going with them," said Donovan.

Vivian was angry that Donovan wanted to go with Killo. "You just came in the house. Why the fuck you want go out so soon?"

But, Donovan had made up his mind … it didn't matter what Vivian said. They left, pulling the door shut, the slam-lock catching tightly, leaving Vivian alone with his hurt feelings.

About three hours later, after dusk had fallen, there was a banging on Vivian's door. It was Killo, followed quickly by Junior Screw. Vivian looked out, but Donovan was nowhere in sight. "Where's Donovan?" Looking at Killo and Junior Screw's reaction, he knew something was terribly wrong.

"Where is Donovan?" he shouted angrily.

Junior Screw answered in a low, sad tone, almost a whisper. "Donovan's dead."

"What!" said Vivian in disbelief. His eyes widened and he started to cry.

"He was shot in his neck," said Killo sadly.

"We didn't tell you, but Screw and I went to rob that weed spot, the one Tony robbed twice, but this time they were looking out, and caught Donovan off-guard outside the store," continued Killo.

"You really mean to tell me that you took my brother … in my wife's car … on a robbery?"

Vivian fell deeply into mourning. He called his wife and she arranged to identify Donovan's body. Valerie made all the funeral arrangements. Only Vivian and Valerie attended. Vivian didn't invite anyone. That was the way he wanted it. Tony was the only other family he had in America, but he was in hospital, under police guard, so he was out of it.

Tony was found guilty of the weapon possession charge and later deported to Jamaica. Within a few months, Vivian made some arrangements and Tony was back in America. Donovan's death took its toll on Vivian's whole family. He did not know how to let his grandmother know what happened to Donovan. When he finally summoned the courage, he called his sister. "Vivienne, I don't know how to tell you this, but I have to." He paused, taking in a deep breath for fortitude. "Donovan's dead."

"Yeah," Vivienne nervously giggled … then there was no one on Vivienne's end of the line.

"Hello? Hello? Hello?" Vivian tried to find a live body on the other end.

A few seconds later, a male voice answered.

"Where's Vivienne?"

"She just fainted. What happened?"

Vivian explained while others tried to revive Vivienne.

The weeks that followed were lousy for Vivian. Tony was back in New York, and Vivian had just secured passage for his aunt to come to New York. He rented an apartment on the Upper Westside of the Bronx, over by Riverdale on Kings Bridge Avenue, where his Aunt Lyn, his wife, and he were living. At least Vivian had a home for his child, which was due in late November or early December 1978.

One night, while Vivian and Valerie were relaxing at home, Valerie realized that liquid was pouring from between her legs. Without hesitation, Vivian took his wife to the hospital and the doctor in attendance immediately admitted her.

"Her water broke," a nurse politely told them. "It's a good thing you brought her in time so we can save the baby."

Vivian watched through a glass partition as Valerie went into labor. The night wore on—Vivan waited, but nothing happened. He figured that she wouldn't deliver their child until the next day, so he went home to rest. The next morning, he rushed up to the floor where his wife was and found out that she'd been moved to another room.

Vivian panicked and searched for the nurse. "What happened?"

The nurse smiled and announced, "Mrs. Blake had a beautiful baby boy."

Excitement spread across Vivian's face as he rushed to Valerie's room. In Valerie's arms was his pride and joy—his newborn son, Duane.

Vivian planned the name for his son for a long time. He would have liked to name his son Vivian Blake Jr., but Vivian is a girl's name in America, unlike Jamaica.

Vivian held his son for the first time that morning—a healthy baby, born without any complications. Vivian and Valerie were beaming with happiness, anxious to take Duane home.

Vivian had already bought a crib and baby toys. Although Duane was a very quiet baby—no fuss at all—about a month later, Duane became ill.

Aunt Lyn was still living with them and told Valerie and Vivian to rush Duane to the hospital. The doctor performed all kinds of tests, but couldn't determine what was wrong. Duane had stopped eating and had to be fed intravenously. His hair started falling out and he could hardly smile.

Vivian was going crazy. He couldn't understand what was wrong with his newborn. He prayed incessantly.

Duane received seventy-seven injections within a fifteen-day period. Even a spinal tap was performed, yet there was no progress in the diagnosis. Valerie started to complain that it was the work of evil spirits and that someone wanted to kill her baby. Vivian thought about what Valerie said and started to focus on his Aunt Lyn.

From back home in Jamaica, he'd learned that his aunt loved to practice *obeah*—a term used for evil doings. Vivian started to wonder if this was his Aunt Lyn's doings. *Why?* Then he came up with a theory. At the time, Vivian was the sole provider of his aunt's son, Andrew. Everything started to make sense to Vivian. *She doesn't want Duane to interfere with the raising of her own son.* He started to build a wall between his aunt and himself. *If my son dies, I will never forgive my aunt.*

After fifteen days, Duane was discharged from the hospital. The doctors did all they could but could not find Duane's problem.

Vivian couldn't eat. He couldn't sleep. He gave no indication of his thoughts to his aunt. Immediately after Duane left the hospital, a girlfriend of Valerie's told Valerie of a young lady in Brooklyn who read the past, present and future of anyone who came to see her, and that she also possessed the power of healing. Valerie, accompanied by her friend, took Duane to see the woman in Brooklyn. Vivian stayed at home, remaining silent.

Later that evening, Valerie returned from Brooklyn, stopping by her mother's house with Duane. She called Vivian. "Vivian, the lady in Brooklyn said that an evil spirit haunts our apartment, so I'm not bringing Duane back up there." They spoke for a while, and then he left the apartment to see Valerie and Duane at her mother's apartment.

Duane was responding more actively than the previous day. The lady had bathed Duane with some special herbs and had given Valerie a little red pouch to pin on Duane's clothes at all times, to keep away any kind of evil spirit. As the days passed, Duane grew stronger. His appetite returned, and his hair started to grow back—he fully recovered.

Vivian, still not saying anything to his aunt, found her another apartment, and she moved. Wanting his family to be with him, Vivian told Valerie to look for another apartment. She was lucky and found a plush, two-bedroom apartment on Riverdale Avenue. The apartment at Kings Bridge Avenue was a single bedroom, so Vivian turned that one over to Tony.

Vivian was hustling steadily now, with a consistent income. He was a kid with big dreams, always wanting more. His aspiration was to be the best at anything he did. Still selling pound-parceled marijuana for Freeman and Pepito, Vivian made a bold move while speaking on the telephone to Freeman in Florida one day. "I'd like to come to Miami and get some of the weed at a good price. I have a wife and a newborn son to support now."

Freeman who'd just been ripped-off by his girlfriend, Dernis, contemplated what Vivian had said. "Yeah, you can come to Miami. I'll buy the weed for you."

This was the opportunity Vivian had been waiting for. He'd saved up thirty-four hundred dollars, so he booked a flight and split for Miami with every penny. When he arrived, he took a cab to Freeman's duplex apartment on 41st St., NW, near 22nd Ave. The next day, Freeman bought eleven pounds of marijuana for Vivian and fourteen pounds for himself with the little cash left after Dernis ripped him off. They both returned to New York that night with the dope.

Upon reaching New York, Vivian had a buyer for his eleven pounds of marijuana, so he sold it immediately. After taking care of the sale, he decided to go see Freeman over by Pepito's apartment. At Pepito's door, he overheard Pepito quarreling with Freeman.

"Why the fuck you let Vivian go to Florida? You know that he's our best salesman. As soon as he gets used to Miami, he might not want to work for us no more."

Vivian listened from outside the apartment door for a while, and then decided to knock. Pepito was all business, but Vivian could see the disturbed look on Freeman's face.

Despite what Pepito thought, Vivian didn't plan to stop working for Pepito and Freeman. He took Freeman's fourteen pounds of marijuana and sixteen pounds from Pepito and was headed out the door when Freeman said, "Drop me down by Manhattan, Vivian."

He obliged Freeman, stashing the marijuana at Big George's apartment in the Bronx first, and then headed to Manhattan. He told Freeman what he'd overheard from outside Pepito's of door. "You don't have to take that shit, man. Let's rent two apartments and start *our* shit."

Freeman liked the proposal and indicated his readiness with a sly grin. "Check about the apartments and let me know."

The next morning, Vivian went apartment hunting. He wanted apartments in the region of Grant Avenue and 167th St., for he knew the area well—a lot of marijuana-buying customers hung out there. He checked one apartment building located a block from Grant Avenue on Morris Avenue at the corner of 167th St. As luck would have it, the building superintendent showed Vivian two apartments in the building; one on the second floor and the other on the fifth—the top—floor; both were one-bedroom deals.

Vivian rushed to a phone booth and called Freeman at a number in Manhattan he'd been given the night before. "Got two apartments, man."

"All right, come see me and I'll give you the money to rent both."

Vivian thought for a second. "You rent one; I'll rent the other. Take a cab and meet me at the Jamaican patty shop on 167th St. and corner of Grant."

In no time, it was agreed that Freeman would take the apartment on the fifth floor, while Vivian would take the one on the second. Vivian would do the selling downstairs, while Freeman would do the storage of the marijuana upstairs. This marked the beginning of a new era for Vivian.

Chapter 7: Morris Avenue

Two huge pieces of rose-colored carpet were delivered by a carpet company located on Fordham Road to Vivian's first pound-parcel marijuana joint. Tony, Caltman, Rudy, and Vivian all started jumping around excitedly as the carpets were placed—still rolled up—on the wooden floor. Vivian couldn't afford to pay the carpet company for installation—he and the guys decided to give it a go themselves.

Rudy, who was the strongest of all four, rolled out the carpet on the floor. Rudy was tall and well built, with very light complexion, his father being a white man.

They gang toiled for hours until finally, the carpet was laid. Vivian went on a shopping spree immediately after the carpet was laid, and bought a TV, pots and pans, and a box spring with mattress. They were ready to roll.

By this time in New York, all of the Jamaicans who sold pound-parceled marijuana were scared to expose themselves to the general Jamaican marijuana-buying population. To Vivian, this was ludicrous; the people were hungry for a service and he planned to offer that service. In those days, you could never get a pound of marijuana from the top man. You had to go through five or six people to get it, which could take from four hours up to two days. Now, the customers had a nickel-and-dime spot to supply them, so the long waiting for the dope caused the old-fashioned top guys—principally elderly, scared men—to lose a ton of business.

Vivian was by now twenty-three, Tony nineteen, Caltman twenty-five, and Rudy twenty-three. They all hailed from Tivoli Gardens in Jamaica. Tivoli Gardens kids were respected by most Jamaicans in the radical world and made their mark as a strong, tightly knit community. Vivian had seen the response from selling pound-parceled marijuana on the streets for Mr. Mel, Pepito and Freeman. He could sell twenty to thirty pounds of marijuana within a two-hour period, right there on the streets. The customers were hungry for that type of one-on-one service. Vivian gave the patients just what the doctor ordered—an apartment to walk in from off the street and purchase pound-parceled marijuana—the first of its kind in New York.

Vivian purchased two brand-new pistols from an American—a chrome Smith and Wesson 9 mm automatic pistol and a .38 revolver. That was all he needed, he thought. He had thirty pounds of marijuana for Freeman and Pepito, so he decided to start off his new business place with it. To Tony and Rudy he instructed, "You two stand guard with the pistols at all times, while Caltman and I sell the weed and count the money, understand?"

Everyone understood perfectly, and business started to roll. Big George was alerted to the starting of business on Morris Avenue, so he sent the customers to Vivian. In an hour, thirty pounds of marijuana was sold. It was a happy occasion for Vivian and the guys—the business started out on a high note.

Freeman had already carpeted his apartment upstairs and was relaxing when Vivian took him his share of the money.

"When we going back to Miami?"

"Tonight, if you're ready." Freeman was all smiles, feeling the wad of bills in his hand.

"I'm ready right now." Vivian was having a ball, comically giving Freeman the go-ahead.

Freeman made reservations for himself and Vivian on a midnight flight with National Airlines and they left for Miami that night. By the next day, they were back with forty-five pounds of marijuana—twenty pounds for Vivian, twenty-five for Freeman. The whole amount was sold the same evening they arrived back from Miami.

A marijuana shortage pervaded the New York area, so no matter how much marijuana a dealer had, it went lickety-split. Because Freeman had the access to a constant marijuana supply, their business thrived. Thereafter, Vivian started buying fifty pounds of marijuana at a time in Miami. After buying his load, he decided to give his brother and his friends a share of it, so that they could start their own businesses.

Returning to the Morris Avenue apartment, he weighed up fifty single-pounds. "This is yours, Tony." He gave Tony ten pounds of marijuana. "This is yours, Caltman, and this is yours, Rudy." Each dealer got five pounds each while Vivian kept thirty for himself.

Vivian flew back and forth, between Miami and New York, buying fifty pounds for himself, while the others were still buying twenty pounds. Freeman bought it by the hundred-pound load. In just a few short weekends, Vivian also made hundred-pound buys.

Money was abundant, and everyone was happy. Vivian was now able to support his family adequately. More friends arrived from Jamaica. Vivian's friends were more or less the sportsmen and working-class guys. The others were Tony's age. Everyone was a part of the Tivoli Gardens community, one way or another.

On arrival in Florida one sunny morning, Vivian sat in Freeman's house watching television. Marijuana was becoming scarce in the Miami area, too. Vivian heard a shout from a Jamaican neighbor—Jingles—for Freeman. Jingles was of average height, dark complexioned, with a pair of very distinctive bowed legs. He lived with his wife, Carmen, a tall and strong, light-complexioned woman who had a masculine way about her. Vivian alerted Freeman and walked with him to the back of the duplex that adjoined Jingles' fence.

"What's happening, Vivian? Didn't know you were here," said Jingles.

"Just got here about an hour ago."

"Anyway, Freeman, a friend of mine has some marijuana," said Jingles, as he handed freeman a sample of the drugs.

Freeman took the sample and smelled it. "How much a pound?"

"Three hundred and fifteen dollars."

Freeman frowned, "Jeez, I ain't paying that type of cash for no ganja." Vivian looked at the marijuana, which was top grade, but said nothing. After finishing the discussion with Jingles, Freeman and Vivian went back inside the house. Freeman was used to paying from $260-280 per pound. "Freeman, the weed looks good." Vivian pleaded with him to make the deal.

"I'm not paying so much money for no weed." Anger was written all over Freeman's face.

Vivian waited until Freeman settled down then said, "Hell, I'm going to buy some of that weed, 'cause I'd like to go back to New York tonight." Then he paused. "Remember, I live in New York with my family, man."

Freeman was upset that Vivian chose to buy the expensive marijuana, but Vivian was a businessman and knew he would still be making money—although less—from the purchase. Rudy was due to arrive in Miami with money to buy his, Tony's and Caltman's dope, so Vivian alerted Jingles and told him that he wanted to purchase one hundred and fifty pounds.

Jingles got in touch with his friend, and then his friend came over. By then, Rudy had arrived with his cash. Jingles' friend—Neville—was very slender and good-looking, with a very light complexion, like Rudy's.

Rudy gave Vivian cash for fifty pounds and in turn, gave Neville cash for the total of one hundred and fifty pounds.

Neville was back with the marijuana in two hours—the best weed Vivian had ever bought in Miami. He and Rudy packed the marijuana in three suitcases and flew to New York that same night on a Delta Flight, connecting in Atlanta and arriving in Newark, New Jersey early the next morning. They arrived on Morris Avenue just in time to start business. Upon seeing the quality of marijuana, one customer—who had come to the apartment before the marijuana arrived—said, "I'll buy the whole fifty-pound suitcase."

In about two hours, the drugs were sold and Vivian was on his way back to Miami. He had a chance to see his son at Mother Will's apartment for only a few minutes.

Freeman still had no marijuana. That was quite unprofessional of Freeman, because Vivian merely upped the price to twenty-five dollars more per pound to take care of the higher costs.

That same day, Freeman received a call from a Cuban lady friend—Angela—who sold him some marijuana. But, Freeman told Vivian that she had no more. He knew Freeman was lying, but said nothing. Vivian saw Freeman packing the marijuana and became angry.

"What you doing, leaving me here? Don't you see I don't know nobody to get any weed from?"

"I'll be back from New York tomorrow."

Vivian knew Freeman was up to no good when he saw the devilish look on his face. Rudy had come down with Vivian and was at Freeman's house, too. Vivian went next door and asked Jingles if Neville could get some more marijuana for him. Jingles replied that the marijuana was sold out, but showed him a sample of some terrible-smoking Jamaican marijuana.

"Shit! That black ugly shit!" said Vivian, turning up his nose. "How much per pound, man?"

"Just two hundred bucks."

Vivian took the sample to Rudy and discussed it. "I'm gonna take a chance, Rudy. Weed's scarce now. Might take a little longer to sell, but it must sell."

Rudy agreed to purchase fifty pounds; Vivian one hundred and fifty of the bad-smoking marijuana. They headed to New York, behind Freeman, just in time to see the last ten pounds of Freeman's marijuana being sold. Pouring out the garbage marijuana on the floor and filling the pound bags, they were surprised that customers started to pour in. By ten o'clock that night, the two hundred pounds of bad-smoking marijuana were sold out. They laughed as they counted the money.

Vivian reached home around eleven-thirty that night by cab—the police had impounded Valerie's LeMans while Carlton was using it, because of unpaid tickets. So, Vivian entered the Riverdale apartment, his traveling bag full of cash from the hot sales. Valerie was still up, feeding Duane. He kissed his wife, then took the bottle from Duane's mouth and kissed him on his lips. Duane started to make a face, so Vivian inserted the formula bottle back and fed the baby until the bottle was empty. Lifting his son from the bed, he held him close to his chest and rubbed Duane's back until he burped. The baby smiled at his daddy, and fell asleep in Vivian's arms.

"My father will look about the car for you tomorrow, if you'll be here," Valerie offered.

"Yeah, sure, I'll be here. Won't be going to Miami until about fours days from now."

The next morning, Valerie and Vivian, with Duane in his arms, took a cab to the William's apartment to pick up her father. They all left—baby in tow—for a Cadillac dealership on Fordham. The car that especially caught Vivian's eye was a '77 Seville, rose-colored. Sevilles had first appeared on the market in '76—the new rage in Cadillacs—small and compact. "That's the car I want."

It was stunning. They took it for a test drive with the sales representative, and then went back to the office to talk about financing. Vivian didn't have a job, so he couldn't qualify for a loan—Valerie's father had to buy it on credit. Everything was approved that same day, and Vivian and the family drove out of the Cadillac dealership in his new Seville.

Driving a Seville back then was like driving a Bentley now. Everyone looked when a Seville cruised by. Two days later, Tony and Rudy pooled *their* money together and bought a Seville. Within two weeks, there were four Seville's around—Killo and Junior Screw had to have one too, even though they couldn't afford them. Junior Screw had to borrow cash to insure his car; Vivian didn't like that, but decided to let him be, thinking that Junior might get the feeling Vivian didn't want him to drive a Seville. Vivian's only concern was for his friends to still have capital to continue business.

Killo was the fly guy, and for him, the most important thing was to drive a flashy car. He didn't care if he had nowhere to live, as long as his car was flashy, Nevertheless, he was one of Vivian's best friends.

Vivian spent the rest of the four days with his wife, son, and, of course, the new car. Time to resume his travels to Florida—he packed a traveling bag with clothes and enough cash to buy two hundred pounds of marijuana, kissing Valerie and Duane good-bye, as he took a cab to the airport.

At Miami International, Vivian took a cab to Freeman's house. It was late, so he went to bed about an hour after arriving. The next morning, Vivian arose early to find that Freeman's brother, Winston, had arrived a month earlier from Jamaica to live with Freeman. The same connection that brought Winston to America was en route to Miami with Vivian's youngest brother, Kong.

About ten-thirty that morning, a cab pulled up in front of Freeman's duplex. Vivian was on the front lawn, and to his surprise, saw Kong peeking out the window, accompanied by a lady. The lady paid the cab driver as Vivian opened the door for his brother—the lady got out on the other side. Kong was Vivian's favorite baby brother.

Later on that day, Vivian was talking to Jingles. They stood in the yard and he pointed to a section of the house. "Who lives in this section?"

Vivian had met the one tenant who rented a room from Jingles—Roy-o—and had become close to him.

"Other than Roy-o on the top floor, the room on the ground floor's empty," Jingles said.

"You renting it?"

"Sure, if you want it, you can have it."

Vivian paid Jingles the rent immediately and took possession of the single room. Now Vivian had his own base in Miami. All he needed was more connections to the wholesale drug sellers. Freeman introduced him to Angela; Vivian already knew Neville.

Rudy came down to Miami that same day and Neville sold them two hundred pounds. They packed their marijuana and left for New York the same evening, taking Kong back with them.

Up in New York, the apartment on Morris Avenue was growing crowded. Some of his and Tony's friends were bunking there—Glasses, Souls, Noukie, Patrick, Pepsi, Baskin, Perry and a guy named Skatta, who was just released from prison in Upstate New York.

Vivian rented another apartment on the fifth floor—beside Freeman's apartment—to store his marijuana and take care of the overflow. Vivian had kept guns to a limit—only two guns were in the apartment, and he owned them both. When Skatta arrived, he tried to advise Vivian that more guns were needed, but Vivian didn't think so. Most of the other guys agreed with Skatta, but Vivian refused to finance the purchase of the guns. Those who had money, bought guns; some even borrowed money to purchase their own.

Vivian didn't like the idea of so many guns in the apartment. He feared that one day, during the heat of a petty argument, guns could be drawn and shots fired, wounding or even killing someone. That would be the end of his business place.

Everyone made money, at least for a while, incident free. The guys from Tivoli Gardens had arrived—they had made their mark on the city of New York, and the Jamaican community in New York had started to recognize that fact. Many of the guys had shiny cars, and wore diamonds and gold jewelry.

Their big night out on the town came at last—a dance being staged by some popular Jamaicans from Brooklyn, in Manhattan at the United Nations Building. The Jamaicans in Brooklyn were real partygoers. They dressed exceptionally well and drove expensive cars.

On a cold winter night in December 1979, every one of the guys at Vivian's apartment put on his double-breasted, pinstriped, custom-made suit for this pre-Christmas party. Vivian had excellent taste in clothes and was always admired as a cool dresser. Years had passed and bright colors were out, so he advised his friends that they were to order double-breasted, striped suits, like those worn in the days of Al Capone. This they did. It was a night to remember.

Vivian led the way in his Cadillac Seville, followed by Tony, Killo, and Junior Screw. Four Sevilles pulled up outside the door of the United Nations Building. It was a stunning affair. Vivian and friends exited the Caddies, dressed immaculately, like a group of mobsters entering a speak-easy back in the old days. Vivian led the way in his brown suit with an Italian-style brown-and-beige beaver hat clinging to his head, beige shirt with brown-and-beige striped tie. To complete the perfect ensemble, he wore a brown-and-beige old-fashioned pair of shoes and brown socks. The other guys were stunning, too, as they walked to the dance entrance under the watchful eyes of the party patrons.

Their presence was felt that night. Murmurs ran through the huge hall and the patrons stared. The girls were taken aback with the attire of these new kids on the block. Before the night was over, Vivian received over a dozen telephone numbers from the beautiful ladies in attendance. An elderly friend—Quitty, who was in attendance with Vivian—did a surprising thing.

Months before the party, a very strong community leader of Tivoli Gardens—Claudius "Claudie" Massop—and two other friends, Indian and Noland, were brutally murdered in Kingston by a group of renegade police officers. Claudie was shot eighty-seven times, Noland seventy-one times and Indian sixty-two times.

Quitty walked up to the DJ playing the music at the dance and took his microphone. He asked the patrons kindly to oblige the Tivoli Gardens community with five minutes of silence for Claudius. Vivian and his friends were shocked when they heard Quitty on the microphone. The crowd paid due respect—if a pin had dropped in that hall during that five minutes, it would have been heard. The new kids on the block had arrived.

The party resumed into even higher gear. Vivian and his friends bought champagne and other drinks for many of the patrons who mingled with them. When the night ended, their drink tab almost reached twenty-five thousand dollars, but it was twenty-five thousand dollars well spent, because they had a ball. That night was talked about for many years after.

The night ended on an incident-free note, which proved to many people that the Tivoli Gardens men were not as barbaric as they were perceived to be. The females swarmed over Vivian and wished him well; the guys were invited to upcoming parties in Brooklyn.

Vivian led the Tivoli Gardens guys out of the dance at daybreak—they boarded their respective vehicles, and headed back to the Bronx.

A new day had arrived for Vivian. As of that night, the overall perception of an ever-smiling, easy-going person—a ladies' man—started to penetrate the different Jamaican communities. In the weeks that followed, Vivian attended many parties, preferring those in Brooklyn, because he was away from the eyes of the Bronx. He feared it would be too easy for his wife to learn of his different affairs.

Business grew exponentially at the Morris Avenue apartment. They could easily sell three hundred pounds of marijuana a day. Vivian needed more help in Florida—more guys were required to go down to Miami to help bring back the suitcases. Some suitcases of marijuana were lost due to theft on Eastern Airlines—baggage handlers sought out the luggage of suspected drug traffickers while they were checking in their suitcases. The handlers marked the suitcases by looking at them, then hurried around the back and took them off the ramp before they were even loaded onto the plane

While in Miami, Vivian was introduced to a guy named Joseph, who worked at the airport. Joseph made a proposal to Vivian. "I'll make sure your suitcases are safely on the aircraft, so no one can steal them, for a fee of three hundred dollars each."

This sounded good to Vivian.

"And, to top it off, I'll give you your claim checks when you deliver your suitcases to me at my home, so no one will see you guys checking in any suitcases at the airport."

Vivian loved this proposal, and immediately decided to work with Joseph. It was one of the best decisions Vivian ever made. No suitcases were stolen again, and operations ran smoothly.

Joseph came to Vivian one day with yet another proposal—to bring marijuana from Jamaica via Air Jamaica. "If you can get suitcases of marijuana on the plane, I can take them off. For my trouble, I'll take half of the marijuana."

Again, Vivian took up the proposal. He wasn't in possession of a Green Card, so his friends in Jamaica sent the marijuana to him in Miami. The operation went well for Vivian with Joseph's connection at the Miami International Airport. Suitcases after suitcases were flown in from Jamaica to Miami, and then transported to New York where huge profits were made.

In 1979, Vivian told his grandmother to find a house in the upper class section of Kingston and St. Andrew, so he could purchase it. She located a house in Manor Park, St. Andrew, so Vivian sent the money.

His grandmother furnished the house and moved in, happy to move uptown in the high-class community on Grosvenor Terrace.

Vivian's grandmother was never a big fan of Tony. She always warned her favorite grandson, "Be careful of that black boy, Tony. Anything too black is not good. He's trouble." Vivian didn't take her seriously, but agreed with her, anyway, to make her feel that her words were important to him.

Vivian's wife became an American citizen, so, instead of traveling to Jamaica or Canada to pick up his Green Card approval, he was permitted to pick it up in New York. Whenever an illegal alien is married to a permanent resident of the United States, the person has leave the United States and go back to their country of birth, or a country designated by the Untied States, to receive the Alien Registration Card approval. In October 1979, Vivian received his Alien Registration Stamp in his Jamaican passport.

An interview was conducted. Many illegal aliens were there who'd paid an American citizen or a permanent resident to marry them, so that they could receive the Green Card—business marriages. Valerie and Duane were with Vivian. Just as the interview was about to commence, Duane, who was in his mother's arms, stretched out to Vivian and shouted, "Dada."

Vivian took Duane's outstretched arms and placed him on his lap.

"I don't think an interview's necessary. I can see that you are all a family," said the immigration officer smiling. "But there's a bit of a mix-up in your police record about your charge on impersonation, so I'd like you to go up to the courthouse in the Bronx and have it rectified." He explained to Vivian what that meant.

Vivian and family left Federal Plaza in Manhattan immediately and drove to the Bronx. He dropped off his wife and son, and then headed down to the courthouse on 161st St.. The document was corrected, and he drove back to downtown Manhattan—Federal Plaza. He reached the Federal Building in the nick of time and caught the immigration officer, as he was about to leave for the day. The immigration officer looked over the papers, nodded his head in approval, turned around, and beckoned to a female assistant, who was about to quit.

"Could you open the safe for me and take out that Permanent Resident stamp?"

Vivian beamed when he heard those words.

"This young man needs to go visit his family in Jamaica."

The assistant opened the safe and brought the stamp to the immigration officer. He took Vivian's passport and stamped the inside. "You can travel with this stamp in your passport until you receive your Alien Registration Card in the mail within the next two months."

Vivian could travel to Jamaica legally, for the first time since his arrival in the United States. Back in 1977, Vivian traveled to Jamaica for a summer vacation, borrowing the Alien Registration Card of his friend and brother-in-law, Big George. Big George had received his Alien Registration Card when he was very young, so it was hard to recognize Big George by the photograph.

Vivian had spent three weeks in Jamaica, and brought back to the United States one of his young brothers, Errol, using another person's Alien Registration Card. To top it off, Donovan and Vivian wore two pairs of shoes to America, each containing a half-pound of marijuana—a total of two pounds all together—undetected.

Before Vivian received his permanent residency in 1979, he paid cash money for a Visitor's Visa for his sister, Vivienne. An immigration officer at the Norman Manley International Airport in Kingston stopped her. The Officer was suspicious of the visa and found it *bogus*. He turned her back. Vivian paid for a similar visa for his Aunt Lyn earlier, and she'd made it through to New York.

With Vivienne busted and the last of Vivian's immediate family left in Jamaica, he decided on one more attempt to get her into the US. He paid a lady from the Bahamas two thousand dollars to fetch Vivienne from Jamaica. Within two weeks, Vivienne arrived in Miami, via Nassau.

The family members left in Jamaica were Aunt Lyn's kids, his grandmother and the father of his brothers and sister—Altiman Bruce. His grandmother was very old and required a legitimate visa, and his aunt was responsible for her own kids, so he decided to help Altiman. Within two weeks, his connection in the Bahamas fetched Alty—as he was called—from Jamaica and brought him to the States. Now, almost all of Vivian's family members were in the US.

Vivienne lived with Vivian, his wife, and son in Riverdale. As it happened, the girlfriend Vivian left behind when he came to America—Norma—was a very close friend of the family. His grandmother loved Norma, but Vivian always thought it was an artificial sort of love. But, Norma was a kind-hearted girl, so that might have been the reason for his grandmother's fondness for Norma. Vivienne and Norma were also very close, so she gave Norma the telephone number to Vivian's apartment where she was also living.

Vivian didn't like the idea. He was now married, although he still had affection for Norma. If Norma called his apartment for Vivienne, he was sure that wouldn't sit well with Valerie. Valerie knew about Norma and felt that Vivian, deep down, was still in love with Norma, so any connection with the girl would worry her.

As fate would have it, while Valerie was home and Vivian was out one day, Norma called the apartment. When Norma identified herself to Valerie, an argument ensued. Norma cursed Valerie in such a nasty manner that Valerie began to weep. When Vivian returned that night, Valerie told him what transpired. He was so upset, he had no alternative but to tell his sister Vivienne she must live with their Aunt Lyn. That way, Vivienne could give Norma her Aunt's number, because Norma was now forbidden to call his apartment. Valerie was pleased that Norma was out of her hair—at least, for the present.

Chapter 8: Back For The First

In December 1979, Vivian went to Jamaica. He packed ten huge suitcases, and hat boxes filled with beaver and straw hats. His grandmother and a few cousins met him at the airport. Three cabs were required to transport his luggage to his new home in Grosvenor Terrace.

It was a very hot and sunny day in Kingston, when he arrived. After paying the cab drivers, he surveyed his new house, which sat on three-quarters of an acre—what a beautiful yard. The lawns were well trimmed with abundant fruit trees in the backyard. His grandmother had readied the room at the back of the house for Vivian—furnished very comfortably by Jamaican standards of the time.

The only television station in the country, the Jamaica Broadcasting Corporation (JBC), which was owned by the government, wasn't broadcasting in color yet. Vivian didn't bother having a TV in his room, because he couldn't get accustomed to the black and white after watching color television for the past six years in America. Video recorders were not even on the market in America, much less in Jamaica.

Vivian conversed with his relatives for a while, and then went out on the patio for some fresh air. News had gotten around in Tivoli Gardens that Vivian had arrived, and most of his friends were expecting him. Taxis and cars started pulling up outside Vivian's house—friends from Tivoli Gardens who hadn't seen him in a long time.

Vivian was the youngest resident of Tivoli Gardens ever to own a house in the upper class neighborhoods of St. Andrew. Lester Lloyd Coke—a.k.a. Jim Brown—was the first, buying his in Arcadia in 1977. Another resident of Tivoli Gardens—Dinnal—was the next one, purchasing one in Roehampton. So, at this time, there were only three Tivoli Gardens' residents who had residences in the upper class neighborhoods. Strangely, all three were very close friends.

Dinnal was a short, dark-complexioned young man, who dressed immaculately by Jamaican standards. He was very handsome and attracted many uptown beauties. The mother of one of his babies was a model with a popular agency in Kingston. He didn't get on very well with the girls in Tivoli Gardens, but that mattered very little to him, because he was such a favorite with so many from uptown. Jim Brown and Vivian nicknamed Dinnal "Beardy," or "*El Beardo*." Sometimes, they'd tease him, calling him "Pussy-Skin" because of his lust for young girls.

Jim, Dinnal and a friend, named Bird Beak, came to see Vivian the day of his arrival.

"Just passing through," said Jim, "heard that you'd arrived."

"Reached home from the airport about an hour ago."

"What time you coming downtown?" Jim wanted to spend some time with his friend.

"In about an hour." Vivian embraced Jim, Dinnal and Bird Beak.

"Later then. We're on a mission. See you downtown." Then, Jim Brown and the guys left.

Vivian talked to his friends and family for a while, before telling them it was time for him to head downtown to his community. He rode in a cab with some of his friends to the Tivoli Gardens community center. Jim, Dinnal and Bird Beak were already there. Carl Mitchell—a.k.a. Bya—and Donovan Jones—a.k.a. Champs—were sitting with the guys. An ex-police officer—Spar—was also present when Vivian reached the center. The friends who rode in the cab with him continued on to another destination in Tivoli Gardens.

Vivian greeted Bya first, paying his respect, before Champs and Spar. Bya was then the community leader of Tivoli Gardens and Denham Town in general. Vivian wasn't close to Bya, but showed him respect as the community leader. Many people who hadn't seen Vivian in a long time were grouped in different areas of the center, looking at Vivian talking to Bya and the others. Sonia—a girl Vivian was in love with ever since they were kids—appeared. Sonia smiled as their eyes met. Sonia's family and Vivian's family were amongst the first twenty families to live in Tivoli Gardens.

Sonia was dark complexioned and good-looking and had a big ass that made her the lust of most men. She was then living with a guy named Molo, who worked at the airport in Kingston. Her only kid was a daughter by Molo. Vivian envied Molo because Sonia should have been his girl … but such was life. Vivian knew all of Sonia's relatives well. There was her mother—Maizey, also called Pinnis—who was short, light complexioned, of medium-built, and wore only male clothes. She was a very strong female community leader in Tivoli Gardens. Pinnis rode motorcycles and bicycles as well as most men. In Sonia's younger days, she was a tomboy, and could skate and play cricket with the boys. Later, she lost interest.

Sonia's brother—Teddy Paul—was light complexioned, slim, and had sleepy eyes from his constant use of marijuana. He was one of the up and coming community leaders. Then there was Shirley—their eldest sister—who kept to herself for the most part. The only time you heard about Shirley was when she was upset with her common-law husband Fitzy—a.k.a. Seelo.

Vivian was delighted to see Sonia, who was wearing a pair of jeans showing off that big ass of hers. He stepped over the railing that separated them, and embraced her lovingly. Jim, Bya and the rest of the guys looked on at Sonia and Vivian with suspiciously, sneaky smiles, because of the affection Sonia and Vivian were showing each other. They all knew the father of Sonia's baby very well.

"I'll be going over to Linette's in a few minutes, so I'll see you over there," Vivian invited.

"All right, I see you then." Sonia smiled broadly and walked away, and Vivian went back to his conversation with Bya and the guys.

Bya, a very short, fairly light-complexioned man of Indian descent said to Vivian, jokingly, "Leave Molo's woman alone, you hear me?"

Vivian laughed as did Jim and the other guys.

"So what, Bya, I can't hug my good friend? This is a civilized world we're living in."

"If it is trouble you came to Jamaica to create, go back to America," joked Jim. Everyone was laughing.

"Listen, I am going to look for Linette and Dorothy," said Vivian, still laughing. "Your woman, Dorothy, Jim."

"Oh, Dave," (a nickname Vivian was called by his friends), "don't call my name to that woman when you see her. We're not on speaking terms right now."

"I am going to tell Dorothy that you want to see her."

"You crazy? Don't tell her that, Dave," concluded Jim, as Vivian walked away.

Dorothy was a tall, dark, well-built woman with a cute face, and she loved Jim Brown to death. She spoke with a voice befitting a very young girl. Linette was the mother of Law's children—fair complexioned, heavy-set, and had very good-looking facial features. Sonia, Linette, and Dorothy were Vivian's closest female friends, although Linette and Dorothy were much older than he.

He had another close woman friend, who lived in another section of Tivoli Gardens—Barbara—the wife of Donovan Jones' brother, Mickey, and mother of his kids. She had a wonderful personality, was well built and fair complexioned, but kept mostly to herself and attended to her kids.

Arriving at Linette's apartment, Vivian saw Sonia, Linette and Dorothy sitting on the verandah on an over-sized bench. He greeted both Linette and Dorothy lovingly, then pinched Sonia on her rear. They looked at each other with that hunger of wanting to be together since childhood. He sat on the bench with the girls and they chatted happily. He spent about an hour with his girlfriends, and then left for the Top Ten—a place where Vivian used to hang out when he was a kid—the sports capital of Tivoli Gardens. All the football leagues and cricket players hung out on there.

His boyhood friends were happy to see him, at least those who were still in Jamaica. Many of his friends had migrated to America with his assistance. Two of his long-time friends—identical twins, Hugh and Harry Cole—were still living on Top Ten. Most people couldn't tell them apart, but being so close to them, Vivian knew their separate identities. They even fooled their girlfriends at times.

Barbara, and the twins greeted Vivian as he entered his old stomping grounds. Seeing his friends and associates, whom he had not seen for a few years, gave Vivian great pleasure.

He walked over to an old lady—Miss Ida, Donovan and Mickey Jones' mother—who was almost totally blind, had a cross-eyed look to her eyes, and was very heavy set, and hugged and kissed her. He was a very ardent supporter of her family. She sold fresh fish most of her adult life, and Vivian ate fish from her table many times. Because she couldn't see him she didn't know who it was at first, but she never forgot his voice.

"Vivian, is this you?"

"Yes, Miss Ida. It's me."

"How you doing, Vivian? I'm glad you remember to come and look for your mother." Tears ran down her cheeks. "Your mother, Miss Ida, can't see too good no more, Vivian … just shadows."

They talked for a while, and then Vivian walked around the Top Ten area, greeting other friends and associates he hadn't seen for awhile.

Vivian hurried to see a family that he was very close to, the family of his best friend, Caltman Daley, over by their apartment. He hugged Caltman's mother, Mrs. Daley, and her husband. It was a joyous occasion for Vivian. Caltman's other brothers—Clive, Ansel, Fitzy, and his sister, Maggie—were there, and he greeted them lovingly. Maggie's daughter, Yvonne, had grown so big that Vivian was surprised.

In that same apartment building were Barbara's kids and her sister, Bibi and her kids. Bibi was looking as good as usual, and her kids had grown up beautifully, especially her daughter, Debbie. Barbara's kids—Julie, Alan, Quincy, and Nicky—were as slick as ever. Barbara and Mickey kept their family tightly knit, and the kids wore the best clothes from the United States.

All in all, it was a very fulfilling first day in Jamaica for Vivian. He was so happy to see his old friends and associates from Tivoli Gardens, and they were so happy to see him. Vivian didn't return home until very late.

The next day, Vivian spent the early part of the day at home. His grandmother prepared his favorite breakfast of brown stew fish with yams, green bananas, and dumplings. Some friends came to visit with him early, so they all had breakfast on the concrete pavement at the side of the house. He had longed for that type of breakfast from his grandmother's kitchen.

Days passed and Vivian was having a ball with the ladies, both uptown and downtown, but the only special lady who was really on his mind was Sonia—unrequited love since childhood. Sonia was not in a steady relationship with Molo, and Vivian grudged Molo, because he wanted Sonia for himself. When they were kids, he dated Sonia's friend Slimo, and then Sonia for a short while. Sonia's boyfriend—Dervon Garvey, a.k.a. Norris—ended up being one of Vivian's friends who lived in the neighboring community.

Vivian decided, one way or the other, if he couldn't have the whole of Sonia, he would settle for a part of her in private relationship, if possible. Vivian approached Sonia and pleaded with her to strongly consider at least a private relationship with him. For Sonia to even start thinking about cheating on her man took a lot of persuasion. Finally, after days of talking, he convinced her.

"Dave, no one can know about our relationship but us, please. I don't want to mess up my relationship with my child's father."

"Nah, Sonia, no one will know. I swear."

"Not even Jim Brown, or Law, Vivian. Nobody."

He convinced her no one would know, so they decided to go about their relationship very discretely. Vivian and Sonia decided that the time had come for both of them to cement their relationship.

"Be on Bustamante Highway. When you see me walk by, you know I am on my way up to your house."

Vivian acknowledged.

That day, at about noon, Sonia walked on Bustamante Highway in Tivoli Gardens and walked past Top Ten. Sonia was looking so sexy. She was dressed in milk-white jeans, which hugged her ass so closely that chills ran up and down Vivan's body. His dick got hard just watching Sonia from behind, as she walked up the highway.

He waited until he felt she'd caught a cab, and then fetched one for himself. They met in the uptown section of Kingston where no one from Tivoli Gardens community would see them, unless sheer bad luck befell them.

Vivian had booked a hotel room early that morning. Anxiety came over him as he walked with Sonia to the hotel room. Sonia was looking excellent. At last, they were in the room and he immediately closed the door. Vivian had his hands all over Sonia, caressing her. He held her around her waist and caressed her ass while sending his tongue deep into her sexy mouth. They stood and caressed each other until they were hot, then Vivian started undressing Sonia quickly until she was naked. He shed his clothes quickly, placed Sonia on the bed, and they gave into their lust.

Sonia couldn't stay away from her house very long, or Molo would become suspicious, so they relaxed in each other's arms, kissing and caressing until it was time for Sonia to leave. She showered, then dressed, and Vivian took her outside the hotel and hailed a cab. Before she took her seat in the cab, he kissed her passionately, then he watched the cab as it drove down the road and out of sight.

In the days that followed, Sonia tried to visit Vivian as often as she could, which, because of her situation, wasn't often. While on her way to see Vivian at his house, there was a surprise. Jim Brown, Dinnal and Bird Beak turned up to visit Vivian. Sonia panicked and hid herself from them. With the help of Vivian's female cousins, Sonia managed to disappear without being seen by Jim and the guys, and away from the compound. They kept their relationship going privately for a long time, without any of their closest friends knowing anything. All that surfaced were merely suspicions.

That Christmas, Vivian, Jim Brown, and Dinnal had a ball at the Rock Nightclub. They had three girls with them, and they partied on until the wee hours of the morning. This nightclub was the fun spot, very intimate—the patrons were mostly middle-class Jamaicans who wanted to have a good time partying. They all went clubbing at the Rock on New Year's Eve and New Year's Night. The Rock Nightclub was where Tivoli Gardens community leaders could comfortably party and have a good time.

There were also nights in Tivoli Gardens, throughout the holidays, where sound systems played to huge crowds from the community and neighboring community. Vivian enjoyed the festive season in his community of Tivoli Gardens and his special nightclub.

It was election year in Jamaica, 1980. The New Year's festivities passed and the New Year began. One evening, after the sun went down at about four o'clock, Bya was sitting on Top Ten, reading the Evening Star—a habit of his. In the evening, this spot where Bya sat, was always cool and breezy. While Bya was reading, a lady walked up to him complaining, "Mr. Bya, excuse me, sir. My daughter was coming home from school yesterday, and I was told that an orange-colored Volkswagen car picked her up, and she has not been seen since … and she is only thirteen years old."

Bya listened carefully. "I don't know what to tell you. Where this happened?"

Vivian and some other friends were keenly listening to Bya and the lady.

"Right in front of my gate on Little King Street." The lady was now in tears.

"All right. I'll find out what I can, and you can check back with me."

"All right, Mr. Bya, I will check back." The woman couldn't contain the tears.

Bya looked at Vivian in a joking manner and laughed. "That little girl went away with her man. Times are hard, so she just started having a man at a very young age."

A few days passed, and the little girl still could not be found. One cool evening, while Bya was reading his Evening Star, with Vivian close by, Vivian saw the lady walking fast toward them and crying out loud, newspaper in her hand.

"Mr. Bya, they killed my daughter! That's her in the newspaper," said the wailing woman as she handed the newspaper to Bya.

He had just finished reading the article, but had no idea it was the same girl this woman had spoken to him about a few days ago. He looked at the paper in astonishment as the woman sobbed in front of him. A crowd gathered as the news of the dead girl spread. The girl's dismembered body was found, and even her head was cut off. The killing was gruesome.

"This has been the fourth killing like this in western Kingston," someone in the crowd shouted to Bya. "And the same orange Volkswagen was sighted."

"A police officer said the orange Volkswagen is linked to Tony Welch," said another person in the crowd as Bya listened keenly to what the people were saying.

"We can't just sit down and let them kill our children, brothers and sisters like this," said a soccer player who had his gear on. "If we have to take to the streets, we're going to do that. Blood for blood! Fire for fire!"

Vivian stood and listened to the people's wrath and concluded silently, *this is going to be the bloodiest election in Jamaica.*

He spent two more weeks in Jamaica, then it was time to head back to America. He'd had a wonderful vacation and planned to visit Jamaica every holiday, or whenever his busy schedule permitted.

Chapter 9: Freeman Robbery

It was back to business. With business going very well and several extra hands to help out, Vivian took Wednesdays off to spend with his kid. He had always taken Sundays off while he was in New York, so now he rested for two days out of the week.

While he was home one Wednesday, Junior Screw—with whom he'd a fallen-out—went with Tony BuzzBee to Freeman's apartment to buy marijuana. Vivian had acquired an apartment beside Freeman's on the top floor, along with the apartment he rented on the second floor. Junior Screw, Freeman's brother—Winston, a.k.a. Bang—and his cousin, Milton Pusey, were there. Junior Screw asked to purchase a pound of marijuana. Bang, Junior Screw and Tony B. were in the kitchen, which was situated at the entrance of the apartment, transacting the business deal. Neither Junior Screw nor Tony B. knew that Milton was in the apartment.

Bang was weighing out the marijuana when he heard a clicking sound.

"Freeze. Don't move or make a sound, or else you're a dead man!" Junior Screw had a gun pointed at Bang's head.

Tony B. also had a pistol pointed at Bang's head. Milton, who was in the bedroom, heard every word Junior Screw said. Milton himself had a .38 Beretta automatic pistol with a magazine containing nine rounds. With the Berretta in hand, he tiptoed to the door and peeked out the bedroom towards the kitchen.

Tony B.'s and Milton's eyes met, and they started firing shots at each other. Milton was hit in the stomach and Tony B. was hit in both legs. Junior Screw panicked in the kitchen.

Milton teased, "I have four extra magazines with fifteen shots apiece … you guys are dead!" He fired a single shot towards the kitchen. Milton was bluffing because he only had one magazine that carried nine shots and he'd used up four shots already. He fired another shot, still teasing the guys.

By now, Tony B. was losing a lot of blood and couldn't walk. They had to get the hell out of the apartment or else Tony B. would bleed to death. Milton had tied a sheet around his waist to staunch the flow of blood from his stomach wound. He was growing weaker and weaker and praying that his bluffing would work, so that the guys would leave the apartment. He needed to get to a hospital soon.

With panic setting in, Junior Screw fired a barrage of shots towards the bedroom, "Cover me!" Junior Screw said to Tony B., as Screw moved towards the exit door.

Tony B. kept firing at the bedroom while Screw opened the door. No one was paying any attention to Bang, who was crouched in a corner of the kitchen. Everyone just wanted to leave the apartment. Junior Screw held off Milton by firing several shots towards the bedroom. "Buzz. Come. Go outside."

Tony B. crept on his hands and knees outside the apartment into the hallway. Milton listened to every word they were saying, and was glad they were leaving, because he'd lost a lot of blood and was now very weak.

Junior Screw fired two more shots from his automatic pistol, and then headed out of the door behind Tony B. He took Tony B.'s gun and ran out of the building, leaving Tony B. to fend for himself.

Tony B. was bleeding badly, so he crawled down the steps, leaving a trail of blood as he moved along, coming to a halt at Vivian's apartment of business on the second floor. He banged on the door. A lot of guys were inside the apartment, including Tony, Baskin, Skatta, Noukie, Patrick, Glasses, Souls, Caltman, and Pepsi. Baskin looked through the peephole and saw Tony B. on the floor, bleeding, and opened the door quickly to assist him.

"What's wrong with you, Tony?"

"I was shot upstairs … in Freeman's apartment."

"Why?"

"Junior Screw and I tried to rob them."

Baskin looked at him angrily while the others looked over Baskin's shoulder.

"You're on your fucking own. Get away from my fucking door," said an angry Baskin as he slammed the door shut in Tony B.'s face.

"Yo, let's get the fuck outta here ... the cops will be all over the place in a few minutes," said Baskin hastily.

Everyone started reaching for their belongings, the marijuana and guns, and they left the apartment.

A trail of blood could be seen as the guys walked down the steps. Reaching the lobby of the building, they saw Tony B. crawling. He looked at the guys and begged pitifully. "Please help me. Remember, we're all from West Kingston."

The guys regarded him with evil eyes.

"You're damn lucky you're from West Kingston, or I'd shoot you in your fucking face right now, motherfucker," said Baskin angrily. "You piece of shit!"

They all walked away.

A few minutes after the guys left, Bang and Milton appeared. Bang had a suitcase with the money, marijuana and a gun in it, while Milton held onto his wrapped stomach, still bleeding. Tony B., by now, was on the sidewalk, begging for help. Milton and Bang saw him, and Milton went over and spat on him, then kicked his wounded leg. Milton caught a cab to the hospital, and Bang took the second cab, leaving the scene like the devil.

Vivian was at home relaxing with his baby when he got a call from his brother, Tony. "Yo, Dave, we got problems, man. We had to leave the apartment in a hurry."

"What happened?" Vivian was alerted by the tone in Tony's voice.

"Junior Screw and Tony BuzzBee tried to rob Freeman's apartment and Milton shot Tony B. pretty good."

"So, you all right?"

"Yeah, we're down by Punky. We cleared out the apartment. Everything's safe,"

"All right, I'll be down by Punky in a few." He hung up the phone, quickly dressed himself and Duane, and left the apartment, baby in arms.

He dropped Duane off at his grandmother's, and then headed to see the guys.

Punky lived on the Grand Concourse at the corner of 165th St. She was an obese woman, but kind-hearted. Vivian had a relationship with an American girlfriend of Punky's, named Pinghe—a light-complexioned, shapely girl. She had a Hispanic look about her, although she didn't have the blood. Pinghe was deeply in love with Vivian at the time.

As luck would have had it, an apartment was available in the same building as Punky's, so Vivian rented it immediately and started his marijuana business *again*.

"I love this house, I'll take it," said Vivian happily to a real estate lady in Miami. He had just agreed to rent a three-bedroom house with swimming pool and two-car enclosed garage in the NW 87th St. area, close to 17th Avenue. He moved from the one room he'd occupied in Jingles and Carmen's house. A bigger place was needed, because more guys were traveling to Miami with Vivian.

The house was rented, furnished, and served its purpose without a doubt. Several friends from Tivoli Gardens stopped by and visited with Vivian and friends. Close by, down on 53rd St. NW, lived an elderly man named Bill—a.k.a. Wild Bill. He was a close friend of Carl Mitchell—a.k.a. Bya—the community leader of Tivoli Gardens. Most of Bya's close cronies stayed with Wild Bill, at Bya's request, when they migrated from Jamaica. At this time, Baskin, Curly Locks, Bucky Marshall, and Skatta were staying at Bill's house. On a regular basis, they visited Vivian's house, swam in the pool, and talked with the other guys from the Gardens.

The guys staying at Vivian's house—Glasses, Ruddy, and Souls—were all hustlers, not radicals like the ones who stayed at Wild Bill's. But, all in all, everyone knew each other from Tivoli Gardens, so it was like one big happy family.

While Vivian was in New York one day, Glasses, Souls, and Ruddy were down in Miami purchasing marijuana. They had taken eighty-seven thousand dollars to buy marijuana for Vivian, Tony, Caltman, and themselves. Vivian and his guys were very close to Jim Brown in Jamaica, but the ones at Bill's house were Bya loyalists.

Bya needed urgent cash in Jamaica at the time, so Bill called Souls at the house. "What's up? You ain't got any money, man? I want to send some cash to Bya in Jamaica,"

"No, not right now."

Bill knew that the guys had come down from New York with money to buy marijuana and thought Souls was bullshitting him. Skatta, Buckie Marshall and Curly Locks were at Bill's house when he made the call, and Baskin and Souls had been asleep at Vivian's house.

Later on that day, while Glasses, Ruddy, Souls and Baskin were at the house, Skatta, Curly Locks, and Buckie appeared, sporting pistols tucked into the waistbands of their pants.

Without pulling their pistols, Skatta said, "Ruddy, Glasses, Souls … we come for the money you guys brought down from New York."

Baskin looked astonished but said nothing. Ruddy gave the guys the eighty-seven thousand without a hassle.

Skatta took the bag with the money, then Ruddy said to him, "Give me back mine. I'm just starting out."

"How much money you have there?"

"Four thousand dollars."

Skatta stuck his hand into the bag, took out four thousand dollars, and gave it to Ruddy. Glasses and Souls asked for their cash, too, but were turned down.

Buckie, Curly Locks and Skatta started to count the thousand-dollar stacks of money they took from Ruddy. After they finished counting, Skatta smiled at Glasses and Souls and said teasingly, "A decent day's work. Right, you all?"

"What's going on, man?" asked Baskin, who was still puzzled. Baskin didn't expect a robbery like this to take place, because everyone was living as one family.

"We're going over to Bill's. You coming?" continued Skatta to Baskin. They packed up the money in the bag, smiling all the while, then left with Baskin following behind them.

The next day, Souls went to Bill's house. Bill, Baskin, Bucky, Curly Locks, and surprisingly, Bird Beak, were there. Bird Beak was close to Bya, but just an associate of Jim Brown.

A few weeks before the eighty-seven-thousand-dollar robbery, Bird Beak paid Vivian a visit at his apartment in Riverdale, because Vivian was assisting Bird Beak in acquiring some cash. Vivian bought marijuana in Miami for Bird Beak on an ongoing basis, and also sold it for him in New York. This particular day, Bird Beak had come to pick up his cash from Vivian. They talked about Jamaica for a while, and then Vivian said, "Jim Brown just phoned. We were talking for about an hour."

Bird Beak's face had a serious look when Vivian mentioned Jim. "Who? That big boy, Jim Brown? He just robbed my friend Bya of some coke." Bird Beak's tone was commanding and menacing.

Vivian was surprised at the way Bird Beak talked about Jim Brown in his presence. "You can't call my friend big boy, Beak."

"Boy's a thief."

Vivian glared at Bird Beak for a few seconds. "Jim told me about that cocaine—it was no good. And, I'm not going to sit here in my house and have you diss my friend to my face like that." Vivian was shouting angrily.

Bird Beak realized he'd made Vivian mad, and tried to tone down the conversation. He'd overstayed his welcome.

Vivian wasn't amenable to any more conversation, so Bird Beak decided to split.

After Souls left Bill's house the day of the robbery, he spoke to Vivian up in New York, and he told Vivian that he saw Bird Beak at Bill's house.

"What were you doing at Bill's house?" Vivian asked Souls.

Souls was caught off-guard. I went to see if I could get the money back."

"You mean *your* money," said Vivian sternly.

"No. *All* the money."

Vivian didn't believe a word Souls told him and upon hearing that Bird beak was at Bill's house, and the way that Bird Beak had disrespected Jim in his presence, he began to put two and two together as he hung up on Souls. *Could Bird Beak be a conspirator to the robbery? Why's he at Bill's house, knowing what happened?*

Vivian called Jim in Jamaica that same day.

"Dave, the tables soon turn. It's not everyday the wind blows one way."

Vivian knew that Bya treated Jim like an underdog, but Jim was his friend. Leader or not, Bya would never be Vivian's friend, because Vivian was hurt by the disrespectful ways in which Bya and his other cronies treated Jim. Bird Beak couldn't have stood in front of Jim and said what he did, but certainly felt confident enough to say it in the presence of Jim's best friend. Vivian realized it wasn't Bird Beak who was really talking to him, but Bya … by way of Beak.

Being the businessman he was, Vivian moved his operation in Miami to Freeman's house until he could find another house to rent. Souls remained at the house in Miami, trying to get his money back, but Skatta, Baskin, Curly Locks, and Bucky took control of the house from Souls, and treated the hapless Souls like their butler.

They brought an Indian man and his pregnant wife to the house while Souls was there. Curly Locks placed the man and the woman on the carpet, tied their hands behind their backs, and teased them menacingly—they were big cocaine dealers from the Manor Park area in Kingston—friends of Jim Brown. They'd promised to give Jim some cocaine in Jamaica.

Jim told Bya that he was expecting some cocaine from the couple to pay Bya what he owed him.

Bya was in contact with the couple many times, but was never offered a deal like they offered Jim, so he made up a false story and telephoned Curly Locks at Bill's. "Those two people that gave Bill the half-a-key … they were the ones who set up Claudius Massop's life."

Bya verbally signed the couple's death warrant. The couple was innocent, but Bya wanted them dead because they were helping Jim.

Curly Locks lifted the man from the floor and slit his throat swiftly. The wife saw what happened and vomit poured from her mouth instantly.

The man fell to the carpet, his reflexes causing him to kick for a few moments, the life slowly draining from his body, while Bucky pressed his foot firmly against the Indian's head.

Curly Locks went over to the pregnant lady. "You don't wanna die, do you?"

Her mouth was gagged, so she shook her head, as tears rolled down her cheeks.

Curly Locks placed the tip of slender knife against the lady's blouse and slit it, revealing her breast. He put the point of the knife on her breast, and then pulled his pistol out. Within seconds, he hammered the slender blade of the knife into the woman's chest with the gun's butt—driving it deep into her heart. Her eyes widened as death engulfed her body. Curly Locks slammed the back of the pistol on the end of the knife, and the point of the knife pierced her back. "Die, woman. You piece of shit, you."

Blood spewed from the wound in the woman's chest onto his face. He smiled and licked the blood with his tongue. His friends' faces were scornful as they watched Curly Locks' antics.

"Stop that shit!" said Skatta.

Souls stood in a corner and trembled. He'd never seen anything like that in his life. Curly Locks, Baskin, Skatta, and Bucky wrapped the dead woman and her husband in the carpet laying on the floor, placed them in a van, and drove away, dumping the bodies in a swamp in the southwest area.

Vivian was still doing business at the apartment located on the Grand Concourse at the corner of 165th St. when he acquired another apartment on McLlelan St. close by, to give Tony's young friends a place to stay. Therefore, Vivian decided to get another apartment where the more mature guys could hang out—this he did about four months before they were robbed of the eighty-seven thousand dollars in Miami.

At this time, they were all concerned about the attempted robbery at Freeman's apartment that had caused them to lose two good business apartments. Junior Screw was now hanging out with a group of guys from a neighboring West Kingston community called the Land Raiders.

They were a very dangerous group of Jamaicans led by a guy known as Bunny Walker.

On hearing that Junior Screw was with the Land Raiders, Vivian, Skatta, and a former Land Raider—who was now hanging with Vivian, and also known as Baggy Man—went to see him. There were about fifteen Land Raiders in attendance, including their leader, Bunny Walker. Then there was Junior Screw.

"Why'd you try to rob Freeman's house, Screw, knowing we and Freeman are friends?" asked Vivian.

"Nobody can't ask me that—I'm my own man," said Junior Screw tight-lipped.

Baggy Man lost his cool and reached for his pistol, but Vivian clapped his hand over it. Baggy Man wanted to kill Junior Screw right on the spot, but Vivian wouldn't have it—it could have been suicidal because they were outnumbered, and the issue hadn't been settled.

Vivian, Baggy Man, and Skatta left, and returned to the apartment on McLlelan. Vivian's sister's boyfriend, Butter, opened the door and let the guys in. Butter had just come from Jamaica and was staying with Vivian.

Vivian's brother Tony nicknamed the McLlelan St. apartment house, the "House of Parliament," because Vivian's guys there weren't as playful as his friends, and were all about business.

About two weeks later, Bob Marley and the Wailers came to New York, straight from Jamaica. He and the band members were staying at the Essex House Hotel on 59th St. in Manhattan, all set to perform five shows at the Apollo Theater in Harlem, with Betty Wright as their opening act. Marley's security entourage included Donovan Jones (a.k.a. Champ), and an ex-police officer known as Spar—both men were from the Tivoli Gardens community.

Vivian and Baskin went to see Marley at the Essex that first night. The trio, plus Jones, Spar, and other Marley groupies, decided to go out on the town, and walked down to 42nd St. to take in the scenery. Gong—as Marley was called—was in high spirits on the trek down there.

Entering a novelty store on Broadway that sold all kinds of gadgets, Marley noticed a lighter in the showcase and said to the store attendant, "Lemme see this lighter."

The store attendant reached for it. "It's not really a lighter—it's a fun gadget that shocks you when you try to light up."

Marley loved that and started to laugh. "I *want* that." He took the fake lighter from the attendant and tried lighting up. The lighter fell from his hand quickly because of the shock. Marley laughed himself to tears while everyone looked on, laughing too.

Back to the hotel—about half an hour later—while Marley, Vivian, Donovan, Baskin and Spar were talking, a white girl came to visit Marley. He remembered the lighter and decided to play a prank. Asking Spar for a cigarette, he called the innocent white girl over, handed her the fake lighter, and said, "Gimme a light."

The girl was glad to oblige, and flicked the lighter quickly. Her eyes widened with shock as the lighter fell from her hands. Marley hugged the shocked girl. "Jes' fooling around," he said, and kissed her on her forehead. A beautiful smile appeared on her face, and he went off to the side of the room to talk to her.

During the five shows at the Apollo Theater, Vivian, Baskin, Donovan and Spar hung around the reggae star. This was the first time Marley had been able to reach out to so many blacks, and they loved every minute of his acts. Marley was suffering though, and while jogging around Central Park, his big toe started acting up.

Marley promised Vivian he would let him promote a few shows—so long as the promotion was done properly, by credible agencies, but the gigs never materialized. He did his five shows at the Apollo, but never lived to see the City again, dying on Vivian's birthday in 1981—May 11.

On that very day, Vivian was hanging a huge portrait of Marley and himself, in his new home on Long Island, when he heard about the star's death. He had known about Marley's failing health, even saw pictures of him after the chemotherapy—Marley's head was bald by then. It was a sad day for Jamaica and the world at large … a great man, and a friend of Vivian had passed on.

Later, Vivian enlarged two more pictures of him and Marley, and hung them in his family room—vintage memories, for his kids to cherish in the years to come. Bob Marley was a great, great man.

In the summer of 1980, Jim Brown flew up from Jamaica to spend a week with Vivian in Miami. Vivian was now living in a house on North Miami Beach—an impressive place with a huge swimming pool in the backyard. At the same time, Bya was also in Miami visiting his friend Wild Bill. Jim asked Vivian to take him down to Wild Bill's digs to see Bya.

Inside Bill's den were Bya, Spar and Waxy—who had just returned from Jamaica, after his deportation in the '70s. Vivian greeted Waxy lovingly. "Didn't know you came back up."

"Came last night."

Vivian had left Waxy in Jamaica earlier in the year when he was vacationing in Jamaica. He and Jim also greeted Bya, Spar and Bill like old pals.

A plate of pure powdered cocaine was on a coffee table. Bya took two snorts, then looked at Vivian, and smiled. "Good … take a hit." He passed the plate to Vivian who took two huge gulps down his nostrils and shook his head.

"Hmmm … the shit!" Vivian said, indicating the potency of the cocaine.

They all snorted for a while and talked. Suddenly, Bya's voice rose during a conversation with Jim. "Where's the rest of my fuckin' money, man? You better get my fucking money, man, or else *we* gonna have problems."

Jim felt exposed and embarrassed. "Bya, you'll get your money," he said softly.

"You better make sure you give me my fucking money, man, or it *ain't* gonna be nice." Bya sounded as though Jim was his child and he was spanking him.

Vivian felt embarrassed for Jim. While he knew that Bya was just showing him who was boss, and that his friend was nothing in Tivoli Gardens, he thought, *you're wrong, Bya. One day tables gonna turn.*

Jim'll be in charge and I'll be right behind him. Vivian wanted to leave badly—he also had a legitimate excuse. He checked his watch—past twelve midnight. "Damn, Jim. Remember? Law's supposed to come down from New York—must be outside the house waiting and can't get in. We gotta leave now."

"Take Waxy with you, Vivian," Bya said. "Let him stay up by you—there's no space down here."

Vivian went against his better judgment and decided Waxy could stay. On the drive up, Jim's eyes teared, but he and Vivian couldn't speak their minds—Bya's confidant, Waxy, was in the car.

They drove in silence until the beach house came into view—Law was sitting outside on his travel bag. "Damn! Look how Law just sitting outside with all that cash," said Vivian, playing the innocent.

He pulled up in the driveway, got out, and led the way in—the others followed. Law dumped the money in the master bedroom, and then joined the others in the living room, while Waxy flaked out in another bedroom that Vivian showed him.

Jim and Vivian walked out onto the pool deck to talk, while Law and his common-law wife's brother, Waxy, caught up on things.

"Dave, that piece of shit, Bya, disrespected me, man. An' this is all because I can't shoot my friend."

"Bya's a pussy, man. I don't like him, Jim. I really don't."

Tears filled Jim Brown's eyes as he spoke. He was hurting inside, badly.

The next day Butter came down to Miami, and joined Law, Jim, Vivian and Waxy at the North Miami Beach house. Law had brought with him eighty thousand dollars from New York—twenty thousand was for Vivian, twenty thousand for Tony, and forty thousand for Jim. Jim's forty thousand was for buying marijuana, which would be sent to New York and sold. Jim intended to take the principal and profit to Jamaica, to run a Crash Program project for the needy, for the Independence Celebration season in Tivoli Gardens, but it was not to be.

Later that evening, Bya paid a visit to Vivian's house, where everyone had drinks and talked. Bya spoke of his ambitions of reopening a theater in West Kingston, known as "Queens Theater".

"Did you know that Jim and I had the same idea to reopen Queens Theater?" said Vivian.

Bya made a sneaky grin, which Vivian and Jim studied.

"We're planning to donate some money to the needy this Independence season," said Vivian, teasing Bya indirectly.

He smiled at Vivian, but what was said didn't sit well with him. He was thinking that if Vivian was behind Jim Brown, Brown could end up with too much power.

Bya left about ten o'clock that night, and Vivian went to sleep in the den—so did Jim Brown. About three o'clock the next morning, Vivian was awakened by talking in the den. He woke up and saw Jim, gun in hand, talking to Perry—a nephew of Bya's. Perry had come to take Jim out on the street with him, to hunt girls at that late hour.

Vivian found it strange, but relaxing, when he saw Jim was onto things, and above all, had the back of his head covered.

The next day, bright and early, Perry and a friend of his—Winny Poop—turned up at Vivian's house, bearing a message for Jim.

"A lawyer friend of Bya's wants to see you down by Bill's," said Winny Poop.

Jim was getting dressed to go to the 163rd St. Mall. "It'll have to wait till I get back from the mall." He resumed dressing, and he, Law, Waxy, Butter, Winny Poop and Perry left together, leaving Vivian alone in the house.

After they were gone, Vivian closed the door, and noticed something strange. Winny Poop and Perry had left their glasses and a hat on the carpet in the den. Vivian thought, *this is a reason for Winny Poop and Perry to come back here ...I don't trust them.* The only reason why Perry and Winny Poop came to Vivian's house was because Jim was there. Waxy had left a pistol with Vivian when he left with Jim and the guys—a pistol that Wild Bill had given to him two nights before. Vivian also had his own piece.

Vivian unlocked the front door so he wouldn't have to move from his sitting position, if Winny Poop and Perry suddenly returned. They could let themselves in, but he would have full view of their entrance. He sat in a chair in a corner of the den, where no one could move behind him, and waited. Time passed, then the doorbell rang.

"Who is it?"

"Perry. We forgot our hat and glasses."

"Door's open. Come in." Vivian clutched both guns in his hands.

They guys walked into the den and Vivian observed them, but didn't do anything to make them suspicious. Perry walked over to the sliding glass door, and absentmindedly hit his head on the door. Vivian still clutched the two pistols and watched the pair. He had them off-guard, not knowing what to do.

Winny Poop's and Perry's plan was to kill him, and take the money that was in the house. No one could've said they did it, because they'd left the house with Jim, Law, and Butter earlier.

But, Vivian had turned the tables on them. With the guns in Vivian's hands, they couldn't afford to get shot—people would know what happened if Vivian died.

The phone rang suddenly. Vivian placed one of his pistols in his lap, and while scrutinizing the pair, answered the phone. The person on the other end was trying to change his voice to sound like a girl.

"Can I speak to Mr. Coke?"

"Mr. Coke is not here." Vivian recognized the voice as Waxy's, but didn't say anything.

Perry and Winny Poop were restless. Waxy's phone call should've been answered by them, because Vivian should've been dead.

Vivian was much smarter than they were.

Suddenly the doorbell rang. "Who is it?"

"Jim."

Recognizing the authentic Jim Brown, Vivian was relieved. "Door's open."

Jim attempted to enter. "Door's locked, Dave."

"Perry, let in Jim for me." Vivian followed Perry to the door.

"What you doing here?"

"We forgot our glasses and our hat."

Vivian laughed to himself.

Jim placed his mall purchases in the den. "I'm going to see Bill now."

Everyone left the house with Jim, except for Law and Vivian. Vivian didn't tell anyone of his suspicions. Ten minutes later, there was another knock at the door. Vivian still had the two guns in his hands as Law answered it. It was Waxy, Winny Poop, and Perry. Waxy walked toward the bedroom as Winny Poop, Perry, and Law walked to the den. Vivian was keenly listening to the sounds coming from the bedroom and heard the back door in the kitchen open. He definitely knew a robbery was in progress.

Waxy sneaked out the back door with the eighty thousand dollars and was putting the bag in Perry's car. Several thoughts ran through Vivian's mind, *am I to start shooting Winny Poop and Perry? No, Law might be killed in the gunfire. Better to lose the money than my friend's life. I don't think Waxy would try anything at this stage to endanger his brother-in-law's life. They'll take the money and run.*

He heard Waxy come back into the house through the back door, and walk to the den. "Dave, let me have my gun."

Vivian passed Waxy's gun to him, nozzle pointing at Waxy while he grasped the other pistol tightly in his right hand. Waxy took the pistol, and then put it inside his waistband. Vivian made a sigh of relief.

"Dave, later," was all Waxy said, then he, Perry and Winny Poop left.

As Vivian heard the car drive away, he looked at Law. "Law, we just got robbed."

Law looked at Vivian with amazement, "What?" asked Law frantically.

"Look in the bedroom for the money, and you'll see," said Vivian laughing.

Law rushed to the bedroom and searched, but the money was gone, then he rushed back to the den. "The money's gone. You mean Waxy did this to us, Dave?" Law was almost in tears.

Vivian just giggled, then he became serious as his thoughts turned to Jim and Butter. "I hope they're not planning on killing Jim and Butter, man."

Jim and Butter took a long time to get back to the house, which worried Vivian and Law. A car pulled up outside, and Vivian rushed to the door and peeked out. Happiness suffused his face. It was Jim and Butter. They got out of the car and approached the house as Vivian stood in the doorway.

"We just got robbed, man," said Vivian.

"Who robbed you?" asked Jim.

"Waxy, Winny Poop and Perry," he said sadly. They all walked inside the house.

"It's that fucking boy, Bya ... he set it up, man." Jim looked as if he wanted to cry.

Bya left for Jamaica early that morning before the robbery, as if that could prove he had nothing to do with it. Jim spent a few more days in Miami with Vivian, Law, Butter and Baggy Man. The same day Jim left for Jamaica, Vivian and Law took a flight up to New York. Vivian went straight home.

He had about forty thousand dollars in a safety deposit box and eighteen thousand dollars at home, and wanted to head back to Miami the next day and start working. Tony had lost all the money he had, and Vivian wanted to give him some. Vivian called Caltman, who told him the previous week that he had ten thousand dollars stashed away. "Caltman, lend me ten thousand dollars until Monday. I want to go down to Miami today."

Caltman hesitated.

Vivian enticed Caltman with, "I have about a hundred and fifty thousand dollars' worth of jewelry you could hold onto until Monday."

"I know somebody who'd buy the jewelry from you."

"You think I'm selling my fucking jewelry?" Vivian shouted angrily.

"All right, I'll call you soon." Vivian waited and waited, but Caltman never called.

As luck would have it, Vivian's phone rang. It was the contact at the airport, Joseph. There had been no marijuana from Jamaica for a while, so Vivian hadn't heard from Joseph in that regard.

"Do you have any marijuana in Jamaica now?" asked Vivian.

"Yes. Two suitcases can come up tomorrow," said Joseph.

"All right, Joseph. I'll try to get in touch with the people in Jamaica and let you know if I got through."

To get Jim Brown in Jamaica on such a short notice would be difficult, Vivian thought, because Jim had no phone. Vivian decided to call a lady in Tivoli Gardens to see if she could find him. When he dialed the lady's number, to Vivian's surprise, Jim answered the phone. "Jim, I was going to ask the lady to try and find you."

"And, I just stopped by to call you."

It was telepathy. "Can you find your man at the airport?"

"He's right here with me."

This was like a miracle; everything just fell into place.

Vivian left New York that afternoon on a one o'clock National Airlines flight to Miami. Caltman had still not called.

About five o'clock in the evening, as Vivian arrived at the airport, he saw Joseph pushing his two suitcases on a trolley towards him. Joseph followed Vivian to his car, placed the two suitcases—fifty pounds of Jamaican marijuana in each suitcase—in the car trunk, and drove away. Butter and Baggy Man were there to meet him at his house. He took the two suitcases out of the trunk. "Fuck Caltman," was Vivian's declaration as he, Baggy Man, and Butter celebrated.

After surviving two robberies and an attempt on his life, Vivian decided to part company with most of the guys he knew from Tivoli Gardens, especially the ones who were under the influence of Bya. In Miami, Vivian had only two friends with him, Butter and Baggy Man.

Baggy man was a young kid, dark complexioned, short, and had a broken front tooth. From a very tender age he'd been restricted from the streets in Jamaica … his mother forced him wear one of her panties—called a *baggy*—to prevent him from going out. He started his life of crime from the age of twelve, in the inner-city community, known as Fletcher's Land—the youngest and most feared member of the Land Raiders—killing two law officers in Jamaica by the time he was thirteen. He spoke with a stutter, which made him upset, because he was unable to express his feelings verbally—so he reacted physically, instead.

When he arrived in New York and saw so many police cars and officers, he panicked. He once ran from the streets to Vivian's apartment on McLlelan Street in the Bronx and said to Vivian very seriously, "When I see police officers, what do I do? Do I kill 'em?"

Baggy Man had asked in all seriousness, and Vivian couldn't help but break into laughter. "Are you crazy? Do you think this is Jamaica? Police officers in America don't really shoot people like they do in Jamaica, so you don't have to fear them; they just do their jobs. So long as you don't shoot at an American law officer, he won't shoot you, even if you have a gun."

Baggy Man laughed, "So if they catch you with a gun, they bring you in alive?"

"Yeah."

"Not in Jamaica. They definitely gonna kill you if they find a gun on you, so you have to try and kill them first."

Vivian laughed at Baggy Man's comments but knew the reality of it.

With all his losses behind him, Vivian decided to put in some hard work in Miami. Along with Baggy Man and Butter, he spent the next three months in Miami, sending suitcases of marijuana to New York. He rolled over his money constantly, not putting any cash aside, taking risks with all he had. It was all or nothing for Vivian. He was now hell-bent on reaching the top.

The last marijuana purchase Vivian made before finally heading back to New York was a thousand pounds. He reached his goal. He'd promised himself that he wouldn't leave Miami until he had a thousand pounds of marijuana. He made it.

He had girls take eighteen of twenty fifty-pound suitcases up to New York. With two suitcases left, he'd ran out of girls, so Vivian boarded the plane with the last two himself.

How he was missing his son, but first he stopped at the marijuana apartment with the two suitcases. By then, half of the thousand pounds of marijuana was sold. Tony handed him a traveling bag with two hundred and fifty thousand dollars. Vivian was smiling from ear to ear. He counted the packages, and then decided that he would sort the money properly when he got home. He called a cab, and two friends escorted him to the cab, both packing two automatic firearms with extended magazines.

"The Ambassador Apartments," he told the cabbie.

Duane—almost two years old—ran to his dad as Valerie opened the door.

"Daddy!" Duane hadn't seen his father for about three months.

Vivian dropped his flight pack, and the traveling bag with cash on the carpet, and lifted Duane—who was already holding onto his legs—into his arms. He kissed Duane, "Hi, Baby. Missed Daddy?"

Duane smiled and shook his head, then hugged his daddy around his neck.

He kissed Duane again, and then looked at Valerie. "Anything to eat?"

"No, I didn't expect you."

"Fix something quickly. I'm hungry. Fix some corned beef and rice." He lifted the bag of money and carried Duane in the other hand to the bedroom. "Bring the flight pack, Valerie."

He put the bag down and placed Duane on the bed, then laid down with his face directly over Duane's face and started playing with Duane. They played for the next forty-five minutes until Valerie shouted.

"Poppy, food's ready."

He picked Duane up from the bed and took him to the dining table. Corned beef and rice was one of Vivian's favorite dishes, so he had a large helping, as Duane sat on his lap, eating from his plate.

After dinner, the three of them relaxed in the living room watching TV, until Vivian decided to sort the money in the bedroom. He sat on the carpet, with his back against the side of the bed, and then emptied the bag of money between his legs on the carpet.

Duane started to take up the money from the floor. "Daddy ... mine."

"Yes, Baby ... all yours," Vivian said happily.

"Boy, why are you so in love with money?" Valerie said jokingly to Duane.

It wasn't long before Duane fell asleep, leaned against his father, and Vivian lifted Duane from the carpet and placed him on the bed. He continued to sort the money until Valerie fell asleep. It was daybreak, just as Valerie was getting ready for work, when Vivian finished.

It was near the end of summer 1980, when Vivian drove out of a Brooklyn BMW dealership in his brand new 320I. BMWs were fast becoming the cars of the future. Only two other Jamaicans drove BMWs—a guy in Brooklyn, known as Darby, and another elderly man in the Bronx, known as Paul Drugs. Driving a BMW meant you were in the *big league*.

Vivian drove through Brooklyn and pulled up on Midwood Avenue at Miss May's, the house of his past girlfriend, Lorna. Danny, one of Miss May's sons, was standing in the front yard when Vivian got out of his new BMW.

"Nice car."

"Anyone at home?"

"Yeah, Momma and Peaches are inside."

Vivian went inside the house. He was dressed conservatively, with a thick, link chain that had a one-ounce gold pendant on it. The initial "V" was on the pendant in white gold. He wore a gold bracelet on his wrist with "Vivian" written with two hundred diamond chips, made by Finey, a friend with whom Vivian shared a partnership in a jewelry store on Nostrand Avenue in Brooklyn.

Miss May greeted Vivian lovingly, and so did Peaches. Peaches was Killo's money tree, since she'd sold off Lorna to Barney, a prominent member of the Untouchables gang. Miss May had also assisted in breaking up Vivian and Lorna by cursing her out, because Vivian wasn't giving any financial support to Lorna.

How things had changed. Vivian was now on top, so people had to recognize that. Miss May, Peaches and Vivian sat in Miss May's living room and talked.

"You look so good, Vivian," said Miss May. "Life looks like it's done wonders for you."

He blushed.

"Whatever happened to you and Lorna?"

He laughed to himself at Miss May's question, knowing she and Peaches damn well knew what happened.

"Lorna would love to see you," said Peaches. "If you give me a phone number, she could call you when she gets home from work."

Vivian was still in love with Lorna and wouldn't mind seeing her again. "How is she anyway?"

"Mostly sad. Barney isn't treating her right," said Peaches.

That didn't sound too good to Vivian's ears. "Make sure she calls me later. I'll give you my number." Vivian was thinking, *this is the same woman who sold Lorna to Barney. Now she's taking Lorna back from Barney and giving her back to me. Oh, what a life.*

Miss May and Peaches walked with Vivian to the outside gate as he was leaving and saw his brand new BMW.

"Beautiful car," said Miss May.

"I just bought it," he said proudly. One of Killo's other girlfriends, Jennifer, had stopped by and was in the yard talking to Danny and also admiring Vivian's car.

Later that night, while Vivian was at his marijuana house in the Bronx, he got the call he was waiting for.

"Lorna here, Vivian. What's happening?"

"You tell me. I've been wondering about you for years. I heard you had a baby an' all."

"Yes, I have a little girl. She's two years old now."

"So what's up? When can I see you?"

"We could get together one day this week, after work."

"So, you still that same sweet Lorna I knew?"

"Well, I haven't changed much, but you can be the judge of that when you see me."

"All right, we'll be in touch."

Two days later, Lorna and Vivian met in Queens close to the Brooklyn-Queens border, where Lorna was living with her baby's father. Peaches was staying by Lorna's house, to cover for Lorna in case Barney was asking for Lorna. Vivian and Lorna had arranged a very romantic evening of beautiful lovemaking that each had been missing of each other for years. He booked a suite at the Howard Johnson by Kennedy Airport, and escorted Lorna to the suite.

On reaching the suite, Lorna went into the bathroom where she spent a while. He watched TV while he waited for Lorna to emerge. When she did, she was a sight to behold ... dressed in a see-through nightgown that showed every curve on her beautiful body. Vivian rose from the sofa in excitement and held Lorna in his arms. He kissed her soft lips passionately, and they both got steamy.

"Let me call Peaches at my house and give her the number for the hotel room," said Lorna with a sexy look in her eyes. She dialed the phone number at her house and Peaches answered. "Peaches, let me give you the number for where I'm at."

"Hold on, let me go into the kitchen for a pen and a piece of paper."

Peaches placed the phone down and then walked to the kitchen, which was in darkness.

Lorna waited on the other end of the line.

Peaches flicked the light switch in the kitchen and the light came on. All of a sudden, Peaches screamed in Lorna's ears at the other end of the line.

"Barney!" Peaches shouted.

Lorna panicked and hung up the phone. Barney was crouching in the dark, in the kitchen, with the other extension of the phone at his ear. He'd heard Lorna tell Peaches that she wanted to give her the number of her location.

That was all Lorna had said, so at least she could try to fabricate a believable story.

"I have to go home, Vivian. Barney's at the house and he heard me talking to Peaches," said Lorna nervously. "I'll deal with it, though. I'll just make up a story that I was at a bar with some friends." She got dressed quickly and Vivian drove her to Brooklyn. He dropped her off one block from her house and she walked the rest of the way.

On reaching home, Lorna found her furniture destroyed, and Barney in a rage. He held her down with his pistol, saying he was going to kill her. He knocked her around for a while in the presence of Lorna's two kids and threatened Peaches, who was a nervous wreck.

The next day, Lorna called Vivian from her mother's house and told him what had happened. She had moved out with her two kids and was staying at her mother's house. He immediately drove to Brooklyn to see Lorna. Miss May's prized son, Robby, was away in the armed forces, so she offered Vivian his room—a gesture that would have been unthinkable in the past. But, Miss May was intent on seeing Vivian and Lorna get back together. She knew Vivian could definitely support Lorna. A few days later, Vivian decided to take Lorna shopping in downtown Manhattan.

Miss May overheard him and Lorna talking and invited herself. "I'm coming along with you guys."

Lorna didn't like the idea of Miss May going shopping with them, but Vivian didn't mind, so they left at about ten o'clock that morning. Vivian opened the passenger door of his brand new BMW, so that Lorna could sit in the front seat, but Miss May took the front seat instead, and Lorna had to sit in the back. Vivian could see by Lorna's expression that she was upset.

At 34th St. in Manhattan, Miss May was the first one to identify something for herself. "I like that pair of working shoes."

"You like it, you can have it." Vivian quickly bought the pair of shoes for Miss May.

She had to go to work that day, so Miss May had to leave. Lorna was more relaxed after Miss May left. They had a fun-filled day shopping afterwards.

That Friday, Vivian was visiting Lorna in Brooklyn. Law was the only person who knew where Vivian was at the time. He spent that whole weekend in Brooklyn, away from his family—something he'd never done before, especially on a Sunday, unless he was out of town.

"How come you're not home? You never stay out on a Sunday," Law said.

"I'm in love, Law. I'm in love."

After Law hung up, Lorna served him breakfast in bed, and then went back to the kitchen to start preparing Sunday dinner.

After breakfast, Vivian laid on his stomach with his right hand under a pillow, propping up his chin, as he watched TV in the room. The door opened suddenly, and his eyes met Barney's. They stared at each other. This was the first time he'd seen Barney since Barney had taken his woman, and this was sweet revenge.

"Hi," Barney said frightened.

"Hi," Vivian said with a victory smile on his face, his hand still beneath the pillow as if he was clutching a pistol. Barney quickly pulled the door and left.

Vivian slammed the door shut and continued watching TV, but was disturbed by a scream.

Vivian jumped out of the bed and rushed outside where he saw Lorna clutching her eyes and Barney running through the front door.

"What did he do to you?" said Lorna's sister, Pauline.

Lorna's face swelled instantly, and her eyes were almost closed.

"What did he hit you with?" Vivian was very upset.

"I don't know." Lorna was still holding her face in pain.

He looked at Lorna's face and felt sorry for her, knowing it was because of him that she was in pain. Pauline wrapped a hot towel around Lorna's swollen face, and she had lay in bed the rest of the day.

Vivian decided enough was enough and asked Lorna to move with her two kids to the Bronx, where she would be close to him. She said yes, so he rented a two-bedroom apartment in the Bronx on 169th St. at the corner of Anthony Avenue, and exquisitely furnished the apartment. Things were cool between Lorna and Vivian at the beginning, until Lorna started hanging out with a daughter of her stepfather, Kick. Kick's daughter lived in the fast lane and had no regard for money.

One day, Lorna pulled out more than a thousand dollars from a savings pool, which people in Jamaica called a *partner*. A partner was a compulsory savings scheme in which a number of persons gave a set amount of money to a designated *banker* on a weekly basis. Every week, each person in the pool would receive the entire funds for that week, until all members were paid off.

Lorna had pulled down her money from her aunt, Miss Gladys, a very lovely lady, may God bless her soul. She went shopping with Kick's daughter, and spent all the cash, buying five winter coats. When she came home and showed Vivian the coats, he was upset.

"Are you crazy? What are you doing with five winter coats?" he shouted. The weekly deposit that was paid to Miss Gladys was his expense, so he was upset. A few days later, Lorna asked Vivian if she could borrow five hundred dollars. Vivian looked at her and shook his head. He ended up loaning her the money but was upset with her. *She just had over a thousand dollars, wasted the money on five winter coats, and is now borrowing.* That put a strain on her relationship with Vivian.

He started visiting Lorna less and less. Lorna eventually packed up the furniture and went back to Brooklyn to be with Barney. Vivian more or less did Barney a favor by breaking off his relationship with Lorna, because Barney was practically going crazy after losing her. Now he was happy again. This time around, though, he treated Lorna better, for fear that Vivian was waiting in the shadows to steal Lorna away from him again. Barney ended up buying a beautiful home in Long Island where Lorna, the kids, and he lived happily.

Vivian, Valerie and Duane lived in a beautiful high ranch house in Freeport, Long island, with an ocean view from the backyard, which had a swimming pool.

"I love this house."

"Me too," said Valerie, very excited. She turned to the real estate lady who was showing them the house and said, "We'll take this one."

The real estate lady smiled and said, "You all can come with me to the office and sign a binding contract where you deposit a thousand dollars, until the purchase agreements are worked out with your attorney and the sellers."

The owners of the house, a husband and wife, were happy to know a buyer was forthcoming. All the legal details were worked out, and Vivian and Valerie closed on their Long Island home in October 1980. Vivian took over the decorating himself and did a fine job. The house was purchased for ninety-eight thousand dollars, with forty thousand dollars as equity, and a mortgage of fifty-eight thousand dollars.

Vivian bought the best of furniture, and when he was finished, the house befitted a king—something out of this world. His master bedroom was off-white and lime green. The drapes in the bedroom were lime green with a semi-circular drape dropping from the ceiling over half of the bed. The wall behind the headboard was padded with the same lime-green drapery material, the width of the headboard. The bedroom set had an antique finish—the base color was antique white, with green and pink flowers, hand-painted in different areas. It was beautiful. The entire living and bedroom areas were carpeted with off-white, one-inch thick carpet. The living and dining rooms also had antique-looking furnishings—the materials that covered the sofas and dining chairs were the same as that used to make the drapes.

Duane's room had cartoon-theme wallpaper covering the walls, and a bunk bed. The wallpaper throughout the house was imported from Italy. Below, the lower level was decorated with antiques—up to a hundred years old. It was breathtaking.

In December, Vivian and Valerie threw Duane's second birthday party, and the house opening, in one gala affair at their Long Island mansion. Everyone in attendance was flabbergasted at the interior decor of the mansion, and the gala affair was a success. He had spent a one hundred thousand dollars to furnish and decorate the place. In 1980, a house worth one hundred thousand dollars was comparable to a two million dollar mansion in the year 2000.

Vivian, the little Tivoli Gardens kid, was now living a life befitting a king, with his wife and his beloved son, Duane, by his side, and he and his wife both drove spanking new BMWs.

The middle of December 1980, Vivian went to Jamaica on vacation. Bya was still the community leader in Tivoli Gardens. Jim Brown picked him up at the airport, and, after stopping at the Oceana Hotel, went on to Tivoli Gardens. Jim pulled up in front of the community center's main gate where Bya, Baskin—who was deported from the United States—Beardy and Spar were sitting and talking.

Bya watched as they walked towards him. "Oh, Vivian. I hear that you were planning to kill me in Miami." Bya was wearing a sly look on his face.

"Me, planning to kill you? How could you hear a thing like that anyway? You are *the* Bya. I would be stupid to have that leak out, knowing who you are. Anyone who told you that is just stirring up trouble."

"That's a fucking lie," said Beardy, defending Vivian. "People don't want to see my friend, Vivian, come in Tivoli Gardens, but if Vivian can't come in Tivoli Gardens, no foreigner can't come in, either," said Beardy to Bya, seriously.

Jim was physically upset at Bya's remark. Vivian said nothing more. He just listened to Beardy cursing at Bya's remarks.

Bya was lying and everyone knew that. He didn't know how to approach Vivian, because he knew that he and his friend, Wild Bill, were behind the two robberies in Miami.

Vivian spent about three hours in Tivoli Gardens, talking to other friends and associates. After he was finished meeting and greeting people, he decided it was time to visit his grandmother in uptown Kingston, so he, Jim, and Beardy drove out of Tivoli Gardens together en route for his grandmother's house.

The West Kingston Charity Ball was a few days away, and Vivian had plans to attend. Every year they looked forward to this charity ball. Every man—both young and old—had to have a suit made or sent from

America for the occasion, and the ladies new dresses. It was like Tivoli Gardens' Independence Day celebration.

Vivian went well dressed, in his custom-made, double-breasted suit, matching shoes and hat. Bya and Baskin were sitting together when Jim Brown, Vivian and Beardy arrived at the ball in the National Arena. They all walked over to the table where Bya and Baskin were sitting.

Bya smiled as they approached, "My friend, Vivian. No hard feelings. It's just people trying to put us up against each other," said Bya, stretching his hand out and shaking Vivian's.

Vivian smiled and said, "I have no hard feeling." But, deep in Vivian's mind, he knew Bya was a fraud, and this handshake was just bullshit.

Baskin rose from his seat and called Vivian aside. "I can't understand how you didn't talk to me in Tivoli Gardens the other day, man. I'm not down with the bullshit that Bya was talking about."

For some reason, Vivian knew Baskin was speaking genuinely. He had always liked Baskin and knew that Baskin wasn't down with the eighty-seven thousand dollars robbery. He was just drawn into it after it took place. Baskin and Vivian then snorted cocaine together in the bathroom and talked. Later, they joined Jim, Bya, Beardy and Spar, who had just arrived at the table. Everyone left the Arena drunk that night.

That Christmas season was fun in Tivoli Gardens. Vivian got to know Spar very well, and they became close. His last name was Blake, like Vivian's, so they hit it off well. On New Year's Eve, Vivian booked two rooms at the Pegasus Hotel. He had two girls—one named Sidoney and the other was Charmaine—who Spar had introduced to him. Vivian was seeing Sidoney, so he invited another friend, Teddy Paul, to tag along with him, and Teddy Paul and Charmaine got on fine.

They dropped the two girls off at the Pegasus Hotel, and walked over to the Sheraton, where they heard Bya and an entourage were having fun in the Jonkunoo Lounge. Bya, Baskin, Spar, Tappa Zukie and Tall P. were snorting away. Tappa Zukie and Vivian had become close friends in Miami, so he was glad to see him.

Baskin looked at Vivian and asked, "You all partying with us tonight?"

Vivian shook his head and said, "No, we have two ladies waiting on us over by Pegasus. Just give me some cocaine, and let me and Teddy Paul go have some fun with the girls."

Baskin took a huge chunk of the cocaine and gave it to Vivian.

Vivian smiled and looked at Teddy Paul. "Tomorrow, you all."

Bya looked up and smiled. "How you all leaving so soon?"

"We have two girls waiting on us over by Pegasus."

"All right, tomorrow."

Teddy Paul and Vivian left the Jonkunoo Lounge. They checked out of the Pegasus Hotel at twelve o'clock the next day, hailed a cab for the two girls, sent them home, then boarded a cab for Tivoli Gardens. At a section of Tivoli Gardens, known as Bumps, Teddy Paul went up to his apartment while Vivian sat by the iron railing on the main highway in Tivoli Gardens, with Champs, Bad Word and Nine Finger Byron.

In a few minutes, three cars pulled up in front of them. Bya and a friend, Bankine, were in Bya's car. Spar was driving his car, and Tappa Zukie was driving his car. Bankine then drove away in Bya's car, leaving Bya.

Vivian noticed Bya's tiredness. "Looks as if you haven't slept all night."

"Boy, my little friend, a lot has been happening," said Bya in a frustrating manner.

"You want some coke?"

"Sure."

Bya looked over at Spar, who was sitting in his car with his feet outside, and said in a serious tone, "Spar, give Vivian some of the coke, but don't trouble it otherwise."

Spar took out the cocaine and started to cut the hard block with his penknife. Tappa Zukie was leaning against his car, facing Vivian and talking to him.

All of a sudden a gun appeared in Bya's hand and Bya was admiring it—a six-shooter .38 revolver. "You see this thing?" Bya said, toying with the gun. "It does a lot of dangerous things." He waved the gun in front of Vivian, Champ, Bad Word, and Nine Finger Byron's faces. "Spar, come here," said Bya, the tone of authority.

Without warning, there was an explosion toward Spar. Bya turned the gun on Tappa Zukie and shot him twice in the abdomen, then fired another shot towards Spar. Tappa Zukie started to run, and Bya fired another shot at him. Everyone panicked and ran.

Vivian's shoe was stuck in the iron railing as he, Bad Word, Champs and Nine Finger Byron ran off, stealing a peek at Bya from the side of an apartment building. Bya held the gun toward the ground and clicked it, but it was empty. Vivian could have sworn, for years to come, that one of the shots came in his direction.

Since the gun was empty, the four of them walked back toward Bya.

"These guys are acting like they're the boss, and *I'm* the boss around here." Bya tucked his pistol inside of his waistband, and walked to the car where Bankine was sitting behind the steering wheel—he drove Bya away.

Vivian looked at Spar's car and saw Spar lying on the ground, bleeding to death, and rushed to his assistance. Spar was lying face down, with a penknife in one hand and the cocaine in the other. "Help me, Vivian, help me." Blood trickled from a gunshot wound to his neck.

"Let's take him to the hospital. He's dying," said Vivian pitifully.

Champs walked up to Vivian and said, "Are you crazy? Next thing you'll hear is that we acted as if we were the ambulance. Leave the man. Let him die. It's between him and Bya," Champs said coldly.

Vivian walked away, watching Spar on the ground, groaning for life. He laid on the ground for four hours until he bled to death.

Vivian, Jim, Champs and Bad Word hid on the fourth floor of a building in a section of Tivoli Gardens, called Java, contemplating what had gone wrong with Spar, Tappa Zukie and Bya the night before. Perhaps it was a paranoid effect from the cocaine that led Bya to cook off like that. No one wanted to venture around Bya until they knew what was happening.

With everyone pondering, Vivian suggested that someone take him home. Jim sent for Tan Tody, who drove Vivian to his grandmother's house in Manor Park, where he spent two days away from Tivoli Gardens until Jim came for him.

Returning to Tivoli Gardens, Vivian saw Bya sitting in front of the community center. Bya rose up as he saw Vivian coming. He had a .45 automatic pistol—in plain sight—jus inside his waistband, the hammer cocked. Bya didn't usually carry a gun.

"Did you like how the old boy handled his gun the other day?" Bya laughed as he pulled out his .45 and examined it.

Vivian watched him carefully and suspiciously, until Bya put the pistol back.

"I knew you knew what you were doing the other day."

Bya went inside a first-floor apartment with Beardy and Teddy Paul, and they started smoking marijuana from a homemade smoke pipe.

Vivian watched them through a window. He, Champs and Teddy Paul were laughing.

"Aren't you taking a pull of the pipe, Dave?" said Teddy Paul teasingly. "Come, man. Stop acting so cowardly."

"I don't want any weed," said Vivian, laughing.

Bya had a *Red Stripe* beer in his hand, and it slipped and fell to the floor, making a sound as though a shot were fired. Teddy Paul ran, and Bya started laughing. "You're talking about Vivian being afraid? *You're afraid.*

"Dave, remember we have to go to Grace Kennedy's," said Donovan.

Vivian looked at Champs, knowing that he didn't know anything about any Grace Kennedy, but Champs winked at him; Vivian realized his friend was panicking and wanted to leave.

Tivoli Gardens was rife with tension during the following days. Everyone was wondering what Bya was up to—with the gun. If you scratched your waist, and he saw you, he would pull his gun, wondering if you were pulling yours. He was paranoid all the time and pulled his gun on Teddy Paul, a prominent community leader—named Johnathan, a friend of his—Mickey Jakes, and many other people on different occasions. He pulled his gun on Baskin, who was his very close crony, and things changed. Baskin went against him—unheard of.

"Tell your uncle, if he ever tries pulling a pistol at me again, I'm going to kill him," said Baskin to one of Bya's nephews.

At this point, everyone knew Bya's reign as the community leader of Tivoli Gardens was finished.

Hearing Baskin's response, Vivian smiled and mused. The table had turned. The next day, after Baskin's historic remarks, Bya was driving on Milk Lane and saw Beardy. He fired six shots at Beardy, missing completely, and said, "You and Vivian want to kill me."

Things went from bad to worse. The next day, Bya fired shots at his best friend, Wild Bill, and ran him out of Tivoli Gardens.

Vivian—as did most of the guys—kept away from Bya. Champs and Baskin had their guns with them—night and day—swearing that if he pulled his gun at them, they were going to kill him. The only two community leaders who didn't wear guns were Jim Brown and Dinnal, although Bya had fired shots at Dinnal, too.

The straw that broke the camel's back occurred in Tivoli Gardens Square one evening, while Jim Brown was talking to a girl. Bya walked across the bridge at Java, but Jim didn't see Bya coming. Vivian was watching from an apartment building. Jim heard a clicking sound behind him and turned around to see Bya, with his .45 leveled at him.

"What's this for?" asked Jim nervously.

"You're the only person in Tivoli Gardens with the power to kill me, so if I kill *you*, there'll be no one who can oppose me," said Bya, blood in his eyes.

"*But we're friends*. I wouldn't try to hurt you … see?" said Jim, lifting up his shirt, showing Bya he had no gun. "I don't even travel with a gun. I'm not against you, Bya. I'm on your side. Nobody in Tivoli Gardens can hurt you so long as I'm alive."

Bya relaxed the hammer on his pistol as Vivian and many others watched. The two spoke for a while, then Jim was able to leave.

This was the end of Bya. Jim went back for his gun, but Bya had left. Bya was given the message that he was no longer welcome in Tivoli

Gardens. He visited a couple of times, with his wife and several kids in the car, so that no one would want to hurt him. No one really wanted to hurt Bya … all they wanted was for him to stay away from the community.

One day, he drove to Tivoli Gardens with his wife and kids, and Champs slapped him in his face. That angered a lot of the guys and the community at large, because no matter what, it was the same Bya who'd been the community leader for over fifteen years. Beardy was upset and cursed Champs badly.

"If Bya wasn't acting stupid, you couldn't have done that, so I didn't see no reason for you to do that shit, man. Total disrespect to the elder."

Shame faced, Champs walked away and that was the last time Bya came back to Tivoli Gardens.

Vivian, witnessing what Champs had done, was saddened and left for the United States the next day.

It was 1981, and Vivian was back in New York. A lot of cash had been spent on his new home, two BMW cars and vacationing extravagantly in Jamaica. All this lavish lifestyle created a dent in his wallet, so hard work was ahead—to recoup the three hundred thousand dollars he'd spent. During the spending spree, he hadn't taken time out to pay Butter and Baggy Man, who'd stuck with him through the trying times, and neither did he pay Law. Vivian's intentions were good, but cash was low.

He had three people to support, so that they could be on their own—Butter, Baggy Man, and Tony. He wanted to go down to Miami and roll over the cash he had, before he paid out, especially to Butter and Baggy Man. Tony was no problem, nor was Law, because they knew him well and trusted his judgment.

Butter and Baggy Man called at his home in Long Island, Butter being the spokesperson for the two. He was disgruntled and expressed it boldly. "We'd like to start our business. Pay us off so we can go on our own."

Vivian loved the fact that Butter was that ambitious, but there was one thing that bothered him—he didn't like the tone in which Butter spoke. It was clear to Vivian that he would have to part company with Butter and Baggy Man.

That day, Vivian drove to Riverdale to the old apartment he'd turned over to Tony and placed the shopping bag with cash on the dining table as soon as he entered. "This is forty thousand dollars. Split it between Butter and Baggy Man. And, I don't want to see them again."

Tony looked at his brother with astonishment. "What's wrong?"

Vivian sat down at the dining table and so did Tony. "I got a call from Butter and Baggy Man this morning, and Butter said they wanted to be paid off. But, that wasn't it. That was okay. They deserved it. It's just Butter …his attitude was too aggressive. Baggy Man was cool—it's just Butter. The good suffers for the bad. I don't want to see neither of them, or anyone they associate with."

Tony listened to Vivian and smoldered. "I told you, man, a long time ago, that Butter was a pussy. I ain't giving them shit, man. I ain't scared of them. Let's kill them bastards."

"Nah, that's not the way. They deserve the money. They worked for it, man. It's theirs."

"Yo, their friends from Tivoli Gardens robbed us, man. I don't give a fuck about none of them Tivoli Gardens motherfuckers! They all should fucking die!"

"You can't blame everyone in Tivoli Gardens for what a few begrudging Tivoli Gardens unscrupulous bandits did. That's unfair."

"All of them motherfuckers from Tivoli Gardens should die."

Vivian looked at Tony seriously, "Just give them the money, okay? It's theirs, and I don't want any problems, okay? War and business doesn't go together. We'll just cool off selling marijuana for now, until we rearrange our operations in Miami and New York—new houses, new apartments—just to avoid any conflicts."

"What the fuck you talking about, Dave? Why go to so much expense? All we have to do is kill those two punks."

Vivian started to laugh. "Do you know that you're crazy?"

Tony started to laugh, too.

"You can't make money while you're engaged in war. It's not possible. You only lose money. Remember, we're giving the public a service. You have to keep a low profile, and that's bad for business. Just give them their money. We'll be fine." He rose from the table. "I'm leaving now ... later."

Later that day, Butter and Baggy Man arrived at Tony's apartment. Tony opened the door, automatic pistol in hand. The shopping bag with the forty thousand dollars was still on the dining table where Vivian had left it. Tony pointed to the bag and said, "There's your money. Count it." Tony kept his finger on the trigger, the hammer cocked, ready to fire. While Butter and Baggy Man were counting the money, all that was on Tony's mind was whether to kill them or not. He decided not to when he remembered what Vivian said to him. "Remember, this apartment's in my wife's name. She'll get in trouble."

Butter and Baggy Man started doing business on their own, using the houses Vivian abandoned in Miami. They acquired an apartment of their own in New York to sell the marijuana, and they convinced Law to work with them.

Vivian took his time setting up his new operation, while smuggling suitcases of marijuana from Jamaica with the help of Jim Brown. He decided he wanted to spend some quality time with his family before he went back full-force into the wholesale buying of marijuana, transporting it from Miami to New York.

Joseph, at the Miami International Airport told him, "We have to cool off the shipment of marijuana from Jamaica for a while. There are some sniffing dogs on the ramp, searching for marijuana. They busted four suitcases today."

This wasn't good news for Vivian. When the marijuana was coming from Jamaica to Miami, Joseph would just send the marijuana up to New York with one of Vivian's girls. That way, Vivian didn't have to travel to Miami. With trouble at the airport, he would have to obtain a house in Miami quickly.

It was summertime in New York when Vivian's friend, Food Head—brother of Freeman—found a house for him in Miami. Freeman had met an untimely death, while in a pool hall in Miami. Junior Screw, the man a few years before who tried to rob Freeman's marijuana apartment in the Bronx, caught Freeman off-guard and shot him dead from behind.

Vivian wasn't ready to go back to Miami, because he wanted to enjoy the summer at his home in Long Island. Duane was almost three years old, and this was the first summer in his new house. He and Duane swam in the pool that overlooked the ocean, and he watched Duane ride his bike down Guy Lombardo Avenue. The Avenue was named after the famous movie star and musician. His house was three away from Vivian's, and the two of them owned the only two houses on the Avenue that had swimming pools. Guy Lombardo was dead by then, but his wife was still living. At the back of Guy Lombardo's house, the boat deck was designed in such a way that a boat could pull up close to the back door.

Unfortunately, summer came to an end. Duane started pre-school in Freeport, Long Island and Valerie, with a bachelor's degree in Nutrition from Lehman College in the Bronx, was still working with the New York City Board of Education as a monitor of the city's school lunch program. So, she had to have an early start every morning, now that school had re-opened. Vivian knew he had to head right back to doing what he did best—selling marijuana.

Chapter 10: The Shower Posse Era

Vivian abandoned all close relationships with known gunmen from Tivoli Gardens, and who resided in the US. His only communication with Tivoli Gardens was directly in Jamaica, not America. Jim Brown was the one and only community leader in Tivoli Gardens. His second-in-command was a young guy, known as Johnathan, along with Beardy and Champs. All were close to Vivian, except Johnathan. He was new and wasn't born and bred in Tivoli Gardens. Then, there were Sexy Paul and Juicy, who had defected from Concrete Jungle along with Tan Tody, who came to Tivoli Gardens from Greenwich Farm. These guys were also close to Vivian. Vivian had admiration for Johnathan as a young leader, because he acted very maturely.

Jim advised Vivian to stay away from a certain bunch of Tivoli Gardens men in America, because all they thought about was to "get rich quicker and by any means necessary." The advice was well taken by Vivian, but he made that decision long before Jim said it.

Many of Tony's friends had come up from Jamaica, and Tony housed them in the first apartment Vivian had given to him on Kings Bridge Avenue, in the Riverdale vicinity.

Vivian was ready to start business again. He rented a new apartment in the Bronx on McLlelan Street, where he'd previously had a marijuana house, but didn't have anyone to help him operate the marijuana business in New York. He and Tony went to the apartment on Kings Bridge Avenue. About ten of Tony's friends were packed into the one bedroom when they arrived.

"Damn! What the fuck is this here, Tony? Ain't you worried about the neighbors seeing so many guys moving in and out the apartment? This is a decent neighborhood. It could look suspicious, like drugs are selling here, man."

Tony just laughed at Vivian as he spoke, even though their youngest brother, Kong, was in the apartment. Vivian looked around and saw three guys in the apartment whose relatives he knew back in Tivoli Gardens. They went to very good schools in Jamaica and were intelligent. Vivian chose two—one named Big Toe, the other Arrow—to help him at the apartment down by McLlelan Street.

Butter and Baggy Man were operating a marijuana business close by. A tenuous tranquillity prevailed among Vivian, Tony, Butter and Baggy Man. Vivian and Tony spoke neither to them, nor their friends. But, two incidents sparked an even deeper divide.

Tony went over to Baggy Man's and Butter's house one day—a guy named Douda, and two other kids were also there—one named Jeffrey. He was like a brother to Vivian and Tony, for his father—Mr. Mills—was a boyfriend of Gloria's. Vivian had arranged passage for Jeffrey to migrate to New York, but Jeffrey turned on Vivian, choosing to side with Butter and Baggy Man in the split.

Seeing Tony entering the apartment, Jeffrey rose from his seat, pistol in his hand and pointed it toward Tony. "Pussy, I need my fucking ring." Jeffrey was definitely trying to impress his friends in the apartment.

"I'll bring the ring to you later. The gun isn't called far," Tony said calmly.

Jeffrey—being an inexperienced gunman—didn't bother to check Tony, to see if he was armed, but instead, replaced his pistol and turned away.

"Jeffrey, you check to see if he has a gun?" said Douda in a low tone. As Jeffrey spun around, trying to pull his pistol out, three consecutive explosions tore his chest cavity wide open. He was looking down the smoking nozzle of Tony's automatic. The impact of the shot catapulted Jeffrey through the living room window and onto the pavement outside. Amazingly, he survived the drop from the apartment to the pavement—another flight would have killed him.

Jeffrey recovered, and he and Tony encountered each other once more in a friend's apartment. This time, Tony didn't hesitate, shooting Jeffrey twice, again, in the chest. Again, Jeffrey lived. Talk about a cat with nine lives.

Because of these incidents, Butter especially didn't trust Tony. But, at no time did Tony worry about Butter—his main concern was Baggy

Man, whom he considered the real shooter. Tony wanted to kill Baggy Man badly, but Vivian always talked him out of it.

Tony and Baggy Man passed on a street corner one day, and even though they spoke for a while, all Tony could think about was wiping out Baggy Man. His body jostled with adrenaline as he spoke to him, but he decided the time wasn't right.

Vivian, Tony, Arrow and Big Toe went inside the apartment, which Vivian had already furnished. The apartment was located on the top floor, and it suited everyone.

Vivian flew down to Miami to his new house, and Food Head drove him around, so that Vivian could purchase furniture for it. Vivian also purchased a cheap car to transport his and Tony's marijuana.

Killo and Glasses joined him in Miami later, and for the next few months, business flourished. On one of his trips to New York, Vivian heard that a very good friend of his, Teddy Paul, was in New York and was staying at Butter's marijuana apartment, so Vivian went over to speak to Teddy Paul, promising him a pound of marijuana.

When Teddy Paul called for Vivian, Vivian had already rushed out of New York to go to Miami earlier that day. A misunderstanding ensued, because Butter told Teddy Paul that Vivian was at the apartment but didn't want to speak with him. When Vivian returned to New York, he didn't hear from Teddy Paul.

About a week later, on a Saturday night, Vivian received a call from a girlfriend— Joy Cash (nicknamed Joy Trash by some of the girls), who was also a girlfriend of Teddy Paul's. Vivian had met her while on one of his many trips to Jamaica—sexy and cute, of Indian descent.

Vivian decided to cross his Teddy Paul this time. He arranged to have Joy locked in a hotel room, close by his grandmother's house in Jamaica for a full two days. He would have sex with her, and then leave.

Teddy suspected what Vivian was doing with the girl, so while Jim and Vivian were planning to sneak away with Joy and her friend, Grace, one night, Teddy and another friend, Johnny—who was Grace's boyfriend—appeared.

Jim was still determined and said to Vivian, "Come on, man. Let's drive out with the girls. We'll worry about Teddy and Johnny later."

"Nah, man. Teddy and Johnny aren't going to like that."

Jim Brown hissed through his teeth immediately.

After they finished talking, they saw Teddy and Johnny walking briskly toward the girls and ordered them to follow them. Joy and Grace looked at Jim and Vivian for help, but the two guys couldn't get involved then.

The girls were taken to an apartment of Teddy's, in the section of Tivoli Gardens known as Bumps. The guys swapped partners, so each guy had sex with the other's girlfriend.

Vivian and Jim Brown were livid when they learned what happened, but couldn't do squat. Vivian decided one way out of the impasse was to assist Joy in migrating to America, but the condition was that they could no longer have a relationship. The news fell on deaf ears. Joy spread the word that Vivian was her main man. He hated it, but she continued, causing embarrassing problems between Vivian and his other girlfriends. She was obsessed.

That Saturday night in New York, Joy, who was at a party in the Bronx, called Vivian on the phone: "Teddy Paul's here, Dave." She handed the phone over.

"How come I haven't heard from you?" Vivian asked.

"I called, but some guy said you weren't there. Then Butter, who was on the other line, said you *were* there, but didn't want to speak to me."

"And you believed that crap?"

"Well, I just arrived in America … I don't know what's happening."

"Teddy, remember one thing, man … you are my friend, and I would never refuse your call. Never." Vivian's tone was convincing.

Two days later, Teddy Paul came to visit Vivian at his marijuana apartment in the Bronx. Vivian, Tony, Big Toe and Arrow were there when he arrived, and Tony played host for Vivian's sake, but made it clear that he didn't want anything to do with Teddy Paul.

This was Vivian's apartment, and Teddy was his friend, so he didn't care how Tony felt about him being a guest. He and Teddy talked for a while and snorted cocaine together with Arrow and Big Toe. Tony didn't use drugs, didn't drink, and smoked, maybe, half of a cigarette a month … perhaps two months … or sometimes as long as a year. He had discipline.

The day ended on a happy note, and upon departure, Vivian gave Teddy Paul a pound of marijuana to take with him.

The next day, Vivian sent Joy to Miami with some cash, to buy two suitcases of marijuana, and return to New York the next day. It didn't happen.

Killo and Glasses were at the Miami house, and called a cab for Joy, who was en route to the Fort Lauderdale Airport with two suitcases of marijuana. While she was at the check-in counter, two narcotic agents approached her, showing their badges. Her suitcases were examined and found to contain marijuana. She was arrested.

Another girl from Payne Avenue in Jamaica—Angela—had been introduced to Vivian by his friend, Food Head, and was also working for Vivian and Tony. She was the girlfriend of Food Head's cousin, Milton Pusey. She also boarded a flight from Fort Lauderdale with two suitcases of marijuana, not knowing that Joy had been busted, but reached Vivian's apartment in the Bronx safely. When the news broke that Joy had been arrested, Angela said, "Thank God, I made it."

Moments later, another call came in—Killo calling in from Miami. "Oh, Vivian, police came to the new house, and I had to run, leaving $103,000 behind."

Vivian had an instant headache. "When it rains, it pours," was all he could say.

"I am going to leave today," said Killo in a panic. "Miami's hot, Dave."

All Vivian could do was laugh.

"You find it funny?"

"It's the nervous way you're acting … why I'm laughing."

More bad news came that night. Killo was arrested at Fort Lauderdale Airport, trying to leave. Everything was in disarray. Vivian couldn't think straight. He'd just lost $103,000, sixty pounds of marijuana, and two people were in jail with huge bail bonds. He'd also lost his two houses in Miami to boot—all in one day

"What the fuck have I done to deserve this shit?" he shouted out loud to no one in particular. "I'm going home to rest. See you guys in a couple of days." He left the apartment in disgust.

Vivian spent two days on Long Island, and then drove to the Bronx. Finally, his mind was clear. He knew he had to take charge of the Miami operations himself. His friends were reckless, and they didn't take the same precautions he took, to safeguard losses. Vivan kept losses to a minimum when he was at the helm, and this was what he intended to do—take the bull by the horn. Tony encouraged him to spend more time in Miami, because everything ran perfectly when he was at the Miami end. What was hampering Vivian was the fact that his son was young, and he wanted to spend more time with him.

With the attraction to his wife at an all-time low, he now made up his mind to spend more time in Florida. He figured that long spells away from the house would bring a new spark to their relationship, and she would feel like a brand new woman to him after spending weeks apart. His son was another story. He didn't want to be away from him for such a long period. Vivian rationalized that when he could spend time with Duane, it would make up for him being away.

Vivian called Angela in Miami. "What's up?"

"When you guys coming back to Miami? I need some work."

"That's what I'm planning to do. But, I need you to rent a house for me."

"That's not a problem, but you can stay at my house until I get a place rented for you."

What Angela said pleased Vivian, because he was ready to go to Miami immediately. He had to get Killo and Joy out of jail, so he needed to some quick cash.

"For real?"

"Yes, you can stay at my house," Angela restated.

"So what will your man think?"

"I'm my own woman. He barely supports me. I pay my own bills."

"It would be two of us coming down—me and Arrow.

"No problem."

Vivian was pleased to be so welcomed by Angela, whom he hardly knew. "Okay, look out for us tonight."

Tony, Big Toe, and Arrow were at the apartment with Vivian while he was talking to Angela. Earlier, Tony suggested to Vivian that he take Arrow with him when he went to Miami, because Arrow indicated to Tony that he wouldn't mind living there.

In Miami, the baby's father of Vivian's cousin—Bobs—was living in Angela's house with Angela's sister, Shirley. That night, Vivian and Arrow boarded the one a.m. National Airline flight from Kennedy to Miami, Arrow carrying Tony's money, Vivian carrying his own.

It was after four a.m. when they arrived at Angela's house on NW 37th Avenue, close to 169th St. Angela gave Vivian a radiant, sexy smile as she let them in

"I hope your man don't wanna shoot me after today now, Angela."

She hissed through her teeth. "I don't have a man. Milton has his lovely woman Donna, who he loves. He don't come about me."

Vivian and Angela talked for about an hour in the kitchen while Shirley and Chris showed Arrow a room. "You can sleep in my room, I'll sleep on the sofa."

"Show me *your* room," said Vivian.

She led the way and he followed. It was well decorated; only the sheets were ruffled because she was in bed sleeping when he and Arrow arrived. "Let me change the sheets for you," she offered politely. She changed the sheets then brushed her teeth in the bathroom.

The mint fresh smell of the toothpaste aroused Vivian. He had no shirt on, just a tank top, along with his pants, and was bare-footed, having taken off his shoes. Angela came out of the bathroom wiping her mouth with a towel. She had answered the door in her nightgown and was still wearing it. Vivian looked straight into Angela's eyes as she emerged from the bathroom and she smiled. "Why you looking at me like that, Dave? If I may call you Dave."

Vivian signed his name on Angela's heart that morning. Milton was now history, and that's how Vivian wanted it. He couldn't have worked comfortably with another hustler's woman. It wouldn't feel right.

In the weeks to come, the assistance from Angela was priceless. With her help, Vivian made money. She was so generous … buying things for Joy, until her bail went down to five thousand dollars, at which point she was bailed out. Killo was bailed out right after her.

Angela drove an old car, using it for Vivian's errands, so Vivian bought her a Toyota Supra. She deserved it, but when Tony heard that Vivian bought Angela a car, he was not amused. "You really mean to tell me you bought that girl a car?" Tony asked Vivian on the phone.

"Yes, and I'd do it again. She deserved it and more, but you don't have to worry, it was my expense, alone, although she did work for you and the guys, too." Vivian was getting upset at Tony's lack of appreciation for a girl who was helping him.

After a few months, Vivian rented a townhouse in the upscale neighborhood of Pembroke Pines, where he and Angela took up residence. Arrow was dating one of Angela's friends. Angela's nephew, who had just migrated from Jamaica, was dating Angela's friend's daughter. So, Arrow and Angela's nephew—Hucky Berry—were constantly together.

After Joy got out of jail and returned to New York, she decided to start trouble. She heard that Vivian and Angela were seeing each other and this upset her. Encouraged by her friends in New York, she called Angela's house on 37th Avenue. Vivian, Angela and a few others were at the house at the time, so Angela answered the phone.

"Hello, may I speak to Angela?"

"This is Angela, who's this?"

"This is Joy Cash, and I am asking you, please, to leave my man, Dave, alone. All you doing in Florida is sucking his fucking dick, dirty Angela!"

Angela signaled to Vivian to pick up the extension.

He heard Joy cursing out Angela, then he interrupted. "Why the fuck you calling my woman and cursing at her, Joy? I won't say another word until I see you face to face!"

"You can't do me shit when you see me."

Vivian could hear some girls in the background where Joy was, laughing, as if they were the ones supporting her in this disrespectful behavior.

Weeks passed, and Vivian remained in Miami, shipping up suitcases of marijuana to New York for Tony, himself, and the other guys. He bought a brand new Volvo and was enjoying the life.

While Glasses was in Miami one day, he stumbled into Butter at the mall on 163rd Street in North Miami Beach. They both spoke for a while, but Glasses didn't like what he heard.

"Dave, last week I saw Butter and we were talking, but he said something I didn't like, man."

"What was it?"

"He said you should die, Dave, and I thought that statement was uncalled for."

Vivian saw red and trembled. This was the first time in his life that someone had coolly threatened his life, and he had to do something about it. He checked around Florida and heard Butter—was in New York, but was unsuccessful locating him. The next closest person to Butter, other than Baggy Man, was Law.

"Where's Butter?" Vivian asked angrily.

Law replied, "He's in New York, but I don't know where to locate him right at this moment. You want me to give him a message?"

"Yeah. Tell him I heard that he said I should die, and that he should have his gun on him at all times, because I'll have mine, and that's all I have to say." He hung up.

Tony wanted to start an all-out war, but Vivian rebuffed him. That would be bad for business, and furthermore, no one else was involved. It was just between himself and Butter.

About two weeks later, Vivian and a friend from the country parts of Jamaica went to Woolworth's on 183rd St. and 27th Avenue NW to buy some suitcases. The guy had driven Vivian to Woolworth's in an old van. Leaving Woolworth's with one suitcase apiece, Vivian saw Butter and another friend of Vivian's—Ruddy—who had taken sides against Vivian. Vivian's friend had a pouch in his hand at the time.

Butter and Vivian's eyes met; Butter proceeded to the suitcase area, while Vivian and his friend left the store and headed to their van. From the van, Vivian saw Butter and Ruddy peeking into the parking lot from inside of Woolworth's. They knew that Vivian had bought a Volvo so they were searching for his car.

Vivian also knew that Ruddy and Butter came to buy suitcases, so when Ruddy and Butter saw the pouch, they must've mistaken it for a gun. In actuality, it was his Bible. His friend was a Christian.

Butter and Ruddy, not recognizing any Volvo in the parking lot, ran swiftly to their car. Vivian and his friend watched them from the van and laughed until tears were in their eyes as they sped away, right behind them.

Vivian had to give up his marijuana apartment on McLlelan because he heard it was under police surveillance, which left him without an apartment for a couple of weeks. One of Tony's friends—Billy—had rented an apartment but was reluctant to sell marijuana for Vivian—he only sold Tony's marijuana.

Vivian found an apartment on 183rd St. close to Andrews Avenue. The real estate company that rented the apartment to Billy was the same company that rented Vivian the apartment on 183rd—the two owners of the company were friends of Vivian's. They told him that the superintendent of Billy's apartment building complained to them that marijuana was being sold from Billy's apartment, and suggested that Vivian tell Billy to be more discreet. Most of Vivian's customers bought marijuana at Billy's house.

He went to see Billy immediately, a different plan on his mind. "Yo, Billy, I just came from the real estate agents and they told me that the narcotics cops are watching this apartment."

Billy's eyes popped open. Billy had some of Vivian's marijuana, which he had stashed away in a closet and was not selling—leaving it to be sold last. Now Vivian had Billy right where he wanted him. Tony was also present in the apartment and laughed at what he suspected was a con game.

"Here's what you do now, Billy. Take all the marijuana over to my house, then send the customers over there." Vivian started to look around as if he wanted to leave the apartment in a hurry. "Where's my weed? I'm leaving here now." Then he started to gather his marijuana.

Billy was nervous and shaking. "So what's going to happen?"

"We'll run the 183rd St. apartment together," said Vivian, who wanted to laugh, but held back.

Tony was still looking straight into Vivian's eyes to find out if he was lying, but Vivian wouldn't meet his gaze.

"Billy, I think Dave's conning you," said Tony, laughing.

"No, Blacks," said Billy, calling Tony by his nickname. "Yesterday I really saw a detective car in front of the building."

Vivian took his marijuana and immediately left Billy's apartment, without looking at Tony. When he entered the elevator, he laughed until tears rolled down his cheeks and onto his shirt like a river. Billy was conned—big time.

Billy directed all the customers to Vivian's apartment, then abandoned his own apartment and took up residence at Vivian's. Vivian, of course, hated the way Billy had treated him by not selling his marijuana. So, after Billy finished selling the marijuana he had at the apartment, Vivian refused to allow Billy to sell any more marijuana in *his* apartment.

Angela continued to send Vivian's marijuana from Florida, with the help of Chris and her relatives. When one shipment came up twelve pounds short, Vivian had to get to the bottom of it, and called her. "The weed's short twelve pounds."

"It is Chris and guys who took it out," she accused.

Vivian called Chris, but Chris denied anyone took it. Vivian knew Chris wasn't lying—it was Angela who'd lied to him. That sucked.

Angela came into the house while Chris was on the phone. Chris asked her, "Why don't you tell Dave we took out the marijuana, when you knew you spent the money?"

"Dave's lying. I didn't tell him that," said Angela disrespectfully, and then grabbed the phone. "I didn't tell you that anyone took your weed. You're a liar." Angela shouted, ranting and raving.

Then Chris said to her, "Watch how you talking to the man, Angela. That's disrespect."

Vivian hung up the phone.

Now he was thinking, *this is going to be the second woman to really feel my wrath. This girl heard what I did to Joy for disrespecting me over the phone, especially in the presence of people.*

After Joy had called and cursed Angela, it took Vivian three months to finally reach New York, and she preyed upon his mind all the time. He was always a gentleman with women and thought that women were God's gift to men—that they should be treated as such.

Something about most girls from the ghetto made them think a man didn't love them unless he whipped them. Vivian thought that was stupid and sadistic, that these girls would provoke a man to such extremes. It was sad.

With Joy on his mind, Vivian dropped off his luggage in Long Island and stopped off in Queens to pick up a rapper friend—Gully Rat—on his way to the Bronx. It was a Wednesday and he'd planned to take Kong with him to Brooklyn that night, only Kong didn't know it yet. It was lobster night at a club named Tony's Table, and Joy would definitely be there with the friends who were laughing when she was disrespecting Vivian.

Vivian realized that he didn't have any money in his pocket when they reached the Bronx. He'd planned on going to Fordham Road and buying a baseball bat to take with him to Brooklyn. After teaching Joy a lesson, he hoped she'd leave him alone for good.

Gully Rat had no money either, so Vivian detoured and went to one of his marijuana apartments on 169th St. They got out of the car, his gun in his pouch, and walked to the apartment building. Vivian rang the intercom bell from downstairs.

"Who is it?"

"Gully Rat," Vivian replied, using his friend's name.

They walked up several flights of stairs to the fourth floor, and Vivian knocked. Someone looked out, but Vivian sensed hesitance.

"Open the fucking door!" Vivian shouted. To his surprise, standing in front of him in the apartment was Joy Cash. Talk about planning to find a bird, and the bird finding you, instead. "Girl, what the fuck are you doing here?"

"I came to see Tony," Joy said nervously.

Vivian, still laughing, punched her to the floor with a solid blow to the face. Joy had a friend with her—Prudence. She was so frightened by the punch, she ran out of the apartment. An artist—Nicodemus—was also in the apartment, so Vivian sent him and Gully Rat to bring Prudence back. They ran downstairs, and caught her just as she was about to leave the building.

Tony's father, Alty, Tony, and one of Tony's friends—Bigger—were also there. Vivian proceeded to punch and kick Joy furiously. He was mad as hell and was laughing at the same time. He hammered her off-and-on for about six hours until her arms required slings.

Prudence nursed Joy's swollen face and body, and in the morning Vivian had a friend of his—Frenchy—who'd come to the apartment later that night—cook her breakfast.

Unfortunately, Vivian had been snorting cocaine all night, thinking of how miserable she'd made his life, and he broke a telephone over Joy's head after she ate. After that final blow, Joy wanted no more hammering and decided to take her own life. She made a run for the window in the bedroom and Vivian gave chase. He caught her as she was about to jump from the fourth floor, which, plus the basement, would've made five floors. Her whole body was out of the window and he held her by her shoulder. She twisted and turned until her neck was in his hands.

No one in the apartment knew what was happening in the bedroom. Vivian couldn't shout for help, because he needed all of his strength to hold her.

"You're going to be charged for murder, you fucking bastard!"

He tried to call for help, but no sound came. He started to pray silently, then a surge of strength from God filled his body and he was blinded for a few seconds. He made a swift pull at Joy's neck and then her huge body swung inside the room and flew to the far end. God gave him the strength of a thousand men at that moment.

She crashed into the far end wall and cried out in pain.

He called to the guys outside and said, "Take her to a hospital. Now!"

Frenchy and Bigger lifted her up and took her.

Vivian sat in the living room on the sofa with Alty and Tony, while he told them what had transpired inside the bedroom.

"Where's my pouch?" asked Vivian.

Tony saw the pouch at the corner of the sofa and took it in his hand. "Dave, what you got in this, a gun?" Tony said, panicking. "Remember, it was just last week the police raided here. We don't keep any guns or drugs in the house."

While Vivian had been on a quick trip to Jamaica to watch Tivoli Gardens play in a soccer finals, a lot of shooting had taken place in the area between guys from Rema, Vivian's family, and associates. A close friend of Vivian's from Rema—Fatman—was brutally murdered when the smoke cleared. Fatman was not a gunman and he didn't deserve death.

Fatman had represented Trench Town Comprehensive High School while Vivian represented St. George's College in the 1971 high school soccer competition, known as the Manning Cup competition.

Vivian and Fatman also had dated two sisters in Jamaica. Vivian didn't know how to look Fatman's wife in the eyes—nor her sister, who'd been his girlfriend—knowing that the people he knew so well had killed him. It was impossible not to face his girlfriend, because she was working at the front desk of the Kingston Sheraton Hotel, where he was staying at the time Fatman died. She knew he had nothing to do with it, but it was still hard for Vivian to look in her eyes when they met at the front desk that evening.

About three months before Angela and Vivian had the argument on the phone, in which Angela had disrespected Vivian, he'd decided to start producing some of Jamaica's famous recording artists. It was time, he thought, to start to find a way out of the illegal drug business—something he'd grown quite accustomed to.

In the summer of 1982, he flew to Jamaica, armed with four 16-track tapes, some cash, and a brilliant idea. He was all about the music business on this trip, and so he headed to the northern coastal town of Ocho Rios, home of the famed sound system owner—Jack Ruby—whom he'd met the year before, and booked a room at the Americana Hotel for a couple of weeks.

Jack Ruby's sound system was one of Jamaica's top five, and many talented young-and-upcoming rappers were attached to it. Bobby Culture stood out in Vivian's mind—one of the most talented rappers in Jamaica, as far as Vivian was concerned.

Jack Ruby warmly greeted Vivian with open arms. They sat together and talked for a while, Vivian telling Jack Ruby of his plans to start producing some of his artists, especially Bobby Culture. Jack Ruby thought it was a good idea—Bobby needed a break.

"There's only one problem … the sound system is going on a tour of the United States in a few weeks." He paused. "You laid your tracks yet?"

"Nah. I'll be going into the studio in two days—Harry J's in Kingston. If I don't get to record Bobby Culture in Jamaica, I could do it while you're on tour in America."

That was fine with Jack Ruby.

Two days later, Vivian was in Kingston at Harry J's, laying tracks. He worked for seven days in the studio with the Roots Radicks Band and laid forty down. The band—Flabba Holt, Dwight Pickney and Steely—was superb and tight, and did a really good job.

As in many Jamaican studios, several artists hung around at Harry J.'s—Louie Lepke, Fred McKay, and an up-and-coming singer, known as Skreechie. They all did songs for Vivian for a fee. After a week of studio work, he was armed with enough tracks to explode into the music business, so he headed back to Ocho Rios. In the days that followed, Vivian made arrangements with Bobby Culture to do an album in Miami.

With music business out of the way, his attention became focused on other things—a girl by the name of Joan Reid, whom he'd met while on a trek with Bobby Moore, who came from Kingston to visit him. Bobby asked Vivian to accompany him to a girlfriend's complex, called Marine Gardens, on James Avenue. There were four fine-looking girls in the house at the time. Vivian was immediately attracted to the eldest one—Joan—and they hit it off.

The next day, they had dinner at the Americana Hotel. Joan showed him around the town—Vivian was without a car—and she occasionally loaned it to him. Days passed with Vivian's lust for Joan reaching its all-time high.

One evening, while Vivian was in the hotel room relaxing, there was a knock on the door. He took his own sweet time, walked toward the door, and looked through the peephole. Standing outside was Joan.

"I was in the lobby, so I decided I'd just drop in and see you."

"No problem. You're welcome to visit any time."

"Any time? I'm scared of being whipped by your many women. I won't drop by like this again without calling first."

Joan was a short, well-built woman, very cute, with a fair complexion. She wore her clothes well, always looking smashing when dressed. That day, she was wearing jeans with a man's shirt. She'd made a knot in the front, and several buttons were undone from the neck down, revealing just a portion of her huge bust. She had setters in her hair, and the scent of freshness was all over her, indicating that she'd just had a bath. This freshness turned Vivian on as he looked at Joan from her head to toe.

"Why're you scrutinizing my whole body?"

She didn't get a chance to say another word....

Reggae Sunsplash—a yearly summer music festival in Jamaica—was only a week away. Vivian's wife and son, along with some of their relatives, were in Kingston. He booked three extra rooms to accommodate them in Ocho Rios, for they all were attending the festival. Bobby Moore was still in Ocho Rios and he was staying in the hotel too.

Vivian got a surprise visit from a friend while at the hotel. Dee had a problem and explained it to Vivian, who had Bobby Moore by his side.

"I have a boat ready to be loaded with two thousand pounds of weed, and I don't have the first dollar to buy it. A friend had promised to furnish the load, but at the last minute, turns out he's bullshitting me. I need your help."

Vivian looked at Bobby, then back at Dee. "Where would the load go?"

"To Daytona Beach, and from there, the people would transport it to anywhere in Miami."

"How soon do you need the weed?"

"The boat has to leave in two days."

"What? You ... can't get that amount of weed so quickly."

Vivian looked at Bobby. "What you think?"

"We could try. Nothing's impossible. It's business ... I should be able to do it," said Bobby Moore, confidently. "You have any cash?"

"I have some, but I'd have to get more from Miami in the morning," said Vivian. "I'll have French bring some money down. That won't be a problem."

Vivian started the ball rolling. He gave Bobby $10,000 so he could start the deal. By midday the next day, French was in Ocho Rios with more money for Vivian, who continued his vacation while Bobby Moore and Dee put the deal together. They made the deadline, and the marijuana left Jamaica for Daytona Beach, as scheduled.

Two days after the boat left Jamaica, Vivian and Dee, along with one of Dee's friend's—Eddie—flew to Miami. Vivian booked Dee and Eddie into the Howard Johnson by 163rd St. in North Miami Beach. He then went home to the townhouse that he shared with Angela.

About two days later, he received a call from Killo, who'd been deported to Jamaica. Killo wanted a favor from Vivian. "A guy in Miami has some cash for me, and I'm sending my baby's mother, Jennifer, to

Miami from New York to pick up the money. All I want you to do for me is let Jennifer stay with you, and then take her to see the guy. She's got the address."

"No problem. When will she be coming down?"

"Tonight. I'll call you back and give you the details."

"I won't be home. I'll be at the Howard Johnson Hotel in North Miami Beach. I'm registered under my name. Just call me there."

That night Vivian instructed Jennifer to take a cab to the Howard Johnson where he had booked a room for her. When she arrived at the hotel, he escorted her to her room, gave her money for food if she needed it, and then left Dee and Eddie's room, next door.

"Is that your girl, man?" asked Eddie. "She looks fucking good."

"Nah, she's a friend … off limits to all of us," said Vivian, smiling, and warning them at the same time. It was time for him to go home, so he left.

The next morning, he checked on the guys at the hotel, then went over to Jennifer's room. Jennifer was already dressed and waiting.

"Ready to go?"

"Yes." She picked up her purse.

They drove to the address Jennifer was given by Killo. A lady came out to Jennifer and told her the guy would not be in until the evening. There was nothing to do but drive back to the hotel. Jennifer was enjoying the warm weather in Miami and looked so relaxed in Vivian's company. He sensed it and was a little scared, so he dropped her off at her room, then went next door. The phone rang a few seconds later, and for some reason, he knew it was Jennifer. Jitters ran through him as he heard her voice. She was so sexy and pretty she made him nervous—tall, fair complexioned, strongly built, and of Indian descent.

"Hello, Dave?"

"Yes, Dave here."

"Have you got anything doing now?"

"No."

"Could you come over and keep me company? Please?"

"No problem." said Vivian, as goose pimples rose on his flesh. He told his friends he'd soon be back, that he was going next door for a few minutes.

He'd given Jennifer the handful of Colombian marijuana that she'd requested the previous night. Jennifer loved smoking her marijuana cigarettes. Her door was ajar, so he just pushed it open and entered. Jennifer was already undressed, wearing only a body suit. A magazine she was using to roll the seed from the marijuana lay between her legs, on the bed. The curtains in the room were closed, making the room as dark as midnight, except for the light coming from the TV—unlike the bright sunlight filling the room earlier that morning when he picked her up. He walked past her bed and sat on the sofa. He was nervous. The darkness and her outfit made him tremble. It wasn't because he was scared of her, but because it was his close friend's woman.

He sat on the sofa for a while, watching TV. If anyone had asked him what was playing on the TV, he couldn't have said—his mind was on sexy Jennifer. No one spoke for almost twenty minutes. Jennifer merely puffed on her marijuana cigarette constantly.

Vivian broke the silence. "Let me have one of your pillows, so I can stretch out on the sofa."

"You can lay down on the bed. I don't bite, you know."

His knees buckled, but he managed to reach the bed and stretched himself out. He turned his back to her and tried to focus on the program. She was facing the wall, still puffing her marijuana cigarette.

"Can I say something to you, Dave?"

"Sure," he said nervously.

"Suppose I asked you to make love to me … how would you feel about that?"

All the nervousness left Vivian immediately and he suddenly was strong and fearless. "How would you expect me to feel, Jennifer? You're a beautiful woman … I'd love to make love to you."

They faced each other and smiled.

"I'll be right back," he said as he rose from the bed. "I have to go tell these guys next door a story."

179

Jennifer laughed.

He went next door. "I've got something to do. See you guys later." Then he left.

He went downstairs and drove his car out of the hotel parking lot, as if he was leaving, then hid the car near some bushes, so his friends would think he left the hotel. Then he sneaked back into the hotel, crept on his knees past his friends' door, and slipped inside Jennifer's room.

By the next night, they had to take a break. Dee told him the marijuana had reached Daytona Beach safely, and that the guys were driving down from Daytona Beach the next day to deliver their half. The split was fifty-fifty between Vivian, Eddie and Dee and the boat guys. Jennifer caught a flight to New York early the next morning, and Vivian packed up his marijuana in suitcases, which were headed to New York via Miami International Airport.

While Vivian had been vacationing in Jamaica, Tony started spending a lot of time in Miami, staying at some cheap hotels on Collins Avenue. Arrow was doing the purchasing of marijuana for Tony. Arrow and Angela's nephew, Hucky Berry, were still dating a mother and her daughter, but Hucky Berry and Arrow had a dispute that outraged Hucky Berry, resulting in the rear ending of Arrow's car.

Hucky Berry was a stubborn and brave kid, not afraid of Arrow, so he didn't think twice about hitting Arrow's car. Although just as brave a kid, Arrow thought twice about approaching Hucky Berry without assistance, asking Tony for back-up to confront this punk kid.

One bright sunny day, about twelve noon, Arrow, Tony and a few others pulled up at Vivian and Angela's rented house on 37th Avenue, where Hucky Berry, Shirley, Chris and her brother Teddy, were living. Hucky Berry was on the lawn talking to a friend named Squeeze, and Tony's crew started firing shots at Hucky Berry. He ran for his life, breathlessly entering the house. Chris, who was inside, heard the gunshots and reached for a gun, and returned the fire to prevent them from entering the house.

Arrow, Tony, and friends retreated, ran back to their car with guns in hand, and sped away. After the smoke cleared, Squeeze was found, lying on the lawn with a gunshot wound to his neck. He was rushed to the hospital. Luckily, he survived.

About two hours later, Vivian pulled up to the house and noticed the blood on the lawn and the shattered glass panes in the front door. He knew something was wrong, so he got back in his car and quickly left the area.

Later that evening, he saw Hucky Berry and Chris, and they told Vivian what had happened. He was upset. "You really mean my brother did that, knowing it was Angela's house and Hucky Berry is her nephew? He's got no respect for me or regards for my feelings. You think I, or anyone of my friends, would have done that at his woman's house? This isn't good for business in Miami. Tony seems as if he came to Miami to wreck the place."

In the weeks that followed there was much tension in the streets. Tall Hunch—a friend of Hucky Berry (both were residents of a community called Payne Land in Kingston, Jamaica.)—was shopping one day when a friend of Tony's—Cracker—was also in the plaza browsing. There was also tension in New York between Tall Hunch, Tony, and his friends because one of Tony's friends had killed one of Tall Hunch's friends—Ox—and had also shot and wounded another by the name of Dunguman.

On seeing Tall Hunch, Cracker reached for his pistol and started to shoot. Unhurt, Tall Hunch ran for cover, and then returned the fire. They exchanged several shots, before Cracker retreated and headed to a house that Tony had just rented close by.

Vivian was in New York when he heard about the shooting. He didn't like it one bit, because the once peaceful Miami was becoming a war zone—all because of Tony. The Jamaican community knew that Vivian wasn't into murder and shooting, but was wondering what was causing this upsurge of violence involving Tony and his followers.

After leaving parties and dances, Tony's friends would fire several shots into the air shouting, "Shower! Shower! Shower!"

Meanwhile, Vivian couldn't forgive Angela for disrespecting him and telling lies about the marijuana shortage. He vowed the relationship was over—she just didn't know it yet. He was busy planning a trip to Jamaica, via Miami to do some studio work with a new artist—a female from Guyana, named Angela. She had done a remake of Denise Williams' *Going to Take a Miracle* for his Clay Pot label and Vivian decided to do an album with her. He flew down to Miami where Angela, the artist, met him.

He stayed in a hotel—not at Angela's house on 37th Avenue. *When I get back from Jamaica, I'll settle the score with you, Angela,* he said to himself, but Angela found out that Vivian was in Miami and tracked him down. She called the Howard Johnson, by North Miami Beach—his favorite hotel—and was connected to his room.

"Aren't you coming home?" she begged.

"I'm going to Jamaica in the morning. I'll be home when I get back."

Angela, the artist, didn't make the flight with him to Jamaica, so he went on ahead and took care of other music-related business. Finishing his business in Jamaica, he returned to Miami, but instead of going to 37th Avenue, checked into a different hotel. He took a cab to the new house that Chris, Shirley, Hucky Berry and Teddy had moved into, and asked for Angela—she was not at the place on 37th Avenue.

"Shirley, where's Angela? She's not at the townhouse."

"She just drove off from here a few minutes ago."

"All right, Shirley. Chris … later." Vivian walked back to the cab.

Chris followed behind him and said, "She's acting scared right now. She thinks you're going to beat her up."

Vivian smiled then left in the cab, which took him to the townhouse. He picked up his Volvo and drove around town, looking for Angela, but couldn't find her. He checked with Food Head's sister, Paulette, who was very close to Angela. If Angela went to anyone, it would have been to Paulette. Vivian turned the charm on Paulette, who had a six-month-old child by one of Tony's friends. He didn't care; he needed to find Angela at any cost, even if it meant making love to her best friend and the mother of Tony's friend's baby.

"It should have been us two together, instead of Angela and I," Vivian lied to Paulette.

"You mean that?" asked Paulette, innocently.

This is the first time I'm going to have to use a woman, Vivian thought. *Forgive me, Lord.* He kissed Paulette on her lips gently, and then started to move his hand up and down her legs.

Paulette was a black girl—very shapely—and was wearing a short nightdress. He slid his hands into her panties and played with her vagina until she was wet. He lifted her onto her bed, and in a quick motion his pants were off. Not even bothering to take her panties off, he used her until he came. They both lay on her bed and he questioned her about Angela.

"Did you know that Angela's seeing my brother, Winston, privately?"

Vivian knew she was telling him, not asking him. "So where's she now?"

"I don't know, but she stops by everyday. If she sees your car, she won't stop. She's looking out for you."

The next day, Vivian stopped by a girlfriend's—Pearl—and borrowed her car. Pearl was also Angela's friend. He drove to Paulette's house and went inside.

"Angela just called me, and I asked her to bring a box of pampers for my baby. She'll soon be here."

Her phone rang.

"Paulette, was that Dave I saw driving Pearl's car into your driveway?"

Paulette indicated to Vivian that it was Angela on the phone. He signaled to her not to let Angela know he was there.

"No it wasn't Dave." Then she hung up the phone.

In about two minutes, there was a knock on Paulette's door. Vivian went behind the door, as Paulette was about to open it. Angela walked in, but as the door closed behind her, she stared as if she'd seen a ghost.

Vivian held her by her blouse and pulled her to him. He punched her twice—not too hard. "You gotta behave yourself, girl. Why you giving me so much trouble?"

He let go of her blouse, left Paulette's house, returned Pearl's car, and went home.

Angela laughed as she said to Paulette, "I thought he was going to really whip me. That was nothing. Shit, I'm going back home in the morning."

Vivian had just finished the breakfast he prepared and was watching TV in the living room downstairs, when he heard a key turning in the front door. There was Angela stepping inside the townhouse. His plan had worked. She took the bait. Since he'd just eaten, he watched TV for about an hour until his food was completely digested.

He heard the vacuum cleaner going upstairs, as if Angela was cleaning the bedrooms, and he went upstairs into the master bedroom where Angela was cleaning. His eyes spat scarlet fire. "Here's the pussy you were talking to on the phone three months ago."

She giggled in panic and looked at Vivian's face. "Dave, forget that. Please?"

As the last word left her mouth, she felt a blow crash against her jaw and she fell to the floor. He mauled her, then dialed the phone number to her sister Shirley's house. He held the phone to Angela's ear, because her hands were in excruciating pain.

"Tell them who I am ... a man or a pussy," he demanded.

She could barely talk, but she muttered, "He's a man."

Then he took the phone. "Shirley, you all come and take her out of my house to the hospital." He hung up. "Your things will be packed by the time your sister comes, you can go and live with Winston."

Her eyes were swelled shut, but she didn't miss the astonished look. She didn't know he had found out about Winston.

When Shirley and Chris reached Vivian's townhouse, Angela's belongings had already to been packed.

"Shirley, your sister's now free to live with your new brother-in-law, Winston."

Surprise registered on Shirley's face at Vivian's remark. He could see that everyone had known, except him.

About a week later, his wife and son visited Miami and stayed at the townhouse. While Valerie was cleaning the house, Valerie found a white powdery substance at the foot of all the drapery in the house. There was also a statue on a mini altar at the rear of the TV that Vivian usually watched in the living room. She claimed the girl was using witchcraft on Vivian, but he dismissed it.

"What good would witchcraft have done? She's out of my life, so that doesn't make any sense."

"They say when it's happening to you, you don't know and you always deny its presence."

He hissed through his teeth, and then started playing with Duane.

Vivian, Angela and her relatives still remained friends, but the intimate relationship had gone. Angela and Winston came out of the closet with their relationship.

It was now 1983, and business was going great . Vivian gave Tony the townhouse in Pembroke Pines and rented a house in Turtle Bay in Miramar. Tension was still in the air with Tony and his friends, against the Payne Land guys, and Vivian was having a lot of problems in New York with the workers handling his marijuana business. On his trips to New York, Tony threatened the guys who remained loyal to Vivian, if they didn't do as Tony said. That bothered Vivian. He knew Tony couldn't do that and get away with it, if he wasn't his brother. Plus, the guys were originally Tony's friends.

Vivian was in Miami waiting on a planeload of marijuana from Jamaica when he realized that the people in Jamaica were stalling. He boarded a flight to Jamaica to straighten things out. He'd already paid a French woman and her husband who lived in Jamaica, to fly the load of marijuana in, so he couldn't understand the problem.

He went to the hotel where the couple was living, mad as hell.

"Why the fuck have you people been stalling with my fucking weed? I'm not begging you to do this shit. I've paid you in full, so what the fuck's wrong?"

The couple started to panic and the woman said, "All right, cool down. We'll deliver the load to Miami in two days. We leave two nights from now."

"I'm not leaving Jamaica until I hear the load's in Miami, you hear?" Then he stormed out of the hotel room.

That night, in Tivoli Gardens Jim Brown introduced him to someone else.

"This is Modeler, Dave ... a little friend of mine. He wanted to know if he could contact you when he reaches America. He's trying to leave the island soon."

"So, you have a visa?"

Jim Brown and Modeler laughed and looked at each other, then back at Vivian.

"No, he just escaped from gun court. He's waiting on some papers from a friend in Rochester, New York."

Then Vivian said jokingly, "If I didn't have to lose two hundred pounds of ganja, I'd put him on the plane day after tomorrow, but I'd have to take off his weight in ganja for him to go on the plane."

They all laughed, then Modeler said, "It's okay. I just want your number, so I can call you when I reach America."

Vivian looked at Jim Brown for approval and Jim nodded.

"He's okay, Dave. You can give him your number."

The planeload of marijuana left Jamaica as scheduled and arrived safely in Miami. Vivian left Jamaica for Miami the following day. He received his half of the marijuana and proceeded to transport it to New York, via Miami International Airport. When all the marijuana had reached New York, he boarded a flight headed in the same direction.

A few weeks later came the call from Modeler.

"Hi, Dave. I got busted at Kennedy and I'm at the detention center. I want to ask you a favor ... I'd like to beg or borrow a thousand dollars. I'm arranging for them to deport me to my country of birth, St. Kitts, but I don't have any cash to travel."

"No problem. I'll come and see you tomorrow."

He took the details from Modeler and wrote them down. The next day, Vivian went to see him at the immigration-holding center and left a thousand dollars on Modeler's record.

A couple of months later, Vivian received a call from Modeler again, this time he told Vivian he was in St. Kitts, and had just acquired a visa to travel to America.

"Can I come stay with you for a little while? Until I get on my feet?

"Sure, just call and let me know when you're coming, so I can pick you up."

A week later, Modeler flew into the Miami International Airport, so Vivian picked him up and took him to his house in Turtle Bay. Modeler caught onto the marijuana trade quickly and was the best assistant Vivian ever had. He was a perfect businessman; he reminded Vivian of himself. He dotted every *i* and crossed every *t*, so Vivian gave Modeler five thousand dollars' worth of marijuana.

Vivian was now opening up new houses in other cities, such as Detroit, Washington and Oakland, along with his New York houses. Modeler wanted to make a niche for himself, so he chose to send his marijuana to his friend—Don D. in Rochester. Vivian respected Modeler for that. "You're going to do well in this business; you're smart." Modeler just smiled innocently.

Vivian had to take a trip to New York, so he asked Modeler to accompany him. This was Modeler's first trip to New York since he was busted at Kennedy—he loved the nightlife in New York, which was much faster than Miami at the time.

Vivian and a young girl he was dating—Jackie Diamond—shared an apartment in New York. This particular night he decided to spend the night in a hotel with Jackie and her friend, Gig Waist, because Jackie's brother, Howard—a.k.a. Howie, also known as Dave Two—was also staying at the apartment. As Vivian left the apartment, he gave Modeler some money, because Modeler and Howie were planning to go clubbing that night.

Modeler borrowed Vivian's gun, and he and Howie went to a disco where they met two girls—Wendy and Debbie. Debbie, once a girlfriend of Vivian's, was an American, dark complexioned, very cute and sexy after she lost several pounds. Wendy was also pretty and sexy, but was quite light complexioned.

Modeler took a liking to Wendy, while Howie clung to Debbie. They partied all night, and Modeler spent all the money Vivian gave to him, buying cocaine and champagne for Wendy, Debbie, and Howie. Modeler was trying hard to impress Wendy—he wanted her that night.

After partying, all four headed to Wendy's apartment in the Bronx, by Creston and Tremont. Wendy and Modeler went into her room with what was left of the cocaine, while Debbie and Howie went into another room. Being a lady's man, and knowing the formula to get through to these black American girls, Howie wasted no time in undressing Debbie.

Modeler heard Debbie scream in excitement as Howie fucked her, and Modeler could hardly wait for Wendy to finish snorting the last of the cocaine, so that he could make a sexual advance toward Wendy. She firmly refused to have sex with him. He made several more attempts but she became livid and shouted, "No, I won't have sex with you!"

This angered Modeler tremendously—the anger showed on his face. While looking at Wendy with an evil grin, he pulled a gun and before she could say another word, shot her in the head. She died instantly. Modeler then walked slowly to the other room, where Howie and Debbie were.

They heard Modeler enter and saw the pistol in his hand. Without saying a word, he shot Debbie in her head as well. She died immediately, too. Howie was trembling, not knowing his fate, whether Modeler was going mad and planning to kill him as well.

"Howie, come on. Let's leave this place. Now," said Modeler coldly. Howie was so relieved he rushed out of the apartment, tumbling down the steps, as Modeler laughed at him.

Modeler appeared at Tony's apartment and told Tony he'd just killed two girls, telling him the entire story. Tony managed to catch Vivian at the hotel by phone and angrily explained to Vivian what happened.

"Dave, your friend Modeler just killed two fucking girls, man. Is he fucking crazy?"

Awakened out of a dead sleep, Vivian's eyes popped open. "What?"

"Yes, man. Modeler killed two girls, and I think that's stupid. Who the hell's he trying to impress?"

"Where is he?"

"I don't know where the fuck he is, man. He left here about half-an-hour ago," Tony spat into the phone.

Later that morning, Vivian found Modeler at the apartment he shared with Jackie Diamond. He left the girls at the apartment and took Modeler out in the car with him. He didn't want the girls to hear Modeler discussing the double murders that took place earlier that morning.

"What happened this morning, Modeler?"

Modeler hissed though his teeth. "Boy, the girl disrespected me, so I killed her, but because her friend was there, too, I had to kill her." Modeler's tone was ice cold.

"What did she do?"

Modeler sighed deeply, and then said, "She used me. She had me spend all of my money on her and didn't want to have sex with me. Her friend gave up some to Howie, and I was left without anything."

"So, Howie witnessed the whole shit?" Vivian wanted to hear that Howie didn't see anything.

"Yeah, he saw everything," Modeler admitted.

"Oh shit." Vivian held his head with one hand, while steering the car with the other. "Yo, man. That shit is fucked up, man. You didn't have to do that shit, man. That's how most of these cocaine snorting girls are, man. You should've just said *fuck it*. You didn't have to go so far, man."

He could see that Modeler was sorry for what he'd done, but it *was* done, and nothing could change that. They had to keep a lid on it—not a word to anyone else.

The next day, Modeler and Vivian boarded a flight to Miami.

Vivian had just returned from a trip to Jamaica and was back in Miami. Several changes had been made since he'd left. He'd turned a decent profit with his business in the hands of Modeler, while on vacation in Jamaica. This was unheard of—he'd always lost money when he left his marijuana business in the hands of Tony's friends. He usually closed down his business while he was in Jamaica and resumed it when he returned. He had a good feeling about Modeler, so he allowed him to continue business while he was away—it paid off. Modeler sent marijuana to New York, Detroit, Washington and Oakland.

Another change was that Tony had taken up permanent residence in Florida, buying a beautiful house in Pembroke Pines, complete with swimming pool—the works—and had purchased a brand new bottle-green sports Jaguar for himself, and a Honda Accord for his live-in, common-law wife, Pavel—the daughter of a famed female community leader, known as Smokey Barbara.

Barbara had four kids—Orville, Duane and a pair of twins, Coco and Pavel. Orville and Coco met their untimely death in Jamaica through gunfire ... Orville shot by a stray bullet on Chestnut Lane in West Kingston, Jamaica, and Coco while crying over her boyfriend who was gunned down by the police on Charles Street, in the western section of Kingston. She was brutally murdered by the same cops.

Smokey Barbara was a tall, strong, fair complexioned, cute, and sexy woman. She was also very ambitious and had just finished remodeling a grocery store at the corner of Charles Street and Chestnut Lane—strangely, the two streets where her two kids were gunned down—and turned the building into an upscale nightclub, known as Smokey Palace. This was the first of its kind in the inner city of Kingston and was expected to be a huge success, based on her popularity in the Kingston environs.

Just before the opening of Smokey Palace, Barbara became ill. She felt a pain in her legs and went to the hospital and never returned to Smokey Palace—at least, not alive. She died in the hospital of complications that puzzled the doctors, even until this very day. Legend had it that a curse of death was placed on her by begrudging associates, because of her unexpected success with the nightclub. Her friends still bemoan her death.

Pavel, as did most of Smokey Barbara's kids, grew up with Smokey Barbara's adopted mother, Miss Ilda, in Tivoli Gardens. She lived in an apartment building right across the street from where Vivian and Tony lived as kids. Under the strict rules of Miss Ilda, Pavel grew up very decently. She came to America and lived with one of her mother's friends—Arlene—in Miami. Pavel was as straight as they came ... she was never ever mixed up in drugs or any illegal activities.

Vivian saw her in Brooklyn one day. He knew that Tony had always had a crush on her since childhood ... he also knew Tony needed a decent woman, so he made a call to Tony and put Pavel on the line. That was the beginning of a long relationship that produced a beautiful daughter, Keema.

Tony was now ensconced in Florida, renting his own marijuana-packing house, separate and apart from Vivian's house. He felt it was time to branch out on his own, mainly because he didn't like Vivian's friends, especially Modeler. Tony knew he couldn't push around these friends of Vivian's the way he did the guys he loaned to Vivian in New York.

Tony took over one of Vivian's marijuana apartments in the Bronx—by force—an apartment left to the care of one of Tony's friends, Oney. Oney was scared of Tony, so when Tony approached him to take over the apartment, Oney put up no resistance, operating the apartment as a marijuana base for Tony.

Tony then went over to another of Vivian's apartments, which was also located in the Bronx, on Anthony Avenue at the corner of Burnside. Tony's associate, Big Toe, was operating the marijuana apartment for Vivian.

"I want you to sell some weed for me, along with Vivian's weed," commanded Tony.

"You would have to talk to Vivian about that. If he gives me the okay, no problem, but other that that, I can't do it," said Big Toe firmly.

Tony pulled a pistol and pointed it at Big Toe's head, then squeezed the trigger. No shots fired—just a clicking sound was heard. Big Toe quickly talked Tony out of a second attempt to kill him.

While Tony was leaving the apartment, he tried to fire the pistol again. This time a shot rang out. "Boy, you are a lucky motherfucker! Sleep on the same side of the bed you slept on last night, because it gave you luck." Tony then walked out of the apartment laughing.

Vivian decided to let Big Toe and a few others, who were helping him in New York, go on their own. He could protect them against Tony … no one else would have taken that chance with Vivian … only his brother. The only other option Vivian had was to kill Tony. He ruled that out, because he loved his brother, no matter the disrespect Tony had dished out to him.

Kong had his own little marijuana business going, but Tony bribed all of Kong's friends to leave him and work for Tony. Tony turned the guys against Kong so bitterly that some of them spoke nasty of Kong behind his back.

In Miami, the tension between Tony, his friends, and the guys from Payne Land was running rampant. Tony put out an order for Chris to be killed—any time, anywhere—in Miami. Chris was born and raised in Tivoli Gardens, and Tony's cousin Bob's baby's father. Chris had to stay around the Payne Land guys, not by choice, but because he wouldn't be safe around Tony and his friends.

Chris wasn't afraid of Tony and it pissed Tony off more. When Tony sent out his threats, Chris sent disrespectful replies to Tony. Tony, of course, grew more and more angry.

After Tony traded in his Jaguar for a 380SE Mercedes Benz, he drove to the Church's Fried Chicken Restaurant on 183rd St. near NW 37th Avenue to buy chicken. He was in the drive-thru line, between two cars, when one of Hucky Berry's friends—Little Hunch—appeared in front of Tony's car, a pistol in his hand, and pointed it at the front windshield.

Tony panicked, but couldn't drive out of the drive-thru because he was boxed in. Six consecutive shots pierced the windshield then the shooter disappeared. As luck would have it, not a single shot hit Tony. Three shots went through his headrest, two through the steering wheel, and the other hit the passenger seat. He managed to drive out of Church's Chicken safely, but he was pissed. He declared war! The streets of Miami were blazing with gunfire for the next couple of days.

Modeler and Vivian didn't venture out to the streets very much. Vivian had just purchased a house in Pembroke Lakes, right on the lake. He still had his rented house in Turtle Bay, Miramar, but he decided it wasn't a good idea to keep it. Although he wasn't involved with the war that was going on, it was better to be safe that sorry.

Chris, at the time, was still staying with Vivian at that house, along with Hucky Berry, so it made good sense to move. He evacuated the

Turtle Bay housing complex.

Vivian was pissed at Tony and his friends.

"All this shit is looking bad on your side, Dave." Modeler hissed through his teeth, shaking his head in disgust. "Punks always give the most trouble."

Friends spotted Vivian's previous girlfriend, Angela, and her new boyfriend, Winston—the brother of Food Head—driving the streets. Angela had just had a baby by Winston, and the infant was in the car. Tony and his friends pulled alongside them and without hesitation, sprayed the car with shots. The car crashed on someone's lawn, and Tony and his pals drove away, thinking they were dead.

But, God was on their side; they only suffered cuts from shattered glass. However, this launched a police hunt for Tony and his friends.

One of Tony's friends was finally arrested. He cried in jail and told the police officers he was innocent. Tony and his other friends got scared, thinking that their friend in jail was going to blow the whistle on them, so they took flights out of Florida immediately. Tony ended up running away from a new house by Flamingo Road he'd just purchased in Fort Lauderdale.

Miami was now on fire. Everyone in the Jamaican community was talking about this newly emerged gang—the Shower Posse.

Vivian and Modeler were sitting in the newly rented house, when they heard about the ambush on Angela, Winston, and the infant. Vivian became angrier and angrier by the minute.

"You see how Tony and his fucking friends are shooting up Miami? No one knows Tony or his fucking friends down here—they only know me. This shit might look like I'm involved with it."

Upon returning from a trip to Jamaica, Modeler escorted Vivian to the new house in Miramar. Vivian was proud of Modeler. He was launching out on his own, and Vivian respected that. Modeler's business in Rochester, New York was brisk. He'd come a long way since Vivian had started him off, for he was sending over two hundred pounds of marijuana to Rochester on a weekly basis, and above all, the price was much higher in Rochester than in the city of New York.

Modeler was in the process of putting on a series of Dancehall events in New York. He hired the service of a popular sound system in Jamaica—Volcano High Power—owned by one of Jamaica's top record producers, Henry "Junjo" Laws. Two of Modelers's friends from Tivoli Gardens, Donovan Jones and Roy Wanliss—a.k.a. Red Roy—had just escaped from the South Camp Road Rehabilitation Center, and had secured visas to travel along with Henry's entourage.

The tour would have been a success for Modeler if it hadn't been for the huge expenses to fly Henry's entourage in from Jamaica and house them in New York. But, Kong seized the opportunity to make a huge amount of money by hiring Volcano while they were in New York.

All the dances were over, and it was back to business for Modeler. He took Red Roy and Donovan Jones—a.k.a. Champs—back to Miami with him. He'd bought a huge house for the guys, and they had individual rooms. Modeler had a live-in girlfriend, Monica, introduced to him by Vivian. Monica turned out to be a wrong choice for Modeler, but he kept her around because she was clean and cooked well. She had two-timed Modeler with Tony. When Modeler found out Monica was pregnant with Tony's child he was outraged and beat Monica viciously until she started bleeding and miscarried.

Immediately, Champs and Red Roy became good at the marijuana trade, and started helping Modeler pack suitcases.

When Tony returned to New York to elude the Miami police, his cronies decided to continue the war with the Payne Land Posse. Vivian vowed that he would never have anything to do with that feud, because it was bad for business. Plus, there was no reason for the war.

Kong had a huge following of youngsters who were always around him, and Kong was the manager of Vivian's drug houses while Vivian was in Miami. To Vivian, the kids were harmless, so he didn't try to dissuade Kong from having his friends, but he *did* insist that the gang of youths hanging around the drug houses drew too much attention from the tenants in the apartment buildings. As a result of the gang of kids always hanging around, Vivian had to change drug houses regularly and suffered severe losses because of drug busts.

Vivian wasn't close to these kids, other than to say *hi* and *bye*, for these kids were Americans and had no roots in the Jamaican community in which Vivian grew up. In any event, Vivian was living in Miami and only visited New York on occasion.

Tony started to recruit Kong's youngsters as the feud with his cronies and the Payne Land Posse escalated. These youngsters were very inexperienced, and were no match for the Payne Land Posse, mostly veterans of gang warfare in Jamaica.

Vivian laughed to see how stupid Tony was. *What a price to pay to be recognized in the Jamaican community.*

The Payne Land Posse was huge, with notable veteran gunmen, like Dunguman, Ox and Tall Hunch. Dunguman was feared by most of Tony's new recruits, because they had previous run-ins with him. At the H.Q. nightclub in the Bronx, Dunguman proved that Tony's cronies were no matches for him. He approached Tony's cronies and snatched a gold chain from around one of the kid's necks, "I'm taking this fucking chain. If you all don't like it, all you've got to do is start the shit. You're all a bunch of pussies."

Nobody responded to Dunguman's action—they were dead scared of him. The kid whose gold chain was taken—Mugs—was one of Tony's top soldiers, but he was scared shitless. Dunguman walked away laughing, the gold chain in his hand.

Months passed after that incident before Dunguman and Tony's cronies met again, in a popular hangout for the Jamaican posses—Disco Fever Nightclub—in the Bronx. Tony's number one shooter, Shower Chris, was there with a group of his posse members, when they all saw Dunguman at the bar. Mugs was pointing at him.

An American girl nudged Dunguman in his side. "Some guys are pointing at you."

Dunguman turned to look in the direction the girl was indicating, and saw Mugs and the other Shower Posse members in the distance, staring at him. Dunguman smiled, then reached into his pocket and pulled out a knife. How he'd managed to smuggle a knife into the nightclub, only

God knew, because there was a thorough search at the entrance for guns, knives, or weapons of any kind.

Dunguman approached the Shower Posse members and fear enveloped them. Seeing the knife in Dunguman's hand, they panicked and started to run for the entrance. Dunguman laughed. The scene was witnessed by several nightclub patrons who made a big joke out of seeing the guys scared and running.

The next day, Vivian received a phone call from New York from one of his soldiers—Kick. "Boss, you heard what happened last night?"

"No, what happened?"

"This piece of shit from Payne Land, known as Dunguman, chased Tony's friends out of Disco Fever with a knife. A girl told me that they were the laughing stock last night. This boy Dunguman has to die. I'm gonna hunt him down myself. It's fucking embarrassing us."

"Nah, you ain't going to do no such thing. That's Tony's friends' problem—not ours. Tony and his punk friends bit off more than they can chew. Let them fucking handle their own shit. I have no problem with the Payne Land guys. I have some good friends who are from Payne Land, so leave it alone," he demanded, and then hung up the phone.

Kong had managed to smuggle one of his schoolmates—Gabriel—from Jamaica to America, and was staying at one of Vivian's houses on the Grand Concourse in the Bronx. Vivian had seen Gabriel once in Jamaica when he delivered some clothes to him from Kong. The second time he saw Gabriel was when he was on one of his rare visits to New York. He'd overslept one Saturday night while in New York at his Grand Concourse drug house, when he heard a knocking on the front door. Realizing he was the only one in the apartment, he picked up one of his guns and walked to he door. Peeking through the peephole, he opened the door and let Gabriel in. Gabriel was looking very upset as Vivian closed the door and walked behind Gabriel to the living room.

"Boss, could I borrow one of your guns?"

"What's the problem?"

Gabriel hesitated a bit, then lied, "A guy just punched me in my face down by Reggae Lounge."

When a guy punched you in the face it was the worst kind of disrespect. Vivian felt it easier to forgive a guy who shot him than forgive a guy who punched or slapped him in the face. To Vivian, bitches and punks were the only people who got slapped around. If that had happened to him as Gabriel said, there would be no hole safe enough for the guy. He might as well kill himself, because Vivian was going to kill him—no matter how long it took.

Vivian sympathized with Gabriel and handed him the automatic pistol he had in his hand. "Make sure that man's dead. Only bitches and punks get slapped around, not men."

Gabriel and Vivian left the apartment immediately. Vivian drove to his house in Long Island, while Gabriel headed back down to Midtown Manhattan, to the Reggae Lounge nightclub. Members of the Shower Posse were eagerly awaiting Gabriel's return. Mugs was outside the club door when Gabriel arrived.

"Is Dunguman still inside?" Gabriel asked.

"Yeah, that pussy's still inside. You've got the gun?"

Gabriel nodded.

Mugs was scared to face Dunguman—with or without gun—so he was glad that Gabriel, a veteran shooter from Jamaica, decided to do the job for them. They all lay in wait for Dunguman outside the nightclub, and concealed themselves in the shadows. Finally, Dunguman exited the nightclub in the company of two guys and two girls. As Dunguman walked toward his car, he saw movement in the shadows, and with quick-reflex action, his hand was inside his waistband, as if reaching for a gun.

His quick action stopped Gabriel in his tracks, assuming that Dunguman had a gun. Gabriel opened fire from a distance, hitting Dunguman several times, and then exited the scene quickly. In Midtown Manhattan, the police responded swiftly to the disturbances.

The next evening, Vivian drove to his drug house from his home on Long Island. He found Kong, Gabriel and two more or Kong's friends in the living room having a jovial discussion.

197

"Dave, Gabriel shot Dunguman last night. He fucked up. Dunguman was shot about ten times in his hands. This piece of shit must have told Dunguman to stretch his hands out. I can't believe this shit!" Kong was beside himself, laughing at the whole debacle.

Vivian was a bit confused for a minute, so he looked at Gabriel. "Was Dunguman the one who punched you in the face last night?"

"Dunguman punched you in the face last night?" interrupted Kong, as he looked at Gabriel.

Gabriel could say nothing, and Vivian realized that Gabriel lied to him the night before in order to get his gun. Gabriel hadn't expected Vivian to be at the apartment when he arrived there the night before, but Vivian's car was parked in front of the apartment building.

Vivian's scornful eyes bore into Gabriel, and he ranted at them vehemently. "That's what you took my fucking gun for, knowing I wanted to have no part in this Payne Land bullshit? Plus, to make matters worse, you've now started a full-scale New York war. You failed miserably to kill one of the main shooters who'll be up your fucking ass—day and night—until most of you motherfuckers are in the ground in fancy pine boxes."

"You give those pussies too much credit," Kong defended.

"No. You're wrong. I don't give them much credit at all. It's just that you and Tony have a bunch of incapable, coward-ass motherfuckers as soldiers, who can only go up against wimps, not real soldiers."

"Dave, you underestimate our soldiers too much." Kong was trying hard to defend their actions.

"Don't get me wrong, I like the guys, but as shooters, they couldn't cover my back. These kids don't have the guts to be real soldiers. They'd fucking panic in an exchange fire, probably killing their own friends."

Vivian laughed, as Kong and Gabriel laughed too. Then, Vivian looked at Gabriel and they both stopped laughing immediately. "I need a new fucking gun from you, Gabriel. I don't give a fuck where you get it—just get it," he continued, and then walked towards the bedroom.

Kong looked at Gabriel. "You shouldn't have lied to Dave. It's gonna be hard for him to trust you anymore."

Sporadic shooting was going on between members of the Shower Posse and the Payne Land Posse. Tony recruited Gabriel, because Kong and Gabriel had a falling-out over a rental car incident outside Vivian's apartment. Gabriel had taken the liberty to drive the rental car without Kong's permission—a simple matter—but Kong was very ignorant and made a mountain out of a molehill.

The following day, not knowing Vivian was at the apartment, Kong arrived and was furious as he approached Gabriel. "Pussy, why the fuck you drove my rent-a-car?"

Gabriel tried to explain, but Kong would accept no explanation. Vivian was in the back bedroom, vacuuming the carpet, when Kong pulled his automatic pistol and Gabriel ran in panic toward the back bedroom. Kong fired a single shot at Gabriel that missed, but which lodged in the bedroom wall, seconds before Vivian stepped into the path of the bullet. A second earlier, he could've been fatally wounded.

Kong and Vivian's eyes met in shock. Kong was so frightened of what Vivian might do, he dropped his automatic pistol to the floor and ran out of the apartment.

Tony capitalized on Kong's problems with Gabriel and recruited him. Tony needed a seasoned shooter, so Gabriel became a lieutenant right away.

A big dance was scheduled at the H.Q. nightclub. The Jamaican partygoers came out in numbers, and in their glitz and glamour—a sight to behold. Gabriel, Mugs, Shower Chris and a few more of the Shower Posse members attended. Members of the Payne Land Posse, along with one of their leaders—Ox—were also there. The members of the Shower Posse saw Ox, but Ox paid no attention to them when he noticed them. Ox had no fear of Mugs, Shower Chris and the others—but, Ox didn't know Gabriel.

Ox was enjoying himself, having a grand time with girls all around him. The Shower Posse guys had Ox outnumbered, but most of them were scared to approach him.

"What's the fucking problem?" said Gabriel, "You all scared of that pussy?"

No one answered. Gabriel looked in Ox's direction. "I'm going to show you all how the fuck you kill bad boys."

Gabriel walked away, and only minutes later, appeared in front of Ox with his automatic pistol pointing at him.

Ox never had a chance to find out who Gabriel was, for his body was peppered with gunshots—flanked as he was, by his girls. He fell to the ground, and died. Total pandemonium broke out, the crowd darting in all directions.

The war escalated. Vivian warned Kong to stop going to the Jamaican club and to stay out of the ongoing war—his warnings fell on deaf ears. Kong went to the same nightclub and was having fun with a bunch of girls. In a dark corner, a group of guys from the Payne Land Posse stood, observing Kong from a distance.

"Let's kill that pussy now!"

They all pulled their pistols and walked towards Kong, who had no idea what was going on until they were almost on top of him. Kong reached for his own pistol, but not soon enough. Gunshots rained in his direction. He fell backwards, managing to fire a few scattered shots before hitting the ground. Female patrons screamed as chaos broke out again.

A telephone call from a female family member in New York awakened Vivian in Miami.

"They killed Kong."

"Wha … who…" stuttered Vivian, as the words filtered through his brain. "What the fuck happened? Anyone identified the body?" Vivian rarely panicked, but this was his brother she was talking about.

"No, that's the thing. There's no body. Only his blood-soaked shirt was found."

"So, how the fuck you come the conclusion that he's dead?"

"So, how we explain the bloody shirt?"

"We don't try to guess. We try to get the fucking facts!" Vivian said angrily. "Shit. You almost scared me to fucking death! Go find out the facts, and when you find out, call me back." He slammed the phone down.

The scene of the shooting was a bloody mess. Two girls, including a pregnant girl, were shot, but Kong's body was nowhere to be found.

Vivian received another call early that morning, and he braced himself for the bad news. "Kong's all right," said the female voice. "It was a pregnant girl's blood that was over Kong's shirt."

"Was he shot?"

"No, he was damned lucky! The Payne Land guys fired a lot of shots at him. Kong escaped death by the grace of God," she concluded.

This was a relief for Vivian, but he was still worried.

By now, it was the end of summer 1984, and one of the popular, yearly Jamaican bus rides—to New Jersey—was coming up. Every Jamaican—from the inner-city area of Jamaica, and now living in the United States—wanted to be a part of it. Vivian gave his girlfriend in Miami, Eleanor, permission to attend, but he wanted no part of it. He stayed home at his Florida mansion.

The night before the bus ride, there was a dance in Manhattan, the home base of the Spanglers Posse. In attendance was a kid, named Duda, who originated from Tivoli Gardens. Duda had a feud with Tony and Kong, because of his disrespectful attitude—he was classified as an outsider and was abandoned by the organization.

At the dance, Duda had an altercation with a kid—Jockey—from the Concrete Jungle Posse, and Jockey was also associated with the Spanglers Posse. Duda, feeling satisfied that he proved his point, went back to his partying. As the party wound down in the wee hours of the morning, Duda decided to leave the party with his friends, so, along with a girlfriend of his, he entered a car driven by his friend, Tommy. Duda and his girlfriend sat in the front passenger seat, with Duda in the middle. Tommy turned the key in the ignition and the car engine roared.

"Pussy, you're a *dead* motherfucker!" came a voice from outside the car.

The trio turned their heads toward the direction of the voice. Duda was looking down the nozzle of Jockey's automatic pistol. Before he could say a word, several explosions cracked the air. Blood spewed all over the passengers in the car, and Duda died instantly. No one else was hurt.

That was the second such shooting in the upper Manhattan area involving posse members. About six months earlier, a reputed Shower Posse member—Stretch—was in a nightclub, along with other members of the Shower Posse. Stretch was drunk, and a Rastafarian Dreadlock had an altercation with him, which erupted into a shouting match. Stretch wasn't about to keep arguing with the Dreadlock, so he pulled his automatic pistol.

"Dreadlocks, why you talk so much?" He shot the Dreadlock twice, and he fell to the floor, crying like a baby from the gunshot wounds.

Members of many different Jamaican posses were at the party, so the environment was already tense. Hearing the two shots, panic ensued, and over two hundred guns were drawn. In a few seconds, over a thousand gunshots erupted, and patrons started to run in all directions. Sirens blared in the distance, heading toward the nightclub.

Stretch—gun in hand—looked at the rest of the Shower Posse members. "We have to leave this club now, or else the police are going to trap us inside here."

He, along with the others, began their short but dangerous journey to the nightclub entrance. Stretch let out a barrage of gunfire from his automatic pistol and the rest of the Shower Posse members followed suit, clearing their way to reach the entrance. All the Shower Posse members rushed out of the nightclub at once, just as the first group of police officers were leaving two patrol cars. Seeing about thirty Shower Posse members, guns in hand, the four uniformed police officers ran, leaving their patrol cars behind. The Shower Posse members managed to escape the dragnet, which netted over one hundred guns and scores of people, all arrested.

The day of the most talked-about Jamaican bus rides came. Jamaicans—from all over America *and* Jamaica—were all hyped up. Activities started early in the morning. Joy, familiar with the Shower Posse, telephoned a girlfriend in Manhattan.

"You going to the bus ride?"

"Yes, why?"

"You heard what happened early this morning?"

"No."

"Spanglers killed Duda, a member of the Shower Posse, and the Shower Posse members are going to retaliate at the bus ride."

Joy Cash couldn't seem to tell the truth. What she told her friend was as far from the truth as the North Pole is from the South Pole. The Spanglers Posse had done Shower Posse a favor by killing Duda. The man who killed Duda deserved a medal, as far as the Shower Posse was concerned.

With this rumor being spread by Joy, the Spanglers Posse decided to arm themselves to the fullest extent. With rumors like that, who could blame them?

Unaware of those rumors, members of the Shower Posse took no precautions. While over thirty Shower Posse members went to the bus ride, only five were armed. This, in itself, indicated that they went to the bus ride to have fun, not to fight a war.

Vivian's wife, her sisters, and Tony's woman attended the bus ride, so a pre-planned gun battle would have made no sense. It could only have caused a disaster, endangering the lives of both their women. The Shower Posse members enjoyed themselves, because that was the reason to go to the bus ride in the first place, but the Spangler Posse was tense because of the rumors.

Because of the tension, different posse members started seeing things that weren't even real, and the tension escalated. Tony's friend—Cracker—was walking with a close friend of Tony's— Lenky-Roy—from the Concrete Jungle Posse. Cracker was straightening the waistband of his pants and a guy from the White Plain Road Posse—not a Spanglers Posse member—thought Cracker was pulling a gun, but Cracker had no pistol on his person.

The guy from the White Plains Road Posse pulled his gun and opened fire on Cracker and Lenky-Roy, killing Lenky-Roy on the spot. Cracker had to dive for cover to save his life.

Pandemonium broke out in the picnic area, even though young kids were all around. Shots were fired all over the picnic grounds, and the

Shower Posse members were caught, ill prepared. Kirk—Vivian's close associate—had to take charge of the situation and assist the posse members, who were mostly Tony's friends. Kirk and Gabriel held the opponents at bay, using handguns against machine gunfire, successfully forcing the opponents to flee the area.

Nearly the entire New Jersey police force swarmed down on the picnic area. Gabriel was firing his automatic pistol in the direction of the unfriendly, when he heard a voice command.

"Freeze! Police! Put that gun down!"

Gabriel froze, dropping the pistol to the ground. The police officer handcuffed him and placed him under arrest. Over three thousand gunshots were fired during that incident, but the Shower Posse was solely blamed for that shooting—totally unfair. All together, the Shower Posse had five guns, with an average of sixteen shots each, making that a total of eighty shots.

It was even said that Vivian was at the bus ride and participated in the shooting, even after his girlfriend, Eleanor, told the public he stayed behind in Florida, and that she called him immediately after the shooting. Rumor had it that Vivian took a private jet back to Miami after the incident.

New Year's Eve, 1984, saw a party in progress on NW 17th Avenue, by the Palmetto Expressway in Miami. The location was the home of a West Indian sports club. Jamaicans and other Caribbean patrons poured into the sports club early, in order bring in the New Year with that party spirit. By eleven-thirty, the sports club was packed. Reggae music blasted throughout the hall. A minute before midnight, the partygoers started the countdown to midnight, then the huge hall erupted in unison: "Happy New Year!"

The New Year arrived. Within the crowd was Dovey, a member of the Payne Land Posse. He was a very decent guy, a former soccer player for the Payne Land community in Kingston, Jamaica and was never really involved in guns. His baby's mother, Patsy, was with him—the sister of a notorious Shower Posse enforcer, Food Head, who was also Vivian's friend.

Dovey hung around members of the Payne Land Posse, but was never an active participant in their war with the Shower Posse. He was spotted in the sports club by an associate of the Shower Posse, who, in turn, telephoned Gladstone Lawrence—a.k.a. Bunny—to say that Dovey was in the sports club. Bunny then proceeded to gather some members of the Shower Posse, and they all headed toward the club.

Upon arrival, Bunny saw Champs leaning on Vivian's 733 BMW, which Vivian had left with Donovan until his return to Miami after the New Year's—Vivian was celebrating his son's birthday and spending the Christmas holidays with his immediate family.

Bunny and the other Shower Posse members walked over to Champs to pay their respect, for he was, in fact, one of the actual leaders of the Shower Posse.

"What's up, Champs?" said Bunny.

"Nothing much."

"I heard that one of the Payne Land Posse members is inside the club. He was one of the guys who fired gunshots into Tony's Mercedes Benz, almost killing him at the Church's Fried Chicken drive-thru on 183rd St."

"You sure he's in there?"

Bunny beckoned to one of the Shower Posse members. "Go look and see if Dovey's in there."

The guy walked towards the sports club entrance. In about five minutes, the guy was back. "He's in there, all right."

"Let's go then," said Bunny. "You three go in through the entrance," he directed. "He and I will cover the rear of the club," pointing to the guy who was going to accompany him.

Champs listened to Bunny as he arranged his operation. This was nothing strange. In fact, Champs was prepared for some fun.

Bunny and one of the Shower Posse members went to the rear of the sports club and walked through the hall toward Dovey, who was standing beside Patsy. The other three entered from the front. Dovey glanced in the direction of the three and recognized them as Shower Posse members. Realizing all three had guns in their hands, Dovey panicked and headed toward the back door.

Patsy saw what was about to happen and followed Dovey as fast as she could. As Dovey exited the back door, he ran right into Bunny and his friend. Bunny's automatic pistol fired, shooting Dovey twice in the upper part of his body, as Patsy looked on. Dovey turned, ran back into the club, and headed to the entrance door. Bunny and his partner chased him through the club and to the entrance door. As Dovey ran toward the Palmetto Expressway, Bunny and the rest of the Shower Posse members crashed out of the sports club entrance.

Champs was still leaning on the car. "Is that Dovey?" He pointed at the figure running down the road.

"Yeah, that's him," said Bunny.

Champs—a left-handed, certified sharpshooter and a member of the Jamaican cadets as a teenager—pulled his automatic, took aim and fired from a distance.

"You really sure that's him?" Champs laughed.

Bunny said, "Yeah, it's him."

Champs, still laughing, aimed again and fired another shot. This time, Dovey fell underneath the Palmetto Expressway. Champs, still laughing, took his time as he proceeded to walk toward Dovey.

Bunny and the other Shower Posse members followed him. They reached Dovey, lying in the street, and Champs pumped another shot into Dovey's head.

He then looked at Bunny and the other Shower Posse members. "You mean to tell me you kids don't know how to kill people yet? The old man, here, has to come to your assistance. Get a grip, youngsters. Never shoot at a man unless you're going to kill him. He'll swear revenge if he's alive. Make sure the only persons that can take revenge are his friends—not *him*. Then his friends are going to be scared, too. Guess why?" He paused as Bunny and the other Shower Posse members looked at him, astonished. "Because you're a fucking killer!"

He turned from Dovey's dead body and walked toward the car. Bunny and the other members of the Shower Posse followed quickly behind, got into their cars, and drove away from the scene of the crime.

Owing to the fact that Dovey was the father of Food Head's sister's baby, that incident was a sad event, especially for the one who organized the hit—Bunny. Champs was an unsuspecting participant in the murder, not knowing who Dovey was. He wasn't as familiar with the situation as Bunny.

Food Head arranged quick damage control by sending Patsy back to Jamaica, so that she couldn't be persuaded by the Miami Homicide Department to testify against Bunny, Champs, or the other Shower Posse members who participated in Dovey's murder.

After a phone conversation with a new girlfriend, Rosie, Vivian drove all the way from Pembroke Lakes down to Carol City where she lived. She was finishing her make-up when Vivian was allowed entrance into the house by a shapely girl of dark complexion, who had a gap between her front teeth. He looked her up and down until Rosie came out of the bathroom.

He left with Rosie, but on their way to the Howard Johnson in North Miami Beach, he couldn't stop thinking about the girl at Rosie's house.

"Who was that girl in the house?"

"My cousin, Eleanor. She just came to Miami."

Vivian didn't ask anything else; he just kept thinking about the girl. When they reached the hotel parking lot, he wondered, *how can I get out of this date with Rosie, without us hating each other?* This was the first opportunity to have sex with Rosie, so he kept thinking, *If I'm to go after Eleanor, it's best for me not to sleep with Rosie.*

Good thought, all right, but to extricate himself from the situation wasn't easy. Rosie made herself comfortable when they reached the room. A thought came to him, *if I turn my beeper on and off twice, it will sound like someone is beeping me.* He pulled the beeper from his belt and pretended to look at a number, and then he reached for the hotel phone, dialing his house number, knowing that no one was there.

"Hello. What's up?" he said to the phone ringing in his ear. "*What?* I'm coming up there right now." He hung up the phone, a disturbed look on his face. "Rosie, I'm sorry about this, but something's come up." He tried to sound sincere. "I'll have to drop you home … pick you up later."

Rosie said sympathetically, "That's all right. I'll be home."

Vivian drove quickly to Rosie's house, dropped her off, and then went by Frenchy's, calling Frenchy away from his girlfriend.

"Dial this number for me and ask for Eleanor." Vivian passed Frenchy a piece of paper with the number written on it. "When she comes to the phone, you give the phone to me, okay?"

They entered Frenchy's bedroom.

"Hello, could I speak to Eleanor?"

"This is Eleanor."

"Hold on." Frenchy handed the phone to Vivian.

"This is Dave. I just picked up Rosie and dropped her back off at your house. You saw me, remember?"

"Yes I did, what can I do for you?"

"You can be my woman for starters."

Eleanor laughed. "This man is a crazy man."

"No, I'm not crazy. I saw you a few moments ago, and all I have been doing is thinking about you. I want to see you."

"What about Rosie?"

"There's nothing going on between me and Rosie. I'll tell you about that when we see each other. Can we meet?"

"When?"

"Now. I'll pick you up down the block from your house in a half an hour."

"Okay, I'll be there."

In half-an-hour, Eleanor walked down the block where Vivian had been eagerly waiting for the past ten minutes. They spent the remaining portion of that evening getting to know each other. Vivian's mind was made up; Eleanor was perfect for him.

"I'm moving you out of that house as of now."

Eleanor looked at him in astonishment. "What will people—"

"What people? I don't care about people. I like you ... and you like me, don't you?"

Eleanor stuttered at his abruptness. "Y-y-yes," she said shyly.

"Well, that's it. We'll be sharing a place together as of now. My friend has an extra room in his house and I'm gonna rent it from him. As of today, we are now seeing each other, okay?"

"Okay, okay. I just hope I'm doing the right thing," she said, a sexy smile breaking across her face.

The next day, Vivian bought Eleanor a bedroom set, which was delivered to Frenchy's house, where he'd rented the room for Eleanor. Frenchy took Eleanor to Rosie's house where she gathered her belongings and moved them to her newly furnished room. Frenchy's girlfriend, Marcia, and Eleanor were schoolmates back in Jamaica, so Eleanor was comfortable with the living arrangement at Frenchy's. Vivian took Eleanor shopping to complete the room decor, and by the end of the day, her little room was like a palace.

Later that night, Vivian took Eleanor to his house in Pembroke Lakes—a beautiful house, exquisitely decorated. His master bedroom was carpeted with off-white plush carpeting and had wall-to-wall, ceiling-to-floor off-white drapes, with thin gold trimmings. The custom-made, extra-king-sized, round bed, padded with off-white crushed velvet and a gold stripe around the base of the bed was awesome. A matching dresser and chest of drawers, with a white floor-model TV added to the opulence. To complete the room, wall-to-wall ceiling mirrors were added.

Black-and-white tiled floors lay in the kitchen and dining areas, the dining room table was white, with black-and-white chairs. The sunken living room floor was covered with rust-colored carpeting, while the room had custom-made, wall-to-wall, ceiling to floor, brown-and-beige drapes, and a cocoa-brown velour, circular living room suite. There were two other bedrooms—one with a burgundy carpet and a white, king-sized bedroom set, the other was carpeted in an electric-blue color, and had a white, queen-sized bedroom set.

Eleanor could hardly believe what she saw. The house was breathtaking, both internally and externally. A huge pool and a gazebo filled the backyard to the lake. They walked hand-in-hand to the backyard and sat in the gazebo for a while and listened to the rippling water of the lake, before returning to the master bedroom, where they watched TV.

Eleanor's body had fascinated Vivian. She had the best hips he'd even seen, and her smile was radiant with that space between her two front teeth. He started playing with the long braids of her hair, and she responded to him. In a few seconds, she was in his arms.

The next morning, he took her back to her room in Frenchy's house. Frenchy was the man in charge of purchasing and packing Vivian's marijuana. So, after a night of pleasure with Eleanor, there was work to be done. Vivian had hired Miss May to cook and clean the house at Pembroke Lakes, and she also lived at Frenchy's. When he dropped Eleanor off, he took Miss May to the house in Pembroke Lakes.

About three months later, Vivian found a house close to Modeler's, in Miramar, and decided to rent it for Eleanor. He furnished this little love nest for Eleanor comfortably.

The packing of marijuana was moved to Eleanor's house. A friend of Vivian's—EasiBoo—plus Eleanor's pregnant sister, Jackie, arrived from Jamaica and stayed with them. It was becoming crowded. Vivian had to make a trip to Jamaica, although he promised Eleanor he'd look for a new place when he returned.

Stopping by Frenchy's house one day, he was greeted with bad news.

"You heard what happened last night?"

"No, what?"

"Police raided Eleanor's house. She, Easiboo and Jackie are in jail."

"Damn! Damn! Damn!"

"Shit man," Frenchy hissed through his teeth. "They found guns, money and weed, man. I'm checking about bail … *if* they are *on* bail."

Eleanor and Easiboo spent about two months in jail, but Jackie was quickly released. Easiboo pleaded guilty to the drugs, guns and money, and Eleanor was released. Vivian had rented another house before Eleanor and Jackie came out of jail, plus a separate house for his packing and storage. He took Eleanor to the house in which Jackie had already set up housekeeping.

A few weeks later, Vivian picked up a girlfriend, Beverly, at the airport, a day before they were scheduled to leave for a Miami–Jamaica–Los Angeles trip. Beverly—a very nice girl, dark and shapely, with an angelic smile, was the sister of Chubby, from Southside in central Kingston, Jamaica.

The next morning, Vivian got up early and decided to head out with Beverly and show her the town. They said goodbye to Miss May, and went out to the car, but the engine wouldn't start. Vivian opened the hood, checked the battery and the terminals, and then tried again. No dice. While he was trying to start the engine, a red-and-black Fairmont passed by, and through the tinted window, he could see the frame of a white man staring at him. A funny feeling came over Vivian, and he rushed into the house to call Food Head's house, as the car disappeared.

Tony's half brother, Tika Shine, answered the phone.

"Tika, do you have a jumper cable?"

"No,"

"Go and buy one and hurry to my house with it. It's very important. Come, now," Vivian urged.

That was a police officer watching my house, Vivian thought.

Tika Shine arrived quickly and gave Vivian a jump-start. The 733BMW engine roared.

"Later," said Tika as he drove away.

Beverly hopped into the passenger front seat, closed the door, and Vivian reversed out of the driveway, driving slowly out to Pembroke Road. He glanced into the rearview mirror and saw a light blue Chevette being driven by a white man at a distance. *That man looks like a cop.* There was a dirty pair of pants and shirt on the backseat, so he decided to find out who the man was. He turned into the Pembroke Pines Shopping Center, and parked around the corner—away from most of the stores. The Chevette pulled into the shopping center, too.

Telling Beverly to come with him, he took the dirty laundry. As they walked away from the car, the Chevette pulled up, about five cars from Vivian's. He and Beverly walked around the corner and quickly entered a same-day dry cleaner, before the white driver could see where they were headed. He gave the clothes to the dry cleaner attendant and told her his name.

"I'll pick them up later. Keep the ticket."

As they exited and headed back to the car, the white man saw Vivian, and he slowed his pace. He reached Vivian, nodded and they exchanged "Hi" greetings. Turning the corner Vivian said, "Run, Bev."

Reaching the car, they sped out of the parking lot. As he glanced back in his rearview mirror, Vivian saw the white man running to his car and he laughed out loud. "You'll never catch me now, mister policeman."

He stepped on the gas and headed to his girlfriend's house, Pearl, to borrow her tinted-window Mustang. While he and Beverly were driving the Mustang, he saw the police officer again in Frenchy's area, so he drove to the Ramada Inn at NW 12th Avenue and the Palmetto Highway.

Later that day, the police raided his Pembroke Lakes house and arrested his helper, Miss May. They took her to the immigration center and Vivian bailed her out for a thousand dollars, and then booked Beverly on a flight to Los Angeles.

Vivian had to abandon his Pembroke Lakes home and rented a house in Carol City at NW 7th Avenue and 198th St. Miss May stayed at the new location.

While relaxing at home one day, Vivian received a call from Jim Brown's son, Jah T.

"What's up, T?"

"All kinds of problems, Dave," Jah T said, in disgust. "Daddy's making me frustrated."

"What's wrong?"

"It's Daddy and his girlfriend, Annette, man. He's acting stupid. He fired about ten shots at her, man. He's acting stupid. You need to talk to him, Dave. He'll listen to you. He need to stop using that cocaine, man. If he continues, he might end up dead ... like Bya and Molla. I want you to convince him to come to Miami and spend a few months. He need to be around someone that doesn't free-base."

Sadness filled Vivian as he listened to Jah T. His best friend was ruining himself in Jamaica. "Where's he now?"

"At Annette's apartment building. I'll go tell him you want to talk to him right away."

"You do that. I won't leave the house until I talk to him."

Jim called Vivian about twenty minutes later and Vivian convinced him to come to Miami to cool out for a while. Jim agreed and made preparations to leave.

Three days later, Jim's girlfriend, Brownie, took him to the Norman Manley Airport and made sure he boarded the plane. Jim possessed an indefinite multiple-entry visa, so he had no problem traveling to the US. At the Miami International Airport, Vivian picked him up. He looked tired, his eyes were blood red from lack of sleep, and his six-foot plus, two-hundred-and-fifty-pound frame looked worn out.

By the time Vivian reached the I-95 Expressway, Jim was fast asleep. Vivian smiled and said to himself, *Bomber, you're really tired.* Vivian pulled into the driveway and tugged on Jim's shoulder to wake him up. "We're home, man."

Jim had a frightened look on his face as he was awakened, but gathered himself quickly. "I'm tired, man."

"I know. Between you and my five-year-old son, I was wondering which one could fall asleep faster in a car."

Jim was cracking up with laughter. They took the luggage out of the trunk and went inside the house.

"I want to sleep tight now, man."

"Come. Let me show you to your room." Vivian led him to a huge guest room decorated with a king-sized bedroom set, carpet, and expansive drapes.

Jim was out cold within minutes, as if he'd taken a sleeping pill. He slept from ten in the morning until seven that evening. Modeler, Champs and Red Roy came to visit, but Vivian told them to check back later that night—his friend needed his rest.

The next day, Vivian's house was buzzing with human traffic. Guys kept coming and going, paying their respect to Jim—it went on like that for about two weeks. On one of the visits, an associate of his—Mikey—brought him a present; at least he *thought* it was a present—a solid rock of crack, weighing about two ounces. He was about to hand it to Jim in Vivian's presence.

"Nah, ah! Nothing like that shit in here!" Vivian's wrath could be felt vibrating through the room. "Jim's here to rehabilitate, and I don't take kindly to you giving him that garbage. Take it out of my house. Go put it in your car. If you're going to be a friend to Jim, do so by helping him kick this habit."

Vivian laid down the law.

Several friends paid Jim Brown homage, bringing large packages of cash—more than enough for him to start a major marijuana enterprise, to purchase a fabulous house, and a fancy car—but he continued to relax at Vivian's house, taking each day as it came.

Vivian took Jim on a shopping spree for jewelry, accompanied by Modeler, Champs and Red Roy. In downtown Miami, they went to the section with all the jewelry stores, where Vivian bought Jim Brown an eighteen-carat gold watch and matching bracelet, an eighteen-carat Cuban-link gold chain weighing a quarter-pound, and an eighteen-carat gold pendant with a likeness of Jesus on it.

Vivian and Modeler also bought themselves expensive jewelry—the same Cuban-link chain and pendant, except theirs had the likeness of the Virgin Mary. Everyone wore their jewelry back to Carol City, and Modeler, Champs and Red Roy visited with Jim for a while before they departed to their home in Miramar.

While Kirk was visiting Miami and staying at Vivian's house, about two weeks later, both Kirk and Jim were watching TV with Vivian in the den. It was about nine-thirty at the night, and Vivian, who went to bed early when he could, started to feel tired and was yawning.

"I'm going to bed."

Jim and Kirk stayed. Vivian's bedroom was at the other end of the house, so when he fell fast asleep, he didn't know that a friend of Jim's— Storyteller—came by and decided to take Jim for a night out on the town. They went down to Liberty City to a crack house, where he was familiar with the man who operated it. There were always several girls hanging out at the crack house, so they had fun smoking cocaine and fucking girls.

When it was time to leave, a man in a customized van pounced on them, pointing a gun, before they could enter their own vehicle.

"Freeze, motherfuckers! I want all your jewelry!"

Jim gave the man all the jewelry and cash he had, and Storyteller complied, too. The robber walked away, taking his sweet ol' time, so Jim quickly approached the owner of the crack house and asked, "Do you have a gun?"

The owner went back inside and brought back a piece. Jim Brown could see the robber a ways down the road, so he held the gun with both hands, aimed, and fired. The robber was hit in the leg, but quickly hopped around the nearby curb on one leg and disappeared.

Vivian was still sleeping when they returned, and Kirk was still in the den watching TV. Champs and Modeler had come to Vivian's house while Vivian was still asleep, and Jim told Kirk, Modeler and Champs what happened. Jim didn't try to wake up Vivian, because Vivian didn't want him mixed up in coke again. *Telling Vivian about this robbery wouldn't be wise.*

After hearing what happened, Modeler convinced Jim to let them go and find the robber, so Jim, Storyteller, Champs and Modeler drove to the crack house and parked in the driveway. Champs remained in the van while the rest approached the door to the crack house, to talk to the owner.

"You have any idea where we can find the boy who robbed us?"

"No, I don't know where to find him." The owner seemed to answer honestly.

Modeler looked at the owner with a vicious look. "How the fuck you mean you can't find that punk?" Swiftly, Modeler pulled his pistol before Jim could stop him from firing a shot into the crack house owner's face.

"What the fuck you doing?" Jim's angry words came too late. Trouble had started and it had to come to an end.

"This boy, here, set you up." Modeler said angrily. He proceeded to the living room where there were five other people—four females and one male. Modeler shot all five at point blank range.

One of the occupants—a teenaged, pregnant girl—begged Modeler to save her life. "Please, sir. Don't kill me."

He had no pity for her. The shot opened her skull.

Jim was mad at Modeler for killing all these innocent people, but it was too late—the bloody bodies lay all over the apartment. While Jim was looking at the dead bodies, one of the girls opened her eyes, and then closed it quickly as she saw Jim staring at her. Now, he had no choice. He had to clean up the mess that Modeler started. He fired one shot into the half-dead girl's head. That was his only involvement in this senseless shooting.

"This was stupid, man. Those people were innocent." Jim was so angry with Modeler he didn't know what to do. They drove back to Vivian's house, and all four dismantled their guns. Vivian was still fast asleep in his bedroom not knowing what was happening in his own house. While burning a gun handle, Modeler accidentally spilled the melted plastic onto Vivian's carpet in the den.

Modeler and Champs left, and Modeler drove to a canal on NW 47th Avenue, between 199th St. and County Line Rd., where he dumped the dismantled guns.

Having had a good night's sleep, Vivian awoke early the next morning, walked into the den and noticed the damaged carpet. Kirk was sleeping in the sofa, so he woke him up. "What happened to the carpet?"

Kirk jumped up, wiped his eyes with the backs of his hands, and barely whispered, "Modeler was burning a gun handle and it melted onto the carpet."

"Why was he burning a gun in my house? What happened to *his* fucking house?" Vivian's voice rose with each word.

Kirk put his fingers to his lips and said, "Shhh. Let's go to your room."

Vivian and Kirk walked to Vivian's bedroom, and Kirk closed the door.

What the fuck is going on? "Why the fuck do I have to be silent in my own house?"

Then Kirk told Vivian everything about the murders the night before. Vivian sat on his bed and pondered while looking into open space.

Vivian was shocked to hear the details. "Shit, man! Why the fuck did Storyteller drive Jim to a crack house, man? If I'd have been up, this shit would never have happened."

"Don't say anything to Jim that I told you. Wait until he says it to you," begged Kirk, then he left the room.

Jim was still sleeping off the cocaine, while the bad news continued to haunt Vivian. He had to talk to Jim, although he promised Kirk he'd wait until Jim approached him. So, Vivian thought of a way to prevent Jim from knowing that Kirk told him anything.

He went to Jim's door, knocked, and entered. Jim wasn't asleep--just lying down. "What's up? What happened to the carpet in the den?"

A sad look came over Jim's face. "It's that fucking boy, Modeler. Some fucked-up shit went on last night, man, and I know you're not going to like it. I don't know what *he* was trying to prove."

Jim told Vivian the whole truth of what happened the night before. "I swear, Dave … I only shot one of the girls, and that was because she got a look at me. She could have identified me, if she'd lived. She was half-dead, anyway, from Modeler's bullets. Those people were innocent, Dave. I'm only a few weeks in Miami, and this man wants to put me in trouble." Jim became increasingly angry as he spoke. "I'm going to stay away from Tivoli Gardens' men while I'm in Miami."

Later on that day, Vivian drove to Modeler's house to see him. He and Modeler sat in the den.

"What happened last night?"

Modeler was adamantly serious when he answered. "The owner of the crack house set Jim up, so I killed him. There were four witnesses, so I killed them, too. They disrespected the big man."

After their discussion was over, Vivian came to a silent conclusion. *For such a smart businessman, Modeler's logic is way off. He definitely was trying to impress Jim.*

On NW 183rd St., near 17th Avenue, a store—Junior's Grocery Store—sold West Indian food products, and Vivian purchased some groceries. Heading out of the store, he saw Chris and two other guys he didn't recognize.

"What's up, Dave?" Chris shouted.

Then one of the two guys looked at Vivian, a fierce expression on his face. In a split-second, he pointed a chrome-plated automatic pistol at Vivian. "Your brother, Tony, fired several shots into my aunt's car while she was driving with her man and baby."

Chris tried to calm the gunman. "What the fuck you doing? Tony and Dave are two different persons. Tony's the one with the problems. Dave's just a hustler."

"If you can't catch one brother, you fuck up who you can catch," said the guy with his pistol, still pointing at Vivian.

Chris stepped between the gun and Vivian. "Watch what the fuck you are doing. It's more trouble that you want to start?"

The gun was lowered and returned to the gunman's waistband.

Vivian took a good look at the guy to memorize his features, and then turned to his car.

Chris didn't want an out-and-out war. "Don't pay him any attention, Dave. He just came to America. He don't understand what's going on."

Vivian stepped into his car without saying anything, and drove away. He dropped off the groceries in his kitchen, handing them to Miss May, then walked to the bedroom, closed the door, and flopped down on the bed. He lay on his back, eyes riveted to the ceiling, while thoughts swarmed around inside his head. *I have the firepower and the men to wage a bloody war in Miami, but is that the right thing to do?* The kid had disrespected him, and he couldn't let that go.

Jim, Kirk and a friend of Vivian's—Junior Blacks—were in the den when he came in from the grocery store, but he didn't tell them about the incident, keeping it to himself. He knew if he'd said anything, they would have wanted to react, even if he objected. Vivian's beeper went off, and he saw it was the number of a friend of his—Denton—when he checked it. He dialed the number immediately and got Denton on the line. "What's up, Dento?"

"Angela asked me to beep you. She wants to talk to you."

"All right, put her on the line."

"I'll have to call her and patch her in three-way." He proceeded to connect with Angela. "She's on the line, now."

"Yeah, Angela. What are you saying?"

"I heard what happened a moment ago out by Junior's. Why didn't you take the gun from the boy and slap him across his face?"

Vivian made a hissing noise, indicating that this wasn't the time for sarcasm.

"Dave, I'm asking you, please, not to react. I've talked to him and cursed him out, telling him that he was wrong to do what he did, and he said he was sorry. Please forgive him, for my sake at least."

Vivian was silent for a while, wondering why she was pleading for a punk kid.

"Say something, Dave. I know how you're thinking, but for my sake, please. I don't want no more shooting."

Then Vivian spoke in a warning tone. "Tell your relatives to leave me out of the war with Tony, his friends … we won't talk on this again … and you have my word. There'll be no retaliation." His statements were definite, calm and sincere.

After he hung up the phone, he said to himself, *now these guys have forced me to carry a gun everywhere I go from now on.*

He told no one of the incident, but advised Jim and Kirk not to be without their guns at any time while out in the streets. His explanation: *just as a precautionary measure against any incidents that could stem from the war between Tony, his friends, and the guys from Payne Land.*

Tony sent down his new guy to Florida—Bugs—and asked Vivian to let Bugs use his address to apply for a driver's license.

"I hope it's not guns he's here to buy," Vivian emphatically replied to Tony.

"Nah, man. I want Frenchy to teach him the ropes so he can buy my drugs for me."

Vivian had no problem with that, so he received Bugs in his home.

When Bugs arrived, Vivian admonished him to do the right thing. "Don't let anyone ask you to buy any guns. It's trouble. You buy too many guns on your driver's license, the FBI might think you're a terrorist. If they check on you, and you can't show the guns that you bought, you'll go to jail. You hear me? Don't let no one ask you to buy any guns for them."

"No, Mr. Blake. Nobody can't ask me to buy any guns for them."

Bugs spent a lot of time around Frenchy until he learned the *ins* and *outs* of Florida perfectly. He helped Vivian, sometimes, but he was totally dedicated to Tony. Soon, he met a girl who was the sister—Sharon—to Arrow's wife. At the time, Arrow was Tony's main man in Miami, and he'd taken up residence in Miramar with his wife, kids and sister-in-law, Sharon.

Bugs started dating Sharon, and after a few weeks, moved in with her at Arrow's house. Tony's two Miami organizers of packing, buying and shipping marijuana were under the same roof. Raggy, who was once close to Vivian—but they had a falling out—was Tony's third in-charge. Vivian had brought Raggy from Jamaica to live in Miami.

One night, Vivian, Jim, Kirk, Junior Blacks and Arrow were in Vivian's den watching TV, when one of Tony's main hit men—Shower Chris—dropped by unexpectedly. He was in Miami on a hunt for Tony's enemies. Chris loved Kirk's company; knowing Kirk was a serious kid, Vivian overheard Chris asking Kirk to assist him.

"I just saw Bummy in a movie theater in Hollywood, and I'd like you to accompany me ... I'm gonna kill him tonight."

Everyone heard Chris and Kirk as they spoke.

Vivian couldn't believe they were discussing yet another killing. "What the fuck you talking about, Chris? Leave Bummy alone. Why does Tony hate the youth? Leave him alone."

Bummy Chris had saved Vivian's life a few weeks earlier, so he couldn't support them in their plans to kill him. Chris and Kirk seemed to scrap the idea, and everyone continued to watch the movie on TV. When the movie finished, Vivian realized that only he and Jim remained in the den. Kirk, Chris, Arrow and Junior Blacks had managed to slip away.

Needless to say, Chris had convinced Kirk to accompany him on his mission to assassinate Bummy. They both left in Chris' car—it had tinted windows—and parked one house away from Bummy's place, and waited for him to arrive. Their wait wasn't long; Bummy pulled up in his car a few minutes after they arrived. Chris and Kirk stepped from their car and sneaked up on Bummy, as he was about to get out. Chris opened fire, discharging fifteen shots until his magazine was empty. Kirk didn't have the chance to fire—not even one shot. For the most part, Chris was eager to kill, because he was always teased about his fear of Bummy.

Bullet-riddled, Bummy staggered from the car and fell into the street, as Chris and Kirk walked back to their car, and then drove in the body's direction. Chris wanted to flee the scene quickly, but Kirk delayed him.

"Stop by the body." Kirk was laughing as Chris slowed the car to a crawl. Kirk opened his door, pointed his gun at Bummy's head, and fired. They sped away.

Kirk glanced back through the rear windshield and saw the body moving. "Stop, Chris … the body just moved … reverse the car!"

He stopped the car and reversed it, nervousness tightening his gut. *Kirk is a cold-blooded killer who takes his ol' sweet time.*

"Just back the car over his head."

"Are you crazy?" Chris didn't follow the command—just put the car in *drive* and sped away.

"You afraid of blood?"

Chris hated the way Kirk laughed at him. "I don't want no blood on my car."

Arrow and Junior Blacks came from the other end of the road and fired more shots at the body as they drove past. Unfortunately several police cars were coming at full speed from the other direction, and they caught Arrow and Junior Blacks red-handed. The guys threw their guns from their car, but the police found them and they were arrested. Luckily, Bummy survived, so the guys were charged for attempted murder, not murder.

A few weeks before the shooting, Jim Brown's common-law wife, Miss Bev was in Miami, staying with Jim at Vivian's house. Jim's daughter, Prudence, was living in Miami by herself in an apartment rented by her father, and Jim and Miss Bev arranged for Prudence to be enrolled in a university in Southwest Miami.

They were all preparing to take Prudence down to her new school, when Vivian whispered into Jim's ear. "We can't travel with any guns in the car. We can't afford for Miss Bev or Prudence to conjure up the wrong idea."

Jim agreed. It had become Vivian's habit to travel with a gun, because of the close encounter he experienced by Junior's Grocery Store. Respect was due to Miss Bev and Prudence, although he felt naked without his gun.

Vivian and Jim sat in the front of the car, Vivian at the wheel, Prudence and Miss Bev sat in the back. As they drove from Vivian's house along NW 191st St., and were about to make a left onto 25th Avenue, a car with five passengers turned off 25th and onto 191st.

The passenger in front was Little Hunch, who'd fired six shots at Tony through the front windshield of his car.

Vivian pointed out Little Hunch to Jim. "That's the guy who almost killed Tony before you came to Miami."

He glanced in his rearview mirror and noticed that the car had turned back and was driving at full speed to catch up with them. Vivian stepped on his gas, picked up speed, and then whispered again.

"The boys are chasing us."

They had no guns, but the guys chasing them *did*, so Vivian accelerated the well-tuned BMW. *I want them to follow me ... I'll just keep enough distance so they won't try to fire any shots ... but will be able to see the car and still continue the chase.* He continued to watch them in the rearview mirror. Reaching the turn for NW 44th Ct., he slowed so Little Hunch and his friends could see where he was going, then sped away and turned a blind corner. Vivian slowed his car across the street and pulled up at Modeler's house, where Modeler, Red Roy, Kirk and Champs were standing outside. The two guys rushed the girls into the house, as the four guys pulled their weapons, and stood in the street, waiting.

Meanwhile, Vivian and Jim found two pistols in the house and rushed back outside, but the car didn't come around the corner. Everyone climbed inside Modeler's and Vivian's cars and searched for Little Hunch's car, but it was nowhere in sight. Likely, they suspected a trap.

After circling for about an hour, they gave up, collected the girls and headed for Southwest Miami to enroll Prudence at the university.

Later that night, Vivian, Jim, Modeler, Kirk, Red Roy and Champs were at one of Vivian's marijuana houses, talking about the incident that took place earlier, when Arrow and Bugs paid them a visit. Hearing the discussion convinced Kirk and Red Roy, who enjoyed shooting, to go with them on the road. Arrow and Bugs had Bummy on their minds, so they took Red Roy and Kirk to a house owned by a man known as Ram, where Bummy would visit often. They purposely kept their intentions from Vivian, because they knew Vivian didn't support anyone shooting Bummy again. However, Arrow and Bugs had it in for him, because Tony wanted him dead, too. Both Arrow and Bugs were scared of Bummy, so they had to convince the two shooters to travel with them.

That night was a disaster. Arrow and Bugs led Kirk and Red Roy on a Tony-planned shooting, as if they were going to get Little Hunch, too, although they knew that only Bummy came to that house. They proceeded to shoot up the house, leaving one innocent man dead and three wounded.

When the incident reached Vivian, he, of course, became hopping mad. The innocent wounded included a past girlfriend of his—Charmaine—another female associate, Eniva, and a male friend, Bunny, with whom he'd grown up. He didn't know who the dead victim was, but the guy surely had his sympathy—another of Tony's crazy schemes that caused nothing but headaches for Vivian—from one extreme to the other.

A few weeks later, on New Year's Eve, another shooting incident took place at a nightclub in Miami. Tony—in New York at the time—relayed the information to Vivian, bragging that one of *his* guys was a killer in the nightclub killing.

Jim was also with Vivian. They had hung out at different Jamaican dances—mainly in Brooklyn—then decided to go to a dance in the Bronx where Tony and his friends would be.

Tony didn't like the way Jim controlled the community of Tivoli Gardens, keeping order. Many of Tony's sidekicks were upset while they'd been living in Tivoli Gardens, because they couldn't shoot anyone, rape any girls, or steal at will. When they came to America, they said all kinds of nasty things about Jim, and Tony supported them.

Vivian retrieved two automatic pistols from the Bronx apartment and took them back to the hotel by La Guardia Airport—where he and Jim were staying—and picked Jim up. Vivian gave him one of the pistols before they left for the dance on Webster Avenue, near Tremont Avenue.

Many of Tony's friends spotted Jim and Vivian, and their eyes literally popped out when they saw the pair. They both walked to a section of the hall where Vivian saw some girls he knew. Across the hall was the bar, and standing there were a lot of Tony's friends, their eyes fixed on them. Chris walked over and greeted them while the others watched. Jim pointed in the direction of the bar.

"Dave, what you drinking?"

"Heineken."

Jim walked across the center of the hall towards the bar. While walking, he fixed his gun in an intimidating fashion, in plain view to everyone looking in his direction. He walked right between some of Tony's friends to the bar, then ordered drinks for Vivian and himself.

Vivian watched Jim all the way to the bar and smiled. *Bomber acts like he is a sixteen-year-old kid.*

Holding four beers with his left hand, close to his body, leaving his right hand free, he walked back between Tony's friends toward Vivian—the gun still in view.

Shower Chris saw Jim's gun and said, "Jim, you can't expose your gun like that. This is America … not Jamaica."

Jim looked at Chris seriously. "I'm Jim Brown. I do this shit anywhere."

He gave Vivian his beers and they started to drink and enjoy themselves. Vivian gave some money to the girls who were standing with them to buy their own drinks.

Jim looked at Vivian and said, "Remember this, Dave ... in front of a dog, I'm a super dog ... but behind a dog I'm just a dog. Guys talk shit behind my back, but when they see me, they don't say shit. They try to befriend me."

Vivian laughed, because he understood very well what Jim was saying.

A few days after the dance in the Bronx, Jim and Vivian went shopping in the Bronx at a store on the Grand Concourse, by Fordham Road, to buy some silk shirts to take back with them to Miami. While selecting shirts, two of Tony's friends—Gabriel and Samuel—walked in. Gabriel made an ugly face, acting like a tough guy, but didn't say anything.

Samuel didn't act like Gabriel, but he didn't pay any respect to Jim, either. He just walked by.

Vivian looked at the two guys with hatred in his eyes. "I don't like those pussies, Jim ... I hate them. You haven't done these guys anything and look how they're acting. We should've brought our guns with us," he said, regretfully.

Jim just laughed. "Dave, don't let those fools raise your blood pressure. To me, they are fools, and they will always be fools as far as I am concerned. I can give those guys a loaded gun and hold my head down so that they could get a good aim ... they wouldn't shoot me. Why you think, Dave? They're afraid to miss, they know they would have hell to pay."

Vivian laughed at what his friend said. They walked to the cashier, paid for their shirts, and left Samuel and Gabriel in the store.

It was 1985, and the year started off with a bang as far as business was concerned. Vivian and Jim bought two townhouses in the Lakes of Arcadia complex. Vivian purchased a house for his live-in girlfriend,

Eleanor, and paid a lady to bring Eleanor's son, Duane—from another relationship—to Miami from Jamaica. A brand new, fire-engine red Honda Prelude, was also given to Eleanor. Now she had everything she'd always dreamed of having. As far as Vivian was concerned, she was deserving of every bit of the luxury.

While living with Eleanor, Vivian also had to have a comfortable family house for Valerie and his son when they came to Miami to stay—a beautiful home in Kendall. His 733 BMW was traded for a new 190E Mercedes that just hit the market.

Jim and Eleanor's houses were only about a hundred yards apart. Jim had let go of many visitors, and was concentrating mainly on his daughter's schooling and the rest of his family back in Jamaica. He was on a rigorous exercise program and ran five miles in the morning and the evening, while sticking to a proper diet.

Vivian hardly recognized him, because of the weight he'd lost, when he returned from a New York trip.

Modeler was doing very well, too—married to an American girl in Rochester, New York. He was planning to bring her to Miami so they could live together. After he was married and started procedures to acquire permanent residence status, he received a call from one of his boyhood friends—Joey—in St. Kitts, who had a proposal for Modeler. Joey had a connection with some Colombians from whom he could acquire tons of marijuana, so he asked Modeler if he was interested in becoming a partner. Modeler accepted.

Modeler checked with his lawyer in New York, who was arranging his permanent residency, and asked whether a trip to the Virgin Islands was possible. His lawyer told him it was okay, so Modeler cemented the deal with Joey and the Colombians, and met Joey in St. Thomas, with twenty thousand dollars.

Glasses—Vivian and Modeler's friend—was handling Vivian's business in Miami, and introduced Modeler to an American girl. Modeler took a liking to the girl, and they started having a whirlwind romance. He bought her jewelry and fine clothing, and even started to trust her with his cash from New York.

One night, the American girl stayed over at Glasses' house after bringing some cash down from New York. Glasses dipped into the bag and stole some of the cash.

The next day, while Vivian was buying some marijuana for Modeler, he discovered a three-thousand-dollar shortage and told Modeler about it.

Modeler was understandably very upset and accused Glasses of stealing the cash, but Glasses blamed the girl, saying, "How could you be trusting an American girl?"

Modeler reached for his pistol, but Vivian held him back.

"You introduced the girl to me saying she was a good girl … now you trying to say she's not a good girl," Modeler lashed out at Glasses. He badly wanted to shoot Glasses, but Vivian put Modeler in his car and drove away.

A few weeks after the flare-up between Modeler and Glasses, a call came for Vivian. Vivian, Modeler, Donovan, Jim, and Glasses were at the house. Arrow was on the line and talked to Vivian.

"I'm down by my Cuban friend's house and he told me that Glasses has been pouring bird seed in your marijuana and taking out the weight of bird seed in marijuana."

Vivian listened carefully to Arrow.

"Two days ago, he took ten pounds of marijuana out of your purchase and replaced it with ten pounds of bird seed."

Vivian told him "later" and hung up the phone. He turned to Glasses who was sitting beside him. "I just heard from Arrow, and his Cuban friend told him that you've been taking out my weed and replacing it with bird seed. Said you did it a couple of days ago at the Cuban's house."

"No, Dave, it wasn't *me*. It was Frenchy … he did it. He wanted to make some extra cash. He was the one who took me to the Cuban."

He knew that Vivian and Frenchy had a falling out and that Vivian would be furious at Frenchy.

"I'm going to Frenchy's right now. I want my fucking weed … *now!*"

He rose from the sofa, grabbed his pistol, and hurried toward the door.

"Dave, I'm coming too," Jim agreed.

Modeler and Donovan followed along, packing their pieces, and headed to Frenchy's in Vivian's car.

On the way, Modeler's beeper kept going off. "It's Frenchy."

Vivian started to wonder why Frenchy was beeping Modeler. They were coming up to Eleanor's house. "Let me stop by Eleanor's so you can call Frenchy and find out why he's beeping you."

Modeler used Eleanor's phone, while Vivian took the other extension.

"What's up, Frenchy?"

"I just got a call from Glasses and he told me that he told Vivian that I took out his weed. That's a lie … *he* did it. You know I wouldn't try to steal from you guys … he did it." Frenchy sounded very nervous.

Vivian, listening on the other extension, interrupted. "Frenchy, Dave here. I'm going to patch in Glasses on the three-way line, but don't say anything until I tell you to."

Modeler put his extension down for a second while Vivian patched in Glasses, then picked the extension back up again when the call went through.

Glasses had left Vivian's residence, and was now at his marijuana house, along with Kirk and Redy Roy.

"Glasses, what you say about Frenchy? Tell me again."

"Yeah, Dave, that boy Frenchy's a thief … been doing this thing for a long time. He should get a gunshot in the forehead."

"Frenchy, you heard Glasses?"

"Yes."

"Oh, fuck! You caught me!" Glasses confessed. "I won't do it again."

"Let me talk to Kirk," Vivian said to Glasses.

Glasses handed the phone to Kirk. "Yeah?"

"Don't let Glasses leave the house … I'm coming there *now*!" Vivian hung up, and all four drove to the house.

Glasses had wanted to leave, but Kirk held his Desert Eagle firearm on him. "Glasses sit down and wait until Dave comes. I don't want Dave to come and see a dead body in the house ... so just sit down, all right?" Glasses definitely understood that Kirk meant business.

The four guys pulled up and went inside. Glasses was sitting on a stool in the living room. Immediately, Modeler pulled his gun, but Vivian took it.

Glasses fell into the trap Modeler hoped for, and Modeler wanted revenge for Glasses stealing his money from the American girl, but Vivian would have none of it—no killing.

Glasses' son, Bum Bum, and Vivian's son were friends and went to the same school on Long Island. Vivian could never have lived with the fact that he was a party to killing Glasses—plus they had grown up together.

After Jim bound Glasses' hands between his knees, Champs kicked Glasses in the face with his instep.

"No, Champs," Vivian commanded.

Modeler, ignoring what Vivian was saying to Champs, kicked Glasses in his eye and blood gushed out.

"What the fuck you do, Modeler?" Vivian grabbed a towel angrily and made Jim take the tape off.

Modeler didn't give a shit about Glasses—he wanted him dead.

Bugs entered the house. Glasses was holding the towel to his eyes, and asked for some tea.

"Here's the tea, Glasses." Modeler poured the boiling hot tea on top of Glasses' head.

Glasses sprang from the ground to the ceiling in pain.

"Nah, this has to end now." Vivian didn't want any torture going on, either.

"The boy's a thief," said Modeler. "You can't be sorry for no thief, Dave."

Vivian directed Bugs to help. "Bugs, come carry home Glasses for me."

"Me and Kirk will carry him home." Red Roy was more than happy to get Glasses alone.

Glasses, like a fool, decided to let Red Roy and Kirk take him home.

"You stupid motherfucker! Didn't you hear I say Bugs will take you home." Vivian couldn't believe the stupidity of this guy.

"Yo, Dave ... you should have made me take him home—to the land of no return." Red Roy laughed at the prospect of killing Glasses.

Modeler and Joey made their necessary connections, and the marijuana was shipped from Colombia, to St. Thomas, then New York. Modeler went to New York and rounded up some girls to receive a thousand pounds of marijuana via Federal Express, arranged by Joey. The deal was pulled off without a hitch. Vivian gave Modeler some phone numbers of his New York City customers, so that Modeler could sell some of the shipment.

Vivian, Champs and Jim were still in Miami, while Red Roy and Kirk were in New York with Modeler. While Jim and Vivian were at the marijuana house, Jim answered a phone call.

"Hello ... who's that?"

"Who do you want?" Jim's tone was direct and to the point.

"Which pussy is this questioning me?"

After realizing it was Jim on the phone, the guy tried to act like he didn't know Jim's voice.

"Oh, Dave ... a boy just asked 'which pussy is that on the phone.'" Jim Brown hissed. "I hung up the phone in his ears."

"You know who it was?"

"No, but it was a long distance call ... sounded like one of Tony's friends. I heard that voice on the phone before.

Vivian quickly dialed Tony's house. "Someone in your house just called here?"

"Yeah, and a pussy hung up the phone"

"Who called?"

"Junkie Tom."

"Well that pussy just disrespected my friend Jim. Fucking faggot ... *he's* a fucking pussy." Vivian couldn't believe his ears ... how much disrespect his brother had.

"He didn't know it was Jim Brown."

230

"This is *my* house, anyone who answers *my* phone is *my* friend, so he meant to disrespect *me*!" Vivian angrily slammed the phone down.

"I'm tired of these motherfuckers, man." Vivian said into the air, as much as he said it to Jim, pacing the floor. "They've shot up Miami and run away ... leaving me to face the heat. Now ... they're fucking disrespecting me, and they ain't nothing but some punks! They walk around firing shots all over the place, calling themselves the Shower Posse and giving me a fucking bad name."

Jim watched his friend helplessly, not knowing what to say. "Cool down, Dave."

"I told Tony the other day that he and his friends are using me as bait. He and his friends are shooting up the place, and people automatically think that I'm involved, because he's my brother. I'm no Shower Posse ... he and his friends are. I don't want to be identified with no stupid gang, and to top it off, they ain't nothing but a group of fools ... it's just that people don't know that. People think it's the Tivoli Gardens men that are the Shower Posse members. They don't realize that it's a bunch of Tivoli Gardens defectors and some strange kids Tony have ... calling themselves Shower." The heat was rising in Vivian with every passing second, boiling, and churning inside him. "I'm gonna teach them motherfuckers a lesson, and when I'm done? ... there'll be no more Shower Posse members left. Tony'll be standing fucking alone." Fuming—the steam seeming to escape through his nostrils—he stood at the window, looking out into the backyard, and stayed there in deep thought.

Jim walked over to his friend. "Dave ... hope you're not thinking what I think you're thinking."

Vivian turned and looked at Jim, his voice becoming low and steady. "I'm going to kill all of Tony's friends, and then there will be no more Shower Posse. Tony'll be left standing alone with no power."

"I know that was what you were thinking, but I want you to think about it carefully ... I'm down with you, with anything, but I want you to think about it carefully, 'cause once it starts ... it can't stop."

"There's a dance in two weeks in New York ... all of Tony's friends will be there. I've thought about this carefully ... been on my mind for over a week. They've just made me decide. That night ... at the dance ... we kill 'em all ... every one of them at the dance."

Vivian walked from the window to the sliding door, and out into the backyard. Jim followed.

"They're all a bunch of punks, Jim. One of our guys is worth twenty of theirs. They love to fire shots ... that's all. They're not killers ... we've got the killers." Vivian looked at Jim and a smile started to crease his face.

He finalized the plans in his mind and related them to his friend. "Bomber, it'll be like taking candy from a baby. I'll notify Modeler in New York and tell him of my plans. You can talk to Champs ... we'll say nothing to Kirk, Preps or Red Roy until we're all in New York."

"I'm down, man ... anything you say, Dave."

Vivian and Jim Brown sent a box with ten guns and ammunition, and told Bugs—one of Tony's henchman—to ship it up to New York with him, not telling him what was in it. Vivian also asked an elderly, short, small-bodied gentleman with a light complexion—Sed, an army veteran who ran errands for Vivian—to receive the package.

When Sed picked up the box at the FedEx office in Manhattan, federal agents surprised him.

"You're under arrest, Mr. Freckleton. You have the right to remain silent. Anything you say can be used against you in a court of law."

That same night, the agents also raided Kong's marijuana house, which was the address on the box of firearms.

The next day, Vivian went to see Jim and told him what happened in New York.

"Bomber, the guns got busted. The guy who picked them up is in jail, and the feds also raided Kong's house—found marijuana and guns."

"What? ... uh ... so, what's next?"

"I'll just have to get some more guns and drive them up to New York if I have to. I'm killing them Shower Posse stooges, man. They ain't getting away."

"There's something I have to tell you. I can't trust Champs on this mission, man. He'll kill Tony."

"What you talking about?"

"I was talking to Champs yesterday, and his remark was … if he sees that black boy Tony, he's not going to leave him alive."

Vivian's head started to pound. He didn't want his brother to die, and for the first time, reality hit him … his brother could easily die in his planned onslaught.

"No, I can't kill my brother, Jim. I'd rather scrap the idea than risk his death. No, I couldn't live with it. Ah, man!" Vivian couldn't bear the thought.

He called off the planned assassination. It would've been the biggest gangland assassination in the history of the United States of America—over thirty Shower Posse members would've been gunned down at that dance.

Vivian told Modeler he'd be up to New York in two days to help him sell his marijuana and would meet him at the Holiday Inn by La Guardia. Vivian's trip to New York was interrupted by a date with a pretty American girl—Duchess—one of the most beautiful girls he'd ever seen. He couldn't pass up the opportunity to sleep with her. He'd been seeing her for over two months and this was the first chance he had to see how she looked naked. She was fair complexioned, had long hair, and possessed a shapely Coca-Cola bottle figure. His date with her was on a Sunday night, a day when he usually stayed at home—unless it was for business.

He lied to Eleanor and told her he had to go out on business. He opted to travel with a neat little gun he'd just bought on the black market—a 9 mm Walter PPK automatic—and left his legal firearm behind. He slipped it in his pouch and left to pick up Duchess. Avoiding the traffic lights on NW 183rd St., he sped by the river on 179th.

The sound of a siren got his attention as he looked in his rearview mirror to see a patrol car pulling him over. The police officer stepped out of his car and approached him.

"Driver's license, please." The officer shone his flashlight through the front windshield.

Vivian complied and stepped out of the car.

The police officer looked at the license, then leaned inside the Mercedes and spotted the gun peeping out from the unzipped pouch under the driver's seat.

"You got papers for the firearm?"

"No," said Vivian calmly.

"Well, then ... I'll have to charge you for illegal possession of a firearm."

Vivian was arrested and taken down to the lock-up. He didn't understand why the officer gave him a bond of only a thousand dollars, since he was wanted as a result of the raid on his Pembroke Pines home. Vivian had fourteen hundred dollars in his possession that the police officers at the lock-up took from him and placed on his record.

"Can I bail myself?"

"Sure ... but all your money's been locked away. It could be done, but you'll have to come back for your remaining four hundred dollars tomorrow. The person who pays out cash won't be in until tomorrow."

"No problem, I'll collect the balance then." *What a break,* he thought.

He asked the officer for a phone and rang Duchess.

"Duchess, I got busted while on my way to pick you up, but I'm working out bail right now. Drive down to the Dade County Lock-up and come pick me up."

The officer processed the paper work and with a huge sigh of relief, Vivian walked out. Duchess was already waiting for him—looking as sexy as ever. She hugged and kissed him, and then drove him to pick up his car.

"You got any cash on you?" he asked Duchess, as they approached his parked car.

"About four hundred dollars."

"Okay, that's good enough. I'll use it until tomorrow. Drive behind me."

She drove behind the Mercedes to the Holiday Inn by the Calder Race Track, and used her cash to book the hotel room.

The jail incident left his mind—all he was thinking of now was sexy, pretty Duchess.

The next day, Vivian drove to Jim's house and told him of his arrest the night before. Champs was also there.

"Modeler got busted this morning too, at his hotel," Jim related to Vivian. "Yeah … Champs came and told me."

"When it rains it pours, huh? Remember … I was supposed to be with him at the hotel room yesterday … *shit*!"

The Air Jamaica jet touched down in sunny Kingston and Vivian stepped off the plane. He was in Jamaica on business but it was close to his birthday, so he thought he might as well mix pleasure with business. It was the last days of April 1985, two weeks away from his birthday.

He'd spent most of his cash on the business he'd come to Jamaica to accomplish, but now that his birthday was close, he wanted a big bash. Tivoli Gardens' new community leader, Jonathan—who'd been remanded in the General Penitentiary in Jamaica—had just been acquitted of murder charges and released. This called for a celebration.

Vivian decided to put on a huge bash to serve both as his birthday party and Jonathan's welcome home party.

He called Jim in Miami. "Bomber, I want you to arrange some cash for me and some clothes for the guys down here for tomorrow. Have Law bring everything down to me."

"All right, I'll arrange everything. Give me the sizes for the clothes. How much money you need?"

Vivian gave him the information.

Law arrived in Jamaica the next night with the clothes and the money—the big bash was planned. Well-known entertainer, Little John, had a sound system—Romantic High Power—which was hired along with the leading Tivoli Gardens sound system, Libra-Tone. All the stops were pulled to make this party a success. Law had also plenty of expensive champagne and other fine alcoholic drinks.

For the first time, Vivian had traveled from the U.S. with a special lady friend along—Andrea—whom he'd met in a Southwest Miami nightclub called Eclipse. Standing in the nightclub, he'd spotted her by the bar. Andrea was of Indian descent, with long black hair. Her complexion was chocolate and she was so cool looking she could almost have lived in a refrigerator. She had a small curvaceous body, and a better word than *pretty* was needed to describe her good looks and smile. She was perfect! He had to have her, so he had one of his friends call her over—the rest is history.

Vivian's birthday was a success. The Tivoli Gardens Community Square was jam packed; drinks and food were free. When the night ended, everyone was drunk and they all had a good time. One item marred the festivities—Vivian attracted the attention of Jamaican law enforcement, which he'd carefully avoided for years. They now wanted to know who this "Vivian" was.

While in Jamaica with Andrea, their nightly fun was cut short when she contracted chicken pox, and had to spend most of the time in the hotel room. Luckily, she didn't contract the contagious illness until after their passionate night of lovemaking on his birthday.

Eleanor heard that Andrea was in Jamaica with Vivian. She tracked him down, found out his hotel room number, and placed a call. Andrea answered the phone.

"Who is this … Andrea?"

"Yes, this is Andrea. Who's this?"

Eleanor didn't mince any words. "This is Dave's woman, Eleanor. Why the fuck don't you leave my man alone? All you're doing in Jamaica is sucking Dave's fucking dick, bitch!"

Andrea laughed aloud at Eleanor. "You're missing the point here, Eleanor. You're a fool … if you were sucking his dick, you'd be in this hotel room with him right now, so you'd better wake up and smell the coffee … and be the bitch that I am, because your man is in love with this little bitch here."

Eleanor was so shocked at Andrea's boldness that she hung up the phone immediately, and didn't say another word.

Andrea told Vivian about the incident, and they both cracked up with laughter at Eleanor's reaction. What Andrea had said to Eleanor was unheard of in the inner cities of Jamaica in the year 1985.

With Andrea still sick with the chicken pox, she flew to Miami to recuperate.

While in Tivoli Gardens, Vivian received a message that his grandmother's residence was raided by police officers from the Central Police Station. They detained one of Tony's friends—Renguy—and took him down to the station.

"I don't want *him*," said the superintendent. "I want *Vivian*—the guy who wears two huge gold chains around his neck."

They released Renguy.

A week later, while Vivian was meeting his grandmother at a different house—one he had in Beverly Hills—her house was raided again. He went back down to Tivoli Gardens. About an hour later, he saw his grandmother driven by a family friend named Mr. Wright, into the Tivoli Gardens Community Square. She had the look of panic on her face.

"Vivian … the police just raided the house looking for *you*."

"Why the fuck they looking for me? I've not committed any crimes in Jamaica."

Later on that day, Vivian learned from a confidential source that they were looking for him in connection with a container of marijuana that was busted a few days back, on Harbor Street in Downtown Kingston. The police claimed that the same container was seen in Tivoli Gardens Community Square, and they thought Vivian had something to do with it. They wanted to have a talk with him.

The police officers left a card at his grandmother's for him to get in touch with them.

"I ain't going to no police station," he said to his grandmother. "If they see me and arrest me … that's okay, but I'm not going to no police station. All they want to see is what I look like."

Another confidential source informed Vivian that the US authorities were also on the alert—looking for him to enter any United States ports of entry—that his name had been placed in the computer. He'd checked out of the hotel and taken up residence in Tivoli Gardens with a girlfriend—Dee—until he devised a plan to reenter America. Vivian's suspicions were that one or more persons were leaking information to the police from within his community—he had to be careful.

He arranged some immigration papers for Dee and booked her on a British Airways flight to Miami, with a stopover in Nassau, Bahamas. He also booked the same flight for himself without Dee's knowledge. Then he called Andrea in Miami and told her to take a cruise to Freeport in the Bahamas, the next day after he would arrive in Nassau, since she'd fully recovered from her illness.

The day of the flight—Wednesday—there was a dance on Wellington Street in West Kingston, so Vivian announced to everyone ... aloud ... that he would be attending the dance that night. He'd already packed his things and arranged for a driver with a van to stick by him the whole day. Early that morning, he sneaked his luggage into the driver's van so that no one would see him leaving with the luggage in the daytime. An elderly friend—Sealo—was going to Miami in a few days, so Vivian turned over his jewelry to him for temporary safekeeping.

That evening, while everyone was preparing for the dance, Vivian sneaked out of Tivoli Gardens in the van and headed straight to Norman Manley Airport. He managed to check through without a hitch—the last person to board the flight. When Dee saw him on the plane, she was, naturally, surprised.

"I just wanted to surprise you. Just consider this a one-day vacation for us in the Bahamas."

The flight was smooth all the way to Nassau. They checked through immigration and customs without a hitch, then walked to the taxi stand and hailed a cab.

"Take me to your best casino resort."

"Get in, sir." The cab driver rushed to stow the luggage in the trunk, and Vivian and Dee were on their way.

The cab driver pulled up to a beautiful casino resort. Vivian paid him, and retrieved their luggage.

"Have a nice stay in Nassau, Sir … Ma'am."

The bellman took them to their suite. After taking care of their luggage, they went back downstairs to the casino and started gambling, having fun and becoming quite drunk. By the time they headed back to their suite, they couldn't wait. Vivian arranged for a wake-up call early the next morning. Then they tore each other's clothes off and were in the king-sized bed. Foreplay didn't last long … they wanted each other so badly.

The sudden ringing of the phone woke Vivian out of a deep sleep, and he nearly tumbled out of bed to answer it.

"This is your wake-up call, Mr. Blake.

"Thank you," he yawned. He wiped the sleep from his eyes and shook Dee's bottom to wake her up.

"What?" she asked through her yawning.

"You have to get up now. Our flight leaves in two hours."

She slowly rose from the bed and headed toward the shower, Vivian following afterward. Dressed and luggage packed, they checked out at the front desk.

"Cab for you both, Mr. and Mrs. Blake?"

"Yes, please."

The bellman hailed the cab, and they both headed to the airport—on two separate missions. Walking inside the terminal, Vivian indicated for Dee, "That's where you check in."

"So, you're not coming?"

"No, I'll see you in Miami in a few days. I have some business to take care of. Have a safe trip. "

They embraced and she walked towards the check-in counter.

Vivian had a different plan to enter the United States—undetected. The US Customs and Immigration at the Nassau Airport was computerized, and if he used his correct name, he'd be busted. Thus, he'd decided to reenter the U.S. at the computer-free Opa-Locka Airport near Miami. His exit point from the Bahamas would be Bimini—no US Customs or Immigration there.

Andrea was in Freeport waiting for him. Since he'd be held up in the Bahamas for a couple of days, who better than Andrea to be with?

He asked one of the skycaps at the airport for information. "Where can I get a flight to Freeport right away?"

"No Freeport flights until this evening, but you can rent a plane if you need to get there immediately."

"How much to rent the plane?"

"Follow me."

Vivian gave the skycap a huge tip of fifty US dollars after he finished arranging the trip to Freeport—a single-engine plane with only one pilot. With no co-pilot in case of emergencies, Vivian prayed all the way to Freeport. Within an hour, they landed. Vivian thanked God.

Andrea was waiting at the Cruise Ship Pier at two o'clock that afternoon. They hugged and kissed as they walked to the hotel that he'd booked in advance.

Vivian arranged another of those single-engined plane flights—to Bimini—the next morning. This flight was much smoother than the one from Freeport, and he and Andrea landed in South Bimini—an uninhabited stretch of land separated by water from North Bimini's population of five hundred, where they were headed later. On South Bimini, the planes and boats outnumbered the total population of North Bimini. An elderly man the natives called The Admiral owned the hotel.

There was no fresh water on the island—seawater was desalinated. The water from the shower was a rusty-brown color. Drinking water was shipped in on a daily basis from Miami. Vivian and Andrea had a hard time coping with the conditions in Bimini, but Vivian was on a mission: he needed a cocaine connection before he left Bimini, because he knew he wouldn't be able to travel out of the United States again.

Low and behold, he was introduced to a Bahamian—Tootsie Roll—who would sell him cocaine at an arranged low price, when Vivian returned to Miami. Phone numbers were exchanged, so Vivian was free to leave, having secured his connection. The next day, Vivian and Andrea boarded a seaplane headed for Opa-locka Airport. Only one immigration officer and one customs officer were on duty, and there were no computers—no hassle—so Vivian made it.

In mid-1985, commercial-grade marijuana sales started to slide, giving way to the new exotic marijuana—sensimilia. However, cocaine sales were on the rise. Most drug dealers who sold marijuana changed to cocaine, because cocaine packages were much smaller to transport compared to the bulky marijuana.

Vivian was an expert in commercial marijuana sales, but a novice to cocaine and sensimilia sales. Times had changed, and he had to make the transition. His marijuana houses in Detroit, New York, Washington and Oakland had to be closed down, and the guys who'd worked with him let go to find new sources of income.

Tony, on the other hand, found a lucrative cocaine market in Philadelphia and was earning big bucks after he ran out of Miami with his friends.

Vivian called up a friend—Carl—in Los Angeles for whom he'd done a favor about a year before. He asked Carl to rent an apartment or house for him in Los Angeles. Carl gladly obliged.

Earlier, Vivian had sent a Killo of cocaine to a guy from the Southside of Kingston—Tilly—who was now living in Los Angeles. Tilly had sold the cocaine but had sent only the principal cash back to Vivian, holding onto the profit. Vivian called Tilly from Miami.

"Where's my profit?"

"Jim Brown took away a trailer load of weed from us in Southside, and I'm taking pay now."

Vivian just wanted his money. "So … that means this is a robbery?"

Tilly didn't answer that question … kept on talking about the type of guns he had in Los Angeles … that no Tivoli Gardens man could enter Los Angeles.…

After Vivian hung up the phone, he said aloud to himself, "Bullshit, Tilly! I'm acomin' into Los Angeles by night … and when you wake up that morning … I'll be in your face."

After Carl rented the house for Vivian, Red Roy, Banana and Red Roy's friend, Vess, went out to L.A. by night. Vivian made contact with

Johnny—a guy who had strong family ties in Tivoli Gardens—and who hung around Tilly. Johnny was Vivian's spy in Tilly's organization. Johnny knew about the house that Carl rented for Vivian, so he was chosen to pick up Redy Roy, Vess and Banana at the airport. Red Roy was chosen to lead the charge in L.A., because he was well respected by many of the guys from the Southside community in Kingston.

The transition was smooth, and they were well received in L.A., even though Tilly had talked his crap on the phone to Vivian. Vivian was informed that everything was okay—that the guys were welcomed with open arms by the Southside guys, and they would also purchase cocaine from Vivian.

As Jim Brown once said, "In the presence of dog, you're a super dog … away from a dog, you're just an ordinary dog."

Thus … business started to roll in Los Angeles. Vivian was bringing in two kilos of coke at a time from the Bahamas as fast as he could, depending on how fast he could arrange for the girls to travel to the Bahamas—which wasn't easy. Consequently, sometimes, he had to buy the cocaine in Miami. Some of the cocaine from the Bahamas was sold in Miami … the rest he sent to Red Roy and his guys in Los Angeles, who opened a nickel-and-dime cocaine apartment, in addition to selling ounces to users on the Southside. The sales of nickel-and-dimes increased dramatically, selling several ounces a day—about ten thousand dollars' worth of revenue. Plans were made to open up four more nickel-and-dime cocaine apartments.

Others joined the Los Angeles organization to accommodate the expansion—Twin, Sugar Belly, and Colleen—all from Tivoli Gardens and neighboring communities.

The increased sales, though, caused more problems and confusion. Red Roy brought his girlfriend, Yvonne, from Florida to Los Angeles, and Vess complained to Vivian and Jim that Yvonne was treating them like kids. Of course, Vess didn't like that. When Red Roy made a trip to Miami to see his probation officer, Vivian and Jim spoke to him about the complaints, and Red Roy promised he would rectify the situation when he returned to L.A.

Red Roy noticed two girls—Debbie and Jane—at Vivian's house. Debbie was preparing to leave for L.A., too, but on a different flight than Red Roy—both reached L.A. about the same time. Jane was scheduled to catch a flight to Detroit with a half-kilo of cocaine to take to Vivian's and Tony's associate—Geego—who'd found a ready cocaine market in Detroit.

Both girls made successful deliveries.

After the cocaine arrived in Los Angeles, Red Roy paid a visit to the cocaine house run by Vivian's friend—Tan Tody. The other guys attended to their nickel-and-dime businesses. He talked with Tan Tody for a while then left.

About a half an hour later, Redy Roy appeared at the cocaine house again.

"Tan Tody, I left with your keys by accident. Here," Red Roy said.

Red Roy invited Tan Tody and the rest of the guys to a nightclub that night, but after two hours, Redy Roy hadn't shown up at the designated club. They all left. When Tan Tody reached home, he looked in the refrigerator to see if the cocaine was still there. The package was there, but he noticed the bag had been tampered with. When he weighed it, the cocaine was fifteen ounces short—thirty ounces instead of forty-five.

The next day, he called Vivian in Miami. "Bossie, Red Roy duplicated my house keys and entered my house when I wasn't here, and stole fifteen ounces of the cocaine. You don't have to worry about your money … I'll pay you from the house sales. I'm just telling you what happened."

"If that's the way Red Roy's acting, he can't talk to me again. He's on his own."

"Hold on, Bossie … Vess want to talk to you."

Before Vivian could say anything, he'd already handed Vess the phone.

"Mr. Blake, you heard what the boy Redy Roy did?"

"Yes … let me talk back to Tan Tody … *quickly*."

Vess gave Tan Tody the phone.

Vivian didn't like anyone usurping his authority. "Did I tell you I wanted to speak to anyone? Why you put Vess on the phone?"

"Sorry, Bossie … it won't happen again. I'll talk to you later."

The next day, Tan Tody called Vivian again … with *more* bad news

"Bossie, this is Tan Tody … I don't want you to be upset, but we just killed Red Roy and Evon down at the coke house."

"What?" Vivian could feel the heat rising, both astonishment and anger. "Don't you know killings are not good for business?"

"He disrespected me, man." Tan Tody tried to defend his actions, ending up with, "I'll call you back later."

Vivan held the phone at his ear for a few seconds before hanging up. "Damn! Just when business started going good, *they had to mess it up!*"

The bad news continued to roll in, with a call from Geego a few days later.

"Dave, an American guy who hung around me stole the half-kilo of cocaine."

"What the …" he sighed, letting his breath out slowly "… they say that bad luck is worst than witchcraft."

"The guy's dead anyway … I killed him."

"That don't help *me* none. His death can't bring back my cocaine," said Vivian angrily as he hung up the phone in Geego's ear.

Bugs, who Tony had been treating badly, invited Tony to send some girls to the Bahamas to pick up some coke for *Tony's* business. Tony's girls were busted, each with one kilo of cocaine, while leaving Nassau for New York, which led the police to the hotel where Law was staying with a girl. He had a kilo of cocaine in the room, so they both got busted, too.

With one thing after another, 1985 was Vivian's worst year ever in the drug business.

Being informed that Law was busted in Nassau, he had to put up bail for his friend.

Bugs's girlfriend called Vivian on his beeper, and he called her back.

"Bugs asked me to call you," the girl said. "He's asking if you could bail him out."

Vivian was angry at Bugs' request. "Tell him to call Tony. That's who he's working for ... *let Tony bail him out.*" He hung up the phone, slamming it on the girl's ear.

"What the fuck he thinks? He think I print money?" Vivian said to himself. "Call fucking Tony. He's got money, too. You're in jail because of *his* drugs—not *mine.*

Vivian was on a downhill slide, with one last iron in the fire. He had sent sixty thousand dollars with a friend who had gone to St. Georges College in Kingston with him when they were teenagers—Leyton—half-Chinese, slender, and very light complexioned, from the upper class neighborhoods in Kingston. Leyton promised to bring a five-hundred-pound-load of sensimilia marijuana to Miami.

Leyton arrived in Miami close to Christmas time, 1985. More bad news. He'd managed to bring only a hundred pounds of sensimilia for Vivian. Most of the marijuana was lost in Bimini due to theft.

I can recover my sixty thousand dollars I invested in the venture, at least. Something wrong had to happen, when I was involved. 1985 just ain't my year.

He'd lost almost a million dollars in twelve months. Earlier in the year,

Vivian suffered a one-hundred-pound loss when ten of his friends were arrested. The night before the arrests, he was hanging out with Andrea, snorting some cocaine at Graces' house—the girl Jim Brown later married in order to remain in the United States permanently.

After Vivian finished snorting, he fell asleep in Grace's den. The next morning, Andrea took his Benz and drove to the clothing design school she was attending, leaving her Bronco Jeep for Vivian. Law, Jim Brown, and his daughter Prudence came to Grace's house early that morning, because Jim had promised to remove a refrigerator for Grace. Law was to take some money to Jamaica for a business deal that very day, too.

They removed the refrigerator for Grace, and then Vivian decided to go home.

"I'm tired, Law. Drive the Bronco and drop me off at the house."

Vivian hopped into the Jeep beside Law, and Prudence rode with Law and Vivian, instead of with her father.

On the way to one of Vivian's houses, he said to Law, "You know what? Drop me by Eleanor's house. I need to get some sleep. I won't get no sleep if I go to the other house."

After Vivian ate something, he went to bed, but immediately remembered something he wanted to tell Law before he left for Jamaica, so he called the house.

The phone rang, and a strange voice answered the phone.

"Let me talk to Law."

"Law's busy. He can't come to the phone right now," said the strange voice.

This person sounds like a policeman. "Tell Law to come to the phone," he repeated.

"He's *busy!*"

Vivian was positive it was the police, and hung up. About two minutes later, his beeper went off, and he returned the call to a female friend.

"I see a police car with Jim Brown."

"What? Jim's arrested?"

"Yes, I just saw him in the police car, and your house at 205th St. is swarming with police."

From that arrest, Donovan Jones—a.k.a. Champs—was deported to Jamaica. On his return from Jamaica, he switched allegiance from Jim to Vivian's brother Tony's .

After receiving the hundred pounds of sensimilia, Vivian decided to head for New York. He'd already packed his marijuana and sent it up. After confirming that the marijuana reached New York safely, he boarded a plane for the same destination. While in the air, he contemplated. *If all goes well, I might just have to spend some time in New York and get my shit together. Too much bad luck in Miami at this present time. I just hope 1986 will be more prosperous for me.*

Two hundred thousand dollars in cash had been lost when it was confiscated from the girls leaving L.A.. He'd lost out on two loads of marijuana from Jamaica—an initial investment of almost two hundred thousand dollars—which would have yielded over eight hundred thousand dollars, and had lost about ten single kilos of cocaine at different locations. Plus, bailing people out of jail, and his arrest the night before Modeler got busted, all took their toll. 1985 was one year that Vivian would remember for the rest of his life, not to mention the senseless killings and shootings of '84.

Chapter 11: New York, 1986

Vivian spent a good Christmas with his family, who were now living in Mr. And Mrs. Williams' home in the Bronx. They had sold their house in Long Island, because Vivian was in Florida so much, plus it was easier to commute from the Bronx. Valerie had also resigned from her job with the New York City School Board and had opened a boutique on White Plains Road.

New York felt strange to Vivian—he'd been away so long. Tody was now in New York, also, and was staying with his girlfriend, Beverly, who was sharing a basement flat with her friend, Jackie Ramsay.

Vivian paid Tan Tody a visit at the basement flat, and was introduced to the two girls—Jackie was Teddy Paul's baby's mother, but Teddy Paul was in Los Angeles and the relationship ended. She was now seeing a young guy named Winston.

"Tody, I have some weed here in New York. I want to get sold. It is over by Kong's weed house, but they're joking that they don't have any sensimilia customers. And, I am worried if the marijuana stays at Kong's, he'll fuck it up somehow."

"You could bring the marijuana up here. I don't think it would be a problem with Jackie, but let me ask her anyway."

He walked away from Vivian and went to speak with her.

"She says it's cool … it won't be a problem."

While talking to Tan Tody, Vivian was eyeing Jackie Ramsay. Tan Tody laughed.

"You're looking at Jackie's sexy shape. The pussy in her jeans looks like it weighs about fifty pounds," he joked.

"Who's her man?"

"She have a kid she's seeing … name Winston … and Shower Chris comes around sometimes … but, your name Vivian, if you understand what I mean."

"So what happen to Teddy Paul?"

"Teddy and her not going together anymore."

Vivian studied Jackie's rear-end and smiled. While he was looking at her ass in the tight jeans, she turned around, caught him staring, and smiled at him invitingly.

"What are you staring at?"

"I'm just admiring your shape ... you look damn good there."

Jackie was fair complexioned, so it was easy for Vivian to see the blush of her face. She was blessed with bow legs, also, which made Vivian want her even more. It would also be better for business if his marijuana was going at her house. He wouldn't want another man to be strolling in where his marijuana was. *He* had to be the man of the house, so he made his move.

Early the next morning, he brought the two suitcases of marijuana to Jackie's basement flat. Tan Tody took the two suitcases from him and placed them in the room that he and Beverly shared.

"Jackie sleeping?"

"She still in bed, but I don't think she's asleep. You want me to wake her up for you?"

"No, I'll do it myself."

He knocked on Jackie's door.

"Who is it?"

"Vivian."

"Come in, door's not locked."

She was laying flat on her stomach under the sheet, and he could see the imprint of her big ass through it as she glanced at him and smiled.

"What do you want with me, Dave?"

"I'm gonna take you away from that man you got."

"Dave, I'm begging you to leave me alone ... I'm not your type of girl." She wasn't really serious ... just toying with him.

"Who's my type of girl?"

"I'm just ordinary Jackie, and your women are pedigree women."

Vivian sat on her bed, pinched her on her ass; she screamed and got out of bed.

"I'll be back soon." She held her nightgown around her body, then went to the bathroom, brushed her teeth, and returned with a big smile on her face.

"Leave me alone ... your wife's boutique is just around the corner ... I don't want any problems."

He laughed as she got back into bed. *This is my girl as of now.* He put his arm around her, and she tried to push him away, but Vivian wasn't convinced that she didn't want him to touch her.

Jackie and Beverly went to Connecticut that morning, leaving Tan Tody and Vivian at the basement flat. A strange thing started to happen to Vivian ... he was missing Jackie from the moment she left until she returned. Vivian was falling for a girl he thought wasn't his type—a typical rebel with a ghetto mentality, a shoplifter who kept more than one man at a time. She was the exact opposite of the women Vivian was attracted to. But, for a very long time, he'd never wanted a woman like he wanted Jackie, after they were together that morning.

He even started acting jealous—something unthinkable for Vivian. Everyone who heard of the relationship thought it was just a fling, but they were wrong.

Jackie and Beverly came back from Connecticut three days later. Vivian was happy to see her. She thought the relationship wouldn't work, but she was wrong. Vivian thought Jackie was a good girl at heart ... all she wanted was a good man who could bring her some respectability in the Jamaican community, and he thought he was the man to do that. He did it for almost three years.

With Jackie back, he went about the business of selling marijuana. Not knowing very many cash customers for sensimilia, he had to give it to a few customers on consignment, and many customers stiffed him. Vivian had come to a decision about which he contemplated for days—to move back to New York.

He had bailed Jim out of immigration, so he was safely in Miami, again. Vivian flew down to see him.

"Jim, I've decided to go back to New York to live ... ain't shit happening in Miami. I'm gonna see what I can get started in New York."

"I think you're making the right decision … both of us can't sit here with nothing to do."

Vivian left Jim, his sister Vivienne, and Eleanor behind. He was on a mission.

Weighing his options, he thought about Tony and his friends, who were already established in Philadelphia. He had no friends in Philadelphia, so he was at a dead end.

Then, a friend—Snowman—who used to take care of the Washington end of his business told Vivian that he had some friends in Philadelphia who could rent a house for them.

Vess and Tan Tody were also in New York, and Tan Tody made a suggestion to Vivian.

"Why we don't let Vess go down with Snowman so that they can find a Philadelphia house together?"

Vivian gave Vess fifteen hundred dollars and a bus ticket to go see Snowman in Washington, but Vess never reached Washington. He surfaced in Los Angeles with the dough.

Snowman decided to use one of his guys to go to Philadelphia when Vivian got a call from Tony at Jackie's house.

"Yeah, Dave … I heard that you and your Tivoli Gardens friends are planning on opening up coke houses in Philadelphia, but let me tell you something … anyone you send to Philadelphia, I'm going to send my friend to kill them. Philadelphia's mine."

Vivian didn't want a conflict, so he decided against opening a coke house in Philly, even though he'd always maintained that Tony's Shower Posse guys were a group of gun-toting kids—not killers. Yes, they killed people, but they were still punks as far as Vivian was concerned. Killings and shootings didn't go well with business and he was a businessman—all he wanted was make money.

One of Vivian's Cuban friends—Carlos—came up to New York, and asked Vivian to help him sell some cocaine and some marijuana. Due to Vivian's assistance, Jackie acquired a much better apartment on Baychester Avenue in the Bronx, and Vivian sold the marijuana from that apartment, which was rather inconvenient. Due to the slight shortage of marijuana in New York, the marijuana sold quickly.

Seeing how fast the marijuana was sold, Vivian decided to open a new marijuana apartment in the Bronx and enlisted the help of two of his customers who had helped sell Carlos' marijuana. As soon as the apartment was officially opened to the public, marijuana sales became brisk, and he ran out. In Miami, Jim and Eleanor bought, packed, and sent marijuana up to New York for Vivian and he was back in the driver's seat.

A two-bedroom apartment was rented in the Parkchester area of the Bronx to facilitate his nine-year-old son, Duane, and his recently born daughter—Dominique, his second child with Valerie. Vivian commuted between his wife's parents' house and the apartment.

Marijuana was in demand in New York, and Vivian found enough to supply his customers, but, in 1987, marijuana sales slowed. The city abounded with marijuana, and every drug dealer and customer was selling pound parcels. Consequently, in the summer of '87, Vivian had to abandon his marijuana apartment in the Bronx.

While Vivian was at his family's Parkchester apartment, a friend—Ricky—called him and nervously told him some bad news.

"Dave, I fired a shot accidentally through the floor of the apartment, and it went into the apartment below."

"Did anyone get hurt?"

"I don't think so."

But, that marked the end of Vivian's marijuana business in New York forever.

Tony, along with his army of Shower Posse gangsters, had taken a long vacation in Jamaica. He'd purchased permanent residency papers in England for the mere sum of seven thousand pounds and was also in possession of an English passport—so were most of his Shower Posse gangsters. He boasted about the fun he had in Jamaica, that it was the best time he'd ever had in his life, hoping to recoup his extravagant spending from business in Philadelphia—Philly was in ruins. His business had come to a complete halt due to the constant killings by members of his gang.

Before he had left for Jamaica, he left some money with one of his cousins—Paulette. With cash low and Philly out of bounds, he asked Paulette to bring ten thousand dollars to him. She came up with several excuses—telling him the section of the bank where her safety deposit box was located was under repair—but disappeared when she ran out of excuses. Tony started spreading the word that Paulette robbed him of *two hundred thousand dollars*.

Vivian ran into Paulette at a grocery, and Paulette told him it was only fifty thousand dollars she spent and that Tony was lying about the two hundred grand. After listening to Paulette, Vivian was convinced that Paulette was telling the truth, and talked her into speaking to Tony on the phone.

They used the phone at the grocery store. Paulette talked to Tony a few minutes, then handed the phone to Vivian.

"Tony want to talk to you."

"Where are you?" Tony asked.

"I'm at the grocery in Parkchester, below Macy's."

"I want to talk to her personally. Keep talking to her until I get there … I'm leaving now."

"Okay." He thought Paulette needed to face Tony and get it over with. There was nothing anyone could do to recover the fifty thousand. Vivian kept talking with Paulette, but after an hour passed, he decided to find out what was keeping Tony, for Parkchester was only twenty minutes away. Tony answered.

"What happen, aren't you coming?"

"Me and Cracker crashed my car on our way there, and the car's totaled. Lyn's witchcraft is strong … if I'd gotten a chance to reach you, I would have shot Paulette point blank in the face."

Vivian's mouth popped open as he hung up the phone, thinking, *Tony would have made me a party to his assassination plot of my own cousin. Fuck that! He would have a guest coming to dinner up in his fucking face and that would have been me, motherfucker!*

About twenty guys usually hung out at Tony's apartment with nothing to do but bullshit. He had visited Tony a couple of times at the Yonkers apartment, but stopped visiting because of the presence of so many guys. Vivian had known by then that the Feds wanted him, so he was taking no chances in an apartment that could be raided at any time, especially if the neighbors were observing traffic at the apartment, although no drugs were sold there. That week, though, Vivian needed to see his brother. Tony was having a problem closing the contract on a house he was buying in Jamaica and needed thirty thousand dollars—Vivian lent him the money.

When Vivian was on one of his infrequent visits to his favorite jewelry store in Brooklyn, he saw a familiar female face of the woman vacuuming the carpet. He walked up to her and whispered in her ear. "Hi, Evon." She turned, smiling.

"Who are you?"

"I'm Dave ... Eleanor's Dave."

She was taken aback, and her hand went up to her mouth to hide her shock. Evon was a friend of Eleanor's, and Vivian had seen her picture in Eleanor's album. Of course, as with every beautiful woman, he'd fallen in love with the picture. Now he was seeing the lady for the first time in the flesh.

"Wha ...what have I done to startle you like that, Evon?"

"You...you are Dave?" asked Evon in disbelief.

"Yes, in the flesh. You want to see identification?"

"No, I just...I just thought...never mind."

"You just thought what?" Vivian insisted with his cunning smile.

"You have far exceeded my expectation of *the* Dave."

"What? You thought that I was this big, black ugly monster of a man?"

"Something like that," she said while blushing.

"You really mean that, ah?"

"Yes."

Her childlike expression endeared her more to him.

"So tell me ... what do you think now? Did I pass the test?"

"With flying colors!"

The ice was broken and they spoke at length.

"Can I call you up sometime ... probably take you to dinner or movie perhaps?"

"If you can get my number you could ... but I ain't giving it to you," she teased.

"I'll get it ... don't worry. You'll hear from me soon," Vivian promised confidently.

That night, Vivian called Eleanor's house in Miami and spoke to her brother, Patrick. "Look in Eleanor's phone book when you get a chance and get Evon's number in New York for me. Call me back immediately when you get it."

It wasn't more than fifteen minutes when Patrick called back.

Evon wasn't home when Vivian called her that night, so he tried again in the morning.

"You see? I got your number."

"Who is this?"

"Your secret admirer ... Dave," he said confidently as she laughed aloud.

"How did you get my number?"

"It's for me to know and for you to find out." They spoke for about half-an-hour before they arranged a date at the movies.

Evon was loyal to Eleanor, so Vivian got nowhere with the relationship. Eventually, he stopped calling. Then, Eleanor and Vivian started having problems, because she began to believe the rumors being spread by her friends in Miami about Vivian and Jackie. Eleanor started nagging Vivian about it and even wanted him to move back to Miami.

"I spent three years with you in Miami, with my family living without me in New York. You were happy. Why can't you understand me being in New York with my family for a while? I think you're unfair." Vivian hung up, too angry to talk anymore. His relationship with Eleanor started to go downhill because of the constant nagging, so he refused to return her calls when she beeped him.

One day, Vivian got a beep from a strange New York number.

"Did somebody there beep me?" he asked when someone answered.

"Who's this? Dave?"

"Yeah, this is Dave. Who's this?"

"Remember me? Evon? Your woman in Miami asked me to beep you. Why haven't you been returning the woman's call?"

"Our relationship's finished. I'll continue to pay her bills, but that's it. I've already given her New York apartment to my brother. That's it for us. She don't think about no one but herself."

"That's sad."

"So, how are you, girl? Long time I haven't seen you." Vivian's spirits were definitely lifting as they talked for an hour, rekindling their social relationship.

They talked on the phone every day until their relationship grew more serious. Evon was dating her long-time boyfriend, Carl Armstrong, and Vivian told her she'd have to stop seeing Carl if their relationship developed.

Vivian booked a room at the La Guardia Marriott, because he wanted to be by himself. He checked in about one o'clock that day, had room service, and watched TV. Later on that night, he spoke to Evon on the phone,

"How are you, babes?"

"Where are you? I tried to reach you on your beeper but was unable to."

"I'm at the La Guardia Marriott."

"Who are you with at that hotel?" she asked seriously and he laughed.

"I'm here alone ... you wanna come over?"

"No, I can't. Carl will soon be here, but I could come see you in the morning if you'll still be there."

"I'll be here waiting for you in the morning. Let me give you my room number."

The next morning, bright and early, Evon was knocking on Vivian's hotel room door. When he saw her through the peephole, his face lit up.

She'd caught him still in bed, so he rushed to the bathroom, brushed his teeth, then dashed back under the covers. Evon sat by the dining table.

"Why don't you come into the bed with me?"

Evon started acting like a kid, blushing and fidgeting.

She looks like she's from the Orient. Such a perfect shape and the prettiest eyes on the planet. She was very light complexioned, cute and intelligent—a sexy thing that could represent Vivian—with an Associates Degree from a New York community college and working part-time as a ticketing agent for a major airline. She was perfect for Vivian if he could convince her to break it off with Carl.

Vivian ordered room service for a wonderful breakfast, and the start of a new affair. He loved what Evon represented and he was playing for keeps, so she agreed to let Carl go.

Word started getting around town that Vivian and Evon were seeing each other, and Eleanor was hopping mad, calling Evon all sorts of nasty names. When Jackie approached Vivian, he told her the truth, even though it hurt her.

"Yes, I'm seeing her now."

Jackie began spending more time around her friends in Brooklyn to ease the pain, and Vivian warned her of it when he took her to breakfast in Queens.

"I don't even want to hear Evon say someone looked at her nasty, you hear me? She's my woman now, and I love her."

"You really love her, Dave?"

"Yes, I love her."

Vivian lied to Jackie that morning—a man can't love two women at the same time.

He was still had deep feelings for Jackie, but the public's perception of Jackie Ramsay was haunting him. Evon was the perfect girl for him, and he knew he could eventually love her, once he had Jackie off his system. Jackie was still the greatest love of his life, but Evon's romance with Vivian was something out of a storybook.

While Vivian was at his apartment in New York, a call came from Jim brown's son, Jah T, who was in Jamaica.

"Boy, Dave. I can't understand Daddy."

"What's wrong?"

Jah T sighed for a moment, and then continued. "I heard that boy, Baskin, and Daddy talking as if they're friends ... Baskin was at Daddy's house a few days ago."

"You lying?"

"Nah, man ... it's true, and Daddy knows what Baskin and Jonathan did to me."

"I'll have to check with Bomber and find out what's up."

Vivian immediately dialed Jim Brown's number in Miami and got him on the phone.

"Bomber, what's up?

"Nothing much ... I'm just here."

"I just spoke to Jah T, and he's hopping mad about you having Baskin visit you at your house."

"What's wrong with Jah T? Baskin visiting me ... doesn't mean a thing."

"I think it does, Jim. Do you know the reason why I don't talk to Baskin or have anything to do with him?" He didn't wait for Jim's reply. "Because Jonathan, with Baskin's support, fired a shot through Jah T's baby's mother's window, and they damn well know that Jah T's family was in the apartment. They did it to intimidate Jah T. Someone could've been killed."

Jim Brown sighed then said, "So Tony's upset?"

"Not Tony alone ... even I am. Baskin and I are enemies only because of Jah T, and I'm not even his father, so can you imagine how it looks to him, you being friends with Baskin. How that feels to me and Jah T?" Vivian was beside himself trying to explain his logic to Jim.

Jim was silent for a while. "Boy, I wasn't looking at it that way, and even then, Baskin and I are not friends. He was just driving through my neighborhood, and I was standing outside my house ... he stopped. It's not like I invited him."

"So what's Baskin doing driving in that area? That's out of his way."

"I don't know ... beats me ... I just saw him appear."

The conversation ended after a while.

Baskin turning up in Jim Brown and Eleanor's neighborhood turned out not to be a coincidence. About a week later, while Eleanor was in New York, Jackie and Eleanor's son were playing in the front yard of her townhouse when two men with guns pounced on her and forced her inside the townhouse. Searching downstairs, they found twenty thousand dollars inside Eleanor's bedroom and stole it, along with all the jewelry that was inside the house.

"Don't come downstairs for the next half-an-hour," commanded one of the gunmen. She was too scared not to comply. When she heard the gunmen go through the front door, she went to the window that faced the street and peeked outside. To her surprise, she saw Baskin a distance away, signaling to the robbers.

Jackie told Vivian what had happened and he called Jim.

That boy, Baskin, sent his friends to rob Eleanor's house."

"What?" asked Jim, in disbelief.

"Yeah, when you saw Baskin in the neighborhood that day, he was casing out Eleanor's house."

Jim had a talk with Baskin who later phoned Vivian at the New York apartment.

"I don't know anything about any robbery. They're telling lies on me."

"Eyewitness saw you outside … down the block," said Vivian calmly. They spoke for a few minutes with Baskin trying in vain to convince Vivian he had nothing to do with the robbery.

About a week after the robbery, Champs called Vivian.

"I heard about the robbery at Eleanor's house. Baskin should die. I have nothing to do with any man from Tivoli Gardens right now," he continued, as Vivian listened carefully. "I got ten pounds of weed, and I'm calling you to see if you could sell it for me." Champs continued before Vivian could respond. "And, Dave, Jim Brown is a fucked-up person, too."

Champs could've said anything but that. "If you want me to sell the weed for you, I will. You don't have to say anything about Jim Brown … Jim Brown's *my friend*."

Champs was silent. He was a member of Tony's Shower Posse Gang and had turned against Jim Brown.

A few months before that call from Champs, a shooting incident took place, the reason being that Vivian's friends, Kirk and Preps, were a cause for sore eyes within Tony's gang. Together, Kirk and Preps were more dangerous and cruel than the whole combined Shower Posse. Tony wanted their allegiance, but Kirk and Preps were dedicated to one man, and one man only—Vivian—the only one who could talk to them and make them listen.

While Vivian was on one of his vacations in Jamaica, Champs tried to talk to Kirk and Preps about something they'd done, and Preps muttered, "Pussy! Only Dave can talk to us. You can't talk to us about *shit*."

Kirk and Preps had guns poised, ready to use them.

Champs complained to Jim that Kirk and Preps disrespected him in the presence of everyone.

Jim then called Vivian in Jamaica. "Oh, Dave … I want you to talk to your two *made* friends, Kirk and Preps. They disrespected Champs terribly today, and Champs is upset."

Vivian started laughing. "Jim, those kids'll listen to you, man. You know that. You don't have to call me to tell me such nonsense."

Jim laughed with Vivian. "Boy, Champs cried—they dissed him real bad."

With Champs in the Shower Posse camp, the hatred for Kirk and Preps intensified, so Tony and Champs planned a night assault on them. Vivian was in Miami and happened to call Law's son—Patrick—in the Bronx.

Patrick told him, "Dave … Kong just told me that Tony, Champs and the rest of the Shower youths are on their way to Brooklyn to kill Preps and Kirk." Realizing he was opening a can of worms by telling Vivian that, he continued to talk to him about other things.

Patrick was Law's eldest son—a tall, slender and dark complexioned guy who was an easy-going kid—never mixed up in any gang banging. Kong talked too much, and *that's* how Patrick came by this information.

Vivian cut the conversation short. *I'll not allow Tony and his Shower Posse punks to murder Kirk and Preps*. He dialed Kirk and Preps' number in Brooklyn.

"Kirk, this is Dave. Listen up. Tony and Champs are leading a group of their friends to kill you and Preps at the apartment, so be on the lookout. They're on their way right this minute."

"What the ... talk to you later," the call ended abruptly.

Kirk told Preps and the other guys in the apartment about the planned attack. Everyone made sure their guns were loaded and they had extra magazines. They went outside the apartment and took position. Some went to the roof; some branched out in the vicinity of the apartment building. The area was desolate, with many abandoned buildings, and at night, the only people moving about were the junkies looking for their next fixes.

Finally, Tony, Champs and the rest of the gangsters arrived. They thought they had Kirk and Preps trapped —a surprise attack. They thought Kirk and Preps would be dead before they could realize what had happened, but they were wrong.

Kirk, Preps, and their other friends waited until Tony and his friends were close to the building entrance, then opened fire.

The opposition was caught off-guard. They scampered in all directions in a panic, not even remembering they had guns. When the smoke cleared, the two main instigators, Tony and Champs, had gunshot wounds to their feet.

Vivian spoke to Tony at his apartment in Yonkers the next day.

"Boy, Kirk and Preps surprised us when we thought we were surprising them."

"Yeah?" said Vivian, as if he didn't know.

"Champs and I were shot in the foot. The wounds aren't bad, though ... they don't require hospital treatment."

Vivian was so happy that his brother wasn't badly hurt. After he hung up the phone, he smiled to himself and said, *to every action there is always a reaction. Remember that, Tony.* If he hadn't called Kirk, there could've been about ten or more dead bodies in Kirk's and Preps' apartment. Vivian knew most of the Shower Posse members were punks, but Champs—commonly called "Board-Heart" by himself and Jim Brown—had no feelings for anyone. He would kill his mother if he had to. Things could have been very messy. Champs would have taken pleasure in killing everyone in the apartment with no remorse shown or given.

All is well that ends well. No lives were lost—just two minor injuries.

After the shooting, Kirk called Vivian. "Boy, Dave. I could've killed Tony ... he was right in front of my nozzle ... but I let him run past and just fired some shots over his head." Then he laughed out loud. "Dave, Tony can *run*. That nigga ran faster that Donald Quarry tonight. *I swear.*" He laughed until it wore him out, and then became serious. "I wanted to kill that boy, Champs, but he ran so *fast. Shit! I* couldn't even catch him."

Still laughing, he hung up the phone.

The year 1988 started badly for the Shower Posse organization. While watching TV at his New York apartment, Vivian was shocked out of his wits to see a picture of Kirk flashing across the screen.

"Kirk Bruce, a member of the notorious Jamaican gang known as the Shower Posse, is wanted for the murders of five Jamaican drug dealers in a small apartment in the nation's capital of Washington DC" said a television reporter.

"Jesus Christ!" Vivian shouted aloud. He sat stupefied, riveted to the news bulletin.

Kirk had arrived in New York from Jamaica in late 1982 or early 1983—one of Vivian's closest associates. On his arrival from Jamaica, he'd stayed in one of Vivian's drug houses in New York with Kong and Valerie's brother, Anthony Williams—a.k.a. Dumpling—and Kirk and Dumpling became very close friends. One was never seen without the other. A few months later, another Shower Posse member and close friend of Kirk's arrived in New York from Jamaica—Preps. Kirk,

Dumpling, and Preps became an inseparable trio. Dumpling—a psychotic who fired bullets instead of words—was reared by different Jamaican posse members in the Bronx.

Dumpling was also nicknamed Mr. Four-five—donned on him by a Bronx police officer—by his close friends, because he always carried a .45 automatic pistol. After Dumpling's fourth arrest, the police officer had examined his rap sheet and realized that Dumpling used a .45 automatic in all four cases.

One Saturday night, Dumpling, Kirk, and Preps went to a dance at a Jamaican nightclub, arriving after several other Shower Posse members were already there. They noticed that off-duty New York police officers were employed by the dance promoter to search all the patrons entering the premises. They therefore left their pistols in their cars. Dumpling wasn't comfortable without his gun, so he discussed an idea with Kirk and Preps. In a matter of minutes, Preps was outside, attaching guns to a long cord that Dumpling extended from a window in the rear of the nightclub. It didn't take long for the news of the guns to be relayed to the rest of the Shower Posse members. Shortly, every one of the Shower Posse members had a gun on his person—inside the club.

Many members of the Shower Posse were in the men's room snorting cocaine, while Dumpling, Kirk and Preps remained in the hallway doing the same. Dumpling got high on the coke and was enjoying the Reggae music. When the DJ spinning the turntable selected a popular Jamaican song known as *Sonia*, recorded by a popular Jamaican singer—Cocoa Tea—also regarded as the Shower Posse Anthem, Dumpling overreacted and pulled his automatic, firing several shots into the ceiling.

"Shower!" Dumpling shouted, in a rollicking, jovial, drug-induced display.

The patrons in the nightclub were not so jovial, though, and chaos immediately broke out, people running and trampling over each other. The off-duty officers panicked, too, and one of them ran into the men's room, gun in hand. Ten Shower Posse members' guns stared back at him.

In shocked disbelief he said, "It wasn't me," and fainted. The gang couldn't hold back their laughter at the sight of the off-duty office passing out from fright. They walked out of the bathroom, leaving the officer on the floor with his gun still in his hand.

Dumpling, Kirk, and Preps made a hasty departure from the nightclub, but when they heard police sirens in the distance, they disbursed in all directions. With the sounds of the sirens nearing, Dumpling ran faster, gun still in hand. Running about fifty yards in front of Dumpling was a white man with a gun in his hand, too—one of the off-duty officers hired to patrol the club.

When the frightened officer turned around, he saw Dumpling behind him, and accelerated like a space rocket, thinking that Dumpling was chasing him. Dumpling almost died of laughter—he was leaving the crime scene, just like the officer.

In 1985, tragedy struck. Dumpling had become one of the most feared members of the Shower Posse, and was also a member of the hit squad organized to assassinate thirty members of Tony's controlling section of the Shower Posse—the ones committing the senseless shootings in New York and Miami. This was, in effect, shining the spotlight on Vivian, highlighting his alleged leadership of the Shower Posse.

Dumpling, accompanied by Smokey, was on his way to visit some guys at an apartment in the Bronx who owed Dumpling some money. When they were told Dumpling was coming, they feared that Dumpling would end up killing them, because they didn't have the money. They devised a plan.

When Dumpling and Smokey stepped out of their car and walked toward the apartment building, a hail of gunfire erupted from the roof. Dumpling was hit in his neck, and Smokey took a bullet in the leg. Dumpling was rushed to the hospital, but everyone knew he couldn't make it. He died.

Vivian was awakened by a phone call at his Miami home.

"Dumpling's dead," Kong informed him. "They ambushed him by the Tremont Avenue area. I heard from a source that three guys were involved. One of the guys was to testify at my murder trial—the one who didn't show up for the trial."

Vivian took a deep breath. He'd not only lost the brother of his wife, and the uncle of his son, but one of his best friends.

The following day, Vivian spoke to his in-laws and his wife. "I won't be coming to the funeral … I want to remember Dumpling as I saw him last—alive and jovial. I don't want to have a memory of him as a corpse."

The funeral was held the following Saturday, and Kirk and Preps didn't attend, either. They had a different plan in mind. They discovered the names of three guys involved in Dumpling's murder, and while Dumpling's funeral was in progress, Kirk and Preps went on the hunt for the killer.

Two Jamaican males exited from an apartment building in the Bronx. As they were on their way down the stairs, they heard a voice behind them.

"Dumpling say to tell you, 'Hi!'"

The two spun around and found themselves looking down the barrels of two automatics. Kirk and Preps opened fire, spraying their bodies with bullets. Walking down to the two guys who were lying on the landing, bleeding, Kirk proceeded to put his pistol to the head of one of the guys.

"No!" screamed the guy, as Kirk squeezed the trigger again, splattering brain fragments and blood all over the landing. Kirk put his pistol to the other guy's head, and fired—his head opened up like a sardine can as the impact of Kirk's bullet propelled his right eye to the back of his head.

"Two down—one to go," said Kirk as he smiled. Both left the scene of the crime.

For Kirk, the action was a gift to his friend, Dumpling, on the day he was being buried.

It wasn't long before they received information on the whereabouts of the third guy involved in Dumpling's murder. Equipped with an address, they climbed the stairs to the third floor, and Kirk looked around. Preps was beside him with a bottle filled with gasoline.

"You light the front door, and we'll go around to the back of the building as this pussy tries to escape," whispered Kirk.

Preps nodded his approval, but noticed that the apartment door was ajar, as Kirk was about to walk away. Preps motioned for Kirk to look.

"Door's open," Preps whispered, and they both smiled.

Kirk used a gloved left hand and pushed the door open softly. To his surprise, he was staring at Dumpling's murderer stretched out on his back, fast asleep and mouth wide open, on the sofa. *How could things be so easy*, Kirk thought. He tiptoed into the apartment, with Preps behind. They both had their pistols cocked, ready to fire. Smiling, Kirk beckoned to Preps to check the only bedroom. Facing Dumpling's murderer, he stuck his automatic pistol inside the guy's opened mouth.

His eyes immediately opened, and a muffled scream escaped.

"You piece of shit!" Kirk laughed as he squeezed the trigger.

His brains splayed out—all over the sofa and the wall.

Preps rushed back to the living room from the bedroom. "Nobody else in the apartment. Let me get a piece of this motherfucker." He bared his teeth in a sinister sneer, and smiled the smile of a killer about to enjoy his craft. Placing his gun to the head, he fired twice, splattering more brain matter throughout the room. *A job well done.*

Kirk and Preps were like two killing machines in 1985, as if killing were a constant companion they took with them wherever they went.

In Fort Lauderdale 1985, Kirk and Preps attended one of the many dances at the Fireman's Hall on State Road 7, right across the street from a sheriff's office. Eleanor's brother—Patrick Dodd, who was staying at Eleanor's house—had just arrived from Jamaica. Vivian had taken Patrick to one of the houses where Kirk, Prep and some of the other guys had taken up residence. Kirk, Preps, Michael Murray —a.k.a. Geego—Food Head and a few other guys were getting ready to go to the dance, and because Vivian wasn't interested in dancing, Patrick opted to go along with the guys.

Some people who originated in Montego Bay, Jamaica were promoting the dance. Kirk, Preps, Patrick, Geego and Food Head were all enjoying themselves at the dance when Food Head excused himself and went outside to talk to a girlfriend. The guys had only brought two pistols with them because they were not expecting any trouble—Kirk had one and so did Food Head. The dance was proceeding on a good note until an altercation erupted between two rival posse members from Montego Bay, the argument leading to guns being drawn by the two individuals. Instinctively, the crowd parted in panic, then shots started to rain in the dancehall. Kirk pulled his pistol as Preps stood behind him.

"What the fuck's going on?

Shots whizzed around them, the smell of cordite filling their nostrils. Preps and Kirk spotted a guy firing a chrome-plated .357 Magnum. Kirk stealthily raised his weapon, Preps enabling him by holding onto his hand, so that Kirk could master a steady aim. Kirk squeezed his trigger, shooting the guy several times and killing him. Shots rained from another section of the hall toward Kirk and Preps, and without hesitation, Kirk opened fire in the direction of the gunfire, with Preps guiding his hand. They hit several patrons.

Outside, Food Head heard the shots. Worried that his friends were in danger, he pulled his own pistol and rushed to the dancehall's entrance, opening fire to clear a path.

"Shower! Shower!" he shouted, remaining at his station.

Kirk and the guys heard Food Head calling out the posse's cry.

"Shower! Shower!" Kirk responded, giving Food Head his location.

"I'm holding off the door. Make your way to the door!" Food Head shouted to Kirk.

Kirk responded by opening up another burst of fire in the direction of the shots fired earlier, and he, Patrick, Preps and Geego headed toward the entrance. Safely outside the Fireman's Hall, they saw a sheriff's car parked across the street, but the sheriff was nowhere to be found. He'd run for cover after hearing the barrage of gunfire, trying to call for assistance from the neighboring precinct.

The year was 1986. Kirk, Preps, and two friends of Vivian's—Tan-Tody and Porter—were occupying a crack house Vivian had seized from a Jamaican drug dealer, known as Twin, as repayment of a cocaine debt. The crack house was located on Church Avenue between East 51st and 52nd Streets in Brooklyn.

Preps was fucking up, becoming hooked on crack and slowly taking Kirk down with him. Needless to say, this was pissing Vivian off and Preps was marked with a black "X," deep inside his mind. To Vivian, Kirk was worth saving from the destructive claws of crack cocaine.

Receiving a phone call from Tan-Tody one night, Vivian took it.

"Boss, can't you speak to Kirk and Preps? Preps is encouraging Kirk to smoke all of the cocaine we have in the drug house, and we can't make any money."

"So why you calling *me* for? If you think that Preps is your problem, aren't you man enough to deal with your own problem? I gave you the entire house … I'm out of it. *Through. Kapute!*"

"Boss, I know how to deal with the problem." There was resolve in Tan-Tody's voice.

"Nah, I couldn't stand by and see anyone hurt them … *especially* Kirk," Vivian jumped in to dissuade Tan Tody's mind from continuing the plan.

"Boss, I'm fed up with them … trust me … Preps is leading Kirk astray, as if he's controlling Kirk's mind."

"All right, I'll talk to Kirk," said Vivian, hanging up and thinking, *problems … always problems.*

Dialing from his New York apartment, Vivian got Kirk on the line and attacked the problem from a psychological point of view. He found out that Preps was really in control of Kirk's mind, as if Kirk were a zombie. Even the Brooklyn apartment Vivian had personally given to Kirk was controlled by Preps. Preps took over the only bedroom in the apartment, and Kirk and Michelle—his baby's mother—were sleeping in the living room on the sofa.

Weeks went by and nothing changed, so, once again Tan-Tody called Vivian.

"Boss, I can't take it no more. I'm fed up with Kirk and Preps!"

Vivian couldn't believe the whining he was hearing. "Why the fuck don't you tell them to leave your shit alone? You know what? I think you're fucking scared shitless of the two kids," he continued, laughing at Tan Tody.

Tan-Tody tried to deny that he feared Kirk and Preps, but Vivian felt otherwise.

"All right, I'll call Jim in Miami and get his opinion."

That night, Vivian called Jim and told him of the problem with Tan-Tody, Kirk and Preps.

Jim was upset. "That little boy Preps ... he can't behave himself. He should know by now how we deal with unruly kids. We spank them. Send them down to Miami, I'll remind them that they're still little kids." He laughed, but wanted to break their legs instead.

"By no means should anything happen to Kirk," Vivian cautioned his friend. "He's a good kid ... just needs some guidance."

Vivian managed to talk Kirk and Preps into boarding a plane for Miami, telling them that Jim Brown had some problem and needed help in terms of firepower. Even though it was a lie, what better way to entice them than setting before them their favorite pastime—firing guns. Vivian arranged for Patrick to pick up Kirk and Preps from the Miami International Airport and take them to Jim's house.

Tan-Tody's relaxing celebration of ridding himself of Kirk and Preps didn't last very long. That night, packaging some crack cocaine, he felt a stick thrust into his side—someone from behind. Spinning around, his eyes widened in horror. Tan-Tody was looking in the eyes of Kirk and Preps. "How you all come back so quickly?"

He scampered out of the crack house, running a fair distance before he stopped at a phone booth and dialed Vivian's phone number in the Bronx.

"Boss, what's *really* going on?"

"What do you mean?"

"Kirk and Preps are back at the house." Tan-Tody could no longer control his nervousness.

Vivian started laughing.

"Boss, this is not a laughing matter. I thought I was *dead*."

Vivian only laughed more loudly, finding much hilarity in Tan Tody's schoolboy's fright.

"Boss, I'm not going back into that house. Those two little pieces of shit *enjoy* killing, and I'm not gonna be their next victim. They said that Beardy was surprised to see them in Miami and assured them that Jim had no problem in Miami...."

Vivian stopped laughing then. "What?"

As Kirk slipped deeper into the crack cocaine addiction, Vivian spoke less and less to him. Finally, he had to cut all communication to Kirk, because nothing could help. When Kirk was arrested for possession of a firearm, he was sent to prison for two years. Vivian heard of Kirk's arrest and sentence and thought it was a blessing in disguise. Maybe Kirk would be able to kick the addiction in prison.

In 1987, Snowman was in charge of distribution for the cocaine and marijuana businesses in the Washington DC and Maryland areas. While Vivian and Jim were in DC with Vivian's close friends, Earl and Stretch, one of Jim's girlfriends—Brownie—and her son Ricky came to Washington to visit with him, and Jim made sure that Ricky stayed close to him so that he wouldn't stray. While Vivian and Jim were on a trip to Los Angeles to pick up some cocaine, Vivian cautioned Ricky not to venture too far from the house—they'd be back in two days. Ricky was left in the hands of Snowman and Stretch.

Snowman had been given a crack house by a girlfriend—Sunshine—which he passed on to Stretch. The day after Stretch and Snowman were given the responsibility for watching Ricky, Stretch decided to have Ricky accompany him to the crack house. Not knowing Ricky that wasn't supposed to handle any guns, Stretch gave Ricky the gun Vivian had left with him.

Ricky tucked the gun in his waistband, as if it was something he was accustomed to doing—which he wasn't. He knew, without a doubt, if Vivian ever saw him with a gun, he would've slapped him so hard he'd probably have shit his pants.

Stretch, on the other hand, having seen Ricky with Vivian all the time, thought Ricky was a gunman, and Ricky made him none the wiser.

Arriving at the crack house, Stretch, with Ricky in tow, was surprised to see some other guys at the place.

"What the fuck are you guys doing here?"

"Snowman gave us this house."

"Snowman couldn't give you guys the house, 'cause he gave it to me. And, as a matter of fact, I'm not arguing with you guys. *Get the fuck outta here.*"

The guys decided they weren't leaving, so Ricky pulled the gun and pointed it at the main guy acting stubborn.

"Get the fuck out of here!" Ricky demanded as if he knew what he was doing, pointing the gun at the guy, ready to fire.

"That's not necessary, Boss, I'm leaving."

Ricky lowered his gun, which was a big mistake, but understandable, for Ricky was no gunman. Ricky didn't search the guys he'd pulled the gun on—a second, and fatal mistake. As Ricky put the pistol way and turned around, the guy Ricky threatened pulled a gun, and shot Ricky in the back. The guy ran, never to be seen again.

Ricky, however, was dead—instantly.

About ten minutes after Vivian arrived from the airport, there was a knock on his door at his DC apartment. It was his Earl, who was wearing a bandana handkerchief tied around his head, and a terribly sad look about his face.

"Damn, man! Damn!"

"What's wrong?" Instinctively, Vivian was immediately suspicious.

"Damn! I can't believe this shit."

Somehow Vivian felt he knew what Earl couldn't say. "It's Ricky … he's dead," said Vivian. But Earl still couldn't spell it out. Finally, he told Vivian what he'd heard.

Vivian was in a daze … confused … unable to think clearly.

"What the fuck am I going to tell his mother? How do you tell a mother that her son was just murdered! *A son who's not a criminal. Tell me!*" Vivian moaned in agony, "how do I explain this? *How* do I tell Jim Brown that his son just got murdered? Tell me … is there any easy way to this?"

Earl had no answer to Vivian's questions.

The next morning, Vivian stood by the telephone for four hours, agonizing over the phone call he had to make. Ricky's mother, Brownie, was in Jamaica. *How am I going to find the courage?*

Finally, he called. Brownie fainted. Vivian held the phone for ten minutes before her daughter, Mizan, came to the phone.

The least he could do was to send airline tickets for Brownie and two of Ricky's aunts, who came to DC to claim Ricky's body and take his body back with them to Jamaica.

That period of Vivian's life was tough, but he was determined to get to the bottom of what took place. Snowman and Stretch didn't intentionally caused Ricky's death, but their mistakes led to it, and Vivian blamed them. Snowman should never have given the crack house to two other people, and Stretch should never have taken Ricky with him, or been stupid enough to give him a gun.

The irony of it all, was that one of Jim Brown's loyal soldiers—Porter—was a friend of the guy who killed Ricky, and was in the same clique—headed by one of Vivian's customers, a crippled Dreadlocks Rastafarian, known as Gillie-Dred—the assassin. He told Vivian everything that had happened, that it was a big misunderstanding, and Vivian truly believed what Gillie-Dread said. *A terrible pity that a life was lost.*

But, that was a part of life, Vivian thought. One thing for certain, he knew that Porter would never condone the killing of a kid, especially one who was like a son to Jim and himself.

Jim Brown accepted Porter's word for it.

When Vivian communicated with Gillie-Dread the next day, he acknowledged, "It's a big misunderstanding, Gillie. Let's put it behind us and go on about our business as usual."

Gillie-Dread was silent on the other end of the phone for a while, and then he sighed. "Boss, no disrespect intended to you, but it can't be business as usual. This mention of the kid being Jim Brown's kid worries me. I mean no disrespect, Boss, but I'll stay as far away from the Jim Brown thing as I possibly can."

Vivian never saw Gillie-Dread again. A few weeks later, Ricky's killer was featured on the television program *America's Most Wanted.*

The narrator of the program stated that he was wanted for the murder of Ricky, the son of one of the Jamaican Shower Posse's most notorious leaders, Lester Lloyd Coke—a.k.a. Jim Brown.

After Ricky's death, Vivian lost interest in Washington DC and went back to New York. He had his eye on Virginia Beach, Virginia.

Released from prison in 1988, Kirk headed to Washington DC to see a close friend—Gillie-Dread. He'd kept close contact with him while he was in prison. Kirk's sidekick, Preps was murdered while Kirk was in prison by a kid he'd under estimated. The kid blew his brain out in a dispute in Brooklyn, at the corner of Lincoln and Troy Avenue. Kirk hooked up with a long-time friend of his known as Carl Dunstan and took Carl with him to Washington DC, where they joined in the Gillie-Dread and Porter's clique.

Kirk was doing okay for a while, making money with Gillie-Dread, but then he started on the crack again. With Kirk smoking crack, Gillie-Dread and Porter began to feel uncomfortable around him, but they were both too scared to tell him to go.

They began to formulate an alternative plan—an assassination of Kirk and Carl at one of their crack houses, arranged by Gillie-Dread and Porter.

Carl, who was having a private affair with Gillie-Dread's girlfriend, got wind of the plot by way of the girl. Gillie-Dread was a cripple from his waist down and was unable to have sex with his girlfriend, so Carl was happy to render that service to her. Not wanting her lover to die, the girl told Carl of the plot to assassinate them.

Carl informed Kirk of the assassination plot and Kirk did nothing but laugh. That same evening, they went to visit Gillie-Dread and Porter at a stash house of Gillie-Dread's. He, Porter, three other guys and Gillie's girlfriend were there. Gillie-Dread and Porter were as courteous as before, since it wasn't the house that they'd planned to use for the assassination.

Gillie-Dread and the guys were all smoking marijuana from a huge smoke pipe, known as a *chilum* pipe in Jamaica. When it came time for Porter's turn, he puffed hard ... then harder ... then inhaled ... then released a burst of smoke that left the living room foggy. When the smoke cleared, Porter's eyes widened—he was looking down the barrel of Kirk's automatic pistol. Carl covered the other three guys, not paying much attention to the girl—after all, he was her lover—and because Gillie-Dread was cripple, Kirk only watched him through the corner of his eye.

"I heard about your plan to kill me, Porter … you and the Dreadlock," Kirk calmly signed their fate.

"No, Kirk, I wouldn't do that," Porter proclaimed, trying to buy time. "We are Shower Posse members … we are *one!*"

Kirk laughed the laugh of a killer about to score, and then his pistol fired. A single shot penetrated Porter's face, exiting through the back of his head, exploding marrow that stuck on the living room wall.

Kirk walked over to Gillie-Dread with his gun pointing at his head.

"No, Kirk!" screamed Gillie-Dread.

"You're a dead pussy!" Again Kirk's pistol exploded another skull, killing Gillie-Dread instantly.

Carl had his pistol on the other three guys, tears running down their faces as they begged for their lives.

Kirk calculatingly reached over and systematically fired three shots in succession—first head, second head, third head. When he was done, Carl pumped one shot each into the three guys' heads.

"Where the fuck's the girl? Kirk bellowed angrily at Carl. "You let the fucking bitch escape just because you were fucking her?"

"She won't say anything, Kirk. Trust me on that one."

"What the fuck are you talking about? You think that fucking bitch can stand police interrogation?" Kirk looked around angrily. "Let's go! We'll talk about this later."

They left, leaving the four dead—gangland style.

Kirk and Carl's pictures were shown on TV and in the newspapers every day. It wasn't long before Carl was cornered in a basement in Brooklyn and arrested. A few days later, Carl led the police to where Kirk was hiding.

The trial was swift. Carl, along with Gillie's girlfriend, turned State's evidence; Kirk Bruce was sentenced to two life sentences without parole. Carl Dunstan received less time for his testimony against Kirk.

Kirk Bruce later confessed to the federal agents that he'd murdered 103 people in his lifetime. The agents investigated the claim and were able to confirm eighty-seven of the murders—sixteen of the bodies were never found.

Back to business again, after the lay-off from Washington DC, Vivian sent a friend—Jack—to a lucrative market in Virginia Beach with a kilo of cocaine, but bad luck haunted Vivian. Jack called him in New York from Virginia.

"Yo, Dave. They stole a half-kilo of the cocaine from where we stashed it, man. I can't find out who took it. What am I to do?"

"What about the other half key?"

"I've got it right here with me. I was planning to take a flight up with it tomorrow."

"Isn't there anyone who would buy the complete half-kilo?"

"Yeah, there's a guy here right now, but he only has half the cash."

"When could he pay the rest?"

"You wanna talk to him?" Jack was eager to have the deal completed.

"Sure, let me talk to him."

"Yeah, man, what's up?" came from the potential customer.

Vivian detected from the accent that it was an American. "I hear that you wanna take the whole shit, yo."

"Yeah, man, but my money ain't correct yet."

"When would you be ready?"

"In about two to three days," said the American.

Vivian detected honesty in his voice and he thought for a few seconds. "What's your name, man?"

"Cal," he said honestly.

"You got a number, address and shit?"

"Sure, man, you want it?"

"Yeah, give it to me."

Cal gave Vivian his address, two phone numbers and his beeper number; Vivian wrote them down.

"I'm gonna give you the half-kilo of cocaine ... give my man the cash you got, and within three days, you bring the rest to him, is that clear?"

"All right, man. Yeah, I'll set you straight ... don't worry about a thing."

Vivian wasn't worried. He felt Cal's vibrations and knew he was an honest guy.

Within two days, Cal brought eight thousand dollars to Jack, and Jack called Vivian while Cal was with him.

"Yo, Dave. Everything's okay. Cal just brought the rest of the cash. I'll be in New York by this afternoon," said Jack happily.

"Is he there?"

"Yeah, you wanna talk to him?"

"Yeah, put him on the phone."

"What's up, boss man?" The sound of happiness rang through Cal's voice.

"Call me Dave, Cal."

"Yeah, Dave."

"Good looking out, Cal. Like the way you do business ... you straight. I'll be in touch with you soon."

"You do that, man, I'll be listening for ya."

With Jack arriving in New York, and not planning to return to Virginia, Vivian began to plot his next move. *I can't sit here like this not doing anything. I've got to start working again.* The cogs of his mind started wheeling and chugging. *What if this guy Cal can move a kilogram of cocaine a week? That could be a start ... pay the bills with lots of cash to spare. I pay fifteen thousand including expenses, per kilo, and the sale price in Virginia is thirty grand, minimum. Good start,* he thought.

Vivian picked up his phone and dialed Cal's house number. "What's up, Cal?"

"Hey, what's up?" They talked casually for a few minutes, each trying to see if they could do business together.

The time for business was at hand. "Cal, do you need anything?"

"Man, I could do with a half-kilo now, man."

"You got the cash for the half?"

"Yeah, man."

"What you think, Cal? You think you can move a kilo in a week?"

"Yo, I've never done it, but I sure can try."

That was good enough for Vivian—a man willing to try. Even if it took Cal two weeks to sell a kilogram, he would still be making at least fifteen thousand dollars every two weeks, and that was better than what most people made in a year.

"I'll see you tomorrow, Cal. Just listen up for me."

The next day, Vivian flew to Norfolk, Virginia and had a girl—Jean—take the bus from New York to Virginia Beach. The night before, he'd checked out the hotel in Virginia Beach, switching to the Plaza Hotel on Mount Trashmore, and told Jean where to meet him. According to Vivian's directions, Jean brought a kilogram of cocaine and his pistol by way of the Greyhound.

Everything went like clockwork. Vivian was in the lobby waiting for Jean when she promptly reached the hotel. He'd instructed her not to speak to him in the lobby—"Just book a room, and I'll follow you there."

She reached her room without a hitch, and he trailed her to the elevator. Jean stayed in the room with the cocaine, while Vivian took his gun from her, and concealed it within the confines of his room.

He called Cal, and within fifteen minutes, Cal was in Vivian's room, toting sixteen thousand dollars. First things first, Vivian counted the money.

"Cal, how soon could you give me money for the next half if I gave you a kilo of cocaine?"

"I don't really know, but I'll try my best to give you the cash by the end of this week ... today's Monday ... or very early next week at the latest."

Vivian liked Cal's sincerity. *Good enough*, he thought. He called Jean's room and told her to bring the cocaine to his room. He turned over the kilo of coke to Cal, who left with a broad smile across his face.

After booking a flight back to New York for Jean, Vivian sent her on her way, giving her the entire sixteen thousand dollars to take with her, and leaving himself with the expense money he used for travel. He planned to spend two weeks in that hotel. He'd already cleared his principal and expense capital from the sale of the half-kilo and made a thousand dollar profit, staying ahead of the game and waiting for sixteen thousand more to come.

The waitress who brought his food via room service to his room was a shapely, young white girl—Ilian—from France, who'd married a black army private while in France, and bore him a son. She was living off base with her husband—now stationed at the Norfolk Army Base in Virginia Beach. Being the only person Vivian knew in Virginia, other than Cal, Vivian invited her out for dinner at a restaurant she'd suggested. They had a wonderful dinner, and then it was time for her to go home to her husband and son. Ilian was one of the warmest persons Vivian had ever met and cherished their friendship.

By Friday morning, only four days after Cal had taken the cocaine, he was back with the total amount of cash. Impressed with the way Cal did business, Vivian inquired, "Do you know any other guys who would wanna buy kilos of coke?"

"Hmmm … I know a guy who pays cash … he buys like two … three … keys at a time. I could let you talk to him. But, let me warn you … he's slick—not a thief—but slick, fast talking nigga … if you know what I mean."

Vivian was shaking his head and laughing.

Cal called the guy, whose name was also Dave, and Vivian spoke to him, agreeing to meet in Vivian's room later on that night. About eight o'clock, there was a knock on Vivian's hotel room door. He saw a tall, dark guy with a single gold tooth, and a very light complexioned girl at his side.

"Who is it?"

"Dave, man, you're expecting me."

Vivian buttoned his shirt to hide the pistol, and then opened the door. This guy was a show-boat … wanted to make an impression on Vivian, that he's *the man* in Virginia. He was dressed *fly*, his beige cashmere coat thrown over his back and walking like he was all that. His pretty lady friend wore a fur coat and was really *expensive-looking* as she strolled behind him.

Vivian closed the door, laughing to himself, and greeted American Dave. "How are you, man? Glad to meet you."

"Glad to meet you too, name sake," he said smiling his gold-toothed smile.

"And who's the pretty lady?" Vivian asked politely.

"This is my lovely woman, Monique," Dave said proudly.

"Hi, Monique. Happy to make your acquaintance. Lovely name for a lovely lady," he turned on the charm as Monique blushed.

"Thank you."

Showing this nigga what class was all about, Vivian kissed her hand politely. There was that look in her eyes that showed Vivian that she appreciated his mannerism far more than he had intended. *I'm a-get this show-boat's bitch*, Vivian thought, as a sly smile began to creep across his face.

American Dave and Monique finally sat down and Vivian sat on his bed facing them. "Never mind my lady, man. She's cool. She takes care of my accounting," American Dave joked, not happy with the smile Monique returned, but not wanting to piss off his potential supplier, either. "Now, down to the business at hand. I like to get straight to the point. What's the price on three keys ... cash up front?"

This guy is not only a show-boat, but he's boasting, right off the bat. Vivian pondered for a while, calculating the price to tell him. "Three keys, ah? Twenty-eight thousand per key," he threw out on the table, wondering if this fly guy would bite.

"Nah, man. I'll pay you twenty-two thousand ... and that's it, man. I've got my cash, man ... any time you ready to deal at my price ... we can do business, yo"

Vivian made a quick calculation in his mind and thought, *I could make seven thousand, three times over in one cash deal. It would be worth it.* "You can't tell nobody I gave you this deal, man," Vivian affirmed.

"I'm a business man, Dave. I don't go around telling niggas my business."

"When do you want it?"

"Monday or Tuesday would be fine."

"All right … you got a deal. But remember, this price is between us."

"Shit! Hell, yeah!"

The both shook hands to seal their business deal, and American Dave gave Vivian all his numbers where he could be reached. The meeting was over almost before it started, but both parties came to an amicable agreement. The pair rose to go.

"Just call me and let me know when you are ready."

"I'll talk to you then." American Dave was ready to roll with his lady friend.

"Nice meeting you, Dave," said Monique in a very sexy tone.

"Same here, Monique." But, as soon as they were out the door he said out loud to the images in his mind, "American Dave, you muscled me out of eighteen grand of profit. I'm gonna fuck the shit outta your bitch. You can bet on *that*!"

Vivian left Virginia and was back by Monday with four kilograms of cocaine. He booked the same hotel as before, and made a call to American Dave's home number.

"Dave, I'm ready for you … three big ones."

"Hey, man, glad to hear from you. My supply was about to run out. Where you at?"

"I'm at the same hotel, room 506."

"All right. See you in a few."

Within an hour, American Dave and Monique were at Vivian's room door. Monique looked sparkling and it sent a tingle through him. As usual, the money came first—thousand dollars stacks, one by one, until all sixty-six bundles were counted.

"Correct," he said, then handed American Dave a plastic bag with three kilograms of cocaine. "Check the cocaine … best you'll ever see." *Why not boast a little?* "And, if you need ten more right away, you got it."

Monique stared at Vivian as he spoke about the amount of cocaine he could provide. He'd provoked her little brain and peaked her interest, which was his main intent for making the statement to American Dave. Vivian sensed that Monique had a passion for the *good* side of life, and he thought, *the bigger the better*, and he was right. He had her attention—all he had to do now was figure out when to make his move.

The next day, Vivian called to see if American Dave was at his office at a used car dealership on the outskirts of town that he owned.

"Hello, could I speak to Mr. David Robinson, please?" he asked, and a female voice responded.

"Could you hold on a second while I fetch him. He's out on the lot."

"Okay," said Vivian, as the assistant put the phone down to fetch American Dave, but Vivian hung up. His plan was in motion. He only wanted to be sure Dave was not at home. He knew he'd blown Monique's mind, and the time to attack was now, with him still fresh in her thoughts, so he dialed Dave's house.

"Hello, is Dave in?"

"No, he's not," said Monique.

"Can you tell him that Jamaican Dave called?"

"Hi, how are you? This is Monique."

He'd set a trap for her—she took the bait. "How are you, you sexy thing?"

"I'm fine, handsome thing."

That was all Vivian needed to hear … now he could really respond to her remarks. "I really called to speak to you."

"Really?"

"Yes, really. Do you know you're a beautiful woman?"

"I'm listening," she said, sexy sweet.

"I like what I saw, and I'd love for you to come and have dinner with me."

"And why would you wanna have dinner with me?"

"Because it would make me a happy man …and above all … I want *you*. You've been on my mind from the moment I saw you. I just keep thinking and thinking about you."

"So … what about Dave?"

"I don't want Dave … I want you."

Monique laughed aloud at his remarks.

"So, can I invite you to dinner later?"

"Well … just dinner … okay?"

"Just dinner," he assured her.

"I'll have to leave here before Dave gets home … about six … so look for me between five and five-thirty," she confirmed.

"Okay, that's fine with me. I'll be waiting. So, see you later my sweet thang."

"Bye honey, until then," said Monique finally.

It was ten-thirty, and Vivian hadn't had breakfast yet, so he ordered room service. Ilian was on duty and delivered it to him; she was genuinely happy to see Vivian and vice versa. She laid the food down on the table then embraced him.

"When did you come back?"

"Yesterday."

"Why didn't you call me?"

"I was planning to call you today," he said politely as he held her and looked into her eyes.

Vivian was still aching when Ilian left, the feel of her embrace arousing him. While he was having breakfast, his phone rang. Cal was in the lobby wanting to see him.

"Come on up, Cal."

In no time, Cal was at his door. "What's up, Dave?"

"Everything's cool," said Vivian while he ate.

"I rounded up eight grand, Dave. That's all I could pick up."

"No problem," said Vivian, as he reached for the one kilo he had left over for this deal. "Just bring the rest when you are ready." said Vivian very confident in his new customer. "I need to get a place to rent. How could I go about that?"

"I've a house coming up in two weeks that I'll be closing on. Started the contract to purchase it when I saw a house that I loved more. I was planning on renting it out, so … you could have it."

"Sounds good. When you say? Two weeks?"

"Yeah, it's empty now. I'll check with the realtor to see if I can get it sooner."

"Do that, Cal, I would surely appreciate it. I kinda like this town." Vivian beamed, his thoughts savoring his newly found outlet for his favorite pastimes—money and women.

Cal gave him the eight thousand dollars and received the kilo.

"I'll talk to you tomorrow, Dave."

Vivian was lost in the movie that was showing on the TV when there was a knock on his door. He checked his watch, seeing it was exactly five-thirty ... *Monique* ... he rushed to the door and looked through the peephole. Outside was Monique, looking stunning. As she entered, Vivian kissed her on her cheeks. "Hi, babes."

"Hi, honey."

Vivian closed the door, and then said politely, "Let me take your coat." While he hung it in the closet, Monique sat on the sofa; he took a position facing her, on the bed. They talked for a while and became acquainted, both laughing happily as if enjoying each other's company. Vivian reached for the room service menu. "You don't mind us having dinner in the room, do you? I think it's more intimate," he asked.

"No, I don't mind, but it's just dinner, right?" she continued teasingly.

"Just dinner," he said studying at the menu. "I can recommend my favorite dish ... I've had it twice since I've been staying here ... honey-roasted duck with Cajun rice ... you'd love it." He handed the menu to Monique.

She browsed through it, but agreed, "I'll try the duck you recommended."

Ilian had already left for the day, so it was safe for Vivian to dine in his room with Monique. They relaxed and talked for a while after they finished eating, and he intended to do exactly what he promised himself he would do to Dave's lady friend.

"You sure do know how to get to a girl, you bad-ass Jamaican, you," said Monique as she smiled and hugged Vivian, feeling overjoyed.

He'd enjoyed Monique immensely and planned to see a lot more of her, so long—whenever she could get away from American Dave.

The next day, Vivian checked out of the Plaza Hotel and booked into the Holiday Inn close by. He'd set up a date with Ilian, who couldn't spend time with him in the hotel in which she worked.

Ilian left work at four o'clock that evening, took a cab to the Holiday Inn, and went straight to Vivian's room where he was anxiously waiting her. They kissed as Ilian entered the room, and greeted each other. Ilian scurried to the bathroom carrying her workbag.

"I'm sticky … gonna take a shower … be right back."

Excitement filled Vivian as she shut the door.

Finally, Ilian stepped out of the bathroom, smelling fresh as a morning breeze, but her attire was something different than Vivian was accustomed to. She wore her work apron and hat, and high-heeled shoes—nothing else. Her long brunette hair curled around her pointed nipples—strange, but very intriguing to Vivian. She walked over to him and said, "You are *mi pasha*. I'm gonna take good care of you this evening. I'm gonna give you the royal treatment."

She started to unbuckle his belt and he tried to assist.

"Just relax, *mi pasha*, this is my treat."

She is now a part of me, he thought, as they relaxed in each other's arms until it was time for her to leave.

I think I'm going to enjoy Virginia Beach.

After a week at the Holiday Inn, Cal took Vivian to the house he was renting, then turned over the keys to him. Being quite experienced in furnishing new places quickly, the tasks seemed routine. Then he called Jack in New York to come and stay with him.

Business boomed in Virginia, and Vivian loved it, but after six months Cal came to him sad faced.

"Yo, Dave, one of my homeboys who covered for me in a shooting is coming out of jail, and he's got nowhere to stay. I promised him a house, so I'm gonna try to find another one for you."

Renting houses in Virginia was very difficult, for people tended to ask a lot of questions. Before a house could be found, Cal's friend showed up, so Vivian stored his furniture in one of the empty rooms and returned the keys to Cal while he was at the house.

"Cal, as soon as you find me another house, I'll be back. Just watch over my furniture. I'm going up to New York today, so if you need more stuff, I'll send it down to you immediately.

"I'll find a place real soon, man. Sorry for this shit, Dave, but I was just in a jam, man."

"I understand, Cal. I would've done the same thing if I were in your situation. I know you mean well."

That evening, Vivian called Ilian and Monique to tell them his situation. They were sad that he was leaving and promised to help look for a house to rent. He caught an evening flight out of Norfolk to New York, where Evon was anxiously waiting his return. He'd been longing to see his son and newly born, so it was a blessing in disguise.

Back in New York, Vivian rented a beautiful two-bedroom apartment in Queens, and decorated it lavishly—a masterpiece his family loved. Duane had white bedroom set with electric-blue carpeting on the floor; the master bedroom was decorated with a mint-green carpet and a king-sized, peach-colored bedroom set.

The décor of the living and dining area was picturesque—gray, black, and fire engine red. The floor was adorned with one-inch thick, charcoal-gray carpet that had a four-inch streak of fire-engine red border around the entire living and dining area. The living room was completed with a black velour, circular living room suite, an ash-gray center table, and a state-of-the-art television and stereo system, made by Fisher. A black dining table with gray-and-black chairs completed the dining area.

A few weeks before Vivian acquired the new apartment, Evon called him at his Parchester apartment in the Bronx. She was panicking on the phone.

"What's wrong, Evon?"

"The FBI was at my house asking about you," she said nervously.

"What?" he asked incredulously?

"Yeah, my sister Charm told me … my daughter's father was also at the house when they came. He was cursing, saying I'm putting his daughter in danger."

"I can't understand that Evon … how would they know that I'm going to your house? If they know that much, they should know everywhere that I go." Desperately, Vivian tried to figure out the possibilities. "It could only be Eleanor. She's the only one right now who would suspect that I visit your house … she's really upset about our relationship."

The possibility that Eleanor would do such a thing upset Evon even more, so she and Charm confronted Eleanor about a set up.

Vivian also spoke to Eleanor, but she continually denied it happened. The circumstantial evidence was there, and Vivian didn't believe Eleanor. The relationship with Evon had just started to blossom, and he'd fallen in love with her; he couldn't bear the thought of not seeing Evon, which was what the situation was tantamount to, if he wanted to stay out of jail. Love conquered his fear, though.

I'm spending Thanksgiving at Evon's house whether the Feds like it or not.

They had to be inventive, so Evon went to a phone booth about five miles from her house to call Vivian every evening. Thanksgiving night came, and Vivian sneaked into Evon's house with only her mom and her aunt knowing his presence. They had dinner in her aunt's top-floor section of the two-family house—alone and without any disturbance.

About a week after Thanksgiving, Vivian decided to spend the night with Evon. She took three different cabs that night to avoid being tailed, then met Vivian in the parking lot of the La Guardia Marriott.

"Are you sure you weren't tailed?"

"No, I'm positive."

They were in the room for only an hour when there were sounds of police radios in the hallway. Through the peephole he saw several police officers walking briskly down the hallway.

"Damn, Evon! You were tailed!"

He looked out the window, but it was too far up to jump—no way out. Vivian gave up and lay on the bed. "What is to be, must be, Evon." he said, then relaxed. He knew the police would be knocking on the door any minute, so he waited and he waited, but the knock never came. The police radio sounds in the hallway ceased—all of the police officers disappeared. He continued to wait a while longer, then bravely opened the door and peeked outside. To his delight, the passageway was clear—no cops—no one at all. The police had been summoned because of a problem next door—false alarm.

Years later, Evon found out that her sister Charm had made up the whole story about the FBI to keep Vivian and Evon apart, and had also convinced Evon's kid's father to go along with the lie to make it more believable. Evon couldn't forgive herself, though, for what she'd put Eleanor through—Eleanor was innocent.

Vivian's life resumed to "normal"; enjoying his wife and kids in Queens, his lovely lady, Evon, and his on-again, off-again relationship with Jackie Ramsay. Because of the hurt she'd felt from Vivian's relationship with Evon, Jackie returned to her two-timing ways.

About a month passed and he received a call from his brother Tony that alerted Vivian's suspicions.

"Yeah, Dave. Can you get any coke to buy?"

"Yeah, my man in California has some." *You ain't gonna use me anymore Tony—nothing for nothing.* "What's in it for me?"

"I've started to operate in Philly again …it's going good, but there's no cocaine in New York."

"Well, let's bring in ten kilos between us per trip, and when my portion arrives in New York, you sell it in Philadelphia."

Tony agreed to the deal.

Vivian figured Tony would agree, because Tony didn't like to lose alone. He'd prefer—if there was to be a loss, bringing in the coke from California—that it would be between Vivian and himself.

Vivian's job was to get the ten kilograms to Tony's apartment in Yonkers. It would be Tony's responsibility to sell it in Philadelphia.

The plan: Vivian would be at Newark Airport by five-thirty in the morning when the cocaine came in from Los Angeles. He'd watch the couriers from a distance, without them seeing him, to ensure that they left the airport safely. He'd then call Tony to tell him that everything was okay, and that the couriers were on their way.

They worked steadily at the plan until Tony found a connection in New York to buy his coke. He didn't need Vivian anymore—greed. He stopped selling cocaine for Vivian without even giving him notice.

When Vivian suspected that Tony had cut the business relationship with him, he approached Tony for the cash due from the last five kilos. It took Tony a week-and-a-half to pay Vivian ... after Tony washed the cash about four times over. Vivian laughed to himself at Tony's game.

The day Vivian picked up the money at Tony's Yonkers apartment, he was astonished at the way Tony was living—his kids were in the apartment, along with twenty of his Shower Posse gangsters, fifteen guns on the floor, kilos of cocaine stacked in one corner of the living room, and thousands of dollars lying around. It was crazy. Vivian was happy to retrieve his cash and leave.

Virginia, here I come. This is probably a blessing in disguise, he thought, as he drove out of Yonkers for the very last time.

Cal had a house ready for him to rent. With Vivian and Tony severing business relations, the house in Virginia couldn't have come at a better time. He packed his flight pack and caught a flight from Newark to Norfolk, then took a cab to his favorite hotel—the Plaza Hotel in Virginia Beach. A few minutes after Vivian booked his room, Cal was at the hotel to pick him up—they went to see the new house.

Cal had decided on an alternate plan, though: he discovered it was much easier to buy a house in Virginia that to rent one. With a down payment of between $1500-3000, a person could easily acquire a home. As business steadily grew, he progressively bought more houses. Not only did he need more stash houses for his cocaine, but also several different, private sleeping quarters for himself—and all of his women.

With the rapid pace of business, he needed two guys to assist him in Virginia. Jack was busy doing his thing in New York, so he enlisted the aid of Tony, telling Tony which two guys he wanted—one of them Brokey-Leeney, whose mother Vivian knew from back in Jamaica, and Student, no gunman, but a soccer player from Jamaica.

Cal had by then introduced Vivian to his friend Tracy, who said he could move a couple keys a week, and American Dave had brought his brother Roy into the picture—he could also move the same amount. Last but not least, he was introduced to Bill—five customers with great potential, all Black-Americans.

These guys wanted to make too much cash from one kilo, so Vivian decided to teach them how to make more money through volume and cheaper sales to customers. The guys took the instructions well, raking in the big bucks. In return, it made more money for Vivian. He was moving four times the amount of cocaine as before, with only five customers. No visible traffic—he was only dealing with five guys—but making money as though he was dealing with a thousand nickel-and-dime customers.

Tony had done him a favor by cutting business relations—Vivian was more relaxed in Virginia. Business, however, started slowing in Philadelphia.

"Yo, Dave. Things are slow in Philly now, man, and I've got some keys sitting. Can you sell 'em?" he asked.

"Sure, just send them down."

By the next day, Tony sent the four kilos. Vivian had some cash on hand, so instead of waiting for Tony's four kilograms to sell, he just gave the courier $112,000 to take back to Tony. Unfortunately, this transaction drew the wrong kind of attention.

As Vivian awoke early one morning, he heard someone talking on the phone. From his upstairs bedroom, he could see down into the living room—it was Brokey-Leaney on the phone, to Tony in New York.

"He sold four keys yesterday, and another guy's buying four today."

Vivian listened until he'd heard enough—Tony had his friend spying on Vivian's business. Vivian coughed and Brokey-Leaney abruptly changed the subject with Tony.

The next day, Vivian sent Brokey-Leaney to New York on an errand. Brokey-Leaney didn't realize he'd spent his last day in Virginia. A few days later, Student, who Vivian also sent to New York on an errand, sneaked back into Virginia and called one of Vivian's customers—Tracey. Tracey called Vivian immediately and told him about the call. Tony was trying to muscle in on Vivian's business—but no dice.

Another call came from a worried Tony.

"Boy, Dave, I have a problem. I asked a girl to buy a car for me, but the cash I used turned out to be marked bills. The Feds in Philly are questioning the people involved in the car deal. I don't like it."

Vivian thought for a while. "You could come up to Virginia and chill out for awhile, but you can't bring any more than two of your guys with you. Virginia Beach's a quiet town. I don't want anyone to start shooting up the place."

That wasn't convenient enough for Tony. Anywhere he went, his Shower Posse gangsters had to be there with him, but Vivian wouldn't stand for it.

Jim Brown had been arrested in Miami by the immigration authorities and deported to Jamaica. He was remanded in the General Penitentiary in Kingston, on multiple murder charges. Tony asked Vivian a favor when he next called Jim.

"I want you to send a message … ask him if I could stay in Tivoli Gardens. I'm planning to go back to Jamaica to live … I don't like this FBI shit."

"It won't be a problem for you to go back to Tivoli Gardens—I don't have to ask Jim that … Jim has nothing against you. All you were doing was following your stupid Shower Posse friends who don't like Jim Brown. They can't go back to Tivoli Gardens, but you can. I can guarantee that. You're my brother, but those other fools can't go back there. They all thought that living in America was forever, but things have changed—only Jim can help them now. They turned their backs on their community."

Tony was silent. Vivian purposely said these things to let him feel bad, because there wasn't any reason for Tony to go up against Jim. Jim had never done him wrong, yet he and his friends hated Jim. Vivian realized it wasn't really Jim that Tony hated; just the fact that Jim was Vivian's friend and not his—pure jealousy. Tony had also hated Donovan

"Champs" Jones when he was a friend of Vivian's, yet when Donovan Jones offered friendship, Tony gladly accepted. During a phone conversation with Tony, Vivian had asked, "Tony, you trust Champs?"

"Why you ask that?"

"I just asked you a question … just give me an answer … yes or no."

"Yes."

Vivian laughed aloud.

"Why you laughing, Dave?"

"Nothing … just something I remembered." He'd remembered that Champs had been the only one in his group of friends who'd ever mentioned that he would kill Tony. Now Champs was beside Tony as his second-in-command.

Summer in Virginia Beach was busy with tourists walking the beach strip—Atlantic Avenue—and swimming. Vivian had asked Valerie to bring the kids to Virginia for a vacation. He'd just purchased a beautiful house in the suburbs that no one knew of—his private haven—where Valerie, Duane and Dominique stayed. Vivian always kept his family safe, away from the drug world, and didn't even allow his friends to socialize with his kids, except for Jim Brown and his son Jah T.

It was the summer 1988. He took the kids to Busch Gardens Water Parks, and all over Virginia—they had a wonderful time before time to returning to New York.

About a week afterward, Evon and her daughter came to Virginia. They spent time with Vivian at his suburban home. While Evon stayed in Virginia another week, Evon's daughter returned, accompanied by one of Evon's friends. Tragedy struck.

Up in Yonkers, some of Tony's friends were at a park on Broadway playing soccer, while Tony watched from the sideline. Some of Tony's other friends were talking outside the park when they noticed something strange. Several Feds gathered on the road, some dressed in jogging suits; others dressed like ordinary guys. Tony's friends saw the agents in the jogging suits were securing their pistols in ankle holsters, before they started jogging, while the others spread themselves out.

One of his friends whispered to Tony, "A lot of Feds around," pointing discreetly to the ones who were jogging. "Those are agents, too," he added, pointing to the plain-clothes agents.

Tony started to panic and sneaked out of the park, reaching Broadway. By the time they realized Tony was gone, the Feds just managed to catch a glimpse of him as he was about to turn a corner. Tony made a run for it. While running, he saw his brother Ticker Shine driving along and jumped into the car. The Feds didn't know where Tony had disappeared. But, Tony was stupid. He went straight to his drug apartment, which was already being staked out—*he was trapped*.

The phone at one of Tony's drug apartments, where Kong was staying, was wiretapped, and agents had heard Tony was planning to leave the country. They also wanted to catch Vivian in their net, but time was running out. They didn't want to lose Tony, so they had to move in on him ... *now* ... knowing that he had discovered their surveillance.

Jah T. had called Vivian from Jamaica and they were talking about Tony going down there. He put Jah T. on hold, then rang Tony's Yonkers apartment.

Tony answered the phone.

"Tony, I have Jah T. on the line. Everything's okay for you to go down to Tivoli Gardens. You want to talk to Jah T.?"

"No ... not now, Dave ... lots of Feds around," he said nervously. "I just escaped from their trap over at the ball park on Broadway, but they're outside the apartment building."

"So why you went back to the apartment?"

"It's too late for that now ... I can't explain ... I have to get out of here," he said nervously.

"So what about the back of the building ... try that way."

"I'll talk to you later," Tony said, and hung up.

Vivian told Jah T. what was happening. *Damn! Tony's phone could be bugged. If his phone were bugged, they would've heard my conversation with Tony and traced the call. I'd better go to another one of my safe houses until I know exactly what's going on.*

He shouted to Evon who was downstairs, "Come help me pack these things. Tony's got problems in New York with the FBI, and I just called him. I don't know if his phone was bugged, so I'm not taking any chances. I'm gonna move to one of my other houses until I see what's happening."

They packed clothes and papers into his Jeep, leaving furniture and everything else, and drove to a little country house he'd just acquired and furnished.

The phone in the country house had never been used, and the beds never slept in. He was even the first person to enter that he knew, so he had no fear—he relaxed.

The next day, he and Evon cuddled up in the den watching CNN when Vivian saw Tony on TV being led in handcuffs to a police car. What popped up on the screen next was even more shocking—a picture of none other than Vivian.

Evon started to cry and her hand went over her mouth in shock and panic, "Dee, oh my God!"

The TV reporter then said, "...the reputed leader of the violent Shower Posse gang, Vivian Blake, escaped the dragnet and is now being sought by the Federal Agents." Then the reporter paused and added, "There's a nation-wide manhunt for gang leader, Vivian Blake ... all airports, bus stations, and train stations have been set on alert. Vivian Blake could be armed and is considered dangerous. Approach him with caution."

Chills ran up Vivian's spine as he listened to the reporter and saw his picture on the screen.

"How could they say such bad things about you, Dave? They want the world to think the worst of you. I know it's all lies, and that's all that matters ... I'll stick with you to the end."

"It's gonna be rough from now on ... think you can handle it?"

"I don't care ... I'll stick beside you."

"What about your daughter?"

"She'll be okay ... my family will look after her."

"You'll have to stay with me until I figure my next move. If you go to New York, the Feds might try to pressure you to find me. So, until then, make yourself comfortable. And … you can't call your house … at least not right now."

They hugged each other passionately.

"Dave, everything's gonna work out just fine. God isn't sleeping … he knows you're innocent of most of those crimes they're saying you committed. I know you're no monster … I wouldn't have been here if I believed that."

Vivian smiled as Evon spoke. "You're stronger that I thought. A lot of girls who act like they are tough would wanna run, but soft Evon has decided to stick with her man." Vivian smiled and looked at Evon lovingly.

"The difference between me and other girls is simple … I love you."

Never in his wildest dreams would Vivian have thought Evon would've been so strong.

In the days that followed, Tony's other Yonkers apartment were also raided and his friends were arrested—including Kong. Vivian learned of all this information by way of CNN News. *To run now wouldn't be wise. The Feds are looking for me everywhere. In a few months, they'll relax a bit.*

Vivian phoned a friend—Peter—in Fort Lauderdale who was a nine-to-five guy.

"When will you be getting vacation time from your job?"

"On the 2nd of December, why?"

"How would you like a one-week cruise to Mexico, Cayman and Jamaica, then back to Miami?"

"I'd love that."

"Okay, book a reservation on Holiday Cruise Lines for the 3rd of December for a week. It could be my lucky day … it's my son's birthday. Find out how much it'll cost, and I'll call you back in two days."

In two days, Vivian called Peter. "You found out the details?"

"Almost three thousand dollars."

"Okay, I send you five thousand and pay for your ticket. But remember, December 3rd's the date."

"Yeah, that's the date I booked."

"I'll be joining you at your house on Saturday morning. I'll be traveling with your on the cruise … and that's confidential—nobody, not even your girlfriend must know."

"You know you don't have to worry about that, Dave."

"I know that … talk to you soon."

Several preparations were needed for his departure from the United States—destination … Jamaica. He sneaked into New York and spent about sixty thousand dollars on clothing. Thirty of it went to one of his favorite clothes stores on 125th St.—A.J. Lester. While shopping there, he saw one of Tony's baby's mothers—Joan—with her boyfriend. She looked at Vivian for a minute, then she whispered to her boyfriend, "That man looks familiar, but I figure where I've seen him before."

Vivian was reading Joan's lips and laughing, saying to himself, *if Joan can't recognize me then almost no one can.* Joan and Vivian grew up in Tivoli Gardens and he used to live with her and her parents in the same apartment in the Bronx.

Joan looked at Vivian again and he called her over, "This is Vivian."

Joan held her mouth in shock, "Jesus Christ, you fooled me. I couldn't place you for nothing!"

She wished him well, and left Vivian to his shopping spree, attended by the only white person working in A.J. Lester at the time—Mona—one of the sexiest white girls Vivian had ever seen … pretty, with long hair and long fingernails. To Vivian, the most significant thing about Mona was her big ass. Vivian and Mona had become close through the years, even going to a movie together in Manhattan.

After leaving A.J. Lester, he went to Leyton's Shoe Store in Midtown Manhattan, and then headed down to the jewelry district to find something special for Evon. He spotted a diamond-and-gold necklace, which was adorned with other precious stones, and fell in love with it. *Nothing too good for Evon.*

After he was finished shopping, he went back to the La Guardia Marriott, to his room and invited a very special girlfriend over—Marcia. No one knew Vivian was seeing her, and they kept it that way—the relationship was very special. Marcia was very pretty—tall and dark complexioned, with a nose as straight as an arrow. Above all, she was very sexy. They ordered room service for dinner, then relaxed in the sofa and watched TV.

After breakfast in the restaurant at the hotel lobby, Marcia left, and Vivian went about packing for his return to Virginia. By noon, he'd checked out and was on his way. During the drive down, he kept thinking about how he'd fooled Joan. It was rumored that he'd had plastic surgery but he hadn't. He'd started wearing a low-cut hairstyle, shaved his beard, and he wore a nerdy-looking pair of glasses. Apparently, those small changes had drastically altered his appearance.

He reached Virginia Beach about five o'clock that evening and drove straight to the house he was sharing with Evon.

"I've been worried ever since you left here, Dave. I couldn't sleep."

He presented her with her gift and she was ecstatic. She immediately put it on, in front of the dresser mirror in the bedroom as Vivian watched her.

"This is beautiful. I love it! I'll cherish it for the rest of my life. Anytime I look at it, I'll always remember you."

She jumped and hugged Vivian with joy, and then they both went into the kitchen. They chose a recipe from their numerous cookbooks—whipped chicken *cordon-bleu* in a cream sauce with white rice—and had a romantic dinner in their little rustic home. After dishes were done, they retired to the den where they cuddled up, watching TV, followed by a night of non-stop passion.

From August until December 1st, the little house was their refuge. Two new recruits—Norris and Souls—came to Virginia before the all of Tony's problems occurred, and they handled his business well. He kept Evon far away from his drug business.

Periodically, Evon and Vivian would drive a few hours to a different town, so that she could call her daughter and the rest of her family, to let them know that she was all right. All in all, it was a very special four months for Vivian and Evon. Their love grew deeper and deeper. The entire four months that Vivian was in hiding with Evon by his side, he kept a keen watch on a program broadcast on Fox television, *America's*

Most Wanted, and prayed that he wouldn't appear on it before he left the United States.

Thursday, December 1st 1988, Vivian and Evon said good-bye, not knowing if they would see each other again. There were tears rolling down Evon's cheeks as Vivian passionately embraced her, kissing her as if he couldn't let go. Before long, he was crying , too.

Two American friends were paid to drive him to Florida. He held back his tears as much as possible, trying not to look back at Evon, but he couldn't keep himself from one last look as the car drove him away. He waved to Evon, who was still crying, and she waved until his car was out of sight.

During the long drive to Miami, precautions were taken. They drove all night Thursday, and then booked into a hotel when it was daylight on Friday morning. Vivian kept himself locked away until nightfall. Well rested, the three hit the road again. Driving at night gave the most cover, for Vivian couldn't afford to be recognized.

He arrived at Peter's house in Fort Lauderdale about six o'clock Saturday morning. The American couple was given cash for plane tickets back to Virginia, plus expenses, because the car they drove was to be delivered to a branch of a rent-a-car company in Miami.

Peter was all packed and ready to go. Peter's girlfriend was new, and didn't know who Vivian was, so Vivian told Peter to have her accompany them down to the cruise pier.

"Does she have a driver's license?"

"Sure."

"Okay … have her drive us to the pier. She and I will see you off on your cruise, but when it's time for us to leave the ship, she'll be leaving alone. I'll remain in your room." Vivian began to laugh at Peter's expression, and then pointed to his suitcase. "I'm stowing away in the comfort of your room. You'll check in that suitcase as if it's yours, okay?"

The trio left at noon. Mary drove them to the cruise ship pier in Miami and Peter and Mary went straight to the Holiday Cruise Ship counter and checked in his luggage. Vivian stayed in the car and waited for their return. The wait was about an hour and Vivian started to sweat. *Everyone looks like a Federal Agent,* he thought, but finally, he saw Mary walking back to the car, and she signaled him to come.

Vivian was the happiest man in the world at that moment. Peter was at the entrance, and Vivian was dying to board the ship and into the room. Peter led the way, and they all entered.

At last! Vivian thought as he sat on the bed, but until the ship left Miami, he wouldn't be able to completely relax. The call came for all visitors to leave the ship, so Mary kissed Peter.

"Have a pleasant trip, honey. You too, Dave … take care."

Peter walked out behind her. "I'll be right back," he said to Vivian.

At exactly four o'clock, the cruise ship left the Miami shore. The coastline grew smaller and smaller as the ship entered the deep ocean—Miami was no more. Vivian jumped for joy.

Later that night, they dressed and went to the casino, the prelude to five days of fun on the cruise line, en route to Ocho Rios, Jamaica.

Chapter 12: Seeking Refuge

The cruise ship pulled into Reynolds Pier in on Thursday morning, December 8th, about seven. Vivian was dressed in his shorts and polo shirt, like the average tourist, straw hat, and camera around his neck. Weird-looking glasses completed the attire. He took the ship pass from Peter—a yellow slip of paper used to re-enter the ship—and it was time for Vivian to depart to the shores of his native land, Jamaica.

He joined a group of tourists who were readying to disembark. The line started to move. He stepped from the ship, nervous on the inside, but with composure on the outside. *I wonder if any police officers are at this pier looking for me?* he thought, as he walked toward the exit gate of the pier behind some other tourists. Finally, he reached the gate, then the sidewalk. Peter was to meet him at the front desk of the Turtle Towers Beach Hotel, so Vivian hailed a cab.

"Take me to the Turtle Towers Beach Hotel, please," he said in an American accent.

"No problem."

The cab driver dropped him at the hotel, where he went straight to the front desk. "I'd like a room for two nights please," Vivian said to the female attendant.

"Name?"

"Percival Johnson"

Vivian had received a passport from Jamaica with his new name—Percival Andrew Johnson. In a few minutes, his room was booked, and he waited by the front desk.

Before Vivian had left Virginia, he'd made arrangements with one of his girlfriends—Pinky—in Canada to meet him at the cruise ship pier, but she wasn't outside when he arrived. He didn't linger, but went straight to the hotel. In about half an hour, Peter joined him at the front desk with his luggage, so they could go to his room.

"Jamaica at last!"

Peter was happy for him and was glad he could help. Peter had done his job well, and Vivian was very thankful. That night, Vivian called

Canada to find out what had happened to Pinky and was given a number for a hotel where she was staying in Jamaica.

"The damned travel agent in Canada booked me in a hotel in Negril, instead of Ocho Rios. By the time I got to the pier this morning, all the passengers were already off the ship. Where are you?"

"I'm at the Turtle Towers Beach Hotel in Ocho Rios."

"I'm taking a cab now … back to Ocho Rios. It'll take about two-and-a-half hours, okay?"

Next he called Virginia. Evon grabbed the phone on the first ring.

"You reach Jamaica all right? I'm fine right now, now that I know that you are okay. I love you."

"I love you too, babes. You can go up to New York now, and call me at the hotel, but use a pay phone okay?"

"I know that, Dave, I'm not stupid."

Vivian called Jah T. and Jim, who was now out of jail, and informed them that he was in Ocho Rios.

Pinky arrived. Vivian was so glad to see her; he was lonely … wanted companionship. He hadn't seen Pinky since 1984, when he was in Canada. Vivian couldn't wait until she was unpacked … he was all over her. Vivian was the only man she ever really loved, and she was always at his beck and call.

The next day after his arrival, he called Valerie and the kids. Her response wasn't what he expected.

"Pappy, your sister Vivienne called my shop and cursed you. She said that your friend Jim Brown and the guys in Tivoli Gardens knew that Tony was gonna get busted, that Jim Brown told you, and you didn't warn anyone. She said that Tony's friend Brokey-Leaney told Tony that you told him so."

"What? And they believe that?"

"Yes, everyone of them's cursing you behind your back … Tony, Vilma and Vivienne mainly."

"That pussy Brokey-Leaney! That fucking pussy, and I never had a conversation like that before. He's a fucking liar. Go over to Brokey-Leaney's apartment right now. I'm going to call him right away."

Without putting down the receiver, Vivian dialed Brokey-Leaney's number. Get Vilma for me on your three-way line."

Brokey-Leaney did as he was told.

"Yes, Dave, I'm here," said Vilma.

"Brokey, when did I tell you that Jim Brown and the Tivoli guys knew that Tony was going to be arrested, and that Jim Brown told me?"

"You never told me that," said Brokey in a panic, as Vilma interrupted angrily.

"Jesus Christ, Brokey! You mean to tell me that you were lying about Dave knowing that Tony was going to be arrested?"

"I didn't tell nobody that," said Brokey-Leaney still panic-stricken.

By then, Valerie was inside Brokey-Leaney's apartment and was hearing him denying that Vivian had told him anything.

"Tell me you're not serious, Brokey. Tell me that Dave really said it."

"Dave never said anything like that to me."

"And you really let me curse Dave so disgracefully," said Vilma.

Then Vivian interrupted, "Well at least I'm glad this came up, or I wouldn't have known how much you, Tony and Vivienne hated me, and wanted me in prison. Just because Tony's in jail … and you all would have preferred it to be me. You were glad to hear any negative thing about me to crucify me. You all never gave a thought to hearing from me first, before you started to throw disrespect at me, in the face of my wife … but let me tell you this, I've learned today that I no longer have any blood relatives. My friends in Tivoli Gardens are my relatives and that pussy Tony is wishing the worst for me, because I wasn't arrested like he was. Well, tell him he's no brother of mine. I don't want him as a brother. With a brother like that, I definitely don't need no enemies," said Vivian, and then quickly changed the subject. "Pussy Brokey, let me talk to Valerie."

"Yes, Dee."

"You heard that pussy Brokey denying that I told him anything?"

"Yes, and I can't believe people would be so evil. And they crucified you."

"Yeah, I'm wondering how some of them gonna sleep tonight. Vilma's on the line, Val. I'm wondering how she's going to sleep tonight … but on second thoughts, she will sleep well because the hatred for me's still there."

"But for what, Pappy?"

"For money. Tony bought them, but I refused to buy people … you have to be genuine."

"That's really sad," said Valerie, as Vilma remained silent in deep shame. "I'm leaving out of this apartment now, you hear. I'll talk to you later."

"All right, later."

Vivian sat on the sofa in the living area of his suite, while Pinky prepared some food in the kitchenette. He couldn't believe what had just transpired on the phone. His brother wanted him in prison.

Tony was the one who started all the violence in America, yet he wants me in prison—that's not fair.

He stretched out on the sofa and tried to rest.

Valerie, Duane, and Dominique flew into Jamaica just after New Year's 1989. Valerie had already arranged for Duane, ten years old, to attend St. Peter and Paul Preparatory School, because his father was Catholic and wanted his kids to attend Catholic schools. Valerie and the two kids lived in Kingston while Vivian lived in Ocho Rios.

Vivian had rented two apartments in Ocho Rios—one, a beach front condominium at Sea Palms on the outskirts of the town, the other in Columbus Heights in town, overlooking the ocean. He'd purchased a car and was trying to become accustomed to the narrow roads in the country. His first two friends in Ocho Rios were two front-desk clerks at the Turtle Towers Beach Hotel—Gem and Angie. After meeting Gem and Angie, he befriended a cab driver who was always at Turtle Towers—Wally. Wally took him anywhere he wanted to go before he bought the car, and eventually became his driver, especially when Vivian wanted to drive to Kingston to see his wife and kids.

When Pinky went back to Canada, Vivian became lonely once again. Janice filled the niche—a beautiful young girl he met while on a stroll in the town, who lived in an out-of-town section of Ocho Rios known as Breadnut Hill. After he became acquainted with her relatives, he hung out there most days.

While on a shopping trip for a gold chain for Dominique, he met a pretty, young Indian girl—Desolee in a pawn shop, where she worked. He bought his daughter's chain and managed to secure a date with Desolee—cute, with a dark complexion and a beautiful head of hair—from a little town in St. Ann, Jamaica known as Bamboo.

Vivian met her mother, who was a very sweet lady, and welcomed him with open arms. He also met her brothers and baby sister, Karri. There was something strange about Bamboo ... it was cold at night, like one of the worst spring days in New York. Vivian loved the cold, but he wasn't dressed for it.

After taking Desolee home from a date, he was invited to spend the night, which he gladly accepted. When it was time to go to bed, he undressed down to his shorts and tank top then sat on the bed.

"Shit, water's on the bed," he shouted as Desolee laughed at him.

"The comforter's just cold ... that's how it is in Bamboo."

Then they both cuddled up under the covers and made sweet love, sleeping in each other's arms all night to keep warm. Desolee had a beautiful body; because Vivian enjoyed that, they dated until their relationship was disrupted by a girl—Little Donna—he met while visiting Jack Ruby's wife, Loma, at her residence up in Tower Isle, close to his Sea Palms apartment. Everyone knew him by his new name—Percival Andrew Johnson—and most people called him Andrew.

Little Donna had just been deported from America and was going with a popular guy in the country parts of Jamaica. Vivian was a man who thrived on competition, so he graciously took on this challenge and won. Vivian invited Donna to live in his apartment in Columbus Heights and she accepted. By this time, Vivian had met Little Donna's very close friend Donna Combs and they became close to one another.

While Donna Combs was having lunch on the patio with Vivian at his beachfront condominium at Sea Palms, she stared at him for a long time, searching his face.

"Who *are* you, Andrew? And, don't tell me that you're Percival Johnson, because I know you aren't."

He almost choked, but covered it with laughter. "I'm Percival Johnson."

"Bullshit! I know you aren't. You don't have to worry about me … you can trust me."

He studied her carefully then stopped laughing. His gut feeling told him he could trust Donna—she had become a very close friend. Vivian hated not being able to his his true self—at least this would be the one person in Ocho Rios with whom he could be honest.

"I'm Vivian Blake."

"Shit! Why did I fucking ask? I'm too nosey. You mean … the *America's Most Wanted* Vivian Blake?"

"Yes, that very same one … live in the flesh."

"Andrew … honest to God … I'm sorry I asked you, but you don't have to worry … your secret is safe with me."

Little Donna had been staying with Vivian at his Columbus Heights apartment while Valerie and kids had come down to Ocho Rios, and were staying at the beachfront condominium at Sea Palms that weekend. They spent a good amount of time at their private beach and had fun teaching Dominique how to swim. After a fun-filled weekend, Valerie and kids left for Kingston.

Vivian realized that Valerie had left her pocket book, so he placed it on a shelf in his closet, then drove down to his Columbus Heights apartment, where Peter was visiting at the time. While Vivian was at the apartment, there was a knock on the door, and Peter went to answer it. Lo and behold if it wasn't Valerie and Duane, who came back to retrieve the purse—the house keys were in it. Peter signaled to Vivian that it was his wife and son, so Vivian hid in the bedroom while Peter opened the door. Valerie knew Vivian had an apartment in Columbus Heights but didn't know the apartment number—she was just randomly checking apartments and got lucky.

Valerie knew Peter and was relieved that she found the right apartment. She'd adopted Vivian's new name and used it to ask for him.

"No, he's not … hasn't been here since the day began," Peter lied, hoping to cover up for his friend. Vivian's jewelry was on the dresser in the room where Vivian was trying to hide, and the dresser could be seen from the living room where Valerie stood, the bedroom door standing open wide.

Valerie saw the same jewelry, which was at the Sea Palms apartment earlier that morning.

"What's his jewelry doing here if he hasn't been here this morning?"

She headed to the bedroom and saw Vivian and Little Donna together—*immediate rage*. She lunged at Little Donna and slapped her. The girl ran and jumped through a bedroom window.

Vivian tried to appease her, but she would have none of it, and she stormed out of the apartment after Vivian told her where he'd placed her purse in the other apartment.

Duane was feeling sorry that he was the one who had knocked on the door in the first place. His father didn't hold that against him, because there was no way for Duane to have known his father was with another woman.

Little Donna escaped bare-footed, so Vivian sent Peter to find her. She swore she wouldn't go back to the apartment, but Peter convinced her that nothing like that would happen again.

A few weeks later, Vivian found a house in Rio Nuevo, St. Mary, not far from the town of Ocho Rios and rented it. Vivian and Donna started having difficulties at Columbus Heights when his helper saw a man driving Vivian's car when he loaned it to Little Donna. Another incident occurred one Saturday night when Donna was dressing to go out.

"Where are you going?"

"Out."

Vivian laughed, an evil laugh. "With whom?"

"Janice and I are going out."

He'd caught her in a lie, because Janice was Loma's daughter.

"But, I just left Janice in her bed, sleeping with her kids," said Vivian, as he chuckled. "Let me tell you something, Donna … if you leave here tonight, don't put your feet back in my apartment. Take your clothes with you."

Vivian had had it with Little Donna, but he'd promised her that he would take care of her, as she'd just been deported. To send her back to live at Loma's house didn't feel right, so he told her she could live in his new house in Rio Nuevo, and he would help her find something to earn a living, so she could be on her own.

Conniving, Vivian made up a story to tell Evon on one of her visits to Jamaica. She agreed to buy several pairs of jeans, jean jackets, sneakers, T-shirts and ornaments to decorate the clothes, which he gave to Little Donna to start a business. Vivian told her she could stay at his house, get her business together, with one stipulation—she couldn't have a man—and made it clear to her that their relationship was over, but he had the privilege of sleeping with her whenever he wanted. If she found another man, the arrangement was over—the other man would have to find a place for her. She understood.

Taking into consideration his grave position in the United States, Vivian had wanted to settle down in Ocho Rios—no womanizing. He couldn't risk being exposed. When Little Donna found out his true identity, she started to love him, which made him sad. Vivian wanted her to love the simple man in the glasses, not Vivian Blake the gangster.

Miami was in turmoil. The infamous Shower Posse trial was about to begin—some had plea-bargained and were already serving, or about to serve time. They were the likes of Locksley Gayle, Michael "Sugar Belly" Campbell, Donovan Jones (a.k.a. Ronald Jones or Champs), Junior "Tan Tody" Wilson, Kirk Bruce, Lloyd Reid, Michael "Geego" Murray, Bugs, Modeler, Barrington "Vess" Anderson, Joy Cash, Monica Davis, Pearl Estreme, Everald French and Delva Gilzeane.

There were only four defendants who went on trial In February of 1989—Tony Bruce, Errol Huslin, Gary Isaacs and Eleanor Davis (a.k.a. Eleanor Dodd); the rest were star witnesses for the prosecution (twenty-seven in all). Vivian, Jim Brown, Richard Morrison (a.k.a. Storyteller) and Chris Bogle (a.k.a. Shower Chris) were still at large. The trial lasted many weeks, the prosecution's main witnesses taking the stand.

Testimony from Kirk, Champs, and Joy was deferred until the arrest warrants of Vivian and Jim had been executed. Other witnesses at the trial included Everald, Tan Tody, and Monica.

Modeler was the prosecution's key witness, spending almost two weeks on the stand. His testimony was spoken with intelligence, as though he was an attorney himself. It was important that he do so, for he couldn't afford to be the reason the prosecution lost this case—he would've been doomed.

Modeler had just finished serving five years in a federal prison and was charged in the Shower Posse indictment. He was facing another sentence in this indictment, plus, one way or the other, he would've been deported to Jamaica. In Jamaica, Modeler was under two life sentences, plus charges for the murder of two police officers were pending. While serving time in federal prison, he called Jim Brown at his office in Tivoli Gardens.

"Jim, you think you could arrange to have me out of the Jamaican prison when I am deported?"

"One thing I know I can do is give you the best lawyer money can buy, but I can't promise to get you out of prison, otherwise."

"The government in America is offering me a deal which would prevent Jamaica from extraditing me. And, since you can't guarantee me to get out of prison, I think I'm going to take it."

"I can't tell you what to do. You have to do what you have to do."

So, Modeler arranged with the Federal government to testify against Vivian, Tony Bruce, Jim Brown and Richard Morrison a.k.a. Storyteller.

Tony Bruce, Errol Huslin, Gary Isaacs and Eleanor Davis were found guilty.

In April of 1989, all four defendants were sentenced. Tony received a twenty-year sentence in a federal institution; Errol Huslin received fifteen years; Gary got a ten and Eleanor five. The trial generated worldwide media attention, and the hunt was intensified to capture and bring to trial the men who Modeler and others testified were the alleged leaders of the infamous Shower Posse—Vivian Blake and Lester Lloyd Coke.

The Jamaican General Elections were held in 1989, and the People's National Party (PNP) were victorious—they took over the government from the Jamaica Labor Party (JLP). Vivian was in Ocho Rios on Election Day and couldn't believe how peaceful it was. The people actually voted calmly, PNPs talking civilly to JLPs while they voted. He thought to himself, *this is how it should be, instead of brothers killing brothers because of political differences.*

Vivian had spent the better part of his life in America, where there was no political violence. The only people who died in politically affiliated crimes were presidential candidates, not civilians. Democrats and Republicans lived in the same households in America without killing each other, talking about policy differences, and agreeing to disagree.

Vivian loved to see the unity that was displayed in Ocho Rios and decided it was where he wanted to remain and set up a business. After the elections, he rented an office space from a sweet lady named Miss Levene, who was like a mother to Vivian. Her husband, Brenton, owned Parkway Restaurant in town, and Vivian met their kids—Leo and Chris—and other family members, Bev and Grace, whom he eventually dated.

Vivian paid rent for the office space for four months until he decided to start a motorbike rental—Manhattan Cars and Bike Rental Company Ltd. at 60 Main St. Peter was back in Fort Lauderdale and bought ten motorbikes, which he shipped to Vivian. There were only two bike rentals in Ocho Rios at the time, so Vivian's business quickly became the leader. Later, he added car rentals at the location, and then branched out into renting jet skis at Turtle Towers Beach.

Sundays were spent in Kingston, but Monday mornings found him back in Ocho Rios—bright and early. In a new housing complex that was being built in Prospect, St. Mary on the outskirts of town—St. Mary Country Club—Vivian became one of the first to own a home.

By then, Donna Combs was his closest friend and confidante, and he also became friends with Bobby, the father of Donna Combs' son Noah—and Simone and Shakeera, her two beautiful daughters. Through the friendship with Donna, Vivian had met two beautiful sisters—Natalie and Yolande, who lived across the street from Vivian's rented house in Rio Nuevo. Yolande was married and had two beautiful kids, but Natalie was the apple of Vivian's eyes. He was attracted to her from the very first time he saw her, but she was in love with a doctor, who didn't return her love. Vivian hated that, for Natalie was true to the doctor and deserved to be loved. He continually told her that he was going to marry her when she got over that doctor—that was a promise. *That girl needs a good man; the doc doesn't deserve her.*

"Remember, Natalie, anytime you are ready to be rid of the doctor, I'm here."

"Andrew, I love that doctor."

That would tear Vivian up inside, knowing that the doctor took Natalie for granted. She was so sweet, with her cool, fair complexion, tall hair, bowed legs and a smile that lit up the sky. She was an independent woman who didn't depend on her man to support her, and Vivian admired her for that. *A charming family*, in Vivian's own estimation, her mother, Nezita, included.

She ended up having a beautiful son by the doctor, but Vivian still didn't give up and kept in touch with Natalie, even after the birth of her son.

For two years, Vivian lived comfortably in Ocho Rios, but was awakened one morning with bad news from Jah T.

"Dave, daddy's in jail … they're planning on extradition back to America. The police tricked him and called him in for questioning on another matter, then arrested him on an extradition warrant."

This sent chills up Vivian's spine—the beginning of the end of his once comfortable life in Jamaica.

"I'll call you later to keep you up-to-date on any new developments," Jah T. said before he hung up.

Myriads of thoughts spun through Vivian's mind, remembering the good times with Jim and his family coming to Ocho Rios for visits. Vivian had only made a one-week visit to Tivoli Gardens since arriving in Jamaica. Jim and Jah T would visit with him at his family's house when he was in Kingston, or he would visit them at Jim's home in Arcadia.

With Jim under arrest—too close for comfort—Vivian had to be very careful. In the months that followed, he kept his eyes peeled and spent more time at his home in the St. Mary Country Club. Wally, his driver, told him that some men, who appeared to be CID [the Criminal Investigation Division of the Jamaican Police Force] policemen, came to Sea Palms asking about him.

About two months after that, Vivian was visiting a girlfriend—Laurel—in an area known as Balmoral in St. Mary, on the outskirts of town one Sunday morning. A friend, known as Don D. appeared at the house, carrying a newspaper—the Jamaica Herald—and showed Vivian the headline. Vivian was on the front page with a huge write-up on the Shower Posse situation.

His head pounded … he couldn't think. One thing for sure, though, he would have to leave the small town of Ocho Rios, where everyone knew each other—not a place to hide.

Vivian spent a few more weeks in town, tying up loose ends. It was hard, but he had to do it for his own safety. A reward of US $25,000—a million Jamaican dollars—was on his head, so he had no choice. Ocho Rios was a one-way in, one-way out kind of town. He packed his bags and left it for good.

"One day, I'll return to Ocho Rios."

Now a strange place to him, Kingston became his place of residence. He'd lost touch with the big city and didn't know the New Kingston uptown area well. Bored to death at home after he'd taken his kids to school, waiting to pick them up in the afternoons, he looked forward to helping them with their homework in the evenings.

Duane passed his common entrance examination and was attending his dad's former school, St. George's College. Dominique was attending St. Peter and Paul Kindergarten. Valerie wasn't as business savvy as Vivian, so he couldn't leave it up to her to "bring home the bacon"—so he had to find something to do, some kind of business to operate in Kingston.

His latest girlfriend Laurel was now spending some time in Portmore, a community joined to Kingston by a bridge. Most of her relatives lived in Portiere, so Vivian started going to Portmore in the daytime. Occasionally, he drove to Tivoli Gardens after he dropped his kids at school, knowing it was risky, but he was bored.

While Valerie and the kids were on a summer vacation in New York, Vivian was reliably informed that the police heard he was living in Beverly Hills. Immediately, he rented an apartment in Worthington Court, and removed his clothes and other belongings from the house in Beverly Hills. Valerie sold the house when she returned from New York and found another place. Vivian hardly ever slept at the family house for fear of being captured and putting his family in danger. But, he picked up the kids in the mornings and took them to school—Valerie picked them up in the afternoons. Sometimes, though, he'd have to take both turns.

While driving through Portmore one day, he noticed a huge vacant hall in Portmore Plaza and made inquiries as to its ownership—Mr. Montique—who had an office in the Plaza.

The hall appeared to have been locked up for a long time. Vivian was thinking of a place to set up a fitness center when he first saw the building, but noticed a huge bar across the rear of the building. *A nightclub! Of course! There is no nightclub in Portmore, the biggest single community in the Caribbean, and an Americanized nightclub should do well.*

Judging by the size—seven times that of the average store in the plaza—the place might be expensive.

"What's the price per month you would want for this building?"

"Six thousand dollars."

"I'll take it."

This was the first time Vivian had ever ventured into the nightclub business, so he didn't know much, but a willingness to try went a long way. He was a good interior decorator of houses and apartments, so he thought he could try his hand at the nightclub's decor. With nothing to its credit but a bar, Vivian had to build the nightclub from scratch.

An old friend in Portmore—Mutt—was very knowledgeable about construction and costs, so Mutt became his right-hand man. The building was in the middle of what used to look like a desert when Vivian was a kid, so he chose a name of a plant, abundant before Portmore became populated—Cactus—a name that soon became a phenomenon in the dancehall genre.

After three months of construction, refurbishment, and decoration, The Cactus had a jam-packed-to-capacity grand opening—Friday, December 13th 1990. The construction was completed the same evening it opened—just in the nick of time.

The first live acts to grace the stage were Junior Reid and Baby Wayne, two days later. Again, the nightclub was packed to capacity, and that Christmas season was good.

Although many patrons frequented the club, it suffered from lack of big spenders. Two nightclubs had opened a few months earlier in Kingston—Godfather's and the Twenty-four Carat Nightclub. Thus, the big spenders didn't come to Portmore as much.

But, The Cactus still did okay. Proper management was very hard to find because Vivian had to keep a low profile. If he could have been able to be upfront as "Vivian," the nightclub would have been bigger than Godfather's or Twenty-four Carat ever was, but he had to stay in the shadows.

While driving in Half-Way-Tree Square, he and Mutt spotted a girl dressed in tight blue jeans and a jeans shirt, walking with a little girl.

"Can I drop you somewhere?"

"Sure" the girl said, and she hopped into the car, along with the little girl.

"Where were you heading?"

"I'm going down to Hagley Park Road, in KingsPlaza to my hairdresser." So Vivian asked her name and home finding out they were Carlene and Portmore, by Garveymeade, respectively.

"Can I see you again?"

"Sure, I'll give you my address and phone number."

Reaching her destination, Carlene wrote them down on a piece of paper and gave it to Vivian.

Vivian watched Caroline's ass in those tight jeans as she walked toward the hairdresser. She was a gorgeous girl who looked half-white, with slightly puffy cheeks, but her skin tone was pretty.

"Damn, she looks good, Mutt."

She felt Vivian watching her and wiggled her ass even more.

While Vivian was by the Cactus Nightclub the next Monday, he finished some paper work, and then dialed Carlene's home number. Vivian had changed his name in Kingston, and had acquired a driver's license in the name of Paul Williams, but was still nicknamed Andrew.

"This is Andrew ... I dropped you off at your hairdresser's Saturday."

"Yes, I remember you, Mr. Andrew ... I thought you were gonna call me Saturday night. I wanted to come over your nightclub."

"You have my apology ... I got so busy Saturday night, I didn't know my head from my feet."

"Your apology's accepted."

"So when can I see you?"

"I'm free now ... you could drop by if you have the time."

"All right, I'll be over there in a few minutes ... I'm at the club."

"Okay, if you say so, Mr. Andrew."

Carlene was standing by the gate watching for Vivian as he arrived. Vivian was introduced to Carlene's sister Pinky, who was also a small, cute girl, of fair complexion. Carlene invited Vivian to her room upstairs, showing him some of her picture albums, which left his mouth wide open. The clothing Carlene wore to parties and dances caught Vivian off-guard. He'd never seen anything like that before—it showed almost every part of her body.

"Goddamn! You're a brave girl to be wearing those clothes out in public. The guys don't try to touch your private parts at these dances and parties?"

"No, never had that problem."

"You know, you can't go out with me like that. You have to have clothes on—real clothes," Vivian said, while laughing and Carlene laughed too.

"If you don't like that dress, I won't wear it if we're going out."

"It's not that I don't admire it, but I just wouldn't want to be having dinner in a restaurant with my lady dressed like that. It's all right for a dancehall, but it's been years since I've been to a Kingston dance. Country dances are different ... the girls just dress ordinary and no shots are fired."

"You scared of gunshots?"

"Hell, yeah! Shooting's are for bad men. I'm a decent man, can't you see? Let's go have dinner. I know a nice private restaurant where I eat, on Port Henderson Road—Temptations—where the food's great and the setting intimate."

"No problem ... just give me a chance to put something on."

"No naked clothes."

She dressed herself in jeans that showed her sexy shape and wore a T-shirt in which she tied a knot to one side, so that it hugged the top half of her body, showing the luscious imprints of her breasts.

They had a wonderful, delicious dinner that evening, and then he took her home. Twice when Vivian made dates for them to make love, he ended up in situations where he had to cancel out. The third time was a charm. He drove to her house, and walked upstairs to her room, where she was sitting on her bed. "How come you're not dressed yet?"

"Remember ... you postponed dates twice ... I wasn't gonna make it a third time. It seems like because I wear dancehall clothes, you aren't interested."

"Don't say that Carlene. I told you the circumstances about those two times. It was just unfortunate, that's all."

"I've already taken my shower. I just have to slip some clothes on. What do I wear, naked clothes? Remember ... we aren't going to dinner now ... I'm going to jump into your bed."

"Are you crazy? You want those people at my apartment to wonder what this decent eye-glassed man's doing with this naked girl? Those people are nosey."

About a month later, he had a fashion show at the Cactus Nightclub with some of Jamaica's top ten beauties. His roster of models stood like this—Sandra Foster, Erica Aquart, Michelle Williams, Millanie Miller and others—with the Fab Five Band on show.

The fashion show was planned by Maureen German of Spartan, Miss Jamaica World's official chaperone, and Vivian. The show was flawless, but it suffered from poor attendance, even though it was well promoted. Vivian and Maureen discussed the poor attendance after the show ended.

"I want to see a different type of fashion show … one with dancehall girls."

"Up against the uptown girls?"

"Not necessarily, but that wouldn't be a bad idea."

"And … I've got just the right girl … name is Carlene … she has other friends. We could put a show on together."

"Check it out and let me know. I'd be glad to talk to the girls about it."

"I'll check with Carlene and let you know by Tuesday."

Vivian paid Carlene a visit the next day, which was Monday.

"Would you do a fashion show … you and a few of your friends … at the club?"

Carlene started to blush. "I've never been on stage before, Andrew."

"You only have to be yourself. You won't have to act like you're a professional model … just act as if you were in the dancehall."

"That shouldn't be hard, then."

"And I know Sharon Rambo would love that … I guess we can also talk Pinky and Lorna into it."

That night, Carlene got in touch with Sharon and Lorna, and they agreed. Pinky was at the house, so Vivian and Carlene spoke to her and she agreed, also.

Vivian got back in touch with Maureen. "Carlene and her friends have agreed to do the show, how about your girls?"

317

"They're all willing, except Sandra Foster. She said it would be a little too much for her."

The show was planned and coordinated by L'Antoinette Stines, a choreographer who rehearsed it at the Spartan Health Center and included some of her dancers. Vivian loaned Carlene his car, and she drove around, promoting the show and selling tickets.

He went to the Gleaner Company and had them place a photographer's pictures of Carlene, Lorna, Pinky and Sharon in their next issue of the Star newspaper. Their pictures were all over town.

Showtime. It was billed "Fashion Clash: Uptown Fashion against Dancehall Fashion." The Cactus Nightclub was packed to capacity. Carlene, Lorna, Pinky and Sharon all had to take a shot of hard liquor to calm their nerves for their first appearance on a stage, but they were superb. The crowd loved them, and the show was a success. From that night on, Carlene was crowned "Dancehall Queen."

Vivian introduced a teen jam on Saturday evenings—the beginning of the end of Cactus for him. The teen jam sessions were very successful, but it turned away too many of the adult customers and killed his Saturday nights.

Several people began to realize that Vivian was the owner of the Cactus Nightclub, and he didn't like that, so he made arrangements to sell the club when he couldn't find proper management to represent him. An advertisement went into the Gleaner newspaper and two guys responded to it—Brian Chung and his partner Carroll.

Vivian decided on a more low-key business venture. Some great things happened through the opening of the Cactus Nightclub, though. Dancehall music was re-established, dancehall fashion was enhanced to a worldwide trend, and Vivian and Maureen created the dancehall queen.

During construction of the Cactus Nightclub, Jah T visited Vivian regularly at the construction site. He'd promised Vivian that he'd be at the club's opening night, but that was not to be. Jah T was arrested and was remanded in custody at the General Penitentiary in Kingston. It was very unfortunate because Jim was also there, pending extradition to the

States. Jim had to face the sad reality and cope with it for nine long months. After nine months, Jah T was acquitted.

Jim lost his full court hearing and filed a motion in the Jamaican Appeals Court, which also proved fruitless. Richard "Storyteller" Morrison, a co-defender with Vivian Blake and Jim Brown was also arrested and, pending extradition, was also remanded to penitentiary. Jim and Richard went to court together, and both lost their motions on appeal, so they went to the final Court of Appeal in an extradition hearing. They filed their motions with the English Court of Appeal, the Privy Council, and awaited their judgments.

While in the General Penitentiary, long before any decision was expected from the Privy Council in England, US Federal Marshals showed up, along with members of the Jamaican Constabulary Force. The US Marshals had legitimate documents, which showed without a doubt, that Richard Morrison had abandoned his rights to the Privy Council in England; therefore, he was at the end of *his* extradition fight. They had come to take him back to the US to stand trial as a member of the Shower Posse.

This caught Morrison by surprise, because he knew, positively, that he'd appealed to the Privy Council in England, along with Jim Brown. He disputed the facts, and told the prison official that he still had an appeal pending in the Privy Council, but that was not what the documents indicated. The US Marshals had official documents from the Ministry of Security that Richard Morrison had waived his right to the Privy Council appeal.

Richard continued to object before Jim spoke some sense into him.

"Story, just go with them … you can't win. The Jamaican police might kill you if you try to resist."

Storyteller gave up his struggle and went calmly.

The US Marshals were perfectly correct in their extradition procedure. The blunder was on the part of the Jamaican Government. After Storyteller was extradited to the United States, the Jamaican Government found out that the mistake in due process was theirs—not the American Government's—and they tried every diplomatic channel to secure Morrison's safe return back to Jamaica, so that it could be completed, a right which the Jamaican Constitution allowed every citizen. It was fruitless. The damage had already been done—the fault of botched paperwork by Ministry's employees within the Government.

Jim Brown was now alone in jail awaiting his fate from the Privy Council. Months passed, then in February 1992, tragedy struck again. Jah T was riding his CBR bike on the way from his mother's liquor store off Eastwood Park Road in Kingston. It happened along Maxfield Avenue, on his way to Tivoli Gardens, where he was going to a dance in honor of one of Tivoli Gardens community leaders—Claudius Massop, who was gunned down in the Kingston Streets by police officers. Jah T was piloting a truck filled with liquor from his mother's store to be sold at his dance, and given in remembrance of the late Massop, when gunshots were fired at him. One of the shots penetrated his side, and he lost control of the bike and crashed, damaging his testicles. Jah T was pronounced DOA at the Kingston Public Hospital. The cause of death was not the bullet, but rather the injury he sustained in the crash.

When the news reached Jim, he completely lost all composure. Vivian was at the Cactus Nightclub that Sunday afternoon when he saw the newsflash on television—a lifeless body on a stretcher, and a lady hugging him. Being like a second dad to Jah T, tears filled Vivian's eyes as he rushed from the nightclub to the new Kingston apartment.

He called Miss Bev—Jah T's mother—but she wasn't home. One of Jah T's sisters answered instead.

"Dave, Tony's dead. They killed Tony!"

It was worse for Jim, locked up, with no family members to console him. He cried until his eyes were swollen shut. In the days that followed, he walked around the penitentiary with Jah T's picture in his hand, and a black piece of cloth tied around his head. He'd lost his first son, Jah T, the second through gun violence. A hail of gunshots at West Street in Downtown Kingston killed his daughter, Mumpie. At the time of her death he'd been free, so he'd dealt with Mumpie's death better. This time he was locked up, and couldn't even attend Jah T's funeral.

Two weeks later, the day Jah T was to be buried, Jim drank heavily and tried to drown his sorrow with whatever drugs he could lay his hands on, hoping it would take away the pain, but the pain remained. Jim Brown had to face it, but he couldn't. At three-thirty that Sunday afternoon, Jim was locked in his cell ... alone ... crying ... and in terrible pain.

Later that evening, a prisoner, located in a cellblock known as B-South saw a ball of fire rushing from Jim's cell—in a section known as F-North.

"Jim Brown's cell's on fire!"

All the inmates in F-North were alerted and proceeded to break down their doors to go to Jim's assistance. The warders on duty started to panic, not knowing what to do. The inmates managed to get Jim out of his burning cell, but he was badly burnt. The warders brought a stretcher and Jim Brown was placed on it, groaning.

It was Sunday night, and they had only a skeleton staff. Most of the higher-ranking officers didn't work on weekends, and decisions were left in the hands of overseers. They were afraid to make a decision about a famous prisoner like Jim Brown—any mistake could cost their jobs. That caused a delay in quickly hospitalizing Jim. He'd even fallen off the stretcher and hit the floor very hard.

The overseers scampered to find someone in a high position to make a decision about taking Jim Brown to the hospital. When police and soldiers arrived, it was too late. Jim Brown, Vivian's best friend, was dead.

Vivian was at his apartment when he got a call from a blood brother he'd recently met since coming back to Jamaica—Junior Blake.

"Your friend's dead."

"I know ... that's been weeks now ... he was buried today."

"No, I'm not talking Jah T ... Jim Brown. He died at GP a few hours ago."

Vivian was just about to make love to a girlfriend—Marie—when the call came and his feelings for the girl went limp.

"Are you serious, Junior?"

"Yes, there's a lot of news on the radio and TV about it, and a lot of people are at the hospital."

Vivian remained silent after he slowly returned the receiver to the phone cradle.

"What's wrong, Andrew?"

Vivian looked at his girlfriend and giggled—an eerie sort of sound.

"I just lost the only true friend I had left ... nobody ever told me that life would be a bitch," he continued, then made that same insane sound that wasn't laughter at all.

The sale of the Cactus Nightclub became final and it was time for Vivian to chart a new course—a short-term loan company to assist those people who wanted small loans, but whom the banks wouldn't help. He opened an office in Heroes' Circle in mid-Kingston, and business immediately showed great potential. Another branch was opened in Savanna-la-mar in rural Jamaica.

Earl, a resident of Savanna-la-mar suggested, "There's a new plaza opening on Beckford Street ... I think some of the shops are still available."

"That sounds good Let's go check it out."

The owner of the plaza guaranteed Vivian a store, so in May 1993, Vivian's second office was opened, managed by Earl. After five months, he decided to expand throughout Jamaica.

His first office in Heroes' Circle was a bit small, so he acquired a bigger office space in a new location in Kingston, on Hagley Park Road. By September, he opened a branch in the old capital of Jamaica—Spanish Town—and business boomed there, as well. By November, Vivian rented an office space in Montego Bay and one in May Pen, Calrendon, one of Jamaica's leading business parishes. Those two offices were slated to open at the beginning of the New Year, 1994.

Vivian's main operational office was the Spanish Town branch where a girlfriend—Marjorie—was the manager. Having a few dates with Marjorie, he convinced her to join his company as a manager, while she was working at an accounting firm that did some work for him. Marjorie had a boyfriend who was very jealous, and he didn't trust Vivian around

Marjorie. When Marjorie's home developed water problems and she couldn't take a shower, Vivian was eager to help.

"You can shower at my apartment, if you don't mind."

During the Christmas holidays, Vivian spent a few days with his girlfriend—Heather—in his apartment. He'd met her one morning while he was driving to his office, catching sight of her behind. She had one of the sexiest strides a man could ever see, and he couldn't help but stop his car to talk to her. She was of average height, with slight bowed legs and very light complexion. Her hair was long, but she wore it up, and had a radiant, shy smile that showed remarkable dimples. She eventually gave Vivian her work number so he could get in touch with her. By Christmastime, Vivian was now seeing her on a regular basis.

That Christmas, there was no lovemaking, for Heather had the ladies' monthly troubles, so they simply enjoyed Christmas, talking and having other fun. He enjoyed Heather's company, so that was okay with him. Valerie and the kids were in New York for Christmas, so he made do without them.

Business at the loan offices resumed on January 3rd, 1994, with the new May Pen office opening on that day. Montego Bay's office was scheduled to open a week later. On the Wednesday, Vivian stopped by the Hagley Park Road office for a few minutes to take care of some business, and was about to leave with the General Manager—Kerene Sheriff—to have a bite at the Burger King on Eastwood Park Road in Kingston, when a call came in her. They where already out the door when a loan officer ran out and called out.

The phone call took longer than Vivian wanted to wait, so he sent one of the employees—Keisha—for a roast beef lunch from the restaurant across the street, telling her to buy some lunch for herself as well.

While Vivian was talking to one of his managers—Miss Henley—four men entered the lobby, identifying themselves as police officers and asking to be let inside. One of the office staff obliged them, and they walked past Vivian, who was sitting by Miss Henney's desk, to the office in the rear, where Kerene was.

When they came back out, one of the police officers asked, "What's your name?"

"Why?"

"What's your name?"

"Percival Johnson."

The police officers looked at a picture one of them had in his hand.

"This is him ... this is Vivian Blake," said the officer named Derrick Powell. Derrick Powell proceeded to put his hands on Vivian's waistband in a hostile manner, but decided against it when he saw that Vivian wasn't resisting.

"I'd come here to kill you, if you tried to resist arrest," Derrick Powell admitted.

The four officers marched out of the office with Vivian, despite the protests of the office staff. Among the arresting officers was Senior Superintendent Garnett Daley.

Powell kept talking to Vivian in an intimidating fashion. "You send your friends to shoot up my friends on Black Roses Corner."

"I don't even know where Black Roses Corner is. Did you see me when you arrested me? I don't have time for guns ... I'm a legitimate businessman."

The police officers placed him in the police car parked outside. All kinds of thoughts ran through Vivian's mind, his kids the most pressing topic on his mind. *How are they going to manage without me?* Vivian was desperate to think of something. "What ... you guys wouldn't take some money to cut me loose?"

Garnett Daley retorted, "No money in the world could make me set you free," as Derrick laughed along with the others.

Then it hit Vivian; *this is a political arrest.*

Vivian was taken to the special Anti-Crime Task Force Office on Ruthven Road in Kingston, placed in Daley's office, and given a seat while Powell hopped about happily and said to Daley, "Boss, I'm going for the warrant right now."

Several policemen came in and out of Daley's office looking at the gangster they'd heard so much about. One officer came up to Vivian and asked, "Mr. Blake, you know me?"

"No, it's the first I ever set my blessed eyes on you."

"Well, my name is O'Connor … they call me Hux. It's rumored that I'm your bodyguard."

Vivian managed a smile. "I don't even know you, much less you be my bodyguard. But, what would I need a bodyguard for anyway? I've also heard that Bigger Ford was my bodyguard, too. I was in a restaurant the other day and walked past Bigger Ford … he didn't even know who I was."

Another police officer came into Daley's office and stared at Vivian. "I'm Tony Hewitt," said the light-complexioned, medium-built man.

Vivian had heard quite a bit about Hewitt, ever since he was a kid. Jim Brown had spoken well of Mr. Hewitt.

"Mr. Hewitt is the best policeman in Jamaica. He's a policeman first, and anything else comes afterward."

So, Vivian had to look at the legend and show his respect. While Hewitt was in the office Vivian asked Daley a question. "Why were you so intent on arresting me, when a lot more guys who are wanted in America, walk the streets freely, and are not hiding like I was?"

"You know anyone you can name?" Daley inquired.

"It's not for me to tell you that … you should know … the people aren't hiding."

Given his one phone call, he called his attorney, Joy Bailey Williams, who, in turn called his criminal lawyer, George Soutar. Soutar arrived quickly. By that time, Detective Powell returned with the extradition warrant—Daley served it.

In half-an-hour, Powell and some other officers took Vivian to his apartment under the watchful eyes of Soutar. Three police officers stayed in the car with Vivian, while Powell, others, and Soutar went inside the apartment. The officers searched it and took some documents.

"What a nice apartment, man. You don't want to eat your dinner that was prepared?" asked Powell.

"No, I'm not hungry."

Chapter 13: Jailed!

The police officers from the special Anti-Crime Task Force took Vivian to the Half-Way-Tree lock-up—the Gulf—in Kingston, where he was placed in a cell with three other inmates. The Gulf stank. Inmates spat and urinated from their cells into the passageway, making it continually wet—two gutters ran alongside the two rows of cells. Vivian had to deal with it—that's what jail was like in Jamaica.

It was one of the longest evenings of Vivian's life, but nighttime finally arrived. He had the shock of his life when he stood at the grilled cell door looking out into the passageway. An army of rats, the size of guinea pigs, appeared, creeping out from the sewer beneath the cells.

"Shit! What the fuck are those?" he screamed while backing away from the grilled door, the three inmates laughing at his frightened state.

"That's how the rats look around here." Burns was a tall, dark-complexioned guy, firmly built. One side of his body was burnt, from head to leg.

Devil, another inmate, was tall, very light complexioned, good-looking with a slender build, from an area in Kingston known as Maxfield, and Vivian got along well with him.

"Big man, where are you from?"

Vivian studied Devil for a while, and then looked him in the eyes. "I'm Vivian Blake. I'm from Tivoli Gardens."

"You're Vivian? So how you look so simple?"

"How should I look? You all read too many newspapers."

All the inmates stared at Vivian in astonishment, as if his ordinary looks amazed them. Shouldn't Vivian look like the monster the newspapers portrayed him to be?

The third inmate—Chicken Chest—was also from the Maxfield area. They cleared off two concrete beds so that Vivian could have them, while two guys slept on the floor.

Vivian didn't sleep well that night, thinking about his children—the two loves of his life—and wondered how they would manage with him in jail. As long as he was confident that they would grow up to be good kids, he could handle being in jail, but if not, that would surely kill him.

To Vivian, parenting was different compared to other parents. His mother died in a car crash in June of '69, and he knew no father, his father having left four months before he was born and never returned to Jamaica. Just before he left America in 1988, Vivian spoke to his father.

"Son, I was one of the unlucky ones who came to England in the fifties, and never made it. I tried to send for your mother so that she could come to England, but she refused. This was the first time Vivian had heard that his father had tried to help his mother, and he started to release the hatred he'd held inside for his father.

"I'm now living on welfare … the Government of England takes care of me."

Vivian broke down in tears. The same day Vivian wired U.S. $5,000 to his dad. His father died in 1994, while Vivian was incarcerated in Jamaica, and he never saw his dad face to face.

Vivian never wanted his kids to live through what he did, and in his mind, did his best to bring them up in the best environment possible, and provide them with the best education money could buy. He loved his kids, but his relationship with them caused a negative impact on his love life. His two kids consumed most of his love, which left very little for the women in his life. He'd lost all love for his wife, but was still in love with his kids—it wasn't exactly fair to his wife, but that's how it was. He'd never change.

It amazed Vivian, though, that his wife didn't love the kids like he did. Vivian was *in love* with his kids—that was the difference. For example, she would be satisfied with the kids going to a public school, while Vivian preferred the individual attention provided at a private school.

The news of Vivian's arrest reached Valerie and the kids in New York the day he was arrested. By the next day, they were in Jamaica. That evening his kids saw him behind bars—one of the worst days of Vivian's life. It hurt so much, but there was nothing he could do about it. Dominique had to stay a little distance away, because she was only seven years old, but eventually he got to talk to her. Duane approached him and started to cry.

"Why you doing that, Duane? You have to be strong for your father; otherwise, I'll break down, too. No crying, Duane. Everything's gonna be all right. You're the man of the family now ... you have to be strong. I never, ever, wanna see you cry when you visit me ... ever. You understand?"

"Yes, Dad," said Duane managing a smile.

Vivian returned the smile to his son. "That's what I want to see ... I want you to promise me that you'll go to college and get your degree."

"I promise, Daddy ... you don't have to worry about that. Just take care of yourself, Daddy ... I love you."

"I love you too, Son. And, there's another thing ... I want you to promise me that you'll take good care of your sister."

"I promise, Daddy." Duane was still trying to keep cheerful above the pain that he was feeling.

Several of Vivian's friends crowded the station yard that day, wanting to see him. The police officers had to keep the crowd under control, but Vivian had the chance to kiss Dominique—that made his day. By nightfall, the crowd disappeared, and he had to face the reality of being in jail.

The court date was set for Friday, January 7th, in the Half-Way-Tree Courthouse in Kingston, presided over by Magistrate Marcia Hughes, a tall, black, serious-faced woman with a cunning smile. That day, the Jamaican Army and senior members of the police force were on guard. Snipers were on the roofs of different buildings looking out for anyone trying to forcibly take Vivian from the custody of the police.

Vivian thought it very unnecessary—overreaction of the Jamaican Government. The media made Vivian an icon, but it paid off for them. The Jamaican newspaper sold more copies when he was a headline story, and the radio and TV stations had more audience when he was the topic, but Vivian hated that, because what they printed was a bad image of him. There was never a news report without it ending with, "The Shower

Posse was responsible for over fourteen hundred murders."—very damaging to Vivian's credibility and image.

After being at the Half-Way-Tree lock-up for a week, the police officers were given strict orders that he should be left alone in his cell for security reasons. About five o'clock that Wednesday morning, while looking through his grilled cell door, he saw some police officers beating an inmate off the steps that led to the second level lock-up.

The inmate fell down the steps, got to his feet again, while the police officer rushed after him as the he stumbled into the desk area. Vivian couldn't see what was happening, but heard the phone and books crashing to the floor, and the desk and chairs being forcefully moved. A few minutes later, Vivian saw some police officers and an orderly inmate pulling a lifeless body past his cell on the messy passageway, his hands and feet limply dragging across the concrete. They took the body to a cell, about four down from Vivian, and tossed the inmate into it.

That guy looks like he's dead or unconscious.

Other inmates raised the alarm later that morning. The inmate was dead. Whether it was the beating or the fall from the steps, one of those incidents killed him.

Later that day, Inspector Reneto Adams came to see Vivian in his cell. "Blake, you saw what happened to the man that died?"

"All I can tell you is that I saw the officers and the orderly put a lifeless body in that cell."

"Someone will be held criminally responsible for the inmate's death."

Vivian found out afterwards that the inmate was a brother of the owner of a huge fast food chain—Mother's.

The following day, a police officer told Vivian to pack his belongings. "They're moving you to the Central lock-up in downtown Kingston."

Vivian was placed in a cell on the second floor, a much cleaner environment, in which he had a view of the yard where visitors would come to visit their friends and relatives. News of his transfer to the Central lock-up got out. When he went to court in Half-Way-Tree the next day, police and soldiers were everywhere; some on the roof tops with high-powered rifles, others in and around the courtyard with similar weaponry. About three thousand friends, relatives and sympathizers were in the courtyard and in the streets, supporters of Vivian's quest for freedom. Some wore T-shirts, which read "Free Vivian Blake," and several pamphlets were distributed, illustrating facts about Vivian's indictment. The crowd protested and shouted, "Free Vivian Blake," and "You can't keep a good man down," and many others. After a brief appearance in court, he was hustled out to a waiting jeep, and was rushed to the Central lock-up.

An hour later, the lock-up yard became very crowded as visitors started to pour into it. The police officers had to cut short Vivian's visits—there were too many—including Duane and Dominique.

Just as he was about to kiss Dominique, a female corporal interrupted, "She can't visit here. She's a kid."

Dominique panicked and walked away from her father, down to where her mother was standing. If a person had sliced Vivian's arm, not a speck of blood would've appeared—so upset was he about the callous actions of the police officer. It was most indecent. She could've said what she had to say more calmly, and it wouldn't have frightened the seven-year-old child. But, such was life. He was their prisoner, and they called the shots. Vivian spoke with his son for a while, then the family left.

The next week, Duane and some of his school friends walked from St. George's College to visit his father. Vivian was always happy to see Duane, but cautioned his son. "Duane, it's too dangerous on the streets for you to walk all the way down here. Don't do it again, and when you leave here, please take a cab home … make sure you hail the cab in front of this police station."

He spoke with his son for a long time that evening.

Vivian's incarceration was made easy by the humane and caring police officers that worked at the lock-up, served his daily meals, and allowed daily visits. Vivian suspected one of the sergeants to be gay. He did his job well, but was criticized behind his back by the other officers. Vivian had spent most of his adult life in America, where gay people were an important part of the American culture, and he'd learned to accept them as people, not treating them differently because of their sexual preferences, as long as they kept their behavior between themselves and their peers. With that understood, he had no problems communicating with them, and he and the sergeant got along well. He was very intelligent, an avid reader, and well versed on most subjects, so Vivian loved talking to him.

After lock-down one night, Vivian observed an inmate—an orderly—was out of his cell. Vivian suspected this inmate to be gay, also, but that didn't bother him. Vivian had spoken with the inmate several times and found him to be an intelligent individual.

This night in question, the gay sergeant was about to lock the gay inmate in his cell, so he led the inmate from downstairs to the upper section, to a cell next to Vivian's. An observant junior police officer realized that he hadn't heard the gate, which separated the two floors, open or close. He became suspicious and slowly tiptoed up the steps. Vivian heard a shout.

"Shit! What the fuck you guys doing?"

About a half-hour later, while the junior police officer was patrolling Vivian's cellblock, he stopped at Vivian's cell. "I caught the inmate rubbing on the front of the sergeant's parts."

The gay inmate heard what the junior officer said. "You're lying. You're making stuff up."

The junior officer complained in Vivian's presence that he wouldn't work with the sergeant again, but they continued anyway.

About two months later, there was a disturbance on the first-floor cellblock at the Central lock-up. The gay sergeant was on duty and rushed to see what was happening. Vivian was downstairs at the time talking with a visitor. The sergeant returned from the cellblock area downstairs with two inmates, and was upset about the commotion they'd caused.

With a swift whack of his baton, the sergeant hit the skull of one of the inmates, and he fell to the floor, blood pouring from his head. This was the first Vivian witnessed a man receiving such treatment that immediately rendered him mentally insane. The inmate started to laugh, then became deadly serious, then laughed again, then serious … it continued for quite a while.

The sergeant didn't know what to do or say.

Then Vivian said to the sergeant, "Can't you see that the blow to his head has left him mentally insane."

The sergeant looked at Vivian with wondering eyes. The inmate was taken to the hospital—from that day onward insane.

While Vivian was in the upstairs corridor of the central cellblock, an inmate—White Ghost—said to him, "Mr. Blake, look … they're bringing in Shinpan."

Vivian immediately changed his focus to the yard, and saw two detectives leading Erick "Chinaman" Vassell to the lock-up. Vivian had heard the name before, but was seeing him for the first time—light complexioned, slender, medium height, oriental-looking and with braided hair. He was placed downstairs in a cell.

The next day, while Vivian was visiting with a friend, a girl—Pepsi—appeared by the grill.

"Hi, Andrew."

"What you doing in here, Pepsi?"

"I came to visit Chinaman."

Chinaman was brought out from his cell to the grill, and Pepsi introduced Chinaman to Vivian. They both had a lot in common. They knew some of the same girls, but most importantly, they were the two most wanted Jamaicans by the US Federal Government, and they were both locked-up because of extradition warrants.

Vivian called to the gay sergeant who was on duty and asked, "Could Chinaman come upstairs?"

"No, he has to stay downstairs."

After the sergeant walked away, Vivian said, "Saturday, I'll try to get you upstairs when he's not working."

"All right."

That Saturday, Chinaman was moved upstairs to a cell next to Vivian, and they enjoyed a wonderful day on the corridor, which included lunch and dinner. The next day, the gay sergeant was at work from eight in the morning until four in the afternoon.

"Stay in your cell, Chinaman. I don't want the sergeant to see you. He might want to send you back downstairs."

The sergeant was an officer who loved to check the cells while he was on duty, so he was upstairs checking the cells when he looked into Chinaman's cell.

"What you doing up here? Get the fuck back downstairs!"

Chinaman came out of the cell with his belongings and walked downstairs, embarrassment showing all over his face.

Vivian was upset at the sergeant for shouting at Chinaman, and cursed all day until the sergeant was relieved at four.

Vivian's family brought a well-prepared Sunday dinner to the corridor, and he ate until he could eat no more. Night had fallen, and he was retired to his cell. About an hour later, the sergeant on duty pulled his unlocked cell door open.

"Blake, some prisoners just escaped from up here."

There was panicked movement among police officers in the yard. They were all scrambling to find the two escaped prisoners, but the inmates were gone. The superintendent in charge of the Central lock-up rushed to Vivian's cell and when he saw Vivian, he was relieved, "Thank God, you're here, Blake. You're a good man." He would surely have lost his job if Vivian had escaped.

The Commissioner of Police—Mr. Trevor Macmillan—visited Central lock-up the next day to inspect the breakout site, accompanied by the gay sergeant, who was smiling from ear-to-ear. The Commissioner of Police commended the sergeant for preventing what they thought was a planned attempt to break out Chinaman and Vivian. The sergeant advised the Commissioner that he was the one who sent Chinaman back downstairs, or Chinaman would have escaped, too.

Vivian thought it so stupid for them to give any credence to such a story, because if he was part of the breakout, why hadn't he gone, too? And, why was he in his cell half-asleep?

With the escape of the prisoners, Vivian and Chinaman made the headlines again. Chinaman went to court the day after the breakout, but never returned. The Central lock-up was full of tension for the next two days, but all the police officers knew that Vivian was not involved.

Suddenly, Vivian was told to pack his belongings. He was transferred without notice to the maximum-security prison in downtown Kingston—General Penitentiary—arriving about midday on a Wednesday, late in August 1994.

The high prison walls were made of bricks—built in the days of slavery and used by the slave masters to store the slaves after delivery by the slave ships. There was a tunnel—now closed—that the slave masters used to transport the slaves from the ship to the holding area. It was not a pretty picture: ninety-nine percent ancient buildings, a primitive sewage system, and a stench from the many gutters that permeated the place. Several prisoners could be seen walking around in full, white calico-fabric outfits.

While in the administration office, an associate of Vivian's—Howie Ninja—appeared. "What's up, Bossie? Where they putting you?"

"They said a section known as H-North."

"Tell them to put you on F-North. H-North is the PNP section."

"Doesn't matter to me."

"PNP or Laborite section … I don't care."

Vivian knew that sometimes it's best to live with strangers, rather than people you grew up with. He was in jail based on false information given to the Fed by people he grew up with. As a matter of fact, he was comfortable with wherever he was going to be living—for God knew how long.

He was taken by a warden—as the correctional officers are called in Jamaica—to H-North cellblock, where he was greeted warmly by mostly ex-death row inmates. He immediately met the prominent PNP activists whom he'd read about in the Jamaican newspapers. Screechy John from Spanish Town and Sprat—a.k.a. Yushman—from the Waltham Park area in Kingston were two of them. Screechy and Yushman arranged a cell for Vivian and made him feel very welcomed. Screechy John was next door.

Vivian also met another guy—Prince—two cells away—who was also fighting extradition, the same as Vivian. The inmates on H-North Block assisted Vivian in settling before the evening lock down, which was three-thirty in the afternoon—the inmates weren't released until nine o'clock the next morning. The cells had no toilet or face basin, so an inmate was equipped with bottles of water, and a bucket in which to urinate and pass feces. An inmate couldn't empty his bucket until the cell was opened in the morning, so he'd have to bear the stench of his own feces in the tiny cell. Vivian lived alone, so he didn't have to deal with a rowdy cellmate—that was a blessing.

Vivian's first morning in the General Penitentiary was a learning experience. Screechy taught Vivian what to do and what not to do. If an inmate didn't mind his p's and q's, he'd be cast amongst the undesirables in the prison, so Vivian had to learn well from his teacher.

After finishing his morning chores, Vivian met some more inmates—Festos and Buckwheel, who were PNP activists from the Dunkirk area; Million, another PNP activist from Hannah Town; Zero, a PNP activist from Waterhouse; and Earl Pratt, a JLP activist from Central Village.

While socializing with the inmates on H-North, Vivian heard someone shouting his name and looked across F-North to find to his delight it was Chinaman.

"What's up, nigga?"

"They brought me here straight from court on Monday."

Vivian and Chinaman were placed under security watch—not allowed to leave their cellblocks to participate in any activities. The warders watched them constantly. At nights, warders with rifles patrolled in front of their cellblocks and fired shots to try to intimidate them, which only caused them to bond more closely.

The superintendent—John Davis—a short, black man who walked with a limp, ordered an extra lock be placed on both Vivian's and Chinaman's cell doors. The pressure in their own country was extreme for Vivian and Chinaman.

Vivian was used to his food being cooked at home and brought to him when he was at the Central lock-up. When his family brought food for him at the prison and they were turned back, Vivian raised hell.

He asked to see the Superintendent and was escorted by two warders to Davis' office.

"Good afternoon, Mr. Davis. Some food came for me today, but the officers at the gate refused to accept it."

"You think this is your house? This is a *prison*. You eat what's served here," the Superintendent defiantly answered.

Vivian studied him carefully and returned in a rude manner, "Anytime I see you eat the dog food served here, I'll gladly eat it, too. Until then, they can shove it." Then he looked at the warders who had taken him to the Superintendent's office. "I'm ready to go back to my section."

John Davis was shocked at Vivian's response. Vivian didn't care about the after-effect, because he knew the superintendent had acted disrespectfully and he would get what was coming to him.

"Take him back to his section," said Davis.

Vivian walked away with the two warders.

"You can't talk to the superintendent like that," said one of the warders, as they walked to the cellblock.

"He disrespected me first; I'm not his boy. He can't talk to *me* like that, and expect me to show him respect. Nah, man ... I refuse to be a punk."

That week, the doctor approved Vivian's home-cooked food, on the basis of health reasons—the permit was given by the Assistant Superintendent, Mr. Sept Hall. The superintendent was hopping mad when he heard that Hall had signed Vivian's food permit, but it was too late. Anything Davis could have done to cancel the food permit would've exposed his extreme prejudice, and he wouldn't want it to be so obvious.

A soccer match was being played at the football field one day, and Vivian and Chinaman were given permission to watch it. About fifteen minutes into the match, Hall approached Vivian and Chinaman. "You both have to go back to your cellblocks. I'm catching hell because I permitted you both to watch the soccer game. I'm sorry about this."

"I understand," said Vivian. "Don't worry about it."

They walked back with Hall to their section.

Vivian was becoming rather comfortable at the prison. Davis left, and a new Superintendent took his place. Vivian obtained permission to paint his cell, and placed plastic tiles on the floor. He had a twin, wooden bed built and painted white, and an electrician wired his cell, adding lights and plug sockets. He could read at nights and listen to his cassettes, and he had a Watchman TV set, with a two-and-a-half-inch screen.

Although he got along well with all of the inmates on his cellblock, some were skeptical. The media blow-ups about him being a very powerful JLP activist was still present in their minds. He was no JLP activist. He was just a pure born-and-bred Tivoli Gardens man who loved his community. Vivian was no politician and didn't like to be identified as one. When he read newspaper articles trying to make him out to be a politician, he became upset. He'd always maintained that he loved his community and was very proud to be a citizen of Tivoli Gardens, that he'd never been a party to anything political.

To Vivian, Tivoli Gardens was more than just politics. Many outsiders would never understand that it was a community of love and unity, because of the bad publicity the community received.

After living on H-North for several months, a long-time JLP activist—Boyork—came into the prison and was immediately placed on H-North.

Many years ago, Vivian had heard a lot about Boyork when he was visiting New York from England. Likewise, Boyork had heard about Vivian and asked to meet him. At the end of the meeting, Boyork asked Vivian if he could assist him with some marijuana. Vivian had given him ten pounds.

Vivian hadn't seen Boyork since that first meeting.

"What's up, Bossie? Long time I haven't seen you. You heard that I was busted with the marijuana you gave me in Upstate New York?"

"Yeah, I heard it in passing. So, are you okay?"

338

"Not really. I was taken with a gun in my possession, and I'm facing five years."

Boyork was familiar with the block, because he'd spent sometime on H-north on a previous arrest.

Vivian had nothing much to talk to Boyork about, because they weren't friends. He was closer to the inmates on the block.

In the weeks that followed, Boyork tried to get close to Vivian, but Vivian dealt with him on a completely social level. That annoyed Boyork, so he started to discuss Vivian with other inmates—those who were skeptical about him. Everyone thought Boyork and Vivian were friends from a long time ago, but nothing was so farther from the truth.

Finally, Vivian and Boyork had an argument, which turned sour. Yushman and Screechy John didn't like what Boyork was starting to stir up on the cellblock.

Boyork was walking from the bathroom, when Screechy jumped from out of nowhere, and stabbed him in the arm. Boyork was immediately removed from the block after he received several stitches, but some of the inmates didn't like Screechy's interference in what they thought was purely a JLP affair.

That night, Vivian clarified the whole misunderstanding. "This is the second time in my life I've set eyes on Boyork. Once in New York, and then here. I am closer to you all than I ever was with Boyork. I don't know him … we're not friends."

Vivian spoke aloud and everyone on H-North heard him. The skeptical inmates changed their attitudes toward Vivian after that night and started to respond more friendly. Vivian wasn't the JLP activist they thought he was.

Screechy was acquitted of his murder charge, and Yushman was granted a $20,000 bond—both left jail. Vivian had introduced Evon's sister—Audry—to Screechy and they started dating.

Back in prison, Vivian and an ex-death row inmate— Festos—from Dunkirk, took to each other. The inmates from Dunkirk stuck together, especially the three ex-death rows on H-North—Festos, Buckwheel and

Fines—and Vivian admired that. They were always together, never entered into anything life-threatening with each other, and were enrolled in the prison school program.

Festos would get mad when they called him "Gullymouth," but he was a very pleasant person. He was black, of medium build and joked a lot. He was a good soccer player. Festos had been in prison for upwards of fifteen years. Fine was tall, dark and strong, and laughed a lot, too. He'd been in prison over ten years. He was also a good soccer player. Buckwheel was the youngest of the three—slender, dark, handsome, and wore his clothes well. He and Vivian had much in common. He was an excellent soccer player, and above all, he'd attended St. George's College, the same as Vivian.

Vivian and these three inmates became so brotherly that they were the envy of many of the inmates from the West Kingston area. That didn't bother Vivian much … just because a person was from West Kingston didn't mean they had to be his friend; associates likely, but not necessarily friends. *There is no community where everyone is friends,* Vivian thought.

Vivian had another close friend—Speedy—from Concrete Jungle in Kingston. He'd lost the appeal of his murder conviction and was transferred from the General Penitentiary to the death row section of the Spanish Town District Prison. Speedy was tall, black, and slender and played soccer well.

Making the best of a bad situation, Vivian decided to teach himself how to write movie scripts and screenplays. He'd managed to sneak a cellular phone inside the prison, so he had unlimited access to the outside world via the telephone. He kept in constant contact with his kids. They'd moved from Jamaica and were living now in New York, and he and Duane planned, and wrote movie scripts together. The first three scripts Vivian wrote by himself; then Duane started to do his thing.

From the prison, Vivian made connection with a Hollywood producer/director named Carolyn Phieffer-Bradshaw, who'd just finished producing a Jamaican movie called *Clash*.

Vivian read *Clash's* script, compared it to the scripts he'd written, and knew that he'd done a better job than the writer of *Clash*. So, he called up the director's wife after sending the three scripts to her.

"Hi, Mrs. Bradshaw, how are you? This is the guy from the prison who sent you those scripts."

"Yes, how are you? I just finished reading the scripts. I'm impressed. You got better as you went on. From reading I could see that *Niggaz from the Bronx* was your first script, then *Drug Connection* and finally *Journey*."

"You are perfectly correct," said Vivian, anxious to know whether the scripts were good. "So tell me, what do you think?"

"Hmmm … they need to be written in screenplay format, but I know someone you could talk to who can write them. His name's Tony Hendricks. I'll give you his phone number so you can talk with him."

A concert was scheduled at the prison, coordinated by a warder named John Hepburn. Vivian and Chinaman were very instrumental in coordinating the artists—Beenie Man, Monster Shack Crew, Lt.Stitchie, Tony Rebel, Admiral Bailey and others. Vivian invited Hendricks to the concert, so they could have a good talk. Hendricks showed up as promised and decided to perform for the 1,500 inmates, their friends and families. The audience was in stitches, and he received a warm reception.

After the performance, he was led to Vivian—who was in the audience. They greeted each other formally.

"How are you?"

"Fine, and how are you, under the circumstances?"

"Just hanging in there."

"I've read the scripts, and I love them, but I think *Niggas from the Bronx* and *Journey* should be merged."

They talked for a long time while the concert was in progress, then Vivian asked the million-dollar question. "How much would you charge to write one of the screenplays?"

Hendricks pondered for a second. "US $20,000."

Vivian was shocked at the price but showed no indication. "I'll be in touch with you about the writing of the screenplay."

The concert was a great success—the inmates, their friends and families immensely enjoying themselves. That night, while Vivian was in his cell he thought about the price that Tony Hendricks had quoted him to write the screenplay.

How hard is a screenplay to write? Vivian thought. *I must be able to do it myself. I have the screenplay for Clash here ... I should be able to teach myself.*

After release from his cell the next morning, he went to the library in search of some kind of text about screenplays. He was in luck. He found a book titled *Formatting Screenplays* and started to scan through it. "Perfect!" he said to no one in particular, then signed for the book and left. He read until daybreak and continued studying the context of the book the following night until he had it.

In the weeks that followed, he wrote the screenplay and sent it to Duane.

Duane called his father that evening on his father's cell phone. "Dad, I can't believe you did this. This screenplay's professionally done. How did you do it?"

"With a little knowledge, dear boy, and determination, you can do anything."

Thereafter, Duane, with the help of his father, would put the scripts together, Duane would come up with the concepts, but his father would actually write the screenplays. To date, they have completed thirty screenplays.

Vivian was an avid sportsman, so during the daytime he participated in sports, and when he was locked away in his cell, he'd write screenplays and American rap songs. The screenplays that Duane wrote were mixed—some about American gangsters and others that were directed at the hollywood movie audience.

The sporting events that Vivian took special interest in were soccer, cricket and table tennis, and he excelled at all three. He was placed amongst the top four cricket and table tennis players in the prison. He'd lost his speed in the soccer arena, but he was still as skillful as ever.

His friends were mostly sportsmen in the prison, because they shared that common bond. His team, H-North, became the envy of most prison teams. He furnished the soccer gear for his teammates and any equipment they needed. This became a problem, though, because inmates started accusing the H-North inmates of being showboats, and a grudge developed.

H-North was the cleanest section in the prison. Even that was becoming a problem for other inmates, so some of them began to hate Vivian, because of the ways in which he showed his love to his friends—they were not part of it. H-North cellblock was one of the blocks on which the warders enjoyed working the most.

When Vivian entered the prison, H-North and F-North were dubbed the most violent blocks. With the emphasis on sports, the inmates on H-North cellblock transformed their violent energy into competitive energy, and the environment became peaceful. Fifteen warders had previously been posted on H-North; eventually, one warder could control the block. The warders loved the change, but there were outside inmates who hated that. The inmates on H-North, however, kept their cool and paid the others no attention.

The superintendent of the prison, a very kind-hearted humanitarian—Mr. Jones—was tall, dark, and well built and wore tested glasses. His corporal—Mr. John Hepburn, a.k.a. Mr. John—was a short, slender, black man who was always laughing, and knew every single prisoner by name. He knew the prison better than any other warder, so Mr. Jones trusted his judgment—he never failed Mr. Jones.

Mr. John had soccer teams from outside the prison come inside the prison walls and play against an all-star prison team, which kept the prison calm. The prisoners looked forward to those regular activities; it kept their minds occupied, and from idle thoughts that could develop into altercations. About every two months, there was a major activity for the inmates to enjoy, which was coordinated by Mr. John and approved by Mr. Jones.

One afternoon, while most prisoners were locked in their cells, the Commissioner of Prisons—Col. John Prescod—was touring the prison yard. He was between H-North and F-North cellblocks, accompanied by Superintendent Jones and other senior officers. Col. Prescod complained to the Superintendent and the other officers about the spiderwebs on the walls, even though there were more pressing problems in the prison. An argument ensued between the Colonel and Mr. Jones—it could be heard on H-North. Two days after the disagreement, Mr. Jones went on leave and never returned to the General Penitentiary.

Mr. John continued with his activities, but didn't receive full cooperation from the senior officers any more. There was a senior officer, the Director of Prison Security—Mr. "Toothpick" Smith—who Vivian had come to hate. Vivian had no idea why Mr. Smith placed so much pressure on him. Mr. Smith hated the General Penitentiary but glorified another prison—South Camp Road Rehabilitation Center.

After Mr. Jones left the GP, Toothpick put a lid on activities, which resulted in minimal entertainment for the inmates. This, along with non-support of other senior officers, forced Mr. John to resign—the General Penitentiary went downhill. The inmates dearly missed Superintendent Jones and Corporal John Hepburn. If Mr. Jones and Corporal Hepburn had remained at the penitentiary, there probably would not have been a riot in August of '97, during which eighteen inmates died.

After Mr. John's departure, the feeling within the prison was of sadness, and the sadness caused frustration. To make matters worse, a search team was formed and violence skyrocketed, instead of declining. Force is not always the answer ... a little public relations with the inmates would have worked much better.

Life had to go on, so Vivian and his friends on H-North continued their sports activities. Grudges among other inmates against Vivian and his friends grew worse, but the H-North inmates continued their sanitary ways and their sports activities.

Vivian was becoming deeply involved in screenplay writing. Realizing the rapid rise of violence in the prison, Vivian, along with Festos, Buckwheel, Fines, and other inmates, formed a committee to combat violence, which was endorsed by the prison authorities. Weekly meetings were held.

In early 1997, Bobby Reds was transferred from the Remand Center in Kingston to the GP.

Chinaman went to see Vivian over at his cellblock. "I have a guy known as Bobby Reds, who just got in the prison. I want you to get a cell for him over at your block and take care of him for me. I don't want him over at my cellblock, 'cause we don't get along."

"No problem. I got to meet him once when I owned the Cactus Nightclub, but he didn't know who I was then."

Vivian and Chinaman busied themselves with Bobby Reds' relocation on the H-North. Finally the okay was granted, and Bobby acquired a cell, two away from Vivian. Vivian was having Jamaica's National Dish—ackee and saltfish—so he offered Bobby some. After Vivian finished eating, he bought a bed from an inmate, placed it in Bobby Red's cell, and loaned him a six-inch colored television and a cassette player. Vivian did everything he could that day to make Bobby comfortable. Everything Bobby Reds needed to feel at home, Vivian obliged.

"I have a cell phone, so if you need to make any calls, I'll lend it to you later."

"Definitely, man, I need to call my woman."

While Bobby was at the Remand Center lock-up, he'd been treated badly by the inmates. They didn't like him because of his miserly behavior, which Chinaman complained about to Vivian.

"He's too cheap. He's a miser."

Bobby was stripped of his cash while remanded at the Remand Center. After a court appearance in the Half-Way-Tree Criminal Court in Kingston, he begged the judge not to send him back to the Remand Center, because he said the inmates had robbed him and wanted to kill him. The judge took sympathy with his plea and remanded him to the GP. Several inmates who had been at the Remand Center were eventually transferred to the GP—where they saw Bobby.

One H-North inmate—Gregory Nose—was one of those incarcerated with Bobby at the Remand Center. He saw Bobby and Vivian sitting together.

"Big man, you shouldn't protect this pussy Bobby Reds."

Vivian looked up at Gregory Nose. "What's the problem with you and Bobby?"

"Me and this pussy can't have any problem ... he's a pussy."

Vivian had heard Bobby Red's name in the street as someone who could at least defend his manhood, but now Vivian was surprised.

Bobby Reds held his head down as Gregory Nose disrespected him to his face and said nothing.

"What the fuck is this?" *Is Bobby Reds a punk?* "All right, Nose, just cool down, man. As you can see, Bobby don't want no problems with you."

"Big man, no disrespect to you, but it's just that this piece of shit Bobby is a punk."

"All right ... finish the argument, Nose ... Bobby's around me now," said Vivian as he escorted Nose away.

"Big man, anytime I see that fat fuck in the streets, I'm gonna kill that piece a shit."

"You and Bobby shouldn't take this shit to the street ... let it end here. You promise me that."

" Promise."

"Big Man, you're the one who's saving that punk, man."

Bobby Reds shocked Vivian by not responding to the disrespect meted out to him by Nose. After Gregory Nose left, Vivian talked to Buckwheel about it.

"Oh, Dave ... don't you see that Bobby belittled himself? He acted like a punk."

" I can't believe that's the Bobby Reds I've always heard about," said Vivian as they laughed together.

Bobby Reds, this strong-built, fair-complexioned, medium-height guy, just stayed to himself, looking into space, after the ordeal.

As the days passed, Bobby and Vivian drew closer, but Bobby said something wrong while talking to Vivian about his arrest. "It was the boy, Paul Burke, and the boy, Tony Brown, who sent the police to my house." Bobby's loud voice caught the attention of the other inmates, and

Vivian interrupted him angrily.

" No, I won't have you disrespecting these big men behind their backs like that. You couldn't say that in the presence of Tony Brown and Paul Burke out in the streets. So, I don't want you to try and impress these inmates. I won't allow it." He seriously challenged Bobby. "Do you know that I have a lot of respect for those two men that you're trying to disrespect? Paul is man that sympathizes with my situation, and I have a lot of respect for him for that. Plus, Jah T loved Paul, and always told me he was a good man. And, as for Tony, the man's a survivor … look at all his trials and tribulations … and he's still around, standing firm. I give that man a lot of respect. I don't want to hear you disrespecting them again in my presence, you understand that?"

Astonished, Bobby looked at Vivian, and couldn't understand why Vivian had come to Paul and Tony's defense. A wedge developed between them, but Bobby didn't figure that out until later.

While Vivian was talking to Buckwheel one day, Bobby walked up and said, "What's up my laborite friend, Vivian? You and your PNP Lieutenant talking?" Vivian got real upset and so did Buckwheel.

"When you see my friend and I talking, don't come here with your political bullshit. I don't want you labeling me as no politician. I would prefer for you to call me your Tivoli Gardens friend. I don't deal with politics. I have never voted in my life."

Buckwheel looked at Bobby in a nasty fashion.

"Everyday … you talk about politics," Vivian said. "All you do is use the PNP Party for financial gains. By tomorrow again, you'll start criticizing them, saying which MP is a whore, from who is not. You talk too fucking much. If the PNP Party hears the things you talk about them in prison, their supporters alone would tear you to pieces."

Bobby was left speechless.

Bobby and Vivian still tagged along, but most of the inmates on the H-North Block started to dislike Bobby Reds. He'd come to Vivian with a proposal to smuggle a hundred pounds of marijuana to America. He told Vivian to arrange for fifty pounds of marijuana, to have someone take it to a house in Kingston on a certain day, and Vivian did as he was instructed. After the shipment of marijuana was supposed to have reached Miami, Bobby said to Vivian, "Your marijuana reached the house in Kingston late, so it didn't get to go to America."

Vivian looked at Bobby and laughed, "But you told me when to bring it, and it was delivered on time."

"Anyway, I'll give you five pounds of hash oil from Miami, because I didn't send any marijuana, I sent eight pounds of hash oil, instead."

Vivian constantly asked Bobby about the five pounds of hash oil, and Bobby gave him a different story every time.

"Where's my fifty pounds of marijuana?" Vivian asked one day when he was really upset.

"It's at the house."

Vivian arranged for the fifty pounds of marijuana to be delivered inside the prison and distributed to his friends. When the marijuana arrived, it was twenty pounds of pure, tasteless marijuana.

"Where's the rest of my marijuana?"

Bobby couldn't give Vivian a straight answer. Vivian's marijuana was sent to Miami, but he didn't want to pay Vivian.
Vivian became impatient. " Just give me the five pounds of hash oil from Miami, and we're even."

Bobby could do nothing but agree. By then, he was on trial at the Half-Way-Tree Criminal Court in Kingston. Returning to prison from court one evening, Bobby commented to Vivian, "Daley came to court and testified against me, wearing a shirt that I bought for him in Miami."

Bobby boasted so loudly that all the inmates on the H-North could hear. He went back to court for two more days and was found guilty for possession of a firearm and marijuana. He'd still not handed over the five pounds of hash oil in Miami to Vivian's designated receiver. A concert was being prepared in the prison and Vivian had told Bobby, " Just sell the hash oil … let me have the cash in Miami. I want to have someone do some shopping for my friends on the block," said Vivian patiently, but was still sidestepped by Bobby's trickery.

After Bobby was sentenced, he obtained a cell on another cellblock—B-South, through a private deal. It wasn't until Bobby was moving off H-North block that Vivian knew he was leaving, of course, because Bobby Reds didn't want to pay up.

Vivian sent two friends—Buckwheel and Bubbler to fetch Bobby. When he arrived, both of them were flanking the chair that Vivian was sitting.

"What happened to my money, Bobby?"

Bobby started to stutter in panic while Vivian spoke to him. He then ran swiftly, shouting, "I'm going to tell the Superintendent you want to kill me."

The trio laughed themselves to tears as they saw the fat man run.

Two warders—Mr. Waugh and Mr. Henry—heard of the problem and called up Vivian and Bobby. The problem was explained to the warders for them to see who was in the wrong and who was in the right.

Finally, Mr. Waugh said, "Bobby, as far as I see, Blake is in the right. I think you should make some arrangements to settle this dispute."

Bobby agreed to give the warders US $5,000 out in the streets, so the money could be turned over to a person of Vivian's choosing at the end of two months. This was agreeable to Vivian, and everything returned to normal.

A concert that had already been planned by Vivian and Bobby was to be held in the prison yard. Approximately three weeks before the concert, Vivian noticed that several inmates were frequently visiting Bobby—inmates who were never friends of his. Most of them didn't like the inmates on H-North cellblock, begrudgingly saying that H-North inmates were boastful.

Vivian called Buckwheel's attention to the gathering and said, "What's Bobby doing ... forming a gang?"

" It seems that way. I've never seen Bobby talking to any of those guys before."

" It must be Sona introducing those guys to Bobby," said Vivian, "So what's Bobby think ... it's cheaper to form a gang than pay five thousand dollars? Bobby don't know it costs a lot to buy friends. Friends must be *earned*, not *bought*. It can get costly."

Vivian and Buckwheel laughed at the folly of such foolishness.

The very next day, a guy who was arrested on an extradition warrant—Tall Ian—was brought to the penitentiary and placed on H-North. He was an associate of Bobby from back in Miami, and boasted that Bobby was scared of him … that Bobby was a punk.

Ian went to visit Bobby on his cellblock, and when Ian returned to H-North, he called Vivian aside and handed him a brand new knife that Bobby had given him.

"Respect is due, Big Man. Bobby's trying to buy me as one of his soldiers. I'm not here for that."

Vivian took the knife, then smiled and called over Buckwheel. "This is one of Bobby's knives. Looks like he's arming the entire prison against us. Just gave this knife to Ian."

"It's true. I heard he's trying to turn the conflict between you and him into a political affair. That way he could win a lot of support from the guys who are PNP affiliates. And … the fools will believe him, because they never really got to know you.

On the morning of the concert, Vivian summoned a warden named Maragh. "I hear that Sona is recruiting inmates for Bobby to form a gang in the prison. Tell Sona to stop it. I took one of the knives from an inmate who said Bobby gave him the knife.

"Where is it?" asked Mr. Maragh,

"I gave it to the warder," Vivian lied.

Mr. Maragh went to Sona to talk about what Vivian had said, and an argument ensued that morning between Vivian and Sona that the warders had to quell. Vivian, Sona, and Bobby were taken to a prison overseer's office and warned that if there were any more problems, the concert would be cancelled.

A civilian—Danny Champagne—who was also instrumental in putting the concert together—was also in the overseer's office, and tried to make Vivian shake Bobby's hand, but he was unsuccessful. Vivian refused.

The day of the concert, Vivian laughed as he saw Bobby walking to the concert with a gang of about thirty inmates—Sona as his US Lieutenant—but the concert went off without incident.

About two weeks later, Mr. Waugh and Mr. Henry went to see Bobby about the agreement he'd made with Vivian, but Bobby said he wasn't going to pay any money. Bobby kept his distance from Vivian after that.

One Wednesday morning in August of '97, the inmates in the penitentiary woke up to a strike action taken by the junior warders. Inmates on H-North cellblock came out of their cells about ten o'clock.

The strike was in objection to a statement made by the Commissioner of Prisons—Col. John Prescod—saying that the warders should be given condoms, which most warders took as an insult. That morning, two inmates who'd left their H-North cellblock on a stroll to another cellblock—Pre-Release—were seen running towards H-North, bleeding. One of the inmates—Audley Brown—said, "Bobby's friends just attacked us."

He'd been stabbed in the back. A few minutes later, Bubbler was seen walking into H-North with a bloody towel over his eyes. "Bobby's friends hit me in the face with a glass bottle."

For the rest of that morning, about thirty injured inmates started limping in to H-North, bleeding, needing medical attention. All of them said the same thing: "Bobby's friends attacked us ... 'we're affiliates of Vivian's and his friends on H-North cellblock.'"

H-North cellblock was packed to capacity, resembling a hospital ward—so many injured inmates. Several soldiers were deployed in the prison, to try to keep the peace.

A prison overseer—Mr. Ser Jue—was assigned to H-North, and visited Vivian that evening. "Blake, I want you to assist me in locking down the inmates in their cells."

" No problem, Mr. Ser Jue. H-North is the least of your worries. It's the other cellblocks you should be worried about.

The inmates on H-North cooperated with Vivian, and he was able to quickly lock them in their cells

The next morning, H-North didn't open until ten-thirty. The previous night, many inmates hadn't gone into their cells and were running rampant in the prison yard all night long. That Thursday evening, Vivian saw a gang of Bobby Reds' friends kill an inmate in front of Bobby's cell, then about a half-hour later, a stiff body—dead for several hours—was thrown into the prison yard from the second floor of a cellblock. The rampant stabbings that Bobby's friends had started the day before, spilled over into Thursday, and several inmates used the opportunity to carry out long-sought vendettas against other inmates.

Again, Vivian assisted Mr. Ser Jue in locking down the inmates on H-North. After lock-down, the inmates on H-North noticed that inmates in other cellblocks were destroying the automatic locking devices that secured the cells—the break-lock system—and in no time, H-North was the only cellblock with intact locks remaining.

A shout came from Tony Jones. "Coach!"

Vivian was called "Coach" by his friends on H-North cellblock, because of his ability to organize the soccer team.

"Yes?"

"We can't stay locked in our cells like this when everyone's out in the prison yard. Remember? They don't like us ... they might come on the cellblock and burn us out."

Several inmates sounded their agreement, but Vivian contemplated that move. *If anything goes wrong,* he thought, *my name would be the first to be called ... the media enjoys making a mess of my name.* "I'm not coming out, but you all can. Don't tear the break-locks down ... just try to get the break room lock off and open the cells without any further damage."

Two inmates forced their way through their cell door. In no time at all, the break room lock was broken and all cells opened, except the ones that were padlocked. The inmates used iron bars to open those, leaving Vivian's padlock untouched.

"Coach, you can't stay inside the cell at this time, man," said Buckwheel. "You have to come out."

"Okay, break the lock."

Within five minutes, the padlock was off, and Vivian was out of his cell. He could see several guys gathered by Bobby's cellblock and talking to him. Night began to fall, and inmates began to run to H-North with injuries, the same as the night before.

"Bobby's friends attacked them," came the continual accusation.

A bunch of H-North inmates gathered around Vivian. "That boy Bobby Reds is the cause of everything happening in the prison now … he came here with his politics after everyone was living in unity."

The group of PNP activists and affiliates echoed agreement with the inmates' remarks. "Let's kill that pussy," said one of the inmates. They all turned in anger and headed swiftly to Bobby's cellblock, while Vivian looked on.

Bobby didn't see the inmates until they were almost upon him, so he ran to his cell screaming, " Murder! Soldier, help me! Murder!"

Vivian could hear his scream from a distance as Bobby held onto his door, begging the inmates, "Please … don't kill me. Murder! Murder!"

In the cell next door to Bobby, one of his gang members was hiding, scared for his life, and decided to make a run for it. On his way out of the cell, he plunged his knife into the side of one of the inmates. Pints of blood began oozing from the stabbed inmate, distracting everyone from Bobby; hence, saving his life.

That night, Bobby's friends, led by a trusted prisoner of the authorities—Sona—broke inside the kitchen, stole all the machetes and knives, and went on a rampage.

Vivian and the inmates living on H-North stayed in their section and kept vigil throughout the night, unafraid, because they realized the soldiers were under order not to shoot anyone.

The strike ended the next morning, and, as the warders were reported to work, they saw a fire in New Building. Vivian and the inmates on H-North watched the blaze from their section. The sergeant on duty that morning—Mr. Robinson, also called Spy Robinson by his colleagues—came into the cellblock and Vivian approached him.

"What's going on down at New Building?"

"Nine inmates were burnt to death."

By midday, the warders had brought some semblance of order to the prison, and police officers came to investigate the murders. Mr. Robinson and Vivian hustled all of H-North inmates into their cells, but most of the cells in the other cellblocks couldn't be locked. Inmates were still on the grounds, milling around the storage area where the food and supplies were kept. H-North didn't sleep that night—they kept watch from their cells until daylight.

The warders were in full force by Saturday, and about two o'clock that afternoon, a warder—Bobby Crimestop—and some inmates had a nasty altercation on the cellblock right above H-North. The inmates rebelled, and chaos broke out again throughout the entire prison.

This time, the warders ran to their armory for high-powered weaponry, and the police force was called in. Shots were fired everywhere. While they were mainly concentrated in one area, other inmates milling around the prison grounds created havoc in another.

Five more inmates were murdered by their brethren. From Wednesday through Saturday, several of Vivian's friends were injured—Buckwheel, Festos, Bubbler, White Ghost, Audley Brown and brother of Producer/D.J. Tappa Zuckie. Two associates were killed—Sammy and ex-police officer, Delroy.

If Bobby hadn't made the calculated decision to turn into a prison gangster under a political banner—rather than a peacemaker—lives would probably been spared. Spurred by the uprising at penitentiary, two other lives were lost at the Spanish Town District Prison, bringing the death toll to eighteen.

By Sunday, police officers and soldiers swarmed through General Penitentiary. Having a large police audience, Bobby and Sona started their propaganda, casting blame on Vivian and the H-North inmates for the uprising, but there was evidence to prove them wrong. Mr. Ser Jue and Mr. Robinson knew otherwise. They could testify to the fact that H-North—the only cellblock with its break-lock system undamaged—was the only calm cellblock throughout the entire four days of rioting. Replacement of a few padlocks was all that was required.

Just before H-Block lock-down that Sunday afternoon, approximately one hundred soldiers carrying high-powered rifles ran into the cellblock, sealing off the entire area.

The commanding officer of the soldiers barked through a bullhorn, "Everyone go inside their cells."

The inmates quickly obeyed the command. About fifty soldiers confronted Vivian's cell. "Come out!"

Dressed in soccer shorts, he managed to grab a shirt as the soldiers searched him.

"Come with us," one of the soldiers said.

Vivian walked away with them, but decided to turn back, to go grab a pair of long pants. A soldier pointed his rifle at Vivian, denying him the privilege. He was taken off the section, unaware of why or where they were taking him. The group of soldiers grew to over a hundred as Vivian was taken to a waiting van. Eight warders with high-powered weaponry stood at the van.

"Get in!"

The soldiers slammed the door behind Vivian, and driver of the van hurriedly pulled away—police cars in front and behind—and headed out the prison gate and into the street. Vivian never got the chance to tell his friends of last four years goodbye. That hurt him.

When they reached their destination—Spanish Town District Prison—most of the cellblocks were already locked down. An assistant Superintendent—Mr. Septie Hall—whom he'd known from General Penitentiary, proceeded to take Vivian to a cellblock when an inmate named Doc called out, "No, Mr. Hall. You can't put him there. Inmates who begrudge him are living on that section … there could be problems in the morning."

Mr. Hall made Vivian sit down on the floor while he conversed with another Assistant Superintendent—Mr. Clines.

"Put him on death row."

Mr. Hall was contemplating the situation when an overseer from the reception area of St. Catherine District Prison—Mr. Mack—said to Mr. Hall, "Why do you let the prisoner tell you where he wants to go, Mr. Hall? Don't listen to the prisoner. Let the prisoner comply and then complain tomorrow."

Vivian looked at the overseer long and hard. He would never forget the face if he survived death row. Vivian didn't know what he would face in the death row cellblock, and thought, *whatever ... death row it is*, as he walked behind Mr. Hall, through the prison yard, toward the death row compound.

Familiar faces of associates from Tivoli Gardens came into view as Mr. Hall led him to the first level of a two-floor death row cellblock. Bad, who was in an upstairs cell said to Vivian, "Tell the officer, you want to go upstairs. It's pure pussies lives downstairs."

Immediately, Vivian seriously resented Bad's intrusive advice. "I'll be all right down here."

All the PNP activists on the first floor warmly welcomed Vivian and assisted him as best they could, which gave him great pleasure. Sammy Dread, Barrow, Golders, Neville Lewis, Blain and many others were among the death row inmates. They gave him magazines to read after they finished talking about nine o'clock that night and gave him a bucket filled with snacks to munch on throughout the long, sleepless night.

He missed his friends—Buckwheel, Festos, Fines, Bubbler, Nicko, and Oneil—and kept thinking about all that had transpired at the General Penitentiary.

Sammy brewed tea the next morning and shared it with Vivian. He talked with the death row inmates until it was time for the warders to open the cell. That was the first time in Jamaican prison history that an inmate on remand was placed on death row, but Vivian said to himself, *the media made me out to be a monster, and this is how the prison system treats a monster.*

After the first night, Vivian didn't mind staying there.

While Vivian was in the death row yard, Sexy Paul, leading a group of inmates to the fence, saw Vivian. "What's up, Dave? You'll have to come over to South Block. We have a cell for you. Ask the warder to take you to the Superintendent, Mr. Jones, and explain to him that you don't feel safe over here."

"But, Paul ... I'm okay. The death row inmates and I are getting along fine."

"I understand that, but I want you beside me."

Vivian laughed at that.

Visitors, that morning, were frequent—long-time friend Speedy, Rat from Spanish Town, Alibaba, whom he'd grown up with, plus a kid from Grants Pen in Kingston—Bus Up.

Vivian was escorted to Superintendent Jones' office, and he explained the situation to him as Sexy Paul had instructed. Mr. Jones laughed, "You're in no danger, but I have to remove you from death row, because you shouldn't have been put there in the first place."

Jones addressed a warder in the office, "Accompany the inmate back to death row, so he can pack his belongings. Then locate him on South Block."

His only belongings were two buckets—one given to him by the prison authority, the other by a death row inmate—and some food. As he was escorted by the warder to the new location, his friends shadowed him in the background, watching his back as he headed toward South Block.

The South Block section of the St. Catherine District Prison had the worst case of overcrowding Vivian had ever seen. Inmates slept in the passageway, because the cells were packed, which caused disastrous arguments and confusion.

First things first—his cell. Gratefully, he had it to himself. This cell was one-and-a-half times the size of the one he'd left at the General Penitentiary. *Redecoration.* He painted the cell white with black borders, and placed plastic black-and-white colored tiles on the floor. A table was painted black, decorated with black-and-white tiles on the top. He was given an ancient, metal spring bed, which he painted black, and then he sprinkled the cell with bits of fire-engine red pieces—a red throw rug, a red Rubber Maid plastic chair, and red tablemats.

To complete the accoutrements, a tape player and a black fan, transported from the General Penitentiary along with his other belongings, graced his new world. An electrician wired the cell, providing Vivian with lights and sockets. The cell looked like a studio apartment.

Robbery was rampant at South Block, especially against the foreigners—mostly Black and White Americans. A group of Jamaican inmates intimidated the foreigners and constantly extorted them for money and possessions. Vivian hated robbery and couldn't stand to see the helpless foreigners and non-violent Jamaican inmates being terrorized on a daily basis. The gang bandits patrolled the passageway at nights, brandishing knives, and stealing whatever they wanted. If an inmate refused, he was either beaten or stabbed.

Vivian watched all of this for the first month, wanting to leave matters to the prison authority, because he felt he had enough to take care of—his pending extradition case. He'd lost his first hearing at Magistrate Court and an extradition order was executed. A motion was filed, pending hearing in the Jamaica Full Court.

As the days wore on, the ill treatment and abuse continued and became more than he could tolerate. He knew he had to do something about it. Most of the foreigners were drug-mules, arrested with drugs in their possession at one of the two major airports in Jamaica.

The bandits on South Block had a lot of respect for Vivian, so his first line of action was to have a one-on-one conference with Sexy Paul. "Paul, how do you allow all these robberies and stabbings to take place on the block, and you don't say anything about it?"

"Dave, I've my own problems to face. I'm serving a fifteen-year sentence. Let the authorities deal with it."

Vivian understood where Sexy Paul was coming from, but thought the situation was still too grave. *A warder can only assist after the crime has been committed most of the time,* he thought, *but a respected inmate can prevent the abuse from occurring.*

"Anything that happens over at South Block while we're here will shine the spotlight on us. And, God knows I can't take no more spotlight. I've had it up to here," he said, moving his hand up to his neck. "No matter what our problems, we can't ignore what's happening to these helpless foreigners and terrified Jamaican inmates."

"What should I do about it?"

"For starters, I want all knives and weapons of any sort to be confiscated from all the inmates in this building."

Vivian gathered those who Sexy Paul had identified as his friends—Mackerel, Foreigner, Donkey, and especially an inmate that Sexy Paul hadn't recommended—Scrap-Iron. Vivian saw leadership in Scrap-Iron and thought he could mold him. As it turned out, he was right.

"Listen brethren, the robberies and violence in South Block have to stop. It's a bad reflection on me, now that I'm here. The authorities, no doubt, will think I'm behind it all, and right now, brethren, I can't take that pressure. You all agree with me?"

Scrap-Iron and Mackerel echoed, "Anything you say, Bossie. Your speech is law around here."

"I want all weapons in the building seized—every single one—today. Then bring them all to me. Scrap-Iron … you, Mackerel and Foreigner are responsible for this operation."

"Anything you say, Bossie."

They started a complete search of the three-story building in which three hundred inmates were incarcerated.

By lockdown that evening, Scrap-Iron, Mackerel and Foreigner, with the help of other inmates, had confiscated over thirty knives—some real, some makeshift. Vivian turned over the makeshift knives to the authority but kept the real ones—just in case he ever needed them. *Better safe than sorry*.

"How did you do it?" asked Sexy Paul as Vivian laughed.

"It's easy … your friends and my friends helped me … that's all."

Superintendent Jones sent a warder to fetch Vivian. "How's everything over at South Block, Blake?"

"Okay so far, Mr. Jones."

"I want you to know that the warders are very skeptical and are expecting trouble from you," said Mr. Jones as Vivian listened intensely. "I told them that they had nothing to worry about with you, Blake … that you're not a trouble maker, despite the media persecution. So, I don't want you to let me down. Those inmates on South Block respect you … I can see that … so, use your influence in a positive way. If I can be of any assistance to you or anyone on South Block, my office is open to all inmates."

"Mr. Jones, I've always respected you. You did for me the greatest thing anyone could have done while I was in General Penitentiary. On your recommendation, Col. John gave permission for me to see my six-year-old daughter. You might not have known what that meant to me. I will be forever in debt to you and the Commissioner, and I'll do my utmost to make you proud of South Block ... and that's a promise. Anything that *does* happen will be a spur-of-the-moment thing, which human beings cannot control, but can adjust to thereafter."

"Well ... that's good enough for me. Just take care of yourself, and I wish you much success in your struggle for freedom."

"All right. Take care, Mr. Jones. I'll let you know if I have any difficulties."

Mr. Jones was the best superintendent Vivian had ever come across throughout his incarceration in the Jamaican prisons. He was very compassionate in dealing with inmates and always had time to talk with them. He brought himself down to the inmates' level when he spoke, so they were at ease. They didn't fear him, but they respected him, and they knew he possessed a stern quality when needed. An inmate could call on Mr. Jones anytime and have an audience with him. He ruled with his brain, not by muscle. Force was his last resort. Moreover, an inmate knew not to try and play him for a fool, because he knew every trick in the inmates' books.

Vivian respected Mr. Jones so much that when Mr. Jones heard about Vivian's illegal cell phone, he didn't try to deny it. "Blake I hear that you've a cell phone in your cell. That true?"

"Yes, Sir."

"Bring it to me right away."

Vivian walked swiftly to his cell and retrieved the phone.

An Assistant Superintendent—Mr. John Ramsey—was a no-nonsense man, but, to Vivian, he was a very good and effective assistant to Mr. Jones. They were the exact opposite in demeanor, but both had the most important thing in common—the proper administration of the prison. Mr.

Jordan, Mr. White, and Mr. Gary Campbell were also Vivian's favorites. They were very supportive in making South Block a crime-free section.

To Vivian, Col. John Prescod was a modern man dealing with an ancient prison. Trying to modernize an ancient prison was tough … and he had a fight on his hands. He was a good choice at a bad time—the veteran warders were set in their old ways.

The only person in the Jamaica prison system that Vivian hated was the Director of Prisons—Toothpick—a tall, slim power-hungry man, who pulled his own warders through the mud if he didn't like them and did the same things to inmates. He also had his own preferences of prison institutions. He loved the South Camp Road Rehabilitation Center for the simple reason that both inmates and warders glorified him there. He was a poor choice as a leader of the prison system—he lacked brains—and above all, was no humanitarian.

A television was once seized from Vivian while he was at General Penitentiary. Seeing Commissioner Col. John Prescod in the presence of Mr. Smith at the St. Catherine District Prison, Vivian had begged Prescod to release the television set to his relatives.

"Blake, I'll release the TV to your relatives, but if it reappears inside the prison, it'll be confiscated for good. Okay?"

Prescod spoke to Mr. Smith and informed him that Vivian's relatives would go to the head office of the prison institution to collect it from Mr. Smith—everything was agreed upon.

The next day, a girlfriend—Nordia—visited Vivian, and he told her to pick it up at the prison office. Director Smith started a conversation with Nordia, discrediting Vivian.

"Vivian Blake is a dangerous man. Don't you know that? I'm scared of him. I don't want him to kill me … thinking that I purposely didn't want to give him back his TV."

Vivian had asked Mr. Smith for his television on several occasions, but always received unfavorable responses. Also, the prison dentist had recommended that Vivian needed emergency dental treatment, but Smith turned it down. Vivian's gums receded. Thus, all these things were on the

Directors' conscience. He'd trampled on Vivian's human rights as though they hadn't existed.

Nordia and Smith conversed for a while before he rudely said, "I'd like to see that fat vagina of yours. I live alone in Wilodene—my wife is away in America. Here's my number. I'm home by seven in the evening. Do you have a phone number I can call you?"

"No, I don't," Nordia lied. She'd only accommodated his rudeness to ensure that she got the TV.

That day, Vivian spoke to Nordia when she returned home from the meeting in the head office. Every word said was relayed. Vivian was really upset, so he went to Superintendent Jones the next day and told him what Mr. Smith had said. Mr. Jones laughed for a moment, then said, "Are you serious?"

"Yes. My girlfriend told me."

They spoke for a while, before Vivian left.

South Block was running calmly at the time. Stabbings had dramatically declined from an average of six a day to one every six months. Vivian had purchased four pairs of boxing gloves, to encourage inmates with problems to settle their disputes the old-fashioned way. A human ring formed in the yard, encircling the fighting inmates, and warders ensured that no serious injuries were occurred. Most of the time, it was a very entertaining event, with as many as five fights a day. At the end of the boxing match, the two inmates would become friends again.

With the assistance of the Jones, Assistant Superintendent Ramsey, Mr. Jordan, Mr. White, Mr. Gary Campbell, Mr. Bedwood, and the entire staff at the reception area on South Block compound, Vivian managed to keep South Block safe for Americans, Europeans, Canadians and inmates alike.

There was another big problem—the ninety percent illiteracy rate of the inmates in South Block Building. Vivian spoke to Mr. Jones, and together with the help of some educated inmates—mainly Preacher—an illiteracy program was founded. Vivian was the first teacher in the program, but immediately turned it over to Preacher after the inmates settled into Monday-to-Friday classes.

Vivian was very proud of this achievement, for although many inmates couldn't read or write when the program began, they improved in their studies every day. If for nothing else, Vivian wanted to be remembered for his role in improving literacy. With the implementation of the classes, news spread to other areas of the prison and classes were formed there.

Just before Christmas of 1998, Vivian was visited by a US attorney—George Soutar. "I have a reporter from GQ Magazine in America, named Jeff Stern, who wants to interview you about your problems in America."

"Sure. I'll give him an interview. Where is he?"

"He's outside. I'll get him."

Vivian had a very refreshing talk with the reporter.

Chapter 14: The Highjack

Vivian lost his full court hearing and the resultant appeal in the Jamaican Appeals Court. Soutar informed him soon afterward that he was denied leave for a hearing in the English Court, or Privy Council. Vivian had reached the end of the road. Human rights organizations and the Jamaican people were his last hope, but he had little time. He was out of options, with no one capable of leading a public appeal to the Jamaican people.

He had no choice but to call on his beloved son, even though he didn't want Duane to become involved in this sort of media hype. Duane was very young, only twenty years old, and had never been exposed to the media spotlight. *But*, Vivian thought, *Duane has the Blake in him. He's very intelligent and an honor roll student at Howard University. He'll learn as the days progress.*

When the school semester ended in May 1999, his father called him.

"Duane, I've just got word that I wasn't granted leave for my Privy Council hearing."

"Damn, man … Daddy, damn. So, isn't there anything else we can do?"

"Well, George Soutar and a human rights lawyer, Hilare Sobers, will be meeting today. Plus, Soutar told me that George Phang, Tony Brown and Paul Burke are in support of my plea for freedom. That's why I called. I need you to catch a flight … the latest one tomorrow … so you can do the running around for me."

"I'll see about a flight right away, Daddy. For your freedom, I'll do anything, even if it means my life."

After Vivian hung up the phone, tears ran from his eyes, and he wondered if it was the right thing he was doing … getting his son involved. But, Duane wouldn't have it any other way.

Duane arrived in Jamaica the next day, and they spoke by phone that night, planning their strategy. That same week, a local television station—CVM—organized an interview with Duane, on an early morning program, *CVM at Sunrise*, with Cliff Hughes. The interview went well, and was seen by most of Jamaica. The news of Vivian's problems spread all over the radio station.

Vivian wrote an article, asking the Jamaican people for their support in ensuring that he was treated justly in the eyes of the Constitution. He offered to pay for the article to be published in the leading newspaper—The Gleaner—but they led him around in circles. No *yes* or *no* was forthcoming. Duane tried other news communications without success, and then approached *The Jamaica Herald* and they accepted. The article was placed in both *The Jamaica Herald* and the *X-News*, grabbing the attention of the entire island. *The Jamaica Daily Gleaner* also ran a follow-up piece: "Vivian Blake begs for Mercy," which greatly upset Vivian and his son.

A popular radio station—HOT 102 FM—asked for an interview with Duane on their morning program, *Breakfast Club*. The hosts of the program—Beverly Manley and Anthony Abrahams—conducted it that morning. It was broadcast live. Midway through the interview Duane said, "There was an article in *The Gleaner*, which said my father was begging for mercy, but I want to set the record straight. My father's *not* begging for mercy. All my father wants is justice." After the interview, Beverly praised Duane publicly for that statement.

Momentum developed in Jamaica, and many organizations rallied behind the "Free Vivian" Campaign—The Ethiopian Orthodox Church, The Higgler Association, The Sound System Association, and entertainers. Songs were recorded by well-known artists—Round Head, Harry Toddler, Zebra, Spragga Benz, John Wayne and many others—in support of Vivian's freedom.

A committee was formed with leading attorneys, such as Gayle Nelson, Hilare Sobers and George Soutar, along with community leaders from the Kingston region. A meeting was held at the King Ital Restaurant in Cross Roads where all communities—both PNP and JLP—were represented. The meeting was a success, and they worked on a manifesto to accompany a delegation to see the Minister of National Security and Justice—The Honorable K.D. Knight.

People from all over the island volunteered their services, and posters were distributed. "Vivian Blake, A question of justice" was plastered on walls, island-wide. The entire island echoed the same sentiment: " Free Vivian Blake." Every day, discussions were broadcast on TV or radio, and another article was published in one of the daily newspapers. Momentum built. Knight asked Vivian's attorneys to meet with him at his office—the date was set for Monday July 5th, 1999, at nine in the morning.

While this was taking place, "The Vivian Blake Committee" was being formed with Louise Frazier Bennett representing the Sound Systems Associations, Jesse Gender, Entertainer, and a man of very strong Rastafarian belief and the Head of the Higgler Association—Mr. Hylton. Out of that committee, a lobby group formed—"The Jamaica Lobbyist Action Enterprise."

The "Free Vivian Blake" groups, backed by members of the dance hall fraternity, residents of the many different, inner city communities of Kingston, Montego Bay, May Pen, and also residents of other rural communities, sought to collect fifty thousand signatures within four weeks, to petition the government to cancel Vivian's extradition order.

A press conference was arranged for Thursday morning, July 1st, at the Terra Nova Hotel. All the media houses were in attendance and the press conference went well.

"What have you got to say about your father's charges?" asked one reporter.

"My dad is innocent of most of those charges. I'm not saying he's an angel, but most of those charges are false accusations by friends and associates of his."

A rally was scheduled at the Nelson Mandela Park in Half-Way Tree Square in Kingston, on Friday, July 9th, at five o'clock in the afternoon. After Duane rented the park, he was recognized as Vivian Blake's son, and administrators tried to cancel the rental a few days later. Louise called up the people responsible and managed to secure a rental of the park sidewalk—not the inside, as originally stated in the contract. A scheduled march was planned for early Monday morning, July 12th, to the Governor General's residence at Kings house.

On Monday, Vivian was represented in the meeting with Knight by attorneys Ian Ramsey, Gayle Nelson and George Soutar—Sobers, was not present. The reason was that Duane accomplished more for Vivian than anything Sobers ever accomplished through any of his correspondence. Sobers' employment was a waste of Vivian's hard-earned cash.

The meeting with the minister continued throughout the day, and Vivian spoke to Soutar the next day, indicating it had gone well. They were awaiting the minister's decision.

"So, George, tell me now … what the fuck is Sobers doing? It's been six weeks now, and he hasn't made any progress. I don't know why you recommended that man to me. This is like a rip-off. If there was no chance for me at the Human Rights Council—he should have told me that from the beginning. It's been six weeks, and not even a word whether The Human Rights Council have decided to take the case or not … knowing we've got zero time."

" I don't know what to tell you on that."

"Tell Mr. Sobers this: return my one hundred thousand dollars, because he didn't earn it. All he did was hop on the gravy train of a desperate man."

Vivian contacted his son that evening by phone, relaying that he'd seen Soutar and that there was no decision by the Security Minister, yet.

"The tension's killing me," said Duane. "I haven't eaten since morning."

"You have to eat, man …I don't have any faith in the meeting with the Security Minister. The decision comes down to me, or American aid to Jamaica … and right or wrong, the government will choose foreign aid over me. My faith is in the people. I just hope nothing happens before the rally on Friday. The government has to listen to the voice of the people."

"Let's keep our fingers crossed."

"Go get something to eat, Duane."

"All right. I love you, Daddy."

"I love you too, Son. Let me talk to your sister."

Duane called out to Dominique and gave her the phone.

"Hi, Daddy. You hear anything yet about the meeting with K.D. Knight?"

"No, not yet … probably tomorrow."

"Daddy, I'm nervous. I can't wait to see you out."

"If it's God's will, I will be soon. But, if it's not, there's nothing we can do but continue the fight."

"I'm praying, Daddy. Duane prayed all day today."

"That's good. You all keep praying. God doesn't sleep. He'll vindicate me somehow. I guess I'll talk to you later."

"I Love you, Daddy."

"I love you too. Later, and tell Duane later."

"All right Daddy, I will."

There was no word on Wednesday, July 7th. Vivian felt confident, that one way or the other, no decision would be made to take him out of the country that week, even if the Honorable K.D. Knight's decision was dishonorable. That would give the people a chance to have the scheduled rally on Friday. A host of entertainers were slated to perform and the road march scheduled for early the next Monday would go on as planned.

By the 8th, Vivian felt even more confident that nothing would transpire in terms of extradition until the following week if Knight's decision was *unfavorable*.

That morning, Vivian was visited by attorney Gayle Nelson, who reaffirmed that the meeting had been favorable to them, and that he expected a decision in their favor.

During the lunchtime break, Vivian was locked in his cell. With thirty hours to go before the rally on Friday, Vivian undressed and lay in the bed, watching his little Watchman TV.

"Blake, you have an attorney visit," said Mr. Murray, a warder.

Vivian quickly dressed, the warder unlocked his cell, and Vivian walked out of the building toward the lawyers' visiting area.

Soutar greeted him. "No decision, yet, from Mr. Knight, but I don't know how to feel about it. Mr. Knight spoke to me on Tuesday, and he was saying that the US Government would not ask for the death penalty on any murder cases that carry the death penalty. I told him that there are a lot more issues than the death penalty, so he said he'll be in touch with me soon. I haven't heard from him since, but, somehow, I don't trust his language on Tuesday."

Vivian wasn't the least bit disturbed, because the people were about to start talking on Friday—only a day away—and the government would have to listen.

"Mr. Nelson was just here."

"What? I told him I'd meet him here, but he never called back to confirm. What did he say?"

"He was talking about some million-dollar fee, which I didn't understand. How much you give him already … $140,000, right?" Vivian asked.

"Yes. I'll talk to Mr. Nelson."

"What's this about a million-dollar fee? My understanding was that his fee was $140,000."

"Don't worry about it … it's just a misunderstanding. I'll talk to Mr. Nelson about it."

Mr. Murray, was waiting to take Vivian back to his cellblock, but was stopped by an overseer—Mr. Patterson.

"No, let me wait here a minute," said Mr. Patterson while turning to Vivian. "Sit in the office where the lawyers visit."

Another lawyer was occupying the office, so Patterson said, "Just stand right here."

Vivian noticed that all the gates leading to the different cellblocks were padlocked, and a warder was padlocking the gate that led to the hospital. *Something isn't right. Why are all these gates being closed? I've never seen them do that before.*

Then he realized that even the gate to the place where the orderlies lived was also closed. *Something's going on.*

Vivian walked over to the other side and stood on the landing below Superintendent Jones' office. He was the only inmate in the locked-off area, with about fifty warders guarding him. He continued walking to where an inmate—Doc—was standing behind the gate of the orderlies' cellblock.

"What going on, Doc? How come they locked all the gates?"

"It's strange ... I've never see them do this before."

Vivian decided to find out if his suspicions were right, so he looked toward the warders and shouted to the overseer. Mr. Patterson. "Mr. Patterson, I have to go take my medication now," Vivian lied.

Mr. Patterson hesitated, not knowing what answer to give Vivian. "I'll allow you to get your medication soon."

Then Vivian realized ... he was being held hostage in the area.

"Doc, this is some extradition thing, you know that?"

"It could be ... this looks weird."

By then Vivian was standing at the South Block Compound gate. He quickly leaped on the gate and went over.

"Blake, don't go over!"

Vivian paid him no attention. He walked to the side of the South Block Building, which was locked, and shouted to Sexy Paul. "Paul, give me my knife."

Before Sexy Paul could respond, Vivian saw about a hundred warders coming through the gate, and into the South Block Compound. He walked from the side of the building to the front and stood by the building gate. The crowd of warders approached, then Patterson said to Vivian as all the warders crowded around, "Blake, come with us. Come over by the Superintendent's office."

"I'm not going anywhere with you."

Then a staff warder from the reception area—Mr. Thomas—said to Vivian, "You think you can beat the charges in America?"

Vivian hissed through his teeth. "What kind of question is that you're asking me at this time?"

"I'm sorry. I'd feel the same way, too," said Mr. Thomas.

An overseer—Mr. Blake—a very Christian man—approached Vivian. "Blake, come with us, man. You know we aren't here to cause you any problem. We're just following orders."

"No disrespect intended, Mr. Blake, but I'll only talk to the Superintendent, Mr. Jones."

Many of the warders retreated and rushed to Mr. Jones' office, while some still stood hovering around Vivian. Vivian looked toward the entrance gate of South Block and saw Jones coming.

"Come, Blake. Let's go talk."

He led Vivian to the side of the Building, away from the warders, where they could talk in private. "Blake, they brought an extradition warrant to take you back to America, right away."

As they spoke, Vivian heard the sound of helicopters and saw two hovering above the prison.

"I don't want you to give them any problem ... I won't let them harm you. Just pray to God, Blake ... God is the savior."

"Okay, I'm ready."

With all the warders following, Mr. Jones and Vivian walked to the South Block exit gate, and then went up the steps to his office. Senior police officers were waiting. Vivian took out the money he had in his pocket and gave it to Mr. Jones. "This is $4,900. Put it with the eleven hundred I have on my record and give it to Sexy Paul. It's for his son's school fees."

Vivian looked over his shoulder and focused on the person he knew was real happy to see him extradited—Director "Toothpick" Smith. It came to Vivian's mind to punch him flat on the ground, but he decided against it because he didn't want to disrespect Mr. Jones. He loved and respected the Superintendent too much to do it—he'd helped him spend his six years of incarceration in a Jamaican prison as comfortably as possible.

"Can I get a change of clothes?"

"Yes," said Mr. Jones, but a senior police officer interrupted.

"We won't have anytime for that."

They immediately proceeded to handcuff Vivian—hands and feet.

"The cuffs on my legs are too tight," he protested, but the police officer didn't care. They hauled Vivian out of the Superintendent's office, without Vivian being able to say goodbye. Dragging him down the steps he shouted, "the cuffs on my legs are digging into my flesh."

But, the police officers didn't care. They were on a mission and they aimed to please their masters. Two large patty wagons were parked in the prison yard, and the police officers, carrying high-powered assault riffles, hoisted Vivian into one of them, and into a cell-like compartment. The door slammed shut.

Sirens blared as the patty wagon drove Vivian out of the prison. Along the road, police officers sported high-power rifles in case there was an incident.

The patty wagon took Vivian to the St. Catherine District Prison—Prison Oval—that was the warder's recreational ground. Armed police officers were stationed on the road to Prison Oval, and inside it. The patty wagon came to an abrupt stop inside the prison, and the door flew open. Armed officers quickly took Vivian out and moved him into the yard.

A crowd gathered on the streets as people watched the maneuvering of the armed officers. A helicopter was parked in the middle of the Prison Oval playing field—its engine running. About ten heavily armed police officers rushed Vivian to it … the cuffs on his legs digging deeply into his flesh. They quickly hoisted him into the army chopper, handcuffing him to the ceiling, and it took off immediately. Four officers accompanied Vivian on the ride, never letting go of their weapons.

In a few minutes, they were over the Manley International Airport, and the helicopter descended to a guarded runway.

Vivian laughed to himself, *what's all this excitement for?* It was as if a movie scene was being filmed.

When the helicopter landed, the officers released Vivian's hands from ceiling and handcuffed his hands behind him. A US Marshal plane, with two US Marshals, was about a hundred feet away. Ten officers with high-powered rifles quickly hustled Vivian into the waiting jet. The police officers guarding the runway were searching the airfield carefully, as if they expected an attack.

Vivian laughed again, *there are only two marshals ... they ain't making a big deal like these Jamaican policemen—as if they were on the mission of their life.*

Vivian was led into the jet, where the handcuffs were removed and replaced with the Marshals' cuffs. Vivian looked through the window as the plane taxied down the runway for takeoff. He laughed at the show they'd put on.

He was on his way back to America to face seventy-seven criminal counts—from racketeering, murder, and drugs, to conspiracy. He reclined in the seat and laughed to himself.

"Why was the Jamaican Government in this rush?" asked one of the Marshals. "They wanted us to come like yesterday when they called. What's happening? Why the rush?"

Vivian laughed and looked at the US Marshals. "Just plain old politics." He closed his eyes and opened them again. "I'm really going back to America," he said to no one in particular. Then he took out a letter he'd received from a lady friend who was serving a life sentence in Fort August's female prison in Jamaica. She was convicted for the murder of a very abusive husband. Her name was Mary O'Doleylynch.

Chapter 15: Miami, July 1999

The small aircraft landed at Homestead Air Force Base at four thirty-five p.m. on Thursday, July 8th, 1999. The alleged leader of the notorious Jamaican Shower Posse gang, Vivian Blake, was extradited to Miami, Florida to stand trial for sixty-two counts of Florida indictments, and a fifteen-count Virginia indictment, which included eight murders and five attempted murders under the RICO Act.

Vivian Blake stepped out of the aircraft in handcuffs and foot-shackles, accompanied by four US Marshals. Two other Marshals standing outside of the plane welcomed him.

"Welcome back to Miami, Mr. Blake," a respectful tone in his voice.

"I can't say it's a pleasure, but thanks just the same," Vivian replied politely.

"We understand perfectly."

Vivian arrived at the Federal Detention Center (FDC) in Miami at about five p.m. that evening, and was processed, searched, and then given a T-shirt, underwear, a pair of socks, a pair of slippers and an orange jumpsuit. Strangely, all the other inmates in the processing center wore green jumpsuits. He was taken to the twelfth floor of the building, where he was searched again, and then placed in a cell by himself. Realizing there was a shower stall, a toilet, and a sink with running water, he was amazed—a huge difference from the crummy cells back in Jamaica. What he *didn't* know was that he was in solitary confinement and would spend the rest of his pre-trial detention locked in it, twenty-four-hours a day. In fact, that was the reason for having all those amenities, in contrast to a Jamaican cell.

The next day, he appeared in court for the first time, having been assigned a public defender. A few days later, he appeared in court for a bail hearing, and was advised by his attorney that he wouldn't be given bail, due to the nature of his indictment. The judge would definitely agree with the prosecutor that he was a flight risk. But, Vivian didn't need his attorney to tell him that—he knew what he was up against.

Wondering why he was placed in solitary confinement, he sought advice and was able to talk with an associate warden—Kapusta.

"You're a security concern."

"What are you?" said Vivian angrily. "Are you a racist?"

"No, I'm not. Just doing my job."

In the months that followed, Kapusta turned out to be one of the nicest guys in FDC, in Vivian's estimation.

Another court appearance was scheduled. In the holding area, preparing for court, he was called to the attorney's visiting booth. While in discussion with the attorney, he noticed a short, fat, black man beckoning to him. His attorney turned around toward guy, who was behind him.

"I'm David Rowe, attorney-at-law. I was sent to see Mr. Blake."

Vivian's attorney turned to Vivian, who looked astonished.

"It's all right, I'm through anyway. Talk to Mr. Rowe. I'll see you in court."

"Your son, Duane, called me and asked me to come to see you. Attorneys George Soutar and Ian Ramsay recommended me to him."

Vivian realized in an instant that Mr. Rowe was Jamaican. He'd heard of Rowe on a Jamaican radio station while incarcerated in Jamaica—he was commenting that Vivian and many Jamaicans were not getting fair trials. Vivian thought for a minute, wondering what the catch was. *Is it money? Is it the publicity Mr. Rowe will get from this case, or is he a genuine attorney?* Because of the publicity of his case, attorneys would try to reap financial benefits, even though the chances of beating the charges were slim. So, Vivian was very skeptical. He thought for a few seconds, and then decided to pick Rowe's brain.

Vivian looked deep into his eyes, studying him. "But, I already have an attorney."

"You can't trust public defender attorneys."

"The man's bright. He's only one of twenty attorneys in Florida certified by the Florida Bar," said Vivian catching Mr. Rowe off-guard.

"Does he know anything about the specialty rules regarding extradition? That you can only be charged for the counts stated in the extradition agreement, which, in your case, was only four counts, of which two will have to be dropped, because there are no such laws in the Jamaican Constitution."

This man had Vivian's attention—it was just a matter of how high Rowe's fees were. An attorney taking him for a ride would try to rip him off to the tune of no less than a quarter-million US dollars, so he decided to bluff, to see how far Rowe would go.

"I'm okay with my attorney. I don't have that type of money to pay any lawyer. The Government's given me an attorney free of cost. All I have to do is guide him."

"The public defender attorney works for the government."

"Where's my son?"

"He's here, I'll bring him to see you tomorrow."

Mr. Rowe and Duane came the next day to the FDC. He was so happy to see his son—they chatted for a while about Dominique and family things, then it was back to the attorney issue.

"Daddy, you need to get a lawyer. Mr. Rowe knows about the specialty rules."

"Nah, it's going to be too expensive, son" Vivian said, still bluffing. He needed Mr. Rowe.

"You haven't heard my price yet" interrupted Mr. Rowe.

Vivian looked into Mr. Rowe's eyes for what seemed like an hour, bracing for at least a hundred thousand. "How much?"

Rowe contemplated for a few seconds. "Thirty thousand dollars. Fifteen thousand within two weeks, and fifteen thousand before trial."

Vivian wanted to jump and shout and say, "Great!" but he kept his cool.

"What do you think, Son?"

"I think that's a good deal, Daddy. You need a good lawyer … especially one that understands the specialty rules."

Rowe and Vivian proceeded with the vigorous work of trial preparation—all the discovery documents in place. Then there was a big scare.

After dinner one night, Vivian started coughing due to a scratchy throat, but couldn't stop. He tried to sleep, but every time he lay down, the constant coughing forced him upright. At about five a.m., he pressed the emergency buzzer in his room. When PA came a half-hour later, Vivian explained about the constant coughing and shortness of breath.

"The pharmacy won't open until eight-thirty. When it's open, I'll bring you something for the coughing."

By seven-thirty that morning, Vivian was worse, and he pressed the emergency buzzer in a panic—there was no response for ten minutes. "I can't breathe," he gasped to a passing counselor.

The counselor hurried away and brought back a lieutenant—Harris—who wasted no time. He shackled and handcuffed Vivian, then escorted him down to the medical department at the FDC, after which Vivian became unconscious. Four hours later, he woke up in a strange environment.

"Where am I?"

"At the Jackson Memorial Hospital," said one of the male doctors in the room.

"What time is it?"

"Eleven-thirty."

"At night?" asked Vivian, and they all laughed.

"No, in the morning."

Later on that day, a nurse came into his room and shook her head. "You're a lucky man, Mr. Blake. I thought you were dead. You came to this hospital ninety-nine percent dead."

He was bewildered. He couldn't fathom what the nurse was saying to him—couldn't believe his ears. Then he remembered something he'd dreamt while unconscious. He was sinking into a dark hole, and when he looked up into the light, he saw Duane and Dominique stretching their hands to pull him up, out of the dark hole. But he was still going down.

"God, please." He'd said in his dream. "I have my two kids to live for. I haven't even seen Dominique through school, yet. Please, God. My kids need me. I can't leave them."

At that point, he floated upward, toward the light, and Duane and Dominique pulled him out of the dark hole. That was when he awoke out of unconsciousness.

Vivian knew he was a lucky man. He had a purpose. God had saved him to fulfill that purpose.

He spent a week in Jackson Memorial Hospital, and was then released into the custody of the US Marshals, who transported him back to the FDC.

As soon as his strength returned, he and Rowe resumed trial preparation. Vivian was feeling upbeat about the trial, knowing that most of the Miami witnesses were all telling lies. They could all be discredited in the Miami courts. He began the quest of gathering witnesses for his defense, people who could prove that he had nothing to do with the eight murders and five attempted murders, particularly, and all the weapon purchases in general.

He received a message from Richard "Storyteller" Morrison, saying that he would be willing to take the stand on Vivian's behalf, because he knew Vivian had nothing to do with the murders of the five people in the Miami apartment—in any way, shape or form. He could identify the killer and sole orchestrator, who'd turned into a Government informant.

Vivian was comforted by that message, so he continued his quest for more witnesses. His attorney told him he needed a character witness. He sent a message to his grandmother in Jamaica—Miss Daisy Woodman—asking her to come to his trial in January 2000 to testify as a character witness. Her reply was that she was sick. Vivian found this very strange—the trial was three months away. How could she say she was sick? It wasn't like the trial was a week away.

Vivian investigated and found out something strange. He was told that his grandmother had made this remark: "I don't know why he asked me to stand up in court for him. I'm not going to do it." Vivian got the picture. Could an old woman be so cruel just for love of money? How money corrupted! *My relatives!* he thought. *This woman has had me up in her heart because I didn't allow her to keep my drug money, like my brother Tony did.* He continued to think, *it's the same way ... she never had a care in the world for my other brother, Kong, because Kong never gave her his drug money to hold for him.*

Realizing there was a huge conspiracy among his relatives—including Tony and Kong—to see him go to prison for the rest of his life, he had to figure out a course of action. First, *Tony and Kong are in close communication with Joy Cash, who's slated to testify against me at my trial,* he thought. *Second, Kong told me that Joy told Tony she wouldn't testify against Tony or Kong, yet all three are still close,* he continued to think. *Third, Joy sent Kong a suitcase with clothes after he was released from prison and he wore the clothes proudly. Something's terribly wrong here.*

Rowe paid Vivian a visit at the FDC, and Vivian relayed the wonderful news that Storyteller was going to testify on his behalf. Mr. Rowe didn't react with approval to what he'd just heard.

"Richard Morrison would be a hostile witness."

"What? How the fuck are you going to get me off, if people who can prove that I didn't murder those five people can't testify on my behalf?"

"You'll take the stand."

"Yeah, the fuck I will, and I'll do the damned best I can. But, I don't think that I, alone, can discredit all those lying bastards ... the ones looking to have their long sentences cut. How come Storyteller's a hostile witness? The man's going to speak the truth. He can't say anything but. He don't know anything bad about me."

The meeting ended abruptly with Vivian having second thoughts about his attorney. *How could he not want Storyteller to testify on my behalf? Is David Rowe working for the government?* He continued to muse in his confusion, hoping that he wasn't right in his negative thinking.

Vivian drew a diagram of his trial—only two months away. He knew all the witnesses the government had in reference to his associates—those who had lied and turned State's evidence—along with some government informants whom he'd never known ... people who were willing to lie in order to have sentences cut. The associates who'd turned against him and agreed to testify were as follows: Cecil Connors (a.k.a. Charles Miller a.k.a. Modeller); Donovan Jones (a.k.a. Champs); Gladstone Lawrence (a.k.a. Bunny); Barrington Anderson (a.k.a. Vest); Kirk Bruce (a.k.a. Kirk); Richard Daley (a.k.a. Lockey); Fuckery Ram; Joy Cash; and Pearl Estreem. Then there were the informants whom he didn't know, or wasn't familiar with—Michael Dodd (a.k.a. Danny Dodd, a.k.a. Spangler Danny) from the Spangler Posse. Danny had lied to the Federal Agents saying that he used to sell drugs for Vivian. He also gave the agents the address of his cousin and former girlfriend—Eleanor Dodd—and *she* was arrested because the Government thought she could be of help to them in Vivian's conviction.

Vivian knew that all these informants were lying, but that it was also risky to go up against so many witnesses. Then there were other associates who'd given damaging statements against him in 1989, like Michael Campbell (a.k.a. Sugar Belly) and Michael Murray (a.k.a. Geego, a.k.a. G-Brown), but they, along with Modeler, were out of the country and not expected to take the stand.

Vivian thought about his attorney. *How are you going to beat this case, David Rowe? You keep saying you're going to beat this case, but you can't show me how. This case, if I go to trial, Mr. Rowe, will make you famous, but it could spell disaster for me. Win or lose at trial, Mr. Rowe wins. Win or lose at this trial, is still loss, because I have to face another indictment in Virginia, which also carries life sentences without parole.* He walked around his cell contemplating. *Damned if you do, and damned if you don't. Vivian, you're fucked. You're up shit creek.* Then he walked to his bed and lay down, saying aloud, "God, I leave everything up to you."

Mr. Rowe returned the next day. "The prosecutor, Mrs. Lee Stapleton-Milford, asked if you would take a plea, but I wrote her, telling her 'no, we're going to trial.'"

"What did you just say?"

"She wants to have a settlement conference."

"Tell her I'll listen. Set up the meeting."

"But—" Rowe stammered.

"But nothing. Set the meeting up … it can't hurt to listen. You never know."

"There won't *be* a settlement … I can guarantee that."

"You never know, Rowe, dear boy, you never know," said Vivian smiling.

"Should I still prepare for trial?"

"Hell, yeah! I told you I was going to listen. I didn't tell you I was going to make a deal."

"Mrs. Stapleton also mentioned that she was willing to merge the Virginia indictment with the Florida indictment by means of Rule 20."

"Wouldn't that be lovely?" His smile grew bigger by the second.

The settlement conference was scheduled for December 14th, 1999. Vivian had already briefed his kids on what was happening, so he went to the meeting with their blessings, and with God. He was escorted to a conference room in the justice building and his eyes widened in astonishment. There were no less than twenty men—mostly white—and a smattering of black guys and Hispanics. Set on easels were charts with *Shower Posse* written at the tops. One chart had a picture of him at the top, with over thirty other pictures beneath his, in different positions, indicating the ranks of the alleged Shower Posse soldiers.

Mr. Rowe attended the conference with his paralegal, Miss Chin. Vivian sat at a table with Rowe, while Miss Chin sat with the men in a different area.

After five minutes of waiting, two beautiful white ladies entered the room. Vivian was very impressed by their beauty and their executive attire. They walked over to where he and his attorney were sitting and one of the ladies introduced herself. "Hi, Mr. Blake, I'm Lee Stapleton-Milford." She beckoned to the other lady, indicating that the she was the prosecutor from Virginia.

"Glad to make your acquaintance," said Vivian nodding politely to the two ladies. Mrs. Stapleton-Milford was swift and to the point, and

Vivian admired her for that. In fact, she won him over with her attitude and her style.

"Mr. Blake, I would like to offer you a plea bargain arrangement for a sentence of forty years, and with the assistance of my fellow Virginia prosecutor, we would merge the two indictments, then run the sentences concurrently under the old guidelines."

That didn't sit well with Vivian. "Forty years is a life sentence, Mrs. Milford. I can discredit all your witnesses. Gladstone Lawrence has lied to the grand jury and I can prove it. Kirk Bruce, Donovan Jones and Vest are all liars and I can prove that, too. That boy, Cecil Connor or Charles Miller—whatever his name is—I can prove that he lied to the grand jury and in the trial of 1989, in which he implicated me in those murders. They're liars … all liars … and I think you know that, too."

Another meeting was scheduled. This time, Vivian was feeling a little more upbeat. Mrs. Stapleton-Milford made a final offer of twenty-eight years.

"I'll have to speak to my kids on Tuesday to see what they think. Tuesday is my visiting day."

It was Friday, December 17th, and the next week was Christmas. No one wanted to be working much in the coming week.

"Couldn't you see them on Monday? I could arrange for the visit here."

"That would be fine." Vivian was anxious to see his kids up close, especially his daughter Dominique, whom he hadn't seen for almost six months.

That Monday was long in coming. He was so happy to see his kids—that was a plus for the prosecutor, and she didn't even know it. Just seeing his kids made all the difference in the world, especially seeing Dominique, who hadn't been permitted to see him because of her age. He explained everything about the deal. They were *iffy* at the inception, but finally came around, and supported their father's decision to plead guilty to twenty-eight years … and it was all over.

Mrs. Lee Stapleton-Milford and Vivian shook hands.

"You have a deal," said Vivian happily.

Chapter 16: St. Kitts

In 1998, former Shower Posse Lieutenant, turned Federal Government informant, now wanted by the American government for drug trafficking, Cecil Connor (a.k.a. Charles Miller, a.k.a. Modeler, a.k.a. Little Nut), was the subject of a worldwide news bulletin. At the time, the US Government was in the process of trying to extradite Miller, as he was then called, from St. Kitts. CNN news reported Miller as saying: "If the United States Government attempts to take me out of St. Kitts, I will kill one American student from Ross University in St. Kitts each day." This statement caused panic at the university, with most of the students trying desperately to leave the island. Since the news was worldwide, it placed Charles Miller in the spotlight again.

Charles Miller—Cecil Connor in 1989—was the prosecution's main witness in a sixty-two-count indictment against the Jamaican Shower Posse. After the trial, which ended with most members of the Shower Posse being found guilty, Connor was placed in the WPS (Witness Protection Program). As the government's star witness, Connor was kept secure and given a new name—Charles Miller.

Vivian Blake, the alleged leader of the Shower Posse, and still at large, left Charles Miller's job for the United States Government unfinished. Restless, Miller decided to make a run for it. He secured falsified papers, and then made an escape from the protective custody of the federal agents.

He turned up in St. Kitts, the land of his birth, in 1993. He was broke and destitute, and hooked up with his long-time boyhood friend, Zambo, who was still living on the island. Zambo did what he could for Miller. With little or no option, he went along with a plan dreamed up by another friend—David "Grisly" Lawrence—to rob a fisherman, who was reported as having a stash of cocaine. Miller had acquired a pistol and was prepared to do anything to survive.

It was impossible to try to rob the fisherman on the docks, so Miller and Lawrence went there one evening and waited until it was quitting time. They tailed the fisherman in their car to a lonely road, and then forced him to stop. Miller left the car, gun in hand, and rushed toward the fisherman's car.

"Where's the fucking cocaine?"

The fisherman nervously pointed to a bag on the back seat. Miller reached for the bag—it contained two kilos of coke.

"Where's the rest?" Miller shouted.

"That's all I have."

Miller looked at the fisherman angrily. "You lying motherfucker!"

He placed his pistol in the center of the man's forehead and pulled the trigger. The result was a foregone conclusion.

Charles Miller's restless compulsion to climb to the top meant he would do anything necessary to attain it. He'd gotten wind that a shipment of marijuana had been brought in from Jamaica and discovered its location and the smuggler's identity—St Kitts is a very small island of forty-five thousand people, so information like that was not hard to come by. Bagga—a Jamaican—was the smuggler, and Miller knew where he lived. He drove an old car—gun at the ready—and, without hesitation, kicked the door in, surprising Bagga and the male owner of the house. Miller held Bagga and owner at gunpoint, as they led him to the marijuana.

"How much marijuana is that?"

"A little over two hundred pounds," said Bagga, trembling.

Miller was still pointing his gun at him and started to laugh. "Bagga, there's a new sheriff in town. Any drugs coming into St. Kitts will have to come through me. You hear that?" Then he kicked Bagga in his ass. "Next time, bring more marijuana, pussy!"

He ordered Bagga and the owner to place the bags of marijuana into his car and drove away, smiling sadistically.

The message finally sunk in about the new sheriff, Charles Miller. Zambo paid him a visit. There was a job to do, but murder would be involved. Zambo was no murderer, but he knew that Charles Miller wouldn't mind, especially when he heard the stakes.

"The Deputy Prime Minister's son, Vincent Morris, is holding over fifteen hundred kilos of cocaine, and I want it," said Zambo. "If you can help me get it, you can have half."

"Where is it?"

"Hidden somewhere on Morris' property. But, that's not the whole of it. Morris will have to die."

Miller laughed. "That's the least of the problem," he said, with a smile. "Are you ready now?"

"No, not today. I'll arrange it."

Miller and friends sneaked onto Vincent's property, looked through the cottage window and saw the Vincent and his girlfriend watching TV. Miller stomped on the door of the cottage and it flew open. Armed with pistols, they rushed inside. The couple screamed as they saw the guns.

"Shut the fuck up! All we want is the cocaine ... then we leave ... nobody gets hurt. You understand? If you decide to be smart-asses, I'll kill the girl first while you watch, fuck face. Understand?"

The couple led Miller and friends to the cocaine buried in the ground. While Zambo and the two other men dug up the cocaine—fifteen hundred kilos—Miller had the couple kneeling in front of him with his pistol pointing at the back of their heads.

Zambo signaled to Miller. "It's all here ... we found everything."

Without hesitating, Charles Miller shot them both, two shots apiece, blowing their brains out. The couple's bodies were found in a burned-out car the next bay, their bodies burned beyond recognition.

Charles Miller was a wealthy man—he had all the money he'd longed for. He was on top. He bought a hotel, a nightclub, part-ownership in a beer-manufacturing plant, a chicken-and-soda distribution business, and built a mansion on top of a hill, overlooking Ross University. St. Kitts weas his to command; the people loved him, the gangsters respected him. His quest for absolute power—the Government of St. Kitts—was his next target.

Charles Miller was a close associate of the opposition party, so he vowed that the opposition party would become the next government of St. Kitts—his campaign money. He mustered enough support for the opposition party that they led the polls by a slim margin, two months before election. On Election Day, the opposition party was victorious. Charles Miller had power in St. Kitts—*he owned the government.*

The St. Kitts police force knew that Miller had killed the former Deputy Prime Minister's son and daughter-in-law, but no one would touch him. He owned most of the police force, except the Superintendent of Police—Jude Matthews. Matthews dug for information to convict Charles Miller for the double murders, and finally arrested him, while continuing to gather information. This was an uphill battle for the superintendent, for every move he made was reported back to Miller in jail by the rest of the police force. Miller decided he'd had enough of the superintendent—a hit was ordered.

The superintendent kissed his wife goodbye one morning and walked out of his house, hurrying toward his police vehicle, when was confronted by Grisly Lawrence. He shot the superintendent several times as his wife watched from her steps. She rushed to her husband's aid but could be of no assistance. The superintendent died on the spot. The assailant was held by the police a couple blocks away, the murder weapon in his possession—an open and shut case, or so it seemed. Despite all the evidence to convict the killer, three different trials resulted in hung juries. The murderer was set free. Charles Miller was arrested on one occasion, but was freed due to lack of evidence in the double murders. Later, he was exonerated—again from lack of evidence.

The entire drug operation on the island of St. Kitts was run by Charles Miller—he was shipping hundreds of kilos of cocaine to a New York Shower Posse member—Oney. Oney was Miller's main distributor in New York, and Miller had cocaine distribution points in Miami, which were controlled by his fellow islanders. His luck ran out, though, when one of his shipments in Miami was busted, and a native of St. Kitts was arrested. Thus, the Government found out it was none other than Cecil Connor (a.k.a. Charles Miller) who had disappeared from the WPS—one of their prized informants, who had turned into a big-time drug trafficker in St. Kitts.

Needless to say, the American Government set out to bring Charles Miller to justice, issuing an extradition warrant to bring him back to the US, to stand trial. The Government didn't know how powerful Connors was in St. Kitts, though, until the extradition proceedings began. With more than conclusive evidence to extradite Miller back to Miami, the judge in St. Kitts concluded there were no grounds upon which to extradite the drug lord. In so doing, the judge denied the American Government's extradition request.

Charles Miller was ecstatic that day, as he exited the courtroom. He'd been declared Commander and Chief of his own little island, where justice was *what he said it was*. But, he was ruffling a lot of feathers in St. Kitts. Business people couldn't adapt to the fact that a gangster was in total control of the island. So, the St. Kitts *Observer* newspaper ran news articles on Miller. He was furious. Some of his hoodlums firebombed the St. Kitts *Observer* office, which quieted the business people for a while.

Meanwhile, the American Government filed an appeal in a higher court in St. Kitts, to overturn the extradition denial. During the interim, Miller continued to further his cocaine enterprise. The Colombians gained confidence in Miller and saw the power that he wielded in St. Kitts—Miller was *the man*. He gave the Colombians the security they needed to operate.

While on one of his rare outings on the high seas, to supervise a huge pick-up of cocaine one night, Miller noticed a yacht. Along with four of his armed friends, he jetted toward the yacht in a speedboat, interrupting the cocaine drop and pick-up. With guns in hand, all five boarded the small yacht. Its occupants were none other than Dr. William Hebert, Ambassador to the US and the United Nations, and five guests.

"Charles Miller, I knew it had to be you. I saw everything," said the Ambassador. "What are you going to do, kill us all? I don't think so."

"I think you're wrong this time. You see too much, Ambassador."

Miller raised his pistol to the Ambassador's head, and shot him through the left eye. The other five guests started to scream as he fell to the floor. Miller and his four friends chased the occupants of the yacht, firing a hail of bullets and hitting all five. One by one, they begged for their lives as Miller walked by them. Without mercy, he shot each of the five guests twice in the head, then returned to the Ambassador and finished the job he'd started—another shot to *his* head.

The Colombians were waiting for the pick-up to be completed and Miller asked their assistance—to dispose of the yacht and the bodies, on their way back to Colombia, which they gladly obliged. The bodies of the Ambassador, his five guests, and the yacht were never found—they vanished without a trace.

While Miller was enjoying his dominion over the tiny island, the US was busy pursuing his extradition and finally became victorious. The High Court in St. Kitts ruled that there should be a new extradition hearing— overturning the ruling of the lower court. That's when Charles Miller got mad. He lied to the American media, saying he was a CIA operative for the American Government in Jamaica, and was working for the CIA in St. Kitts. He stated that the CIA was turning against him. All of this was complete falsehood. Miller lost his head, making threats against American citizens—power had irreversibly corrupted him.

Miller was neither a CIA operative, nor a political activist in Jamaica. It was impossible for CIA operatives to penetrate the inner cities of Jamaica—plus, there'd be nothing to gain. Any knowledge the US needed on Jamaica was easily accessible through the Jamaican Government and its police force. Miller was merely trying to tarnish the CIA's reputation.

Victory was short-lived for the Americans. For the second time, a judge found insufficient evidence to extradite Miller, and the request was denied.

Miller decided to play defensive, though, and closed down some of his businesses, going into seclusion in his hilltop mansion. Twenty guards equipped with M-16s were hired to patrol his home twenty-four-hours a day. He was ready for war with the American Government and vowed that he'd fight until the death—never to be taken out of St. Kitts alive.

Chapter 17: End of the Shower Posse Saga

Saturday morning, February 19th, 2000, the end of Vivian Blake's Shower Posse saga was nearing. The guilty plea hearing was scheduled for Wednesday, February 23rd. He was in his cell at the Miami FDC, reading the novel *Bloodline*, by Sidney Sheldon.

"Mr. B.!" someone shouted.

He recognized the voice as that of Patrick Aikens, an alleged member of the Jamaican Moscow Posse. In the FDC, Vivian had also met his two brothers for the first time—Ian Moscow and Roland.

"Yeah!"

"Modeler's here."

"What?" said Vivian, not clearly understanding what Patrick was saying.

"Modeler ... he's in Miami."

"That's bullshit! I heard he was shot several times in St. Kitts last week, and he ran to the hill with a bunch of his friends. As a matter of fact, he could be dead. He was badly hurt."

"I have the *Miami Herald* in front of me, with a picture of Modeler and some DEA Agents, taken at Fort Lauderdale Airport yesterday."

"What? Let me see the paper."

About an hour later, Vivian received the newspaper from Patrick via a correctional officer—it was true. Charles "Modeler" Miller had finally returned to the US. Vivian had one thing to be happy about—the fact that he decided to plead guilty— because he'd have still been on trial when Modeler arrived in Miami. There was no doubt in his mind that Modeler would have taken the stand against him, and would have lied so perfectly, convincing the jury, as he'd done in trial of 1989, which ended with the conviction of nearly thirty Shower Posse members and associates.

Miller's demise had long been coming. Elections were due in St. Kitts and Nevis, and the prime minister was favored by the voters, but he had one major problem—Charles Miller. The love the ordinary citizens of St. Kitts had for Miller was dwindling, though. He was generous and they praised him for that, but his murdering ways were becoming intolerable.

oples' patience was wearing thin. In late January 2000, they'd had
ugh.

Toney Fetherston was wealthy Englishman who lived in England, but
also had a mansion in St. Kitts. He was an influential friend of the St.
Kitts government. He'd opposed Charles Miller's hold on the island and
made no secret about it. Opposition to Miller's absolute power was also
building among the people. The St. Kitts *Observer* blasted him again, and
his cronies started to pull back. Cocaine connections shied away from
him because of the publicity he was receiving in the American press.

The Fetherston and his wife were vacationing on St. Kitts. Miller
conceived a plan, arranging for two of his cronies to go to the
Englishman, under the guise of robbers. In actuality, Miller arranged a
hit.

The two masked hit men, visited the Fetherston's house and rang the
doorbell.

"We want money."

"I have no money."

Then one of the men shot Fetherston in the head, killing the
Englishman in cold blood, never attempting to search the house for
valuables.

It was common knowledge in St Kitts that Charles Miller had
arranged the hit on the Englishman, but no one had any proof. The Prime
Minister, the St. Kitts police force, and the citizens of St. Kitts were
outraged. Everyone was distancing themselves from Miller, even his
boyhood friend, Zambo.

Things came to a climax when Miller visited a farmer and an
argument developed. Miller pulled his pistol and the farmer ran—several
shots were fired at him. This didn't sit well with some of the citizens of
St. Kitts, and a group of (usually) non-violent citizens decided to take the
law into their own hands. They armed themselves with pistols and
decided to search out Miller, ridding the tiny nation's problem, once and
for all.

While they were in their car, four guys caught sight of one of Millers thugs. They opened fire on him, hitting him several times, leaving him to die.

At the same time, Miller was on a different mission. Along with four of his cronies, he entered the office of the St. Kitts *Observer*. Miller, automatic pistol in full view, created panic amongst the staff.

"I'm not here to hurt anyone; I just want you to stop printing the lies that American Government is reporting about me."

He took a cassette from his pocket and ordered that the staff play the tape on their cassette player. After the message was finished, he proceeded to take photographs of the staff, as a form of intimidation. Then he left the office.

Charles Miller was now a deranged man—he knew he'd lost. The people who'd loved him, wanted no more part of him. He'd gone too far. This once-peaceful little island had a zero murder rate until he showed up on its shores.

In 2000, the people of St. Kitts could take no more. The government of St. Kitts had tolerated Miller for too long … now it was time to shape up or ship out. The election was just around the corned. If Miller was still in St. Kitts on Election Day, the present government, although favored, stood a chance of losing at the polls.

While driving his car a few days later, the St. Kitts police intercepted Miller and found an automatic pistol on his person when they searched him. He was arrested. That turned out to be Charles Miller's last day of freedom on the streets of St. Kitts. The St. Kitts Government forced Charles Miller out, barring him from ever returning.

While in jail, police officers—former friends—advised Miller to give up fighting extradition to America and go voluntarily. He was told that it was either that, or die on the streets.

"The citizens, the Government, the business community, the churches, and the police force are all against you," one of the police officers told him.

Miller conceded to his defeat. He'd fallen from king to peasant. "I'll waive my rights to extradition proceedings. I'll go back to Miami voluntarily."

arles Miller was incarcerated in the Special Housing Unit on the
wing while Vivian Blake was on the west wing of the same unit.
ller went for his first hearing on the February 21st, 2000.

On February 23rd, Vivian Blake stepped into the Miami courtroom smiling. He'd made the right decision. He quietly pleaded guilty to two counts of the Florida indictments: count 3—conspiracy to commit racketeering, and count 4—Racketeering. No evidence was presented regarding count 3, sections E-1 through E-13, which involved the eight murders and five attempted murders. He also pleaded guilty in the court to two of his fifteen counts in the Virginia indictment: counts 12 and 15—both possession with intent to distribute cocaine. All other counts were dropped on both indictments, including the eight murders and the five attempted murders.

RIPTION AND PRESENT STATUS OF CHARACTERS

IAN

was a well built, of average height (5ft 10ins), weighing 218 lbs. He was fair complexion.

PRESENT STATUS

He is now serving thirty years in a Federal Prison. He was born and raised in Tivoli Gardens area, Kingston, Jamaica.

KIRK

was a young, kind, slender, from Indian descendant. He was about 5ft 10ins tall and had an angelic smile, very soft spoken. He was of fair complexion.

PRESENT STATUS

He is now serving two life sentences in a Federal Prison for the killing of five Jamaicans in an apartment in Washington, D.C. He had admitted to the F.B.I. that he had killed one hundred and two Jamaicans. Eighty-seven of the murders have been documented but fifteen bodies cannot be found. He was a rogue killer who lived in many different communities in Kingston, Jamaica. He lived in Fletcher's Land, Southside, Rema and lastly Tivoli Gardens.

SKATTA

was a six footer and very slender with a bow leg, weighing about 140pounds. He was of dark complexion.

PRESENT STATUS

He was shot and killed in a gun battle with some Black Americans in Overtown, Miami, Florida. He was known to have killed over forty people. He died in 1983. He was from Tower Hill in Kingston, Jamaica then Tivoli Gardens.

BASKIN

was about 6ft 2ins tall. He was of fair complexion. He wore tested lens because of a shot he received in his face from a security guard in Jamaica.

PRESENT STATUS

He was shot in the leg and bled to death. He died while being treated in the Jackson Memorial Hospital in Miami. He was a strong area leader for the Tivoli Gardens community, Kingston, Jamaica.

CURLY LOCKS

was of light complexion over six feet tall . He was very slender weighing about 140 pounds.

PRESENT STATUS

He was murdered in Jamaica by one of his cronies whom he had threatened to kill days before. He was known to have killed over one hundred people. He had also shot and killed his pregnant girlfriend and got her younger sister pregnant thereafter. He was a community leader of Rema in Kingston, Jamaica.

BUCKY MARSHALL

was of medium built, dark complexion, 5ft 9ins tall, weighing 170lbs.

PRESENT STATUS

He was shot and killed at a dance in Brooklyn, New York. He was one of the initiatorS for the Peace Treaty in Kingston, Jamaica in the 70's. He was a strong area leader in the Rose Lane and Matthews Lane communities.

SOULS

Was of light complexion, weighed 180 lbs. He had a big mouth, and was about 5ft 9ins tall.

PRESENT STATUS

He was shot and killed in Harlem, New York in his apartment. He was from Tivoli Gardens, Kingston, Jamaica.

RUDY

was very tall and strong, weighed over 200 lbs.

PRESENT STATUS

He is presently residing in England. He was from Tivoli Gardens, Kingston, Jamaica.

WILD BILL

was an elderly man, dark complexion, short with gray and black hair, and a small body.

PRESENT STATUS

He was shot several times in Miami, Florida and was confined to a wheelchair. Origin in Jamaica unknown, but he was a Tivoli Garden's community leader, Bya's main man in Miami.

GLASSES

fair complexion, of average height, medium built and wore a pair of thick lens glasses.

PRESENT STATUS

He was deported to Jamaica in the 90's and is now living on the island. He is from Tivoli Gardens.

PERRY

A tall, dark and handsome guy. He was very slender, over 6 feet tall, weighed about 180lbs

PRESENT STATUS

He served ten years in a state penitentiary and was deported to Jamaica where he is now living. He was from Tivoli Gardens, Kingston, Jamaica.

WAXY

Very dark about 5ft 7ins tall, medium built, weighed about 150 lbs and good looking.

PRESENT STATUS

He was shot and killed by the police in Kingston, Jamaica. He was said to have killed over two hundred people. He was from the Tivoli Gardens community in Kingston, Jamaica.

WINNY POP

Slender, fair complexion about 5ft 8ins tall. Fairly good looking.

PRESENT STATUS

He was found shot to death with a friend of his named Scarps in a car trunk in Miami, Florida. Both guys were from Tivoli Gardens.

BUTTER

big and stocky. He was of dark complexion, about 5ft 10ins tall.

PRESENT STATUS

He served time in a federal prison and was deported to Jamaica where he is still living at present. He is from Tivoli Gardens, Kingston, Jamaica.

BAGGY MAN

was very short, dark complexion and was always smiling. He had a round face and spoke with a bad stutter.

He was assassinated along with his girlfriend in his home in New Jersey. He was known to have killed over fifty people including the assassination of two police officers on Windward Road in Kingston, Jamaica. He was a member of the Land Raiders group, and then later took refuge in Tivoli Gardens, Kingston, Jamaica.

TONY

black in complexion, well built, about 5ft 10 ins tall and weighed about 200lbs. He was handsome and loved to wear jewellery, they sometimes called him Mr. T.

PRESENT STATUS

He is now serving 12 years in a federal penitentiary. It was said that he was the leader of Breakaway group of guys from Tivoli Gardens, who was the real Shower Posse, a group that opposed Jim Brown leadership in Tivoli Gardens. He was from Tivoli Gardens, Kingston, Jamaica.

KONG

Short and well built, with fair complexion. The brother of Vivian and Tony. Kong had a very close resemblance to Vivian.

PRESENT STATUS

He served 10 years in a federal prison, where he had to undergo severe psychiatric treatment. He was later deported to Jamaica, where he was shot and killed in cold blood by the Jamaican police. He was from Tivoli Gardens, Jamaica.

LAW

A tall, dark and slender elderly man, who was always smiling.

PRESENT STATUS

He served eight years in a federal prison and was deported to

Jamaica where he now resides. He was from Tivoli Gardens, Kingston, Jamaica.

MODELER

was a fair complexion, medium built guy. He was handsome, weighed about 180 lbs and was 5ft 9ins tall.

PRESENT STATUS

He served five years in a federal prison and when he was to be deported to Jamaica to stand trial for two police officers he brutally murdered, he decided to turn a federal witness against his friend in exchange for not being deported to Jamaica. He had also escaped from the South Cam Road Rehabilitation Center in Kingston, Jamaica while he serving two life sentences. He is a native of the tiny island of St. Kitts, but lived in Jamaica for a long time. He spent time in Tivoli Gardens, Kingston, Jamaica. He is now serving a life sentence in a federal prison.

DONOVAN JONES

dark complexion, handsome medium built elderly man. He had a twisted leg that rubbed against the other as he walked.

PRESENT STATUS

He served time in a federal prison and was released. Present location, unknown. He was a cold-blooded killer who was called Board-heart. He was from Tivoli Gardens, Kingston, Jamaica.

RED ROY

Of light complexion and short. He spoke with a stutter. He had a small body.

PRESENT STATUS

He was assassinated in Los Angeles, California along with his girlfriend, Yvonne. He had escaped in the 80's from the South

Camp Road Rehabilitation Center. He was serving a life sentence. He and his girlfriend were both from Tivoli Gardens, Kingston, Jamaica.

RICHIE

Tall, slender, dark and handsome guy, who was from the upper class group of Kingston, Jamaica.

PRESENT STATUS

He was sentenced to twenty-four and a half years in a federal prison where he is still serving time. He was from the upper class neighborhood of Norbrook, St. Andrew, Jamaica.

JAH-T

Tall, dark with a strong built and had a pleasant smile. He weighed over 200 lbs and dressed well.

PRESENT STATUS

He was shot while riding his motorcycle on Maxfield Avenue in Kingston, Jamaica. He later died as a result of the crash that took place after he was shot. He was the son of Lester Lloyd Coke "aka" Jim Brown. He lived in Tivoli Gardens, Kingston, Jamaica. He was a strong community leader.

Arrow

Big and fat and tall. Black in complexion with an ugly face.

PRESENT STATUS

He served 10 years in a state prison and was deported to Jamaica. He had returned back to America and was living in the New York area. He was from Tivoli Gardens, Kingston, Jamaica.

BUGS

Short, fair complexion and handsome. He was a medium built

guy, weighing about 140lbs.

PRESENT STATUS

He served time in a federal prison and was admitted to a federal witness protection program after he left prison. He was from Tivoli Gardens, Kingston, Jamaica.

FRENCHY

Short, fair complexion guy with bulging eyes.

PRESENT STATUS

He served time in a federal prison and was later deported to Jamaica. Where abouts unknown.

JUNIOR BLACK

Short, black complexion and handsome. He was medium built, weighing about 150 lbs with a patch of gray hair in the front of his head.

PRESENT STATUS

He served 10 years in a state prison and was deported to Jamaica. He returned to the U.S.A. where he was shot and killed by some Americans who robbed him.

GABRIEL

Average height, medium built, of dark complexion.

PRESENT STATUS

He served 6 years in a state prison for a shooting in New Jersey at a bus ride. Whereabouts unknown.

SAMUEL

Very short, dark complexion, dressed well.

PRESENT STATUS

He was deported to Jamaica where he is still living.

SHOWER CHRIS

Average height, of dark complexion, fairly handsome, weighing 150 lbs.

PRESENT STATUS

He was shot and killed in New York City.

CHRIS "aka" BUMMY CHRIS

Average height, dark complexion, slender, weighing about 135 lbs._

PRESENT STATUS

He was deported to Jamaica.

TALL HUNCH

over 6ft tall, dark and handsome, very slender.

PRESENT STATUS

Unknown

LITTLE HUNCH

Short, black and ugly with a small body.

PRESENT STATUS

He was shot and killed in Washington, D.C.

FOOD HEAD

dark complexion, medium built, and handsome and weighed 175 lbs.

PRESENT STATUS
He was shot and killed in Kingston, Jamaica.

MILTON
Light complexion, average height and built, with a baldhead.

PRESENT STATUS
He was and killed in a restaurant in Miami.

HUCKY BERRY
Light complexion, well built, handsome guy.

PRESENT STATUS
Unknown

CRACKER
average height, black and handsome of Indian descent.

PRESENT STATUS
He was shot several times and left for dead, but survived and presently incarcerated.

BIG TOE
Fair complexion, average height and built and also handsome.

PRESENT STATUS
Unknown

TEDDY PAUL
Fair complexion, short and slender, with a lot of kids.

PRESENT STATUS
He was deported to Jamaica, where he is now operating a legitimate business.

SEXY PAUL

Short, stocky, dark, handsome guy.

PRESENT STATUS

He is serving fifteen years in a Jamaica prison.

JOHNATHAN

Short, fair complexion, neatly built a community leader for Tivoli Gardens.

PRESENT STATUS

He died from an overdose of cocaine.

JUICY BADNESS

Short, stocky, average looks and black.

PRESENT STATUS

He was killed in a shoot out with the police in Kingston, Jamaica.

BYA

Average height, average weight, dark complection.

PRESENT STATUS

He died in hospital from an overdose of cocaine.

LESTER LLOYD COKE aka "JIM BROWN"

Tall with dark complexion

PRESENT STATUS

He was burnt to death in his cell at the General Penitentiary in Jamaica while awaiting extradition to America.